REFORMED THEOLOGY
IN AMERICA

REFORMED THEOLOGY IN AMERICA

A History of its Modern Development

Edited by
DAVID F. WELLS

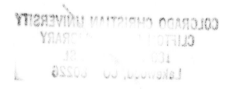

GRAND RAPIDS, MICHIGAN
WILLIAM B. EERDMANS PUBLISHING COMPANY

Copyright © 1985 by Wm. B. Eerdmans Publishing Company
255 Jefferson Ave. SE, Grand Rapids, Mich. 49503

Library of Congress Cataloging in Publication Data
Main entry under title:

Reformed theology.

Dedicated to Roger Nicole on the occasion of his seventieth birthday.
   1. Reformed Church—United States—Doctrines—History—Addresses,
essays, lectures. 2. Presbyterian Church—United States—Doctrines—
History—Addresses, essays, lectures. 3. Calvinism—United States—
History—Addresses, essays, lectures. 4. Nicole, Roger R.—Addresses,
essays, lectures. I. Wells, David F. II. Nicole, Roger R.
BX9424.5.U6R44 1985   230'.57'09   85-16013

ISBN 0-8028-0096-3

To Roger Nicole

A man of God

CONTENTS

CONTRIBUTORS

James Montgomery Boice is the pastor of Tenth Presbyterian Church, Philadelphia, Pennsylvania. He speaks on The Bible Study Hour, and chairs the International Council on Biblical Inerrancy and the Philadelphia Conference on Reformed Theology. He is the author of *Foundations of the Christian Faith*, 4 vols. (Downers Grove, IL: InterVarsity Press, 1978-1981); *The Gospel of John*, 5 vols. (Grand Rapids: Zondervan Publishing House, 1975-1980); and *Genesis*, 2 vols. (Grand Rapids: Zondervan Publishing House, 1982, 1985).

James D. Bratt is Assistant Professor of Religious Studies, University of Pittsburgh, and author of *Dutch Calvinism in Modern America: A History of a Conservative Subculture* (Grand Rapids: Wm. B. Eerdmans Publishing Company, 1984).

Gabriel Fackre, Abbot Professor of Christian Theology at Andover Newton Theological School, is the author of *The Christian Story* (Grand Rapids: Wm. B. Eerdmans Publishing Company, 1985); *The Religious Right and Christian Faith* (Grand Rapids: Wm. B. Eerdmans Publishing Company, 1975); *Word in Deed* (Grand Rapids: Wm. B. Eerdmans Publishing Company, 1975); and *The Rainbow Sign* (London: Epworth Press, 1968).

W. Robert Godfrey is Professor of Church History, Westminster Theological Seminary (Escondido, CA), and a contributor to *Discord, Dialogue, and Concord*, ed. by Lewis W. Spitz and Wenzel Lohff (Philadelphia: Fortress Press, 1977); *John Calvin, His Influence in the Western World*, ed. by W. Stanford Reid (Grand Rapids: Zondervan Publishing House, 1982); and *Scripture and Truth*, ed. by D. A. Carson and John D. Woodbridge (Grand Rapids: Zondervan Publishing House, 1983).

W. Andrew Hoffecker, Professor of Religion at Grove City College, has penned *Piety and the Princeton Theologians* (Phillipsburg, NJ: Presbyterian and Reformed Publishing Company, 1981).

Douglas Floyd Kelly, former editor of the *Journal of Christian Reconstruction*, ministered at the First Presbyterian Church, Dillon, SC, and the First Presbyterian Church, Raeford, NC. Currently he is Associate Professor of Systematic Theology, Reformed Theological Seminary, and cotranslator and coeditor of *The Westminster Confession of Faith: A New Edition* (Greenwood, SC: The Attic Press, Inc., 1979 [1981]).

George M. Marsden, Professor of History at Calvin College, is the author of *Fundamentalism and American Culture* (New York: Oxford University Press, 1980), and *The Evangelical Mind and the New School Presbyterian Experience* (New Haven: Yale University Press, 1970); coauthor (with Mark Noll and Nathan Hatch) of *The Search for Christian America* (Westchester, IL: Crossways Books, 1983); and editor of *Evangelicalism and Modern America* (Grand Rapids: Wm. B. Eerdmans Publishing Company, 1984).

C. T. McIntire, Associate Professor of History, Trinity College, University of Toronto, has edited *God, History, and Historians* (New York: Oxford University Press, 1977), *Herbert Butterfield: Writings on Christianity and History* (New York: Oxford University Press, 1979), and *History and Historical Understanding* (Grand Rapids: Wm. B. Eerdmans Publishing Company, 1984). He also is the author of *England Against the Papacy, 1858-1861* (Cambridge: Cambridge University Press, 1983).

Mark A. Noll, Professor of History at Wheaton College, has coauthored (with George Marsden and Nathan Hatch) *The Search for Christian America* (Westchester, IL: Crossways Books, 1983), and has edited *The Princeton Theology, 1812-1921: Scripture, Science, and Theological Method from Alexander to Warfield* (Grand Rapids: Baker Book House, 1983), *The Bible in America* (New York: Oxford University Press, 1982), and *Eerdmans' Handbook to Christianity in America* (Grand Rapids: Wm. B. Eerdmans Publishing Company, 1983).

Malcolm Andrew Reid is Professor of Philosophy and chairs the philosophy department at Gordon College. He has contributed to *Eerdmans' Handbook to Christianity in America* (Grand Rapids: Wm. B. Eerdmans Publishing Company, 1983), and the forthcoming *Reality of Christian Learning: Strategies for Faith-Discipline Integration,* ed. by David L. Wolfe and Harold Heie.

W. Stanford Reid is Professor Emeritus of History, University of Guelph (Guelph, Ontario), formerly Lecturer and Professor of History at McGill University (Montreal, Quebec, 1941-1965), and founder and chairperson of the Department of History, University of Guelph, 1965-1970. He is the author of *The Church of Scotland in Lower Canada: Its Struggle for Establishment* (Toronto: Thorn Press, 1936), *Skipper from Leith: The Life of Robert Barton of Over Barnton* (Philadelphia: University of Pennsylvania Press, 1964), *Christianity and Scholarship* (Nutley, NJ: Presbyterian and Reformed Publishing Company, 1966), and *Trumpeter of God: A Bi-*

ography of John Knox (New York: Charles Scribner's Sons, 1974; Grand Rapids: Baker Book House, 1980).

Wesley A. Roberts is Professor of Church History at Gordon-Conwell Theological Seminary.

Morton H. Smith has been Stated Clerk of the General Assembly of the Presbyterian Church in America from 1973 to the present. He was Professor of Bible at Belhaven College (Jackson, MS) from 1954 to 1963, and Professor of Systematic Theology at Reformed Theological Seminary from 1964 to 1979. He is the author of *Studies in Southern Presbyterian Theology* (Amsterdam: Campen, 1962), and *How Is the Gold Become Dim* (Jackson, MS: Continuing Presbyterian Church, 1973).

Dennis N. Voskuil, Associate Professor of Religion and religion department chairperson at Hope College, has authored *Mountains into Goldmines: Robert Schuller and the Gospel of Success* (Grand Rapids: Wm. B. Eerdmans Publishing Company, 1983).

David F. Wells, Andrew Mutch Professor of Historical and Systematic Theology at Gordon-Conwell Theological Seminary, has authored *Revolution in Rome* (London: Tyndale, 1973), *The Search for Salvation* (Downers Grove, IL: InterVarsity Press, 1978), *The Prophetic Theology of George Tyrrell* (Chico, CA: Scholars Press, 1981), and *The Person of Christ: A Biblical and Historical Analysis of the Incarnation* (Westchester, IL: Crossways Books, 1984).

Luder G. Whitlock, Jr., is president of Reformed Theological Seminary (Jackson, MS), and formerly its Associate Professor of Christian Missions.

Henry Zwaanstra is Professor of Historical Theology at Calvin Theological Seminary, and the author of *Reformed Thought and Experience in a New World: A Study of the Christian Reformed Church and Its American Environment 1890-1918* (Kampen: J. H. Kok B.V., 1973).

PREFACE

ONE of the quirks of American theology is that it is frequently unaware of being American. German theology, of course, is the result of the ponderous and enormously thorough German academic machinery from which it has emerged. British theology, with its keen interest in historical accuracy, fair play, and civility, obviously reflects the virtues of the middle and upper-middle classes in which it is largely nurtured. South American theology makes no bones of the fact that it is South American. It wears its heart on its sleeve. North of the border, however, this is not so. Here, we simply do theology!

Our assumption, then, is that the North American context and its psychology have not significantly shaped the way we think. Sometimes this assumption is justified in the interests of preserving truth, for if the social context of a theology determines that theology then each theology is only true relative to its context. The concern for truth, therefore, has sometimes led us to deny that the context shapes the ideas. But perhaps more commonly we are simply not aware of how the interplay between Christ and culture is actually going on, nor are we aware of how we are resolving the relationship. This unwillingness to be self-critical is further exacerbated by the fact that often our concern has not been with creating theology but with erecting new churches, carrying forth new enterprises, mounting new programs, sending more missionaries, and sustaining a whole assortment of institutions and agencies nearly or remotely related to the churches. As Americans we have placed more value upon action than upon thought and seen in reflection a virtue that is secondary to that of doing. Not even the Reformed tradition has been immune from this.

It is no surprise, therefore, that one encounters in the essays that follow a most astonishing variety of expression in Reformed thought. These essays are, in fact, a microcosm of the nation. It is erroneous to assume that immigrants are quickly and easily melted in the national pot. They are not. Ethnic interests are preserved through language and social customs but these interests are held within a wider, more diffuse sense of also being American. So it is in this book. There is a broad sense of what it means to be Reformed in America but within that sense special interests are also served. Some of these are ethnic in origin, others have developed—for good or bad—from the intellectual alliances that have been made en route, still others have been deeply affected by parts of the American experience, and most bear the stamp of the towering figures who shaped the tradition.

The recognition of this diversity is in itself an objective that this book has sought to reach. Accordingly, it examines what we have seen to be the five major schools or traditions in Reformed theology. For each school there is a general essay followed by essays on the two major theologians in the school. To limit the scope of the book, we have concentrated on the twentieth century. We have, however, also included some theologians from the nineteenth century. The justification for this is that the school or tradition in which we find them could not be understood without taking account of their work.

The very structure of the book, therefore, lays bare the fact of diversity in Reformed theology. In so doing, it invites those who are Reformed in theology to consider again the reasons for this diversity. Are they differences that the Word of God itself mandates or are they really the result of casual alliances with culture? What does it now mean to profess belief in the Reformation principles of *sola scriptura, sola gracia,* and *sola fidei,* given the fact that we live in a context of modernity with its accompanying secularism?

With this book we also honor a man who has addressed such questions with great energy and ability and in so doing not only has upheld and influenced American Reformed theology but also has justified the nation's wisdom in opening its doors to talented immigrants. His name is Roger Nicole.

Roger was born in Charlottenburg, Germany, in 1915 of Swiss parents. His father, a pastor, served for many years in evangelical churches and rejoiced that his two sons, Jules and Roger, followed in his footsteps as preachers of the gospel and lecturers in church history and theology.

Roger received the A.B. at Gymnase Classique in Lausanne, Switzerland; the M.A. from the Sorbonne in Paris; and a diploma from Institut Biblique in Nogent/Marne in France. At Gordon Divinity School he was awarded the B.D. in 1939, the S.T.M. in 1940, and the Th.D. in 1943. In 1967 he received the Ph.D. from Harvard University, and in 1978 Wheaton College conferred on him the D.D. degree.

Roger began teaching at Gordon College in 1944, and since 1949 he has been Professor of Theology at Gordon Divinity School and Gordon-Conwell Theological Seminary. In 1976 he was appointed to an endowed chair as the Andrew Mutch Professor of Theology. For over forty years he has been a tower of strength to the institution and an inspiration to its students.

Blessed with a remarkable memory, Roger comes to the teaching rostrum equipped with an encyclopedic knowledge of systematic theology in all its divisions. He is bolstered in his task by an equally uncommon grasp of church history and Scripture. He is a man of firm convictions and yet with a sensitive awareness of the positions others might hold. His students and those with whom he discusses views variant from his own are happily surprised at his fairness. Frequently, after he has presented his position with conviction he will then list cautions that are intended to ensure the biblical balance and to guard against an extremism that could easily lead to error. Across several generations he has endeared himself to students by the thoroughness of his coverage, his perspicuity in presenting subject matter, and his evident warmth of manner and love for students. Students are very aware that he is teaching the truth in love and that he is an example of the reality of that truth.

Throughout his career Roger has given special attention to the doctrine of Scripture, beginning with his B.D. thesis in 1939, "Jesus and the Bible with Reference to Inspiration." He played a major role in writing the Statement of Faith of Gordon College and Gordon Divinity School in 1950 and was responsible for the insertion of the words, "The sixty-six books of the Bible, as originally written, were inspired of God, hence free from error." The latter phrase has been a guide to the position of the Seminary in difficult times of theological debate.

Roger has been an indefatigable worker for evangelical causes. As a member of the committee for the New International Version he helped in providing a superior translation of Scripture. His knowledge of languages, his studies in the Old and New Testament, and his wider range of theological learning benefitted this significant Bible project.

Roger was also a founding member and is an active participant in the Evangelical Theological Society, serving as Vice President in 1955 and as President in 1956. His papers and committee work have been a constant encouragement to the society. He was a presenter at the Wenham Conference on Biblical Inerrancy in 1966, held on the Gordon Divinity School campus, and has been active in the discussion that has followed.

As a member and a contributor to the summit meetings of the International Council on Biblical Inerrancy, Roger assisted in shaping and writing its articles. The 1978 meeting produced the important Chicago Statement on Inerrancy.

Roger is a dedicated and unrepentant bibliophile! His own personal library has over 26,000 volumes (not counting some 6,000 mysteries!).

Included are many rare volumes from the sixteenth- and seventeenth-century Reformed divines of Germany, the Netherlands, Switzerland, France, and Scotland. This same interest lies behind his two fine publications, *A Bibliography of Benjamin Breckinridge Warfield, 1851-1921* (Nutley, NJ: Presbyterian and Reformed Publishing Company, 1974), and *Moyse Amyrault: A Bibliography, with Special Reference to the Controversy on Universal Grace* (New York: Garland Publishing, Inc., 1981).

The sovereignty of God, expressed in grace and in judgment, has always been at the center of Roger's vision. It has led him to think globally. He has always been a strong supporter of missions because he is confident that God is great enough to accomplish his saving purposes worldwide. It has also led him to walk humbly because he knows that in our human fallenness resides no spiritual life. To know this is to be liberated from the clutches of that exaggerated and false sense of self-importance which, in the end, undermines all human well-being. And it has given his life a serenity and stability that have been an example to his colleagues, students, and the administrators with whom he has worked. In times of crisis, he has been a source of wisdom; in turbulence, a source of strength. His unerring instinct for what is noble and good has touched those who have known him and has ever pointed to Jesus Christ, "the pioneer and perfecter of our faith."

In December 1985 Roger will celebrate his seventieth birthday, and to mark this occasion we are proudly dedicating this book to him.

D. F. W.

REFORMED AND AMERICAN

GEORGE M. MARSDEN

WHAT sense does it make in late twentieth-century America to talk about being "Reformed"? For most Americans the word conveys no clear meaning. Very few would think of it as a religious designation at all, and most of those would think it referred to Judaism. Even if, as in the present work, we limit the audience to those who have some notion of "Reformed theology," we are left with the problem that even among such a select group, "Reformed" has numerous differing connotations. In the United States alone there are about a dozen Reformed denominations and perhaps another half-dozen with a Reformed heritage. Within each of the Reformed denominations varieties of meanings are given to being "Reformed." These may reflect European traditions, such as Scottish or Dutch, or continental neoorthodox, as well as a variety of American developments. Each such type includes differing subtypes. For instance, within the Reformed Church in America alone, ten distinct approaches to the Reformed faith have been identified.[1] Differences across denominational lines may be sharper. A strictly confessional member of the Reformed Presbyterian Church in North America (Covenanters) might be most unhappy with the preaching at Robert Schuller's Crystal Cathedral. A fundamentalist Bible Presbyterian would refuse fellowship with almost any member of the United Church of Christ. And within most of the larger Reformed denominations, conservatives and progressives are locked in intense struggles over the true meaning of the faith.

A major purpose of this essay is to cut through the bewildering confusion of the many meanings of "Reformed" by reducing the categories to the three major Reformed emphases that have flourished in the American cultural setting. Not every Reformed heritage can be subsumed under these categories and the categories are ideal types or models rather than fully nuanced representations of the growth of each type. Nonetheless, these are the major subgroups that have been prominent among the Reformed throughout American history. So if we understand some-

1

thing of these three developments and emphases we can gain a fairly good picture of the main varieties of being "Reformed" in the American cultural setting.

Perhaps an illustration from my own experience can make clear the characters of the differences among these major American Reformed traditions. Most of my life I have lived in one or the other of two communities that placed great merit on being Reformed. The central meaning of "Reformed," however, has differed greatly in these two communions. The Orthodox Presbyterians, among whom I was reared, meant by "Reformed" strict adherence to Christian doctrine as contained in the infallible Scriptures and defined by the standards of the Westminster Assembly. Only Christians whose creeds were fully compatible with Westminster's and who viewed subscription to them as paramount were fully within the pale. Other factors were important to Christian life, especially a proper emphasis on the law of God as the central organizing principle in the Westminster formulations. But the operative test for "Reformed" was, with this important practical proviso, always doctrinal.

In the other community in which I have spent many years, the progressive wing of the conservative Christian Reformed Church, being "Reformed" is also taken seriously, but with very different meaning. There, a "Reformed" Christian is one who has a certain view of the relationship of Christianity to culture. She or he must affirm the lordship of Christ over all reality, see Christian principles as applicable to all areas of life, and view every calling as sacred. Although subscription to the authority of the Bible and classic Reformed creeds is significant in this community, the stronger operative test for admission is support for separate Christian schools at all levels (except, oddly, the graduate university), where the "Reformed" world-and-life view can be exemplified and taught.

I have also spent some time at institutions of mainstream American evangelicalism, such as Trinity Evangelical Divinity School and Fuller Theological Seminary, where one finds still another meaning to being "Reformed." In this context being "Reformed" must be understood in the framework of being "evangelical." "Evangelical" is a word with a more elusive meaning than "Reformed." Basically it refers to anyone who promotes proclamation of the gospel of salvation through the atoning work of Christ and has a traditional high view of Scripture alone as authority. Evangelicalism is thus much larger than just the Reformed tradition. Within American evangelicalism, however, there is an important subgroup that might be called "card-carrying" evangelicals.[2] These are persons who think of themselves primarily as "evangelicals" and who, as such, identify at least as much with evangelicalism as a movement as with their own formal denomination. Billy Graham, *Christianity*

Today, Eternity, Inter-Varsity Christian Fellowship, Wheaton College and its imitators, and seminaries such as Trinity, Fuller, and Gordon-Conwell have been prototypes of this influential interdenominational evangelicalism.

In this evangelical fellowship the dominant theological tradition is Reformed. It is by no means, however, the only tradition. One trait of this type of being "Reformed," unlike the other two, is that it is tolerant of diversity to the point of keeping close fellowship with persons of other traditions. The operative tests for fellowship among the Reformed in such communities are those of the broader American evangelical-pietist tradition—a certain style of emphasis on evangelism, personal devotions, Methodist mores, and openness in expressing one's evangelical commitment. To be "Reformed" in this setting means to find in Reformed theology the most biblical and healthiest expression of evangelical piety.

The differing emphases of these three communities suggest that in America there are at least three major meanings to being "Reformed." There are, of course, also a number of other Reformed traditions and styles in America. These include the southern, ethnically and racially defined groups, smaller denominations, progressive Reformed in mainline denominations, and some neoorthodox. Nonetheless, the three we have begun with suggest classically distinct types of emphasis that give us some working categories. Many of the developments of America's Reformed groups can be understood as variations on these typical themes.

For convenience' sake, we shall designate these three types as doctrinalist, culturalist, and pietist.[3] In doing so, it is important to remark again that the terminology refers to "ideal types" or descriptive models emphasizing one dominant trait. In reality all three groups typically embody the traits dominant among the other two. Thus a "pietist" is not typically a person who is lax in doctrine or lacking in cultural concern. Similarly, to call people doctrinalists or culturalists does not imply lack of the other two traits.

The Puritan Stock

The oldest major Reformed community in America was the Puritan, which combined strong elements of each of these emphases. Stress on strict Calvinism helped distinguish these early American settlers from their Arminian Anglican opponents. And Reformed orthodoxy was retained in most New England pulpits for at least a century and a half, to the time of the Revolution.[4] Puritans were also characterized by intense piety, often keeping close records of their spiritual health. Moreover, New England's Puritans were America's most successful Reformed culture builders. Virtually free from outside control during their formative first half-century, they built the closest thing humanly possible to their conception of a biblical kingdom. This impressive effort had a lasting impact on the ideals of American civilization. It is ironic that "Reformed" has so little meaning in America today when in fact the culture has been so shaped by that heritage.

The lasting culture-shaping impact of seventeenth-century Puritanism is rivaled by the long-term influence of its eighteenth-century style of piety, epitomized by the Great Awakening. The eighteenth century was generally an era of widespread resurgent pietism, emphasizing personal commitment to the Savior more than Christian culture building. The Great Awakening in New England was part of a wider Protestant pietist awakening that had begun in Germany and spread to most of the Protestant world. In England its largest manifestation was in Methodism. In America it appeared first primarily as pietist revivalism in Reformed churches.

At the height of the first surge of the Great Awakening in America, around 1740, the classic patterns of American Reformed divisions began to emerge. By this time the other major Reformed group, the Scotch-Irish and Scottish Presbyterian, was on the scene. The often changing relations of the Scottish churches to the state, and the sometimes troubled colonial experiences of the Scotch-Irish in the north of Ireland, fostered among Presbyterians in America varieties of views, or perhaps an ambivalence, concerning culture shaping. They inherited the Calvinist impulse to establish a Christian commonwealth; but they also had enough experience of religious oppression to be suspicious of religious establishments, especially when they were living, as in America, under British rule. The Christian commonwealth would be built by persuasion and education.[5]

The symbol of Presbyterian distinctiveness and unity was thus not a social-political program (except that they were militantly anti-British during the Revolution) but doctrinal orthodoxy. Strict confessionalism was a major trait of the largest party of Scotch-Irish and Scottish Presbyterians from their first appearance in the colonies. Presbyterianism in America, however, was from the outset fed by some other streams, not of Scottish but of English origin. English Presbyterianism itself had become tolerant of doctrinal diversity by the early eighteenth century. More importantly, New England Puritans, especially those in Connecticut, viewed themselves as close allies of Presbyterianism in the Middle Colonies and in the early eighteenth century were providing the newly formed (ca. 1706) Presbyterian Church with personnel and leaders. By the time of the Great Awakening, the New England party was closely linked with the more pietistic revivalist group of the Presbyterians. In

1741 this revivalist "New Side" group split from the antirevivalist Scotch-Irish or Scottish "Old Side."

Remarkably, these two Presbyterian "sides" reunited in 1758, thus suggesting that pietist revivalism and doctrinalist confessionalism were compatible. But the tension between these two emphases repeatedly reemerged. The classic instance was in the Old School/New School schism of 1837-38, in many ways a repetition of the Old Side/New Side conflict. The Old School was clearly the stronghold of Scotch-Irish and Scottish elements and found its unity in strict confessionalism. The New School, on the other hand, represented an alliance of more strongly pietist or prorevivalist Presbyterians with New England Congregationalists.

The Growth of Reformed Branches

By this time, however, a number of other issues surrounded this renewed confrontation between confessionalist and pietist axes. The New School was the more typically American of the two groups, its distinctive characteristics reflecting the tendencies of the ethos of the dominant American evangelicalism. This meant that they were more tolerant of theological innovation and variety than had been their predecessors in the seventeenth- and eighteenth-century American Reformed camps. This doctrinal latitude, however, was not a liberalism that involved intentional concessions to secularism (as in later modernism). Rather, it was an outgrowth of pietist zeal for revivalism. In politically liberal America, such zeal translated into some mildly anti-Calvinist (or semi-Pelagian) doctrines emphasizing an unaided human ability voluntarily to accept the revivalists' gospel message with its culminating summons of "choose ye this day." Such doctrinal innovations were held more closely in check by the New School Presbyterians than by their revivalist Congregationalist allies, such as Charles G. Finney. Moreover, they propounded these innovations in the name of greater faithfulness to Scripture alone, as opposed to what some saw as an unhealthly traditionalism of the Old School.

Openness to practical innovation also characterized the New School pietist strand of the heritage. Finney's "New Measures" for promoting revival in the manner of the high-pressure salesman were only the most prominent examples of evangelicalism's openness to departures from tradition. The spread of gospel music perhaps best exemplified the new evangelical style. Especially notable was a new emphasis on personal experience. Controversial also among the Presbyterians was the New School enthusiasm for working through ecclesiastically independent societies (what are now called parachurch agencies) for missions, evangelism, publication, education, and social reform.

This latter issue of social reform was creating a new source of controversy concerning what it meant to be "Reformed," a debate over what we are calling its culturalist heritage. Prior to the nineteenth century, questions concerning social reform had not been conspicuous, divisive issues. Until that time almost all the Reformed groups seem to have been working on the basis of a vaguely formulated, but deeply entrenched, tradition that, ideally, the religion of a nation should be exclusively Reformed. So they assumed that being Reformed accordingly involved transforming the moral ethos and legal system of a people so that it should comport with God's law. The Puritans, as we have seen, worked these principles out most fully in practice. By the early nineteenth century, however, these Reformed principles had to be translated to fit a pluralistic and democratic situation. The question therefore became that of how much emphasis the Reformed Churches should put on shaping the legal structures of a society they did not otherwise control. Was it not the case that the true mission of the church was to proclaim a pure gospel and be a model moral subcommunity within the larger community, leavening it rather than attempting to legislate morality for all?

Finding answers to these questions was complicated by the fact that sometimes the resolution to moral issues could have as much to do with where one stood politically as it did what theological principles one held. Thus, whereas regarding Sabbath observance most nineteenth-century Reformed groups could unite in supporting legislation, on the issue of slavery they were sharply divided. Moreover, opinions on the slavery issue varied strikingly with geography. In the deep South, Reformed people were adamantly opposed to any interference with the practice of black slavery and emphasized aspects of the tradition that favored confining the activities of the church to strictly "spiritual" issues. In New England, by contrast, Reformed Christians often took the lead in insisting that the churches should unrelentingly urge the state to enact immediate emancipation. In the upper South and the lower North, opinions were more varied and often more nuanced. New School Presbyterian leaders, having New England connections, were typically moderate antislavery types, while the Old School sided with the theologically conservative South in wanting to sidestep this and other social reform issues.

"Old School" and "New School" outlooks had thus emerged as the two leading American patterns of being Reformed. The Old School was most characteristically doctrinalist, while the more innovative New School combined pietist revivalism with a culturalist emphasis, inherited from the Puritans, looking for a Christianization of American life. These divisions were not confined to Presbyterians, although they took their clearest shape among them. A number of smaller denominations, including some Baptists, were strictly Reformed doctrinalist groups. Other groups, among whom were some Baptists, the Reformed Church in America, and especially the majority of New England's Congregationalists, were clearly in the New School camp and part of the Reformed wing of the formidable American evangelical coalition that stressed pietism and culturalism. Through the Civil War era, these two schools of Reformed were not irreconcilable, especially once the slavery issue was removed. Most notably, after the war, in 1869 the New School and Old School Presbyterians in the North reunited.

The South, on the other hand, remained separate, holding on to its predominantly Old School tradition and urging the church to stay out of politics. Ironically this apolitical stance of the southern church was deeply mixed with defense of the southern way of life. Accordingly, during the next century the Old School doctrinalism of the Southern Presbyterians was associated with (at least local) cultural influence. In the North, on the other hand, confessionalism lost much of its social base and became more and more associated with a remnant mentality.

The New School heritage, on the other hand, emerged by the end of the century as the stronger of the two traditions in the North. The New School, however, was a combination of two emphases, pietist and culturalist, and these were separable. The divorce between them occurred under the pressures associated with the rapid modernization and secularization of American life between 1870 and 1930. Industrialization, urbanization, immigration, and pluralization undermined the social basis for the old evangelical (and often Reformed) religious quasi-establishment. Moreover, liberal democratic ideology, emphasizing human freedom, ability, and essential goodness, undermined the distinctly Calvinist doctrines. Even more basically, the new naturalistic science and history of the day challenged the authority of the Bible.

Broadly considered, evangelical Christians who responded to these crises moved in one of two directions. One group adjusted to modern times by toning down the supernaturalistic aspects of the gospel and stressing rather those parts of the Christian message that could be realized by developing natural (although God-given) human individual or cultural potentials. On the other side, conservatives reemphasized the fundamentals of the faith, which stressed God's supernatural interventions into history. Thus in the Reformed communities, as in many other areas of American life, a new division was superimposed on existing patterns.

The modernist accommodations to prevailing ideas and ideals fit least well with doctrinalist emphases and best with culturalist. Such theological liberalism was in principle compatible with some pietist emphases (as in a romantic religion of the heart), but in the long run piety proved difficult to sustain from generation to generation without a strong sense of radical divine intervention.

In the New School traditions (including Presbyterian, Congregationalist, Reformed Church in America, Baptist, and other heirs of the nineteenth-century evangelical mainstream), where doctrinalism was not especially strong, the new liberalism flourished, at least among some of the denominational leadership. It grew first, in the late Victorian era, as a version of evangelical romantic piety. In the progressive era, following the turn of the century, it also blossomed as part of the theological basis for the social gospel movement. By this time liberal Protestantism was moving away from crucial parts of traditional evangelical doctrine, repudiating emphases on personal salvation through trust in Christ's work of substitutionary atonement and rejecting the infallibility and reliability of Scripture. These liberal notions alarmed some of the heirs to revivalist pietism. Ecclesiastical warfare broke out and eventually brought a long series of splits between the two camps. Since the social gospel was associated with the modernist tendencies, the "fundamentalist" opponents tended to reject all "social gospels," or culturalist emphases. Such rejections, however, were seldom consistently sustained. New School revivalists also had a heritage of aspiring to Christianize America on a voluntary basis. Thus even when, especially after about 1920, fundamentalists decried the social gospel, they typically still endorsed a politically conservative culturalism that involved efforts to return America to nineteenth-century evangelical standards, as was seen in the anti-evolution and prohibition movements.

The supernaturalist or fundamentalist party among the Reformed included major elements of Old School or doctrinalist heritage as well as the successors to New School evangelicalism. The Old School party, centered first at Princeton Theological Seminary and after 1929 at Westminster Theological Seminary, provided intellectual foundations for defending the traditional faith. The common enemy, modernism, brought these strict confessionalists into close alliance with Reformed people of more New School or pietist-revivalist heritage for a time. Thus by the early 1930s the strictly confessionalist Presbyterians who followed New Testament scholar and apologist J. Gresham Machen were closely allied with Presbyterians among the more strictly revivalist fundamentalists, such as those at Wheaton College or Moody Bible Institute.

The groupings among these theologically Reformed fundamentalists were complicated by the presence of still another major new camp— the dispensationalists. Dispensationalism was essentially Reformed in its nineteenth-century origins and had in later nineteenth-century America spread most among revival-oriented Calvinists. Strict Old School confessionalists were, however, uneasy with dispensationalists' separation of the Old Testament dispensation of Law from the era of Grace in the church age. Dispensationalism, accordingly, was accepted most readily by Reformed Christians who had a more New School, or revivalist-evangelical, emphasis than among the various Old School, or doctrinalist, groups. During the fundamentalist controversies, however, these two groups were thrown into each other's arms.

The union, however, did not last. In 1937 the followers of Machen who had just left the Presbyterian Church in the U.S.A. split roughly into Old School and New School camps, with the more revivalist group, led by Carl McIntire, favoring dispensationalism and total abstinence from alcoholic beverages. About the same time, doctrinalist Southern Presbyerians took a stand against dispensationalism in their denomination.

Another, less separatist branch of the New School evangelical party survived well in the "new evangelicalism" that grew out of fundamentalism after World War II. The new evangelicals were largely Reformed in leadership and had moved away from strict dispensationalism. Institutionally they gained strength at centers such as Wheaton College, Fuller Theological Seminary, Trinity Evangelical Divinity School, and Gordon-Conwell Theological Seminary. *Christianity Today*, founded in 1956 under the editorship of Carl F. H. Henry, gave them wide visibility and influence. Inter-Varsity Christian Fellowship, InterVarsity Press, and the ministry of Francis Schaeffer also added substantially to the outreach of this Reformed evangelicalism. Keeping cordial relations with many individuals and groups not Reformed and with evangelicals both within and outside mainline denominations, this New School tradition has emerged as one of the most influential expressions of evangelicalism today.

The Old School, though smaller, also remains active. It has wide influence through Westminster Theological Seminary and similar conservative schools. Denominationally, it is especially strong in the Presbyterian Church of America and in the conservative wing of the Christian Reformed Church. It is also found among Reformed Baptists and in other smaller Reformed denominations.

Of the three strands of the heritage, the culturalist emphasis is the least unified today. Nonetheless, it is perhaps as prominent as it ever has been. This continuing emphasis, that Calvinists should be transforming culture and bringing all of creation back to its proper relationship to God's law, has been resurgent due to the convergence of a number of developments. Most clearly articulating these views have been the North American Kuyperians, followers of the turn-of-the-century Dutch theologian and politician, Abraham Kuyper. Kuyperianism was brought to America largely by the Dutch-American Christian Reformed Church, where a hard-line Kuyperianism also developed among the admirers of

Dutch philosopher Herman Dooyeweerd. Dooyeweerdianism has enlisted non-Dutch disciples, but the widest influence of Kuyperianism spread in a mild form through the neoevangelical movement after World War II. The fundamentalist tradition, said neoevangelical spokespersons such as Carl F. H. Henry, had not sufficiently recognized that the Christian task involves relating a Christian "World-and-life view" to all of culture and politics.[6]

By the 1970s such moderately conservative emphases were converging with the resurgence of conservative politics among American fundamentalists and fundamentalistic evangelicals. Fundamentalists had their own, vaguely Reformed, traditions of wanting to Christianize America. Versions of Kuyperian Calvinism such as those suggested by Francis Schaeffer in the influential political ministry of his later years helped articulate the new fundamentalist conservative political emphases of the Moral Majority. Schaeffer drew many of his political ideas from the work of the politically conservative Dooyeweerdian thinker, Rousas J. Rushdoony. Rushdoony also contributed to the emergence of the hyper-Reformed "theonomist" movement, which insists that Old Testament law should be the basis of American civil law.

The irony in this resurgence of Reformed culturalism is that the culturalists, who are often united in theological theory, are so deeply divided in practice. Cutting across the culturalist movement is a seemingly insurmountable divide between those who are politically conservative and those who are politically liberal. Many of the American followers of Kuyper have been politically liberal and these had an impact on the politically progressive evangelicalism that emerged during the 1960s and early 1970s.[7] Moreover, the politically liberal Reformed culturalist camp includes Reformed Christians in mainline denominations whose traditions still reflect the political progressivism of the social gospel days. In addition, the neoorthodox heritage in such denominations has contributed, especially via the work of H. Richard Niebuhr and Reinhold Niebuhr, to generally Reformed culturalist sensibilities tempered by a Lutheran sense of the ambiguities inherent in relating Christianity to an essentially pagan culture.

The American Reformed community today, then, still includes substantial representation of the three classic emphases, doctrinalism, pietism, and culturalism. These three are, of course, not incompatible and the unity of Reformed Christians in America would be much greater were this compatibility recognized and emphasized.

The question of unity, however, is complicated by the twentieth-century divisions of modernists and fundamentalists that have cut across the traditional divisions. Neoorthodox and dispensationalist variations add further complications. Moreover, among those who are primarily culturalists, conflicting political allegiances subvert Reformed unity. Nonetheless, there remain a substantial number of Reformed Christians whose faith reflects a balance, or potential balance, of the three traditional emphases. It is these Christians who need to find each other and who might benefit from reflecting on what it should mean to be Reformed.

They can also learn from considering the characteristic weaknesses, as well as the strengths, of their tradition. Perhaps the greatest fault of American Reformed communities since Puritan times is that they have cultivated an elitism. Ironically, the doctrine of election has been unwittingly construed as meaning that Reformed people have been endowed with superior theological, spiritual, or moral merit by God himself. The great irony of this is that the genius of the Reformed faith has been its uncompromising emphasis on God's grace, with the corollary that our own feeble efforts are accepted, not because of any merit, but solely due to God's grace and Christ's work. The doctrine of grace, then, ought to cultivate humility as a conspicuous trait of Reformed spirituality. A strong sense of our own inadequacies is an important asset for giving us positive appreciation of those who differ from us.

Yet too often Reformed people have been so totally confident of their own spiritual insights that they have been unable to accept or work with fellow Reformed Christians whose emphases may vary slightly. Perhaps some review of the rich varieties of theological views among the Reformed in America today will contribute to bringing tolerance and search for balance. Moreover, the unmistakable minority status of the "Reformed" in America today should help foster the need for mutual understanding and respect. Above all, however, a revival of the central Reformed distinctive—the sense of our own unworthiness and of total dependence on God's grace, as revealed especially through Christ's sacrificial work—should bring together many who in late twentieth-century America still find it meaningful to say "I am Reformed."

Notes: Reformed and American

1. I. John Hesselink, *On Being Reformed: Distinctive Characteristics and Common Misunderstandings* (Ann Arbor: Servant Books, 1983), 2 and 113.

2. This concept is elaborated in *Evangelicalism and Modern America,* ed. George M. Marsden (Grand Rapids: Wm. B. Eerdmans Publishing Company, 1984).

3. These categories are roughly those suggested by Nicholas Wolterstorff, "The AACS in the CRC," *The Reformed Journal* 24 (December 1974): 9-16.

4. Harry S. Stout, *The New England Soul: Preaching and Religious Culture in Colonial New England* (New York: Oxford University Press, forthcoming).

5. The Reformed efforts to build a Christian culture are well described in Fred J. Hood, *Reformed America: The Middle and Southern States, 1783-1837* (University, AL: University of Alabama Press, 1980).

6. Carl F. H. Henry, *The Uneasy Conscience of Modern Fundamentalism* (Grand Rapids: Wm. B. Eerdmans Publishing Company, 1947), 10.

7. See Robert Booth Fowler, *A New Engagement: Evangelical Political Thought, 1966-1976* (Grand Rapids: Wm. B. Eerdmans Publishing Company, 1982), for an account of this relationship and other developments in evangelical political thought.

I. THE PRINCETON THEOLOGY

THE PRINCETON THEOLOGY

MARK A. NOLL

THE Princeton Theology was a distinctly American and a distinctly nineteenth-century expression of classical Reformed faith. Misunderstanding results if we regard it either as a simple restatement of Augustinian Calvinism, untouched by its surroundings, or as a simple product of American culture, haphazardly garnished with traditional Reformed words. During the nineteenth century—which in America may be regarded as that period stretching from the inspiring moments of the Revolution to the disillusionments of World War I—the Princeton theologians functioned as a loyal opposition. On the basis of their Calvinism, they questioned American myths about the power of the self, the American trust in consciousness, the American rejection of the past, and the American idolization of democracy. Yet they also took their stand as cultural insiders. They spoke Calvinism with an unmistakable American accent. With most other intellectuals of their day, they relied on a Common Sense approach to truth, they assumed the value-free character of scientific investigation, they were suspicious of high-flown ideas from the continent, and they took economic and political self-reliance for granted. The men who articulated the Princeton Theology, the convictions that constituted it, and the institutions in which it took shape were much more than functions of nineteenth-century American culture. But neither were they ever less than that. This paper attempts to place these men, convictions, and institutions in proper context before making an assessment of this important theological school, both in comparison to other varieties of Reformed faith and with regard to its relevance today.[1]

Men

Of the many individuals who contributed to the Princeton Theology during its long life from the founding of a Presbyterian seminary at Princeton, New Jersey, in 1812, to the reorganization of that institution

in 1929, three were clearly most important: Archibald Alexander, founding professor; his pupil, Charles Hodge; and Benjamin Breckinridge
Warfield, who in his turn had studied under Hodge.

Archibald Alexander's experience before coming to Princeton and
his initial leadership of the seminary set the course that his successors
followed.[2] Alexander (1772-1851) arrived at Princeton in 1812 after a full
career as revivalist, educator, pastor, and theologian. During the 1780s
and 1790s he witnessed and led revivals in his native Virginia. As a
result he remained more disposed to value "enthusiastic" religion than
was normally the case at Princeton. Yet even as he took part in the practical renewal of the church, he was also putting his mind to use. Alexander studied privately with the Rev. William Graham, one of the most
ardent disciples of John Witherspoon, then president of Princeton College. What Graham taught Alexander especially was to think for himself,
to distrust learned authorities in favor of the testimony of his own experience. Alexander, however, soon went beyond Graham's instruction
to embrace as well major expressions of historic Calvinism. Early in his
ministry he eagerly read Jonathan Edwards, especially Edwards's treatment of the will. Alexander later worked through several seventeenth-
century Reformed dogmaticians for his own benefit. When he came to
Princeton, after service as a pastor in Virginia and Philadelphia and a
stint as president of Hamden-Sydney College, he carried the intellectual
resources and the practical concerns that would mark that seminary long
after his passing.

Charles Hodge (1797-1878) and B. B. Warfield (1851-1921) receive
separate treatment in this book, so it is not necessary to outline their
careers here.[3] Suffice it to say that Hodge fleshed out the framework
Alexander had established in a wide-ranging collection of works: exegetical commentaries, popular exhortation, denominational history, lectures, and eventually a massive textbook in systematic theology, but
above all polemical periodical essays. Although not as comfortable with
revivalistic piety as Alexander nor as technically brilliant as Warfield,
Hodge was the most complex of the major Princeton theologians. He
succeeded in bringing together more elements from the Reformed heritage, American culture, and pastoral concern than anyone in the tradition. Warfield, for his part, faced a different range of challenges than his
predecessors, including wholesale intellectual defalcation from the evangelical Protestantism that was a cultural given in the America of Alexander and Hodge. Warfield set himself to expose the fallacies of modern
alternatives to historic Christianity, a task that he carried out in hundreds
of essays and thousands of reviews. His mind was discriminating, and
his heart was faithful to historic Calvinism. Warfield did not have the

same pastoral or ecclesiastical instincts as Alexander or Hodge, but he was no less a warrior for the convictions that they held dear.

A. A. Hodge (1823-1886), who taught at Princeton for ten years between the old age of his father and his own death, heads the second rank of Princeton theologians. He was a master of summation and popular presentation, rather than of the polemics that Charles Hodge and Warfield mastered. In this regard his service resembled that of many other Princetonians who augmented and expanded the major insights of Alexander, Hodge, and Warfield, including especially James Waddel Alexander (1804-1859) and Joseph Addison Alexander (1809-1860), sons of the founder who carried out a myriad of intellectual and practical services to the Presbyterian Church, Princeton College, and the seminary; Lyman Atwater (1813-1883), a transplanted New Englander who shouldered the major burden in replying to the theological errors that Princetonians perceived in his native region; William Henry Green (1825-1900), a professor of Old Testament who held firmly to traditional ideas about the Bible even while he appreciated new scholarship on the Middle East; and J. Gresham Machen (1881-1937), a New Testament scholar who led a remnant of the Princeton Theology out into the wilderness after the directors of the seminary altered its course in 1929.[4]

The leaders who formulated the Princeton Theology were men of intelligence, theological insight, pastoral concern, and practical wisdom. Yet what set them apart in their day, and what makes them intriguing objects of inquiry after their passing, is the beliefs they held, the methods they used to propagate those beliefs, and their efforts to preserve them for later generations.

Convictions

The Princeton Theology was not as simple as either proponents or opponents liked to make it. Princetonians sometimes spoke of themselves as Francis Landy Patton did in 1912 at the seminary's centennial: they "simply taught the old Calvinistic theology without modification." Those who doubt the wisdom of Old Princeton sometimes perceive an equally simple, if contrasting picture. One of these was Frank Hugh Foster who, writing of Charles Hodge as representative of the school, suggested in 1907 that Hodge "may be safely left by the historian of a progressive school of theology to the natural consequence of his own remark that during the many years of his predominance at Princeton that institution had never brought forward a single original thought."[5]

The reality was something different. Princeton did maintain a Reformed position in continuity with previous generations of Calvinistic theologians. But the Princetonians did not always organize their efforts, or emphasize the same relationships, as their Reformed predecessors had. Old Princeton often took procedural and methodological questions for granted, even when these exerted considerable influence on the shape of its thought. In these and other ways the theology that developed at Princeton was as complex as that of any of the other major bodies of Christian thought in nineteenth-century America. The strengths and complexity of Princeton stand out more clearly in an examination of those convictions that were most important to the school.

1. *Reformed Confessionalism.* "Calvinism," wrote Warfield in 1904, "is just religion in its purity. We have only, therefore, to conceive of religion in its purity, and that is Calvinism."[6] The Princetonians would no doubt have been distressed had they known that theologians in the late twentieth century would study them primarily in regard to their technical views on the Bible or for their use of the Scottish Philosophy of Common Sense. While they certainly held firm views on Scripture and philosophy, these matters were parts of a larger enterprise, to proclaim the dignity, necessity, and cogency of the Reformed faith. Warfield's words spoke for them all.

Princeton theologians freely employed the riches of the Calvinist heritage in setting out their own faith, although they did not draw equally from all varieties of Reformed tradition. Charles Hodge, for example, admired both the Thirty-Nine Articles of the Church of England and the Heidelberg Catechism, but seems to have made slight use in his *Systematic Theology* either of these documents or of the theological traditions they represent. Yet their wide-ranging use of Augustine on salvation, of Calvin, of several major Puritans, of Luther and orthodox Lutherans, of the Westminster standards, and of Swiss dogmaticians after Calvin suggests the breadth of their Reformed commitments.

The winsome proclamation of this Calvinism was the heart of their concern. Nowhere was Charles Hodge more eloquent than when defending Reformed views of human nature or of divine sovereignty in salvation—as, for example, in polemics directed at Charles Finney or the New Haven Theology of Nathaniel W. Taylor. Warfield was constrained to write scores of articles upholding a broadly orthodox view of the Bible's inspiration, but he wrote even more on specifically Reformed concerns: defending Calvinistic views of revelation (against evangelical perfectionists as well as against Catholics and modernists), offering the views of Calvin and Augustine for modern inspection, and detailing the intended purposes of the Westminster divines.

Princeton Calvinism shared the main emphases of the Reformed tradition: The Fall perverted a perfect creation, led to divine condemnation, and established human guilt. Adam's sin was imputed to all humans, who properly deserve the condemnation which that sinfulness entails. The same process of imputation that rendered humanity doomed in Adam justified the elect through faith in Christ. God expressed his saving purposes in covenanting to offer salvation through Christ. Sinners, turned from God by rebellious natures, were "bound" to their own sinful desires until God changed their hearts through Scripture, Christian nurture, preaching, and the sacraments. Redeemed sinners, though hamstrung by the lingering effects of the Fall, yet were fitted by the Holy Spirit for fruitful service in the Kingdom of God. These principles made up the solid core of Princeton belief to which all other major concerns were attendant.

Questions do remain, however, about the nature of Princeton's Reformed faith. The school tended to assume that positions drawn from various Reformed sources, shaped by the questions of the nineteenth century, and applied in modern polemics were simple restatements of an undifferentiated Reformed orthodoxy. In other words, Princetonians regarded theology as a static entity not affected to any appreciable degree by historical development. Arguments first made by Augustine against Pelagius, by Calvin against the Council of Trent, or by Francis Turretin against his opponents in the late seventeenth century were, to them, parts of one dogmatic whole. They did not consider the possibility that previous Reformed theologians may have individualized aspects of the biblical revelation even as they put the Scriptures to use in their respective eras.

This relative lack of sensitivity to historical conditioning, much more than a supposedly servile use of Turretin, is the most important question concerning the place of Princeton in the history of Reformed thought.[7] No doubt can exist that they were important spokesmen for that tradition. Some doubt may arise as to whether they always represented the tradition to its best advantage. The Princeton assumption that it was possible simply to restate tested and true positions for the present arose from both their confidence in the truth-telling character of Scripture and their particular beliefs in philosophy and science, convictions that deserve individual attention in any overview of their theology.

2. *Scripture.* From first to last the Princeton theologians held to a high view of the Bible's inspiration and authority. At his inaugural in 1812, Alexander preached on John 5:39, "Search the Scriptures," in order to establish the Bible as the foundation for the seminary's existence.[8] In 1915 Warfield summed up a lifetime's work on the same subject by contending in a magisterial interpretation of "Inspiration" that "the Scriptures are throughout a Divine book, created by the Divine energy and speaking in their every part with Divine authority directly to the heart

of the readers."[9] This conviction undergirded the long history of the theology.

Charles Hodge was called upon to make the first major restatements of Alexander's views on Scripture as the claims of Higher Criticism began to enter the United States at mid-century. Yet even in his *Systematic Theology*, which was finally published in 1872-73, Hodge offered his teaching on Scripture mostly as a corrective to deficient positions that he had encountered early in the century, especially those of Roman Catholics and subjectivist pietists. It fell to his son and Warfield to scrutinize the new criticism more thoroughly. They did this most completely in a memorable essay published in 1881, entitled simply "Inspiration," in which they upheld the church's historic confidence in the letter as well as the spirit of the Scriptures, described presuppositions on both sides of the contemporary discussion, and contended for the traditional view on the basis of the Bible's own testimony concerning itself.[10] In later essays Warfield explored numerous facets of the issue, laying especially heavy emphasis on the way in which the Bible's inspiration did not detract from its character as a thoroughly human (though errorless) book. Princeton's fidelity to the plenary inspiration of the Bible was consistent; each generation refined the position that it had received. The effort throughout was painstaking, careful, scholarly, and learned.

The Princeton adherence to strict views of inspiration does not, however, answer every important question one can ask about Scripture. Why, for instance, should we believe the Bible and a biblical faith? Charles Hodge sometimes said, as in quoting a German source in 1840: "Faith is no work of reason, and therefore cannot be overthrown by it, since believing no more arises from arguments than tasting or seeing."[11] Alexander and Warfield were more likely to suggest that irrefragable testimony and close logic can demonstrate that the Bible is God's word and that we should base our faith on that reasonable certainty.[12] Or again, why do the Princeton theologians usually act as if the Bible existed primarily for the formulation of dogma? As George Marsden points out in this book, other Reformed communities, though not despising dogma, have used the Scriptures as much to inspire piety or guide cultural reformation. For their part, the Princeton theologians usually considered biblical piety a strict product of correct biblical dogma. And they were largely silent about the Bible's potential for cultural reformation.[13] Yet rarely did Princetonians reflect directly on their preference for a dogmatic approach to Scripture.[14] A further question concerns relationships between the "book of God" and the "book of nature." Charles Hodge felt that ideas of design, which he found in Scripture, negated Darwinism. A. A. Hodge and Warfield, on the other hand, both felt that the Bible could be read in such a way as to make peace with Darwinism.[15]

To summarize, the Princeton teaching on the nature of Scripture was consistent and very clear: the Bible was God's written word; it was a genuine product of human activity that could be studied historically; yet the Bible was also the presentation of the most perfect truth in all that its human authors (under the inspiration of the Holy Spirit) meant to affirm; it was effective in doing the converting and sanctifying work of the Spirit. On questions about the place of the Bible in apologetics, its place in the church's life more generally, and its interpretation in relationship to general revelation (as in science), the Princeton testimony on Scripture was less unified. Such unanswered questions do not detract from their positive testimony on Scripture, but rather suggest that the many good words from Princeton on the Bible did not include the last word.

3. *Scottish Common Sense Philosophy.* Although it had long been recognized that the Scottish Philosophy of Common Sense played a leading role at Princeton, it was not until the publication of Sydney Ahlstrom's seminal essay on the general subject in 1955 that this dimension of the theology began to receive careful attention.[16] Since then it has become a commonplace to hold that Old Princeton was heavily, even uniquely, indebted to this philosophy. There are several plausible reasons for doing so.

John Witherspoon (1723-1794), the instructor of Alexander's mentor William Graham (1746-1799) at Princeton College, had trained his students in the convictions of the Scottish philosophy. And Graham was among its most ardent exponents.[17] From study with Graham, Alexander adopted many of the principles that Witherspoon brought with him to America from Scottish thinkers like Francis Hutcheson (1694-1746) and Thomas Reid (1710-1796). These philosophers were attempting to rescue the English "moderate" Enlightenment of Isaac Newton and John Locke from the skepticism of David Hume and the idealism of George Berkeley.[18] As Alexander came to express these positions, they included an affirmation that the "common sense" of humankind could verify the deliverances of the physical senses and of intuitive consciousness (i.e., the "moral sense"). It was second nature for him to think, as illustrated in his earliest lectures at the seminary and in his last, posthumously published book, that this "common sense" provided the basis for an irrefutable apologetic concerning the existence of God and the reality of biblical revelation.[19] Along with Witherspoon, Graham, and their Scottish mentors, Alexander was an enthusiast for empiricism and induction. Scrupulous investigation imitating methods of the "natural philosophers" would lead to the same kind of success in ethics and theology as the great Newton had enjoyed in studying the physical world.[20]

Charles Hodge imbibed the Scottish Philosophy from Alexander, as well as from the pastor of his youth, Ashbel Green, who became president of Princeton College in 1812, the year that Hodge began his studies there. (Green's major educational change at the college was to restore Witherspoon's lectures in moral philosophy as the integrating text for the undergraduates.) Hodge's debt to the Scottish Philosophy appears most clearly in the opening pages of his *Systematic Theology* where, in oft-quoted lines, he likened the construction of dogmatic systems to scientific exploration: "The Bible is to the theologian what nature is to the man of science. It is his store-house of facts; and his method of ascertaining what the Bible teaches is the same as that which the natural philosopher adopts to ascertain what nature teaches."[21] Warfield learned the Scottish Philosophy from James McCosh, the last prominent defender of the system, who in 1868 came from Scotland to Princeton College as Witherspoon had a century before. That was also the year in which Warfield began his undergraduate studies. Other spokesmen for the Princeton Theology asserted Common Sense convictions aggressively or, like A. A. Hodge, simply accepted them as the natural axioms for theological inquiry.

When this eighteenth-century philosophical position was added to Princeton's Reformed convictions, the result was not always propitious. Princetonians could be overconfident in assuming that the deliverances of their own consciousness equaled the common intuitions of all humanity. They were naive in thinking that chains of apologetical reasoning could begin with no moral preconditions in the seeker and no predetermined assumptions about the end of inquiry. And although their Calvinism pointed in an opposite direction, their philosophical allegiance could at times leave them sounding like scientistic positivists.

Yet this is not the whole story. Princeton's accommodation to Scottish Common Sense Philosophy was neither total nor comprehensive. While harboring few reservations about epistemological and methodological aspects of the Scottish position, they regularly resisted its ethical implications, at least on major doctrines.[22] They were not like their theological contemporaries in New England who substantially altered traditional Reformed views of human nature and divine sovereignty on the basis, in E. A. Park's words, of "the fundamental laws of human belief," those "ethical axioms, which so many fathers in the church have undervalued," which are derived from "*the philosophy of common sense.*"[23] By contrast, the Princeton theologians never allowed the deliverances of refined Victorian conscience to overwhelm basic Calvinistic beliefs in human moral incapacity or to replace supreme confidence in the sometimes "unenlightened" pronouncements of the Bible.

Thus, the Princeton investment in Common Sense Philosophy did not lead to a comprehensive reordering of traditional Reformed theology as it did for N. W. Taylor. Rather Princetonians merely added Common Sense to their more traditional theological convictions. The result was a system with more internal stress and less methodological rigor than Taylor's New Haven Theology; and it was a system that did not come to terms with religious experience as forthrightly as did Horace Bushnell.[24] Yet for all these weaknesses, the very naiveté of Princeton's Common Sense convictions was a disguised blessing. Acting intuitively, Princeton made profitable conjunctions where Common Sense really did support traditional Reformed positions (as in the impossibility of living as if there were no God who maintained the physical and moral worlds). To be sure, they muddied the waters when discussing the first principles of ethics by clumsily intermingling Scottish beliefs about universal human capacities with Reformed convictions about the moral effects of the Fall.[25] But Common Sense intuitionism was never the last word, especially when it came to teachings on the sovereignty of God over human consciousness and the superiority of divine revelation to the inner voice of the self. And these were convictions that were fading during the nineteenth century almost as fast among American evangelicals at large as among the champions of the new theologies.[26]

4. *Religious Experience, The Work of the Spirit.* In spite of their reputation as scholastics or rationalists, and in spite of their fidelity to the objective works of God, the Princeton theologians constantly stressed the importance of religious experience and the need for the work of the Holy Spirit. The Sunday afternoon "conferences" with seminary students that lasted from generation to generation throughout most of the century, their occasional sermons, and especially the commentaries and selected polemical essays of Charles Hodge testify to consistent efforts at giving the supernatural work of the Spirit its proper place in the life of the individual believer and of the church as a whole.[27] As Reformed theologians, the Princetonians always insisted that the Spirit worked through "means."[28] Yet none of them neglected the importance of religious experience, even if they insisted that such experience not be opposed to the propositional testimony of Scripture and the intellectual structure of the confessions.

The pertinent question for the Princeton theologians is not whether they had a place for religious experience and the work of the Holy Spirit. As Professor Andrew Hoffecker's fine recent book makes clear beyond cavil, they certainly did.[29] The question is rather where this religious experience, where the work of the Holy Spirit, fit into their theology. It is hard to escape the conclusion that on this score, as in the Princeton appropriation of Common Sense Philosophy, no entirely satisfactory integration occurred. The Charles Hodge who laid such great store by "facts" and "scientific method" could also argue for the priority of inner convictions over external argument in the reception of religious truth. And as David Kelsey has pointed out, even Warfield, the most carefully logical of the Princeton theologians, often described his belief in Scripture as arising more from the internal power of the written word than from conclusions out of a neutral chain of argument.[30] At issue is not their seriousness about religious experience, but the incorporation of that seriousness in their theology as a whole.

The quickening power of the Holy Spirit, manifest through divinely ordained means, was a principal feature of Princeton religion. That this element of the Princeton Theology seems to stay in the background is the responsibility first of these men themselves, since they seemed less clear about the place of the Spirit's work in their theology than in their lives. But it is also a result of a historical failure to realize that occasional Princeton statements that ignore or play down the importance of religious experience were not necessarily the foundational axioms of the theology as a whole.

Institutions

The convictions of the Princeton theologians are the main reasons for their continuing importance. Yet historically considered, the institutions that embodied those beliefs were nearly as impressive as the doctrines themselves. The ideas gave the theology its direction, but the institutions made it influential in America.

Princeton Seminary, the second major American school devoted to postgraduate theological education, was, quite naturally, the place where the Princeton Theology received its fullest institutional expression. The way the seminary came into existence had more than a little influence on the course that the Princeton Theology would take.[31] The seminary was founded in 1812, five years after the establishment of Andover Seminary, in response to a feeling that America was undergoing a cultural crisis of unprecedented seriousness. Its founders—Ashbel Green and Samuel Miller as well as Alexander—had several related purposes for the school: to fit clergymen to meet the cultural crisis, to roll back what they perceived as tides of irreligion sweeping the country, and to provide a learned defense of Christianity generally and the Bible specifically. The conserving character of the institution did not change during the life of the Princeton Theology. As its centennial in 1912, the seminary had enrolled over 1,000 more students than any other theological school in the United States. A total of 6,386 students studied at Princeton from Alexander's inauguration to Warfield's death. Some of them became famous theologians, educators, and ministers in their own right (by 1912 the alumni included fifty-six moderators of General Assemblies and five bishops of the Protestant Episcopal Church). Even more impressive was the steady infusion of ministers into the ongoing congregational life of the nation, ministers exposed to a powerful expression of American Calvinism and, much more often than not, its advocates as well.

The Princeton Theology spread outward through seminary graduates, but even more visibly through the printed page. A vast cornucopia of essays, commentaries, treatises, reviews, and pamphlets—on an incredibly diverse range of topics—tumbled from the presses of Philadelphia, New York, and Princeton itself to present this theology to the public. Many of these books, like Charles Hodge's *Way of Life* and his *Systematic Theology*, or the theological compendia of A. A. Hodge, reached wide audiences throughout the nineteenth century. A remarkably large number of Princeton books remain in print to this day.

Significant as the books undoubtedly were, the Princeton Theology received its fullest expression in periodicals.[32] Their learned and extensive reviews contained the fullest exposition of Princeton positions, the most vigorous attacks on rivals, and the most thoughtful reflections on great national events and significant intellectual milestones. The greatest of these journals was Charles Hodge's *Biblical Repertory and Princeton Review*, begun in 1825 in an effort mostly to transmit European theological scholarship to America, but changed over the years, and under a series of titles, to a mighty instrument of theological instruction. Although he had assistance in editing its pages, as indicated by the long lists of articles contributed by the Alexanders, Lyman Atwater, Albert Baldwin Dod, and other stalwarts, this was the supreme vehicle for Charles Hodge's convictions.[33] After managing the review for nearly forty years, he called his labor "a ball-and-chain" borne "with scarcely any other compensation than the high privilege and honour of making it an organ for upholding sound Presbyterianism, the cause of the country, and the honour of our common Redeemer."[34] Yet even foes recognized the power of the work in the journal, like the editor of Lyman Beecher's autobiography who said it was "the most powerful organ in the land." Friendly voices were even more extravagant, like the *British Quarterly Review*, which in 1871 called Hodge's journal "beyond all question the greatest purely theological Review that has ever been published in the English tongue."[35]

What made the *Princeton Review* so powerful, and what also contributed to the influence of the journals that A. A. Hodge and B. B. Warfield managed, was the Princeton ability to enlarge a parochial controversy into a full-blown defense of Reformed doctrines. For depth of treatment, clarity of argumentation, and seriousness of purpose, there is simply nothing in twentieth-century American religious life to match the theological discussions in nineteenth-century periodicals. And the

Princeton Review took a leading role in many of these. Whether Hodge
was debating the relationship between intellect and feeling with E. A.
Park (7 articles, 265 pages, over 18 months, in the *Princeton Review* and
Park's *Bibliotheca Sacra* during 1850-52), tilting with Horace Bushnell
(three lengthy articles over a twenty-year span), or addressing more particular issues of interest only to Presbyterians, the journal demanded
reading.

After Hodge's day, changes in the American academy reduced the
influence of the theological journals. Still, A. A. Hodge in *The Presbyterian Review* (1880-1889) and Warfield in *The Presbyterian and Reformed
Review* (1890-1902) and *The Princeton Theological Review* (1903-1921)
reached nearly the same degree of seriousness and comprehension.

The final institution of the Princeton Theology was the Presbyterian
Church. Although the seminary never enjoyed the confidence of the
entire denomination, its influence made it a power to be reckoned with.
It maintained consistent Old School views in the schism of 1837, urged
caution in the reunion of the northern Old and New School denominations in 1867, arrayed itself at the turn of the twentieth century against
innovation on the Confession and theological inclusiveness as a denominational strategy, and in general sought to keep the denomination close
to its confessional Calvinist roots.[36] From 1835 through 1867, with but
one exception, Charles Hodge reported on the year's General Assembly
in the *Princeton Review*. This quickly established Hodge as one of the
most visible arbiters of Presbyterian opinion in the century. "There is
no inducement," one of Hodge's allies once wrote, "to prepare a good
article for the July number, because every one turns at once to that on
the General Assembly which absorbs all interest."[37]

The expression of Princeton convictions in these institutions—the
seminary, their books and journals, the Presbyterian Church—was *the*
Princeton Theology. Many convictions of Old Princeton deserve a place
among the church's perpetual beliefs. But a judicious definition of this
theology as a concrete historical entity must always come back to the
institutions in which the Princeton beliefs took shape during the nineteenth century. To say this, however, raises the question of the Princeton
Theology in relation to its times.

The Nineteenth-Century Context

Many of the supposed defects of the Princeton theologians, and
some of their vaunted triumphs as well, become less striking if the work
of the school is placed in its historical context. To study Princeton only
in relationship to twentieth-century theological developments, or, from
a different perspective, to ignore the centuries between Calvin's activity

in Geneva and Alexander's in Princeton, is to short-circuit sympathetic understanding of these theologians. It may even be that the genuine contribution of the Princeton Theology will only be apparent when it is placed against the background of its times.

To do this shows immediately that much of the Princeton Theology was simply a singular expression of the ordinary affirmations of their day. For example, the Princetonians used Scottish Common Sense Philosophy mostly because it was America's common intellectual coinage of the nineteenth century. Early in the period orthodox Congregationalists at Yale as well as Unitarians at Harvard embraced this perspective nearly as enthusiastically as did Presbyterian Princeton. Common Sense assumptions later became commonplace in the theological pronouncements of an incredibly broad range of American theologians: revisionist Calvinists like N. W. Taylor, more consistent Calvinists like E. A. Park, New School Presbyterians like Albert Barnes, Disciples of Christ spokesmen like Alexander Campbell, Unitarians like Andrews Norton, and so on. At least for much of the nineteenth century, the Princetonians' Scottish Realism shows us more how they moved with their culture than against it.[38]

Once again, Princeton defended the authority of the Bible because for most of the century almost all evangelical Protestants took this for granted. In the last third of the century, the Princetonians came to stress more the cognitive than the affective veracity of Scripture. But even here the fact that these later Princeton proposals received such wide support from non-Calvinist groups would suggest that there was nothing peculiarly distinctive about the positions. And for the first two-thirds of the century, as essays by Randall Balmer and John Woodbridge have shown, it is hard to distinguish the Princeton views on the Bible from those of the American evangelical world at large.[39]

Similarly, Princetonians advocated a naive empiricism in the construction of theology because most American intellectuals approached theory-formation like this. During the nineteenth century historians, public servants, social scientists, and even artists, geniuses, and crackpots, all looked to simple scientific generalizations as the path to truth.[40] In this climate the Princeton methodological naiveté was part and parcel of a more general epistemological innocence in America.

For most of the nineteenth century, then, the Princeton theologians merely shared widespread cultural values in their convictions about the Bible, Scottish Common Sense Philosophy, and scientific empiricism. The distinctive Princeton achievement was to absorb these cultural assumptions into their Calvinism without losing that Calvinism. To be heard in the nineteenth century, it was necessary for Princeton to adopt the intellectual conventions of the day. Schools of theology that did not do this, like the Mercersberg theology of J. W. Nevin, are of considerable interest to twentieth-century scholars, but they were close to nullities in their own day. The truly remarkable thing about the work of the Princetonians was that so much historic Calvinism remained even as they adjusted their thought to accommodate American intellectual conventions.

Perspective: Princeton, Jonathan Edwards, and the Dutch

To assess the accomplishments of the Princetonians as well as their deficiencies, it is helpful to compare them with other representatives of Reformed theology. Two obvious candidates for such a task are Jonathan Edwards, who forged the most powerful engine of American Calvinism during the eighteenth century, and the Dutch followers of Abraham Kuyper, who through immigrant communities had established a presence in America by the end of the nineteenth century.

The many striking contrasts among these Reformed theologians can loom larger than their commonalities, even if their agreements were far more extensive than their disagreements. Though later theologians and historians have belabored their differences, the compliments that Princeton and the Dutch paid to Edwards and to each other were sincere.[41] The three represented different geographic regions and ethnic origins— New England from English stock, middle American from largely Scotch-Irish background, and immigrants from Holland—and they possessed very different temperaments, but the three shared a remarkable resemblance in efforts to do theology and approach life in a Calvinistic way.

Yet the differences were major. Edwards and the Dutch, first, showed much more concern for the intellectual framework of theology than did Old Princeton. The former wrestled with these questions as full-scale theological issues in their own right. Opinions differ concerning the success of these efforts, but they still resulted in a great deal of insight concerning method and a more obviously Christian grasp of procedural problems than the Princetonians displayed. By way of compensation, Princeton's relative lack of sophistication on such matters left its theology more accessible to a wide audience—at least so long as their assumptions about method corresponded roughly with those of the general populace, and that was for nearly one hundred years.

Second, the three differed in how their approach to Scripture affected their picture of the Christian's task in society. Princeton used the Bible to construct dogma, while it was content to accept the cultural conventions of the merchant-yeoman middle class without question. To Edwards the Bible was a resource for reflective piety, for discovering the divine and supernatural light that graciously converts the darkened heart; his absorption was so thorough on this theme that he seems to have given little thought to the late-Puritan society in which he lived. The Dutch, by contrast, almost defined themselves by their capacity to find scriptural principles for cultural formation, whether in education, politics, voluntary organizations, or economics. These varied uses of Scripture have appeared complementary in some circumstances and competitive in others.

Finally, the three differed in their ability to adapt to America. In spite of the combination of his genius and his piety, Edwards's Calvinism did not long survive his death. Within seventy years of his passing, "Edwardseans," though following his lead in some methodological and ethical matters, had stood on their head most of Edwards's basic affirmations about human nature, the process of salvation, and the relationship between Christ and the elect. Dutch Calvinism has sustained itself better in America, but at a price. The precepts of Kuyper and Bavinck remain a beacon for their theological descendants. Yet these descendants are still largely isolated, still relatively unconcerned about the wider American scene and only just beginning to exert an influence in that larger arena.

The Princeton Theology, by contrast, proved both consistent and influential. Of major American seminaries besides Princeton, only the Harvard Divinity School could claim that its teaching remained relatively stable over the first century of its existence. But unlike Princeton, the Harvard Divinity School was not a national force. The Calvinism of Princeton, on the other hand, was remarkably powerful for more than a century from 1812 on. This is a major achievement when viewed as a chapter in Reformed history, not for the trivial reason that lack of change somehow implies virtue, but for the much more important reason that the undeviating Princeton convictions were largely Reformed. Everything in the nineteenth century conspired against Calvinist views of humanity and of divine sovereignty. In holding to these positions, the Princeton theologians may have uncritically imbibed a good bit of the American self-determination, especially on matters epistemological, that they professed to repudiate. They may have responded woodenly to a changing philosophical situation. Nonetheless, the constancy of the Princetonians in steadily proclaiming the weakness of human nature and the divinely originated path of salvation, not to speak of their success at shaping institutions to embody this message, testifies to a Reformed vigor the like of which has never been seen in America.

Perhaps it is sufficient to conclude this comparison by saying that Edwards, the Dutch, and Old Princeton each faced cultural-theological crises of considerable magnitude, that each chose somewhat different ways of responding, and that these choices lent each school its distinctive character. Edwards chose to give himself unstintingly to intellectual toil of the most fundamental sort. As a result he left few genuine successors, for those who followed in Edwards's train lacked his powers of insight and his unreserved dependence upon a sovereign God. His books, which have remained to inspire a theologically promiscuous host, constituted his enduring legacy. The Dutch chose the path of cultural formation on a European model. The result was great internal strength, but only slight impact in America at large. Princetonians chose to pour their energies into a seminary devoted to dogmatic inquiry. The result was considerable ambiguity in relationship to American thought and social conditions, but also extraordinary influence within the American milieu.

The Princeton Theology Today

The steady reprinting of books from Old Princeton as well as a continuing, if not overwhelming, flow of critical attention testifies to the vitality of this school among Reformed and evangelical Americans at the end of the twentieth century. Nonetheless, it is no revelation to say that the unique blend of concerns and institutions that constituted the Princeton Theology has passed away. A brief survey of the conservative Reformed denominations, where one might naturally expect to find a continuing Princeton Theology, testifies instead to its absence. Within the Orthodox Presbyterian Church and at Westminster Theological Seminary, great respect remains for the Princeton Theology, but the presuppositional apologetics of Cornelius Van Til has largely replaced Old Princeton's commitment to the Scottish Philosophy of Common Sense, and so unhinged one of its crucial elements. In the Christian Reformed Church, which lacked organic historical connections to Old Princeton to begin with, other varieties of Dutch epistemology—from Kuyper, Bavinck, or Dooyeweerd—take the place of Princeton beliefs about apologetics and religious knowledge. Theologians in the Presbyterian Church of America (PCA) speak kindly of Old Princeton, but here again, philosophical, apologetic, or intellectual tendencies exist that distance members of this body from the Princetonians. The ecclesiology of Thornwell and Dabney, the prospects of Christian Reconstruction, or even a spirit disinclined to sophisticated academic endeavor provide alternative theological foundations in the PCA to those that Old Princeton affirmed. Only a scattering of individuals today combine Augustinian Calvinism, empirical realism, evidentialist apologetics, and piety based on propositions in the manner of the Princeton theologians.

This is not to say that individual parts of their theology do not remain influential. The historical work of Ernest Sandeen, as well as the ongoing efforts of the International Council on Biblical Inerrancy, shows how important the Princeton views on Scripture, especially as refined by Warfield, still are.[42] In addition, the apologetic strategies of the school enjoy considerable currency; some evidentialists who emphasize the reliability of consciousness, logic, and history in demonstrating the truthfulness of the faith make their debt to Old Princeton explicit.[43]

In all this, however, a historian may be pardoned for wondering if the burden of the Princetonians, the critical position that made them a great force for the faith in the nineteenth century, has not been overlooked in our day. Helpful or harmful as their particular views on inspiration and apologetics may be, the Princeton theologians looked upon these matters as subordinate constituents of a more general theology whose end was to glorify God in his greatness and rejoice in the mercies of his salvation. As with so many things in our century, the tendency is to concentrate on means and slight the end. During the nineteenth century the Princeton Theology stood for divine grace, it stood against human pretense in self-salvation and self-revelation, it proclaimed the moral weakness of humanity, and it championed a salvation won for us by God himself. These are the themes that the latter-day friends of the Princeton Theology too often neglect and its latter-day critics too often avoid. But these are also the themes that, if they could be revived, might constitute the greatest gift of Old Princeton to the contemporary world.

During his great debate with E. A. Park in 1850 over the intellectual apprehension of Christianity and the role of the feelings, Charles Hodge paused to summarize the foundation stones of his faith, for which he was prepared to battle without ceasing: "That a sentence of condemnation passed on all men for the sin of one man; that men are by nature the children of wrath; that without Christ we can do nothing; that he hath redeemed us from the curse of the law by being made a curse for us; that men are not merely pardoned but justified." Hodge continued that, by dividing the mind and the heart, Park was preparing "a weapon" against these beliefs. He then closed with a word of hope that Hodge applied to the doctrines themselves but that an admirer can apply to the Princeton version of these convictions as well: "Our consolation is that however keen may be the edge or bright the polish of that weapon, it has so little substance, it must be shivered into atoms with the first blow it strikes against those sturdy trees which have stood for ages in the garden of the Lord and whose leaves have been for the healing of the nations."[44]

Notes: The Princeton Theology

1. Some of the themes developed in this essay are similar to those that introduce the anthology *The Princeton Theology 1812-1921: Scripture, Science, and*

Theological Method from Archibald Alexander to Benjamin Warfield, ed. Mark A. Noll (Grand Rapids: Baker Book House, 1983). This anthology also contains a detailed bibliography and fuller notes than are possible here.

2. See James Waddel Alexander, *The Life of Archibald Alexander* (New York: Charles Scribner's Sons, 1854); and Lefferts A. Loetscher, *Facing the Enlightenment and Pietism: Archibald Alexander and the Founding of Princeton Theological Seminary* (Westport, CT: Greenwood Press, 1983).

3. The basic biography for Charles Hodge is the life by his son, A. A. Hodge, published by Charles Scribner's Sons in 1880. In the absence of a good biography for Warfield, John E. Meeter and Roger Nicole, *A Bibliography of Benjamin Breckinridge Warfield 1851-1921* (Nutley, NJ: Presbyterian and Reformed Publishing Company, 1974), is invaluable.

4. On these individuals, see *The Princeton Theology 1812-1921,* 14-16.

5. Francis Landy Patton, "Princeton Seminary and the Faith," in *The Centennial Celebration of the Theological Seminary of the Presbyterian Church in the United States of America at Princeton, New Jersey* (Princeton: Princeton Theological Seminary, 1910), 349-50. Frank Hugh Foster, *A Genetic History of the New England Theology* (Chicago: University of Chicago Press, 1907), 432.

6. B. B. Warfield, "What is Calvinism?" in *Selected Shorter Writings of Benjamin B. Warfield,* ed. John E. Meeter, 2 vols. (Nutley, NJ: Presbyterian and Reformed Publishing Company, 1970, 1973), 1:389.

7. On Turretin's role at Princeton, see *The Princeton Theology 1812-1921,* 28-30, 116. On the Old Princeton understanding of history, see George Marsden, "J. Gresham Machen, History, and Truth," *Westminster Theological Journal* 42 (Fall 1979): 157-75.

8. Archibald Alexander, *The Sermon, Delivered at the Inauguration of the Rev. Archibald Alexander* (New York: J. Seymour, 1812).

9. B. B. Warfield, "Inspiration," in *International Standard Bible Encyclopedia* (Chicago: Howard-Severance, 1915), as reprinted in *The Works of Benjamin B. Warfield,* vol. 1, *Revelation and Inspiration* (Grand Rapids: Baker Book House, 1981), 96.

10. A. A. Hodge and Warfield, *Inspiration,* introduction by Roger R. Nicole (Grand Rapids: Baker Book House, 1979).

11. Hodge, "The Latest Form of Infidelity," *Biblical Repertory and Princeton Review* 12 (January 1840), as reprinted in Hodge's *Essays and Reviews* (New York: Robert Carter & Brothers, 1857), 90.

12. For example, Alexander, *Inaugural Address;* Warfield, review of Herman Bavinck's *De Zekerheid des Geloofs* in *Princeton Theological Review* 1 (January 1903): 138-43, reprinted in *Selected Shorter Writings of Warfield,* 2:117-22.

13. See William S. Barker, "The Social Views of Charles Hodge: A Study in 19th-Century Calvinism and Conservatism," *Presbyterian: Covenant Seminary Review* 1 (Spring 1975): 1-22.

14. A good discussion of these different approaches is Richard J. Mouw, "The Bible in Twentieth-Century Protestantism: A Preliminary Taxonomy," in *The Bible in America: Essays in Cultural History,* eds. Nathan O. Hatch and Mark A. Noll (New York: Oxford University Press, 1982), 139-62, with 143-44 on the doctrinal emphases of Old Princeton.

15. See, in general, James R. Moore, *The Post-Darwinian Controversies: A Study of the Protestant Struggle to Come to Terms with Darwin in Great Britain and America, 1870-1900* (Cambridge: Cambridge University Press, 1979); and, more specifically, David N. Livingstone, "The Idea of Design: The Vicissitudes of a

Key Concept in the Princeton Response to Darwin," *Scottish Journal of Theology* 37 (1984): 329-57.

16. Sydney E. Ahlstrom, "The Scottish Philosophy and American Theology," *Church History* 24 (1955): 257-72. An early work commenting on Princeton's use of the Scottish Philosophy was Ralph J. Danhof, *Charles Hodge as Dogmatician* (Goes, The Netherlands: Oosterbaan and le Cointre, 1929). The fullest consideration of this subject is now John C. Vander Stelt, *Philosophy and Scripture: A Study in Old Princeton and Westminster Theology* (Marlton, NJ: Mack Publishing Company, 1978).

17. See Wesley Frank Craven, "William Graham," in *Princetonians 1769-1775: A Biographical Dictionary*, ed. Richard A. Harrison (Princeton: Princeton University Press, 1980), 289-94.

18. For an excellent general picture, see Henry F. May, *The Enlightenment in America* (New York: Oxford University Press, 1976).

19. Alexander, "The Nature and Evidence of Truth," in *The Princeton Theology 1812-1921*, 61-71; Alexander, *Outlines of Moral Science* (New York: Charles Scribner's Sons, 1852).

20. The best study of this enthusiasm for the new science among theologians is Theodore Dwight Bozeman, *Protestantism in an Age of Science: The Baconian Ideal and Antebellum American Religious Thought* (Chapel Hill: University of North Carolina Press, 1977).

21. Hodge, *Systematic Theology*, 3 vols. (Grand Rapids: Wm. B. Eerdmans Publishing Company, 1946), 1:10.

22. The different uses of this philosophy by evangelicals is discussed in Mark A. Noll, "Common Sense Traditions and American Evangelical Thought," *American Quarterly* 37 (Summer 1985): 216-38.

23. Park, "New England Theology," *Bibliotheca Sacra* 9 (January 1852): 191-92.

24. For comparison, see, on the power of the New England Theology, Bruce Kuklick, *Churchmen and Philosophers: From Jonathan Edwards to John Dewey* (New Haven: Yale University Press, 1985); and on Bushnell, Daniel Walker Howe, "The Social Science of Horace Bushnell," *Journal of American History* 70 (September 1983): 305-22.

25. See especially the discussion of Alexander's ethics in D. H. Meyer, *The Instructed Conscience: The Shaping of the American National Ethic* (Philadelphia: University of Pennsylvania Press, 1972), 55-58.

26. On the more general trends, see Nathan O. Hatch, "The Christian Movement and the Demand for a Theology of the People," *Journal of American History* 67 (December 1980): 545-67; and Hatch, "Evangelicalism as a Democratic Movement," in *Evangelicalism and Modern America*, ed. George M. Marsden (Grand Rapids: Wm. B. Eerdmans Publishing Company, 1984).

27. A thorough recent discussion of these emphases is Steven L. Martin, "The Doctrines of Man, Reason and the Holy Spirit in the Epistemology of Charles Hodge" (M.A. Thesis, Trinity Evangelical Divinity School, 1984).

28. Warfield's discussions of the human elements in biblical inspiration and of natural processes in the creation of the natural world illustrate the sophistication of this useful theological construction. See *The Princeton Theology 1812-1921*, 268-79, 293-98.

29. Hoffecker, *Piety and the Princetonians: Archibald Alexander, Charles Hodge, and Benjamin Warfield* (Phillipsburg, NJ: Presbyterian and Reformed Publishing Company, 1981).

30. Kelsey, *The Uses of Scripture in Recent Theology* (Philadelphia: Fortress Press, 1975), 17-24.

31. See Mark A. Noll, "The Founding of Princeton Seminary," *Westminster Theological Journal* 42 (Fall 1979): 72-110; and *The Princeton Theology 1812-1921*, 18-20, 51-58.

32. See *The Princeton Theology 1812-1921*, 22-24, for a discussion of the various Princeton journals from 1825 to 1929.

33. To obtain an overview of the work of this journal, see *Biblical Repertory and Princeton Review. Index Volume from 1825 to 1868*, 3 vols. (Philadelphia: Peter Walker, 1870-71).

34. Charles Hodge, "The *Princeton Review* on the State of the Country and of the Church," *Biblical Repertory and Princeton Review* 37 (October 1865): 687.

35. Cited in A. A. Hodge, *Life of Charles Hodge*, 257, 259-60.

36. A good modern treatment of Old Princeton positions is to be found, emphasis of the title notwithstanding, in George M. Marsden, *The Evangelical Mind and the New School Presbyterian Experience* (New Haven: Yale University Press, 1970).

37. *Biblical Repertory and Princeton Review. Index Volume*, 2:206.

38. See Noll, "Common Sense Traditions and American Evangelical Thought," *American Quarterly*.

39. Randall H. Balmer, "The Princetonians and Scripture: A Reconsideration," *Westminster Theological Journal* 44 (1982): 352-65; Balmer and John D. Woodbridge, "The Princetonians' Viewpoint of Biblical Authority: An Evaluation of Ernest Sandeen," in *Scripture and Truth*, eds. Woodbridge and D. A. Carson (Grand Rapids: Zondervan Publishing House, 1983). Woodbridge and Balmer rightly criticize Sandeen for suggesting that Old Princeton invented the concept of biblical inerrancy (see Sandeen, *The Roots of Fundamentalism: British and American Millenarianism 1800-1930* [Chicago: University of Chicago Press, 1970]; and "The Princeton Theology: One Source of Biblical Literalism in American Protestantism," *Church History* 31 [September 1962]: 307-21). Still, a modified version of Sandeen's argument—that Princeton refined, clarified, and emphasized certain aspects of the common evangelical heritage concerning Scripture—is quite defensible. Sandeen's work on fundamentalism, as well as other standard treatments of the subject that document the eager fundamentalist use of Princeton's views on Scripture (e.g., George W. Dollar, *A History of Fundamentalism in America* [Greenville, SC: Bob Jones University Press, 1973]; George M. Marsden, *Fundamentalism and American Culture* [New York: Oxford University Press, 1980]), suggests two things: (1) that fundamentalists recognized the Princeton formulation as a powerful statement of their sometimes inarticulate convictions, but also (2) that A. A. Hodge and Warfield were in fact highlighting in a new, effective way elements of an earlier, more amorphous confidence in Scripture.

40. On this widespread trust in a simple scientific epistemology, see, among many others, Bozeman, *Protestants in an Age of Science*; Henry Warner Bowden, *Church History in the Age of Science: Historiographical Patterns in the United States 1876-1918* (Chapel Hill: University of North Carolina Press, 1971); Foster, *New England Theology*; E. Brooks Holifield, *The Gentlemen Theologians: American Theology in Southern Culture, 1795-1860* (Durham, NC: Duke University Press, 1978); Herbert Hovenkamp, *Science and Religion in America, 1800-1860* (Philadelphia: University of Pennsylvania Press, 1978); Daniel Walker Howe, *The Unitarian Conscience: Harvard Moral Philosophy, 1805-1861* (Cambridge: Harvard University Press, 1970); May, *The Enlightenment in America*; Meyer, *The Instructed Conscience*;

Alexandra Oleson and Sanborn C. Brown, eds., *The Pursuit of Knowledge in the Early American Republic: American Scientific and Learned Societies from Colonial Times to the Civil War* (Baltimore: Johns Hopkins University Press, 1976); Douglas Sloan, *The Scottish Enlightenment and the American College Ideal* (New York: Teachers College Press, 1961); and Laurence R. Veysey, *The Emergence of the American University* (Chicago: University of Chicago Press, 1965).

41. The best work I have seen in comparing Princeton and the Dutch is by Stephen R. Spencer of Grand Rapids Baptist Seminary, "A Comparison and Evaluation of the Old Princeton and Amsterdam Apologetics" (Th.M. Thesis, Grand Rapids Baptist Seminary, n.d.). On connections between Edwards and the Princetonians, see Mark A. Noll, "Jonathan Edwards and Nineteenth-Century Theology," in *Jonathan Edwards and the American Experience*, eds. Nathan O. Hatch and Harry S. Stout (forthcoming); and on relations between Warfield and Kuyper and Bavinck, *The Princeton Theology 1812-1921*, 302-07.

42. Sandeen, *The Roots of Fundamentalism*; at least two recent books by the Inerrancy Council feature consideration of Old Princeton: see John Gerstner, "The Contributions of Charles Hodge, B. B. Warfield, and J. Gresham Machen to the Doctrine of Inspiration," in *Challenges to Inerrancy: A Theological Response*, eds. Gordon R. Lewis and Bruce Demarest (Chicago: Moody Press, 1984); and D. Clair Davis, "Princeton and Inerrancy: The Nineteenth-Century Theological Background of Contemporary Concerns," in *Inerrancy and the Church*, ed. John D. Hannah (Chicago: Moody Press, 1984).

43. For example, R. C. Sproul, John Gerstner, and Arthur Lindsley, *Classical Apologetics: A Rational Defense of the Christian Faith and a Critique of Presuppositional Apologetics* (Grand Rapids: Zondervan Publishing House, 1984).

44. Hodge, "The Theology of the Intellect and That of the Feelings," *Biblical Repertory and Princeton Review* 22 (October 1850): 674; reprinted in *Essays and Reviews*, 569.

CHARLES HODGE

DAVID F. WELLS

THE mainstay of Protestant orthodoxy in the nineteenth century, both within Presbyterianism and the wider evangelical movement, was Princeton Theological Seminary. And Princeton, during most of these years, was identified substantially with the work of its most formidable representative, Charles Hodge. Hodge taught there from 1822, ten years after the founding of the Seminary, almost to his death in 1878, except for two years of study abroad in Germany. The celebration of the fiftieth year of his professorship in 1872 was without precedent in American academic life. Even the shops in Princeton closed on this day to honor a patriarch, a theologian, and a teacher of more than three thousand ministerial students.[1]

Hodge's theological views were formed remarkably early, and in the long and unremitting struggle with the New School thinkers, a struggle that occupied him for much of his life, he defended his convictions unflinchingly and unswervingly. It is true that his *Systematic Theology*, written late in his life as a replacement for the Latin text that had been used at Princeton—Turretini's *Institutio theologiae elencticae*—does evidence a mellower tone than his essays published earlier in *The Biblical Repertory and Princeton Review*, but changes in his theology were few and far between. It was the stout consistency of Hodge's theology and the rigorous defense he gave of it that earned him an almost oracular standing among Old Schoolers. And, with the passing of the years, it created an identity between Hodge's outlook and that of the Seminary. "Princeton theology" in the early years was really Charles Hodge's theology.

Posterity, however, has not always dealt kindly with Hodge, and certainly the perspective in which we now view his theological accomplishments is quite different from that in which his contemporaries viewed them. This is particularly evident at three points. First, we usually identify Hodge's theology with his three-volume *Systematic Theol-*

ogy; his contemporaries for the most part did not. They knew him principally as an essayist and polemicist. Long before the thick volumes of his *Systematic* appeared in 1872 and 1873, he had forged his place in American church life with his incisive and rigorous excursions in the *Biblical Repertory* and its successors. There is a passion and liveliness in these essays that is sometimes absent from his systematic theology.

Second, the cultural and ecclesiastical context in which Hodge was writing has today largely been forgotten. In part, of course, Hodge is himself responsible for this. The fact that he was living in a time of dramatic social and intellectual change within the country is not always evident in the pages of his *Theology;* indeed, he often ignored the world around him much as Jane Austen's novels did the Napoleonic Wars. Yet it is this context that actually engaged Hodge all of his life. He and his colleagues at Princeton worked within the lengthening shadow of the country's "infidelity," against those who were perceived to have been tainted by it theologically, and alongside those through whom revival was occurring but whose means and methods were creating ecclesiastical chaos. Hodge cannot be understood adequately if he is divorced from this context and yet, paradoxically, his *Systematic Theology* gives us insufficient help in understanding it.

Third, the argument that biblical inerrancy was a Princetonian creation has resulted in an obsessive interest in the formulation of this tenet and it has skewered our assessment of Hodge. A contemporary of Hodge would have noticed that while he affirmed his belief in the integrity of Scripture, he spent relatively little time formulating and defending it. Hodge's theological interests lay elsewhere. They were interests foisted upon him by his religious and cultural context. The hotly contested issues, the questions that called forth his great polemical powers, were, as Earl Kennedy has noted, "the doctrines of the imputation of Adam's sin, original sin, inability, and regeneration."[2] These were the issues on which Hodge forged a distinctive position as he stated his opposition to New Schoolers like Nathaniel William Taylor, revivalists like Charles Finney, the "progressive orthodox" like Horace Bushnell, the Unitarians, and, beyond them, a culture turned self-confident in its post-Enlightenment rationalism.

It is this obscured Hodge, the forgotten Hodge, the polemical Hodge, upon which this essay is focused, not the Hodge of later years who is reflected—and, some say buried—in the stout volumes of his *Systematic Theology.* First, then, I want to develop the Princetonians' perceptions of the religious state of the country and consider some of the consequences of these perceptions. Second, I will elaborate upon the contest between the Old School and New School theologies but especially as this was focused in the contest between the faculties at Yale and Princeton.

Third, I want to examine Hodge's view of the atonement, which, with its closely related issues, was at the center of his debate with Nathaniel Taylor of Yale.

Declension and Infidelity

At the beginning of the nineteenth century much of American Christianity was at the nadir of its fortunes. This, at least, was the view of many of the influential orthodox clergymen. The 1730s and 1740s, when the whole eastern seaboard had glowed with the incandescent light of the Great Awakening, were followed, as they saw it, by five decades of lethargy and declension. In these years, the Church was graced with few great divines and even fewer reports of revival. The scenes of uproar, repentance, transformation, and exultation that had marked the days of Edwards and Whitefield were not repeated; they passed into the faded corridors of Christian memory where they quietly expired.

At the same time, Enlightenment ideas were flooding into the country. Colonial militia found themselves in the company of British and French troops whose Christian views were at best uncertain and whose morals were invariably loose. The Revolution opened the door still wider to various forms of rationalism, for the French, many of whom according to Timothy Dwight were possessed "of ardent minds and daring speculations," sided with the aggrieved colonists. "No knight errant ever offered himself to an affrighted damsel with more generosity as her protector," Dwight complained, "than they to the human race."[3] The Revolution, he claimed, brought with it "a long train of immoral doctrines and practices which spread into every corner of the country."[4]

This became the common perception among ministers at the turn of the century and provided the impetus for many a sermonic foray on a Sunday morning. In a typical analysis, Joseph Lathrop reminded his congregation in 1798 that:

> In these American States, there has, for many years, and more especially since our late revolution, been a visible tendency to infidelity, and an observable growth in impiety and immorality. Family religion is falling into disuse; the ancient strict observance of the Sabbath is mightily relaxed, social worship in the church, as well as in the family, is sinking into neglect, not to say contempt. . . . In this state of general indifference, the barriers against infidelity are fallen down, and the way is open for its swift and easy progress.[5]

Lathrop went on to speak of how swiftly and easily infidelity was actually progressing. Licentious books were multiplying and circulating "without modesty," even finding their way into the stacks of "social libraries." Other people, trafficking in "indecent ridicule and malignant satire," had attacked the Bible itself. Ministers spoke of the corruption of justice that had resulted, of the growth of taverns and of tippling, of sabbath desecration, of the abuse of children, and of riots and licentiousness.[6]

The alarm thus sounded, the faithful rose as one to defend the land against further intrusion of infidelity. But what was quickly discovered was that there was no single enemy. Infidelity was a synonym for the whole range of departures from Christian faith, be they small or large.

The most flagrant expression of infidelity was found among the devotees of irreligion who followed in Thomas Paine's footsteps, although they never posed a serious challenge to more orthodox faith. In 1825 the Free Press Association was formed with its literary outlet, *The Correspondent*. A freethinkers society that deliberately profaned the sabbath by sponsoring lectures on that day, sprang up in New York. By 1830 it was rumored that twenty thousand people had been attracted to these lectures. Although this figure appears to be an exaggeration, it is undoubtedly true that anti-Christian sentiment was gaining popular support. Similar societies began to appear in other cities. In 1831 Boston saw the creation of the First Society of Free Thinkers, which was dedicated to the pursuit of "useful knowledge" such as the education of children "without regard to religious opinions." In 1835 these and other societies were linked together in a national network through the creation of the United States Moral and Philosophical Society.

The specter of unbelief, organizing itself, capitalizing on the economic disorders to enlist support for its socialism, and breeding communes and subversive ideas, greatly alarmed Christian leaders, who exaggerated its importance. Horace Bushnell, who did not panic easily, wrote in 1835 of the "considerable number" of societies of freethinkers, which were growing with "fearful rapidity." He thought he discerned why the movement was gaining ground. By opposing religion, private property, and marriage, he asserted, "they unite irreligion, rapacity and lust."[7] Therein lay their power. However, just as the movement began to gather momentum it began to disintegrate from within. By the early 1840s it had expired, the victim of apathy, inertia, penury, a bad reputation, and the devastation of the Second Great Awakening. Those who might have lent a hand to freethinking now called themselves "liberals" and abandoned the movement to its own failing devices.

The transition from "liberalism" to Unitarianism took place between 1805 and 1819. In 1805 Henry Ware was elected to the Hollis chair of theology at Harvard. In reaction to this appointment, Andover Theological Seminary was founded in 1807 to preserve and defend Christian orthodoxy, its two most distinguished faculty recruits being Moses Stuart and Leonard Woods. Orthodoxy and Christian "infidelity" were thus becoming entrenched on opposing sides of the battle.

The controversy with the emerging Unitarianism was sparked in 1815. A book inspired by Jedadiah Morse was published and reviewed by the orthodox journal, *Panoplist*.[8] This drew a response from William Channing, the Unitarian luminary, that was answered by Noah Worcester. Channing then wrote two additional letters and Worcester wrote three.[9] In 1819, the controversy was suspended, but not before the orthodox had achieved their aim. "Unitarianism," observed Wisner, "which had before operated and spread in secret, was brought to light."[10] The entire subject was illumined still further by Channing himself in that same year, 1819, when in the course of an ordination sermon he systematically defended Unitarianism.[11] For the first time, responded Taylor, the world was informed about what Unitarians *did* believe rather than what they *did not* believe! Instead of "sneers and insinuations," the orthodox had some solid arguments to oppose. And oppose them they did. Channing's defense precipitated several rather complex literary duels between himself and Stuart, between Leonard Woods and Henry Ware,[12] and, in 1821, between Samuel Miller, Charles Hodge's colleague at Princeton, and the Unitarian movement as a whole.[13]

From 1821 to 1827 the New School Connecticut Calvinists spearheaded the assault on this, the latest form of Bostonian liberalism, but two new elements were added to the controversy. First, the battle was taken to Boston itself by Lyman Beecher. The object was to deprive Unitarianism of its popular support by bringing the city under the sound of revival preaching. Second, Nathaniel Taylor, professor of theology at Yale, who was most dissatisfied with the approach of the Andover theologians and offered the opinion that they had set the cause of orthodoxy back by fifty years, developed a new apologetic by softening the doctrine of human depravity, which was the most important bone of contention. Taylor was also changing direction, it needs to be noted, because he accepted the estimate made of human nature by the Scottish Common Sense realism.

Beecher's responsibility in checking Unitarianism was to advance to Boston with the Christian gospel, but when he arrived he came as a man of peace; he had honey on his tongue. Not one "knocking down" sermon was preached, he informed a friend. "I have not felt *once* the spirit of rebuke; have not uttered an ironical or sarcastic expression; have not struck one stroke at an antagonist."[14] What was needed, he said, was "luminous exposition" that wooed rather than battered, because ordinary Unitarians were not so much opposed to Christian orthodoxy as ignorant of it. They had never really had a chance to reject it. The strategy was most effective. "New cases of inquiry and of hope appear every week," he wrote, "and an impression is made among the Unitarian population too deep and solemn in favor of the revival to allow their ministers to preach against it."[15] A little less irenically, he later exulted that "orthodoxy in Massachusetts is becoming a phalanx terrible as an army with banners, and that our adversaries shall no more be able to frame iniquity by law, and draw sin as with a cart-rope."[16] Thus were his opponents left to splutter feebly as their congregations were wooed away and the ground was cut from beneath their feet. Here was Beecher, by his own admission "a man of war" from his youth upward, melting impenitent infidels with his soft words while from afar his friend, Nathaniel Taylor, was drawing their blood with his sharp treatises. It is an arresting picture.

This context deeply affected the form and direction that Hodge's theology took. First, the debate with Unitarianism, in which the Princetonians also participated, set up a deep cleavage between the New School and Old School divines. New Schoolers like Beecher and Taylor were embarrassed by the defense of Old School Calvinism made by Hodge, Woods, and Stuart. Hodge, in turn, was scandalized by the defense offered by Taylor. What the Yale divine was advocating seemed to be indistinguishable from Pelagianism. Thus were the battle lines drawn within Presbyterian and Congregational circles.

Second, the alarming situation in the country awakened the Princetonians to the need for a defense of Christianity as a whole. This was present incipiently in Hodge, although it was not to come into full bloom until a little later when Francis Patton and B. B. Warfield began their work. The emergence of apologetics as a fundamental and central concern, not merely as a peripheral exercise, was a nineteenth-century interest; more precisely, it was Princeton's innovation. It was born in a deep commitment to defend biblical faith in all of its essentials. It was this commitment that really explains Charles Hodge.

The New Theology and the Old

A reviewer of E. A. Park's *The Atonement*, a volume of considerable importance for New England theology, declared optimistically in 1854 that "there is general agreement in these views by Evangelical Christians—certainly here in New England."[17] There was, as a matter of fact, general agreement on Park's collected essays neither in New England nor anywhere else. A century earlier, there had been unanimity but for those of a more traditional bent all of this had changed when Taylor had been appointed at Yale and, according to Ebenezer Porter of Andover, had volunteered to shed darkness on the world. It was not long before the "old paths began to be called in question," another dissatisfied author said, "and the ardor of youth began to be enlisted in making new discoveries in the polar regions of speculation," especially, he noted, with respect to finding "a channel of communication between Calvinism and Pelagianism."[18] Likewise an anonymous Presbyterian speaking for the Old School charged that the New Haven divines, philosophizing to faith rather than from faith and trafficking in Scholasticism's "subtle questions," "endless logomachies," and "absurd barbarisms," had unfortunately drifted into "Arminian, Socinian, Arian and Pelagian errors."[19] This was a new turn of events, for as late as 1755 President Clap had claimed that all tutors at Yale were, as a matter of course, examined theologically and, if found guilty of Arminian or "Prelatical principles," were summarily suspended. The "New Scheme of Divinity," which Clap himself had assembled from various New England divines, was not, to judge from Hodge's review of Clap,[20] altogether above suspicion, but certainly Taylor had taken prevailing tendencies to an extreme. And when the Yale divine made his coy retreats into doubt—"it may be no one can prove" or "how do you know?"—it seemed to many Old Schoolers that he was using phrases that, "like a magic wand, have made truth and error appear alike."[21] Consequently, Charles Hodge argued that the bearers of the authentic Edwardsean mantle were the Princetonians, despite the fact that Edwards's Idealism made them a little nervous. The tradition of Dwight, Emmons, and Hopkins was being substantially preserved at Princeton and substantially subverted at Yale.

Hodge took the long view as to why this conflict had arisen. He argued that from its inception Christianity had been plagued by the conflict between two competing doctrinal systems. The one, he said, "has for its object the vindication of the Divine supremacy and sovereignty in the salvation of men; the other has for its characteristic aim the assertion of the rights of human nature. It is specially solicitous that nothing should be held to be true, which cannot be philosophically reconciled with the liberty and ability of man."[22] These competing outlooks, Hodge believed, were again at war in the nineteenth century, each claiming to be the true representative of biblical faith and both asking for the allegiance of the church. Subsequently, of course, historians have come to see that there were many other factors involved in this growing bifurcation, yet it is undeniable that at its center was a contest between two types of Reformed theology and two different estimates of the degree and consequences of human corruption.

In 1820 Taylor judged that the moment was ripe to attack the Unitarians. His objective, however, was only partly that of exposing them for the infidels he judged them to be; his other aim was to hoist to the flagpole of orthodoxy a different kind of Calvinism from the one that the Unitarians had so confidently been mocking.

The point at which Taylor entered the fray was after the ground had been cleared by the debate between Woods of Andover and Henry Ware of Harvard. Taylor now took on another Harvard divine, Andrews Norton.[23] What Taylor sought to show was that the opponents of Calvinism "never fairly attack its doctrines, as they are stated by Calvin himself, or exhibited in the creeds of the churches, or in the writings of the authors which bear his name";[24] these opponents attacked straw men! Specifically, they held up to ridicule a doctrine of human nature that even the sects would consider to be injurious and false. Calvinists in fact believed, said Taylor, that "mankind come [sic] into the world in such a state, that without the interposition of divine grace, all as soon as they became moral agents, sin in every accountable act."[25] This belief in depravity, he said, must be distinguished from "theories" about it. Among these theories was the notion of "the imputation of Adam's sin to his posterity."[26] Sin is not imputed; at least, it is not imputed in the way that Old Schoolers like Hodge imagined. All are born with a corrupted nature, Taylor affirmed, but this is not in and of itself sinful. This corrupted nature only provides the occasion for our sinning when the agent is of a morally accountable age. Furthermore, people sin inevitably, said Taylor, but not necessarily. This was a subtle distinction that the Yale professor would be called upon to defend more than once in the ensuing controversy. But it allowed Taylor to argue that his Calvinism, which he believed to be historic Calvinism, differed from that espoused at Princeton.

Posing the issue in this way appeared to Beecher to be a stroke of brilliance, and it is undeniable that it did relieve the Connecticut Calvinists of some hard apologetic tasks. Unitarians, for example, had been able to expose the harshness of Calvinistic doctrine by picturing hell as paved with the remains of innocent babies.[27] This could now be denied *fortissimo*. To Beecher Nettleton wrote: "I believe it to be a matter of fact that you and I are *really* a different kind of Calvinist from what the Unitarians have imagined or been accustomed to imagine."[28] He suggested that the New Haveners should argue that they had no interest in defending "old Calvinism"; their sole concern was with the "evangelical system." Beecher apparently accepted this as sound advice. Late in 1829, he went up to Boston to deliver a series of discourses on political atheism. On that subject, as he said, he "opened the ground tier; and let out, without let or hindrance, all the caustics in the locker."[29] He also let out a few caustics on "old Calvinism." Referring to the old view of Adam's solidarity with the human race and the imputation of his sin to all people, he said: "It is my deliberate opinion that the false philosophy which has been employed for the exposition of the Calvinistic system has done more to obstruct the march of Christianity, and to paralyze the saving power of the Gospel . . . than all other causes beside."[30] By an unnatural collusion, the Connecticut Calvinists seemed to be uniting in part with the Unitarians against the more traditional Calvinists like Hodge. This was a maneuver fraught with danger, as they were soon to discover. For while the emancipation from "old Calvinism" might be used to discomfort Unitarians by denying them their best arguments, it could also be used against those Calvinists who were thus emancipated. Unitarians seemed to grasp that the sword had two edges far more rapidly than did Taylor and his friends.

Initially, the new twist that Taylor was trying to put into Calvinism was hailed by the Unitarians as a sign that Taylor was in full flight. Realizing that "old Calvinism" was indefensible, Taylor had moved on to new ground. Then the full implication of what was taking place seemed to dawn on them even more fully. In the same year that Taylor was concluding his debate with Norton, the *Christian Examiner* decided to review a sermon of Beecher's. The reviewer spoke of "its decidedly *anti*-Calvinistic leaning." What he meant, the reviewer went on to say, was that Beecher had denied some of the "peculiarities" of Calvinism and had distinctly asserted none of them. As to particulars, the author argued that Beecher had asserted "in as strong and unqualified language as was ever used by an Arminian or Unitarian, the doctrine of man's actual *ability* and *free agency*. . . . On the doctrine of *original sin* and *native depravity*, our author is hardly less unsound in his orthodoxy." Even the doctrine of atonement, he added, "might also be adopted by all Unitarians of whom we have any knowledge."[31]

The new apologetic must have appeared almost heaven sent to the Unitarians and they were quick to exploit it. Yale was played off against Andover, then against Princeton. In the meantime, Taylor's own Calvinism had clarified further in the new direction. The 1828 *Concio ad Clerum* that he delivered to the Congregational clergy of Connecticut was a manifesto for, even an explication of, the new position. With flamboyance and subtlety, he spelled out in some detail what Calvinism meant vis-à-vis the issues raised in the debates. The Unitarians hailed the address as "able and satisfactory." They saw sure signs everywhere that Calvinists were "silently but surely advancing towards the very opinions they so eagerly condemn."[32] More embarrassing accolades could not have been heard. Disquieted and anxious about Taylor's views, many Calvinists began to have second thoughts about New Haven theology. In the following year, 1829, the Unitarians were given a break that was not altogether unexpected. The orthodox divided against themselves.

Taylor's address, *Concio ad Clerum*, had served as a call to arms for the Princetonians. Alexander fired off a broadside against Pelagianism. This was followed by a heated exchange between Hodge and Goodrich, who had earlier purchased *The Quarterly Christian Spectator* as a literary outlet for the Yale divines and as a voice for the New Theology. The debate was over what, from a historical point of view, constitutes historic Calvinism. Goodrich was simply taking Taylor's defense against the Unitarians and turning it into an aggressive offense against the Princetonians. In this he was modestly successful, for he was able to show that Hodge was not as competent historically as he was in other ways. Hodge had participated in an evolution within Calvinism without being fully aware of the reasons for or results of that change. Goodrich's success, however, had only a little to do with the theological issues at stake, and on these matters Hodge was unmovable.

The inevitable parting of the ways came in 1837. In that year, the General Assembly, at the instigation of the Princetonians, and especially of Hodge, abrogated the Plan of Union of 1801, thereby excising approximately sixty thousand church members and ministers from four synods, most of whom were predominantly under New School influence.[33] Sympathizers of the New Schoolers like Leonard Bacon expressed their outrage, complaining that "their titles to all their church property [were] put at hazard without the form of a trial, without the citation of a witness, without the opportunity of defence, after having been reproached in mass, as disorganizers and heretics, and after measures had been commenced leading to a judicial investigation of the charges preferred against them."[34]

Technically, this was correct. Nevertheless, it needs to be remembered that the grounds for the excision were largely theological and these theological issues had been extensively debated in the church during the two decades that preceded this event. It is doubtful whether further debate in 1837 would have provided new light or changed very many opinions. In a roundabout way this was conceded by the New Schoolers who were Congregationalists. They decided in 1852 that Congregationalism should go its own way without any further alliances with the Presbyterians, a preponderance of whom were Old Schoolers. It is this context, of painful theological debate and wrenching ecclesiastical schism, which must be allowed to form the backdrop for Hodge's theological life.

Polemics and Convictions

In the first half of the nineteenth century, down the eastern seaboard at least, ecclesiastical life was much affected by the Second Awakening. What dominated discussion, consequently, were the practical issues that evangelists had to confront. How should conversion be presented? What is a legitimate use of persuasion? What about the Anxious Bench? Can all accept the gospel? Should it be offered indiscriminately to all? These were, of course, the questions provoked in particular by Charles Finney and his "New Measures," and the answers Finney developed had an uncanny resemblance to many of the things that Taylor had been elucidating at Yale.

Hodge was deeply concerned with this development because he saw in its resurgent Pelagianism the supposition that conversion is a merely human work. That being the case, Christ's work on the cross was being emptied of any serious significance. He explained his concern in this way:

> The constant exhortation is, to make choice of God as the portion of the soul, to change the governing purpose of the life, to submit to the moral Governor of the universe the specific act to which the sinner is urged as immediately connected with salvation, is an act which has no reference to Christ. The soul is brought immediately in contact with God, the Mediator is left out of view. We maintain that this is another Gospel. It is practically another system, and a legal system of religion. We do not intend that the doctrine of the mediation of Christ is rejected, but that it is neglected; that the sinner is led to God directly; that he is not urged, under the pressure of the sense of guilt, to go to Christ for pardon, and through him to God, but the general idea of submission (not the specific idea of submission to the plan of salvation through Jesus Christ) is urged as the making a right choice. Conviction of sin is made of little account, Christ and his atonement are kept out of view, so that the matter of salvation is not distinctly presented to the minds of the people.[35]

Hodge saw clearly that soteriological conclusions arise from anthropological premises, that a deficient view of the atonement could not be corrected until the inadequate doctrine of sin had been attacked. It was this that was at the root of the problem and it was this that was attacked with a devotion to principle that was unswerving.

The debate now centered on whether people can be held accountable for what Adam had done. The reverse side of this coin, of course, was whether people could be acquitted by what Christ had done. In each case responsibility was being interpreted corporately, for in each case there was representation of the many by the one. But there were complexities in this that needed to be resolved.[36] In Scripture, condemnation and justification are sentential acts. We are not made unrighteous by being pronounced so any more than we are made holy by being declared justified. We are declared righteous when Christ's righteousness is forensically imputed to us, but does this similarly mean that we are unrighteous only by the judicial reckoning of Adam's sin to us? To allow that this might be so would be to allow a Unitarian conception that we are all natively innocent, that unrighteousness is a matter merely of divine decree and not of human constitution. The idea of condemnation as judicial pronouncement therefore had to be given underpinning in a doctrine of the actual transmission of sin from parent to child. This, however, disturbed the symmetry between the two Adams and their representative roles, for in the one case we are declared righteous without ever actually being so whereas in the other case we are declared unrighteous and we are actually so.

Hodge's solution was forged in direct opposition to the idea of mediate imputation favored by the New School divines. They argued that Adam's posterity was not involved in his sin either because they were in his loins, philosophically speaking (as the Edwardseans believed), or because this sin was simply reckoned to them as the Princetonians said. Imputation, rather, is the transmission of the consequences of that Adamic sin in the legacy of tainted human nature. Sin is, Nathaniel Taylor said, in the sinning. No one sinned in Adam but we do sin because of Adam. We are therefore pronounced guilty when we become culpable for our own sinning and never because we have a connection with Adam's sin. But as this solution was developed both in respect to conversion and in relation to Christ's work, its tendency to become a form of works-salvation, dependent ultimately not on what Christ did and does but upon what we do, became unmistakable. Hodge rejected it unconditionally.

In developing his own view of Adam's federal representation, Hodge was aware that he was taking an unpopular and unfashionable stand. The Old School doctrine, which he only belatedly discovered was not entirely identical with his own, was subjected, he said, to "execration and contempt" from the New School men and a little earlier Alexander had said that they treated it as "so absurd" that they did not condescend to discuss it. This was a provocative statement, for the New School divines were seldom reticent to discuss Old School absurdities!

Hodge dismissed the Idealist's notion of a universal humanity, a generic life common to all people, as "a mere hypothesis,"[37] perhaps not so much out of theological considerations as from philosophical. He was also dissatisfied with the consequent notion of imputation. Edwards's theology used the old word but it had none of the old doctrinal content. But what Edwards had that Nathaniel Taylor lacked was a doctrine of "native depravity"; it was Hodge's agreement with Edwards on this point that he felt entitled him to be called an Edwardsean. It was the deviation from this point by the New Haven theologians that made them usurpers of the Edwardsean heritage. Hodge nevertheless found himself at odds even with the more traditional Edwardseans in explaining how we are culpable for Adam's sin. People have a common nature, Hodge countered, only in the sense that they have a common origin, belong to the same species, have generically identical rational and moral faculties, and are commonly alienated from God at birth. Adam "was an individual man, with no more of the generic life of the race than any other man."[38] Thus Hodge might loudly claim his Edwardsean heritage when in debate with New Haven theologians, but his claim became a good deal more muted when he was in discussion with more conservative followers of Edwards! Indeed, with them Hodge saw his differences with Edwards as more important than his similarities, whereas with Taylor Hodge accentuated his similarities and passed over his differences in silence.

The Protestant Reformers, but in particular John Calvin, included under the single term original sin both the imputed guilt of Adam's sin and the inherent depravity consequent upon it. Hodge believed, however, that it was the latter aspect that the Reformers emphasized. He suggested that this was partly because Roman Catholic theologians at the time held an inadequate view of human corruption and partly because Calvin wanted to affirm that we are not innocent creatures condemned merely because Adam sinned. Hodge himself was to assume Calvin's perspective but only as a result of being embroiled in this extended debate on the subject. Initially he stressed the former aspect, the imputed guilt of Adam's sin, and declared that evangelical religion would survive only if this emphasis was maintained.

The idea of imputation, that one person suffers the penalty for another's sin, he saw to be the working principle of the universe. This principle would still be part of the warp and woof of life even if the Fall, the Bible, and God were to be denied. No man is an island. No one lives out his or her life in a vacuum. The individual acts of one person always touch and affect others. It was the perception of this truth that redeemed Bushnell's study *Christian Nurture*, and it was the failure to see this by the late followers of Edwards that was subverting "the whole evangelical system." For they contended that God could not justly condemn a person for sins other than his or her own. How then, Hodge asked, could he justify a person for righteousness other than that person's own?

The notion of federal representation came into its own when the idea of covenants began to be important.[39] The notion of a probationary period in which the human race was on trial through its representative, Adam, was then advanced. Because of this covenant, only Adam's first sin was imputed to his posterity, for at this point the covenant was abrogated. This was the basis of Hodge's view that, he said, was also stated with "extraordinary unanimity" by both Lutheran and Calvinistic confessions and could be summarized thus:

1. That Adam, as the common father of all men, was by divine appointment constituted not only the natural, but the federal head or representative of his posterity. The race stood its probation in him. His sin was the sin of the race, because the sin of its divinely and righteously constituted representative. We therefore sinned in Adam in the same sense that we died in Christ. 2. The penalty of death threatened against Adam in the event of his transgression was not merely the dissolution of the body, but spiritual death, the loss of the divine favor and of original righteousness; and the consequent corruption of his whole nature. 3. This penalty came upon his race. His sin was the judicial ground on which the favor and fellowship of God were withdrawn or withheld from the apostate family of man. 4. Since the fall, therefore, men are by nature, or as they are born, the children of wrath. They are not only under condemnation, but destitute of original righteousness, and corrupted in their whole nature. According to this view of the subject, the ground of the imputation of Adam's sin is the federal union between him and his posterity, in such sense that it would not have been imputed had he not been constituted their representative. It is imputed to them not because it was antecedently to that imputation, and irrespective of the covenant on which the imputation is founded, already theirs; but because they were appointed to stand their probation in him.[40]

We all, therefore, sustain a twofold relationship to Adam. He is both our natural head and our federal representative. In all of his writings prior to the publication of the *Systematic Theology* in 1872 and 1873, Hodge insisted that it was on the grounds of the latter relationship, federal headship, that we are made liable to the penalty for Adam's sin, a penalty that consisted in the deprivation of righteousness, the suffering of inner corruption, and exposure to God's wrath. Hodge was forced to take this position because of his creationist views—namely, that the soul was not derived from the parents as the body is, but was given individually by divine fiat. The soul comes fresh from the hand of God and at the moment of birth becomes liable to punishment for Adam's sin. Some of Hodge's critics believed that this was a curious position for a Reformed divine to take, but it should be noted that Hodge could claim some company among the Reformed. It seems to court the idea that there is perhaps a moment of innocence in the life of each person before the sentence of guilt begins to be implemented. Furthermore, it reduces the idea of original sin to something less than Protestant theology has usually held out for; original sin, it seems, is not really an inherent corruption transmitted from parent to child, but a corruption inflicted upon people by God. The link is not a common nature, nor yet a universalized humanity, but a decree of God. To deny that we were in some sense acting in Adam through a common nature was to make the same denial that the Remonstrants had uttered. The belated concession by Hodge, then, that we are condemned not only because of federal representation but also because of natural relationship may have been an indication that the Princeton theologian realized some of the difficulties to which his theory was leading, but it is doubtful whether the concession alone, without any serious modifications to the entire doctrine, could save him from the charge, ironical as it was, that he had inadvertently espoused Arminian tenets.[41]

In view of this, it is necessary to examine in some detail the exegetical grounds on which Hodge's views of representation were built. The principal writing in which this is made plain is his *Commentary on the Epistle to the Romans*. It was no accident that Hodge chose to write on this letter. Both Moses Stuart and Albert Barnes produced commentaries on it and in the process slighted the view of immediate imputation espoused by Hodge.

In Romans 5:12-21, the central argument according to Hodge is contained in verses 12, 18, and 19, verses 13-17 being a parenthesis. This in itself cut across the grain of Barnes's and Stuart's argument, for it suggested that the passage did not intend to dwell on the disproportionate blessings of Christ's righteousness compared with the evils occasioned by the Fall. The apostle, rather, was arguing for the similarities between Adam's representative and Christ, not for their dissimilarities. The crux is verse 12, "As by the offence of one all are condemned, so by the righteousness of one are all justified," verses 18 and 19 being its amplification. The apostle sets out to show, however "contrary to the common mode of thinking among men," that God dealt with mankind in this representative. For if a penalty has been inflicted on men, a law must have been transgressed. Sin is not imputed where there is no transgressed law. The law in question, however, could not have been Moses' Law, since there were many who died before it was given (v. 14); it could not be nature's law written on the heart. Therefore, "as neither of these laws is sufficiently extensive to embrace *all* the subjects of the penalty, we must conclude that men are subject to death on account of Adam; that is, it is for the offence of one that many die, vs. 13, 14."[42] Thus is Adam a type of Christ.

The key to understanding the critical words in verse 12 is to understand the word *death* not in a physiological sense, but a penal one. In that case, the verse could be paraphrased thus: "All men are subject to penal evils on account of one man; this is the position to be proved, (v. 12) that such is the case is evident, because the infliction of a penalty supposes the violation of a law. But such evil was inflicted before the giving of the Mosaic law, it comes on men before the transgression of the law of nature, or even the existence of inherent depravity, it must, therefore, be for the offence of one man that judgment has come upon all them to condemnation."[43] Hodge maintained this causal link between Adam's sin and our condemnation without using the Augustinian device of translating the *eph' hō* as *in whom (in quo)*, in which case it would read: By one man all men became sinners, and hence death passed upon all men, *through that one man*, in whom all sinned. He settled for the simple statement "All die for that, or because that, all have sinned." He insisted, however, that the last phrase is to be interpreted as meaning that "all men are regarded and treated as sinners" on account of Adam's act. Interpretations that sever the causal link between Adam's act and God's subsequent treatment of mankind under conditions of condemnation are to be rejected. Thus Stuart suggested that the verse be rendered "As Adam sinned and died, so in like manner death has passed on all men, because all have sinned," and others proposed: "As by Adam, sin (corruption of nature) was introduced into the world, and death as its consequence, and so death passed on all men, because all have become corrupt." The point of this verse, Hodge countered, is not to contrast Adam and Christ, showing that corruption sprang from the one and holiness from the other, nor to show that Adam was the reason for our condemnation as Christ is for our justification. It is true that inner corruption comes from Adam, but this is neither the truth that is in view nor the basis on which God pronounces his judgment on us. Unless this is granted, the biblical doctrine of justification falls away.[44] Union with "Adam is the cause of death; union with Christ is the cause of life,"[45] and in both cases the principles of representation, of imputation, of federal union, are identical. In the one case human beings are treated as judicially guilty without respect to their actual condition, and in the other case Christians are treated as judicially innocent without respect to their actual condition.

That the ground of imputation of sin was man's federal relationship to Adam, rather than natural union, is clear from the fact that Jesus was part of Adam's natural posterity yet Adam's sin was not imputed to him. The fact that Jesus was regarded as sinless "supposes that the federal, and not the natural union is the essential ground of the imputation; that the sense in which Adam's sin is ours is a legal and not a moral sense and that the sense in which we sinned in him is that in which we act as a representative and not a literal sense."[46] Inner pollution was not transmitted to Christ, not because the Virgin Birth interrupted its transmission, but because Adam had not represented him and therefore God did not inflict him with this depravity.

The symmetry between the two Adams is almost perfect in Hodge's theology. We are justified and declared free from penal sanction not for what we do, but for what Christ did for us, just as we are declared liable to punishment not for what we have done, but for what Adam did as our representative. Hodge summarized his doctrine thus:

> 1. That Christ, in the covenant of redemption, is constituted the head and representative of his people, and that, in virtue of this federal union, and agreeably to the terms of the eternal covenant, they are regarded and treated as having done what he did and suffered what he suffered in their name and in their behalf. They died in him. They rose in him; not literally, so that his acts were their acts, but representatively. 2. That the reward promised to Christ in the covenant of redemption, was the justification, sanctification, and eternal salvation of his people. 3. That the judicial ground, therefore, of the justification of the believers is not their own personal righteousness, nor the holy nature which they derive from Christ, but his obedience and sufferings, performed and endured in their name, and which became theirs in virtue of the covenant and by gracious imputation of God. 4. That the believer is not only justified by the righteousness of Christ, but sanctified by his Spirit.[47]

The work of Christ, then, was centrally that of satisfying the demands of justice, thereby enabling God to be just when justifying sinners. To do this, Christ represented us in our sin, as a priest offering himself sacrificially in our stead. He bore our sin, propitiating the divine wrath that it called forth.

The atonement led naturally into considerations of theodicy, for Hodge believed that the justice of God required an atonement and the atonement made possible the preservation of the moral structure of the world. The character of God was on trial and remains on trial, for his justice demands that he treat his creatures as they deserve. If he is moral, he will favor what is good and show his disapprobation for what is wrong. This disapprobation, Hodge believed, is administered not merely as a deterrent to society, nor as a form of rehabilitation of the sinner, but because it is deserved. And because it is deserved, only Christ's interposition could preserve us from that calamity which the vindication of God's character would produce.

Here lay the crux, so to speak, of Hodge's differences with the New School thinkers. For they believed, in most cases, that in God's government of the world punishment was used but the purpose was to prevent sin and to correct the sinner. This attitude led naturally to the assumption that the chief goal of existence is happiness, and holiness is simply the best way to get there. But, countered Hodge, "we know that holiness is something more than a means; that to be happy is not the end and

reason for being holy; that enjoyment is not the highest end of being."
This results in our viewing ethical choices in commercial terms. A choice
is made, not because it is the inherently right thing to do, but because
it produces profit of some kind and avoids loss. Virtue becomes expe-
diency. The end justifies the means. And human beings are degraded
because their moral capacities are reduced to being merely the instruments of happiness.

The debate between Hodge and Taylor represented the collision
between two entire theological systems. At the center of one was the
representative view of the atonement, of which Hodge was the chief
proponent, and at the center of the other was the governmental theory
whose most articulate advocate was Taylor. And related to each view
were different understandings of human nature and of God's moral relationship to the world.

Hodge's view was obviously constructed around a symmetry between the two Adams. This had the twofold advantage of providing a
cutting edge in the debate over human nature and placing justification
at the center of Christ's work, for both doctrines—that of sin and that
of justification—depended upon the idea of imputation. In the one,
Adam represents us convenantally, being the federal head of the race,
and in the other Christ represents us in his righteousness and through
that righteousness redeems us from the law's sanction, bearing it in
himself in our stead.

The parallel was not of course precise in every detail. The sin of
Adam, as Hodge came to stress, was not only imputed to us by means
of a sentence or declaration, it was also transmitted to us by nature. We
are sinners both by what we are and by what we did in Adam our head.
On the other hand, we are justified not by what we are—that is the
Roman Catholic view—but by what we are declared to be in Christ. The
chronology of these aspects, in other words, is not paralleled on the two
sides of the equation. The declaration of human sin followed after it,
whereas the declaration of the Christian's righteousness in Christ pre-
cedes its actual existence. In Hodge's thought, however, this parallelism
was greatly complicated by the fact that he was a creationist. This meant,
then, that the depravity of Adam was handed on to succeeding generations as much by divine decree as anything. This is quite unlike the
manner in which our actual righteousness is transmitted to us by Christ,
which occurs, not by divine decree, but by union with him.

Taylor's view was, of course, quite different. He opposed the view
of depravity as believed by Hodge and though he on occasion used the
word *imputation,* it was never in a Hodgean sense. The atonement was
for Taylor the ground upon which God could forgive sin. What, then,
was this ground? Was it that Christ bore the sin of those whom he

represented, suffering vicariously for them? Not at all. Rather, he held as had Grotius before him that an equivalent manifestation of God's justice is made in Christ's death. This means that the Cross was the occasion upon which God showed his general displeasure about sin. Having done so and thereby sustained his own moral government of the world, he had secured for himself, as it were, a free hand to forgive all or any without requiring of them a strict equivalent of punishment in Christ for sins committed.

This principle was taken a step further in Bushnell, who articulated a view held more or less in common with Auguste Sabatier, A. Ritschl, A. Harnack, Hastings Rashdall, and R. S. Franks. The essence of the idea, originally stated by Abelard, was that through the incarnation, God illumined the world by his wisdom and aimed to excite in us a love for him. The atonement is important, not for what was done objectively on the Cross, but for the *effect* that it has on us subsequently and subjectively; the atonement, in other words, takes place in and with the human response that it evokes. It is this principle that Bushnell clarified. Love, he said, provided the identity between God and sin; we do not look to the vinegar and gall and the writhing body of Jesus as the grounds for forgiveness, but to that divine love in the depths of which our sin is borne and absorbed. The Cross, therefore, is a declaration, not of the satisfaction of our sins in Christ, but of their cancellation within the being of God so that, having expressed his displeasure over sin and painfully accepted the consequences, his moral government of the world is still intact. But such a solution does mean that by grounding the principle of sacrifice solely in love, even if the character of God is magnified in the process, Bushnell leaves his readers with the impression that the work of Christ is not unique. There is, he says, a Gethsemane and a Calvary in *all* love, the mother who tearfully suffers over her child, the husband who mourns the premature death of his wife, those in the nation who sorrowfully bear in their spirits the weight of collective calamities and follies. Love, he declares, suffers the adversities and pains of others, taking on itself the burden of their evils. This is true not only of divine love, but also of human.

Nathaniel Taylor, therefore, represents a halfway house between Hodge and Bushnell. In Hodge the work of Christ, even if it has to be appropriated subjectively, is nevertheless firmly objective; in Bushnell it is largely subjective. In Hodge the law in accordance with which the universe runs is an expression of what God is; in Taylor and Bushnell there is more than a hint that this law is outside of God, and hence of itself arbitrary. In Hodge the work of Christ, relative to the expressed character of God, is unique; in Bushnell it is not.

Conclusion

It was Hodge's calling to live in a time of extraordinary intellectual transformation in the nation, a time when many of its structures and institutions were in disarray, and when the church itself was in some disorder and perplexity. The church stood at a crossroads, and Hodge pulled mightily in one direction while Taylor, aided by the changing climate in the country, pulled equally insistently in the other. They were both victorious. Hodge succeeded in excising the New School cancer from Presbyterian church life, but Taylor succeeded in opening the door to theological views that would soon spread far and wide and be the ruin of evangelical faith, Reformed and Arminian. Taylor was the stepping stone to the next generation's Liberalism, and that in turn would produce the countermovement of Fundamentalism. How very different subsequent American church life might have been if Hodge had prevailed in expunging Taylorism not only from Presbyterian circles but also from Protestantism in general! As it was, he slowed the inevitable march toward a theology resonant with human self-confidence, as was the culture, but he could not halt it.

It is not difficult to see Hodge's weaknesses. He was not a great historian; only when he was stiffly debated about his claims to historic Calvinism did he grudgingly allow that he believed many things Calvin never taught. He did not recognize as matters for serious theological reflection what was going on in the culture. His *Systematic Theology*, as a result, reads like a piece of eternal wisdom, albeit gathered from European divines, which could be deposited in any age or place with equal ease. He was more astute philosophically than his readers may realize, but he was prone to treat philosophy with the back of his hand. At the same time, he drew heavily off philosophical writers. He also imbibed the interests of Common Sense realism, which was, after all, an Enlightenment philosophy. This occurred almost without recognition on his part.

All of these things are true. But these weaknesses occurred within a man who at times almost alone held back the floodwaters of a sickly cultural theology and who, as a result, must be accorded a place in the annals of church history that cannot be erased. He was a man of very great integrity who followed single-mindedly his calling to obey the teaching of the biblical Word, and through this to live his life to God's glory. And in this he succeeded.

Notes: Charles Hodge

1. The creation of Princeton Theological Seminary had originally met with considerable resistance among ministers. Philip Lindsley spoke of the "popular

clamour [sic] so extensively raised against our school" because of the fear it
would become "an engine of political power" and undercut the role of practicing
ministers in training future ministers (Philip Lindsley, *A Plea for the Theological
Seminary at Princeton, N.J.* [Trenton, 1821], 19, 18). Despite its successful establishment, as well as that of other seminaries, the preparation of ministers lagged
far behind the need. Timothy Dwight, who was appointed President of Yale
College in 1795, noted that between 1700 and 1801 the population had doubled
every twenty-three years. In 1801, however, of 1,008 active churches in Massachusetts and Connecticut, only 749 had ministers. This pattern persisted through
the nineteenth century. In 1828, the *Journal of the American Education Society*
reported that among 960 Congregational churches, 240 had pastoral vacancies;
among 3,723 Calvinistic Baptist churches, 1,146 were vacant; among the Protestant Episcopal churches 112 of the 598 churches were vacant. The next year Hodge
reported that between 600 and 700 Presbyterian congregations out of 1,880 were
"destitute of regular pastors," and he went on to note that "the proportion of
ministers, to the population of the United States, is every year rapidly diminishing" (Anon. [Charles Hodge], *Articles on the American Education Society* [Phila-
delphia, 1928], 7). In 1846 the American Home Missionary Society issued a "loud
call" for men for the West and South; Ohio needed 11, Indiana 14, Michigan 13,
Wisconsin 11, Illinois 16, Missouri 9, Iowa 10, Georgia 2, Kentucky 4, Tennessee
2 (*Thirtieth Annual Report of the Directors of the American Education Society* [Bos-
ton, 1846], 47). The fear that Hodge expressed, that the proportion of ministers
relative to the population was declining, was paralleled in some figures Ebenezer
Porter published in 1821. In his survey of college graduates, he had found that
between 1620 and 1720, approximately 1 in 2 became ministers; between 1720
and 1770, the proportion dropped to 1 in 3; between 1770 and 1810 to 1 in 5; and
between 1800 and 1810 to 1 in 6 (Ebenezer Porter, *A Sermon Delivered in Boston,
on the Anniversary of the American Education Society* [Andover, 1921], 5).
    2. Earl William Kennedy, "An Historical Analysis of Charles Hodge's Doc-
trines of Sin and Particular Grace" (Ph.D. diss., Princeton Theological Seminary,
1968), 17.
    3. Timothy Dwight, *A Discourse on Some Events of the Last Century, Deliv-
ered in the Brick Church in New Haven, on Wednesday, January 7, 1801* (New Haven,
1801), 23. Cf. Dwight's attitude toward the French Revolution in his *The Major
Poems of Timothy Dwight (1752-1817), With a Dissertation on the History, Eloquence,
and Poetry of the Bible* (Gainesville, FL: Scholars' Facsimiles and Reprints, 1969),
384.
    4. Dwight, *A Discourse*, 19.
    5. Joseph Lathrop, *A Sermon, on the Dangers of the Times, from Infidelity and
Immorality; and Especially from a Lately Discovered Conspiracy Against Religion and
Government, Delivered at West Springfield and afterward at Springfield* (Springfield,
1798), 12.
    6. Characteristic assessments are found in Lyman Beecher, *A Sermon, De-
livered in the North Presbyterian Church in Hartford, May 20, 1813, On the Evening
Subsequent to the Formation of the "Connecticut Society for the Promotion of Good
Morals"* (Hartford, 1813); R. D. Mussey, *An Address on Ardent Spirit, Read Before
the New Hampshire Medical Society at their Annual Meeting, June 5, 1827 and Published at their Request* (Boston, 1929); Leonard Bacon, *Total Abstinence from Ardent
Spirits, An Address Delivered by Request of the Young Men's Temperance Society of
New-Haven, in the North Church, June 24, 1829* (New-Haven, 1829); James Dana,

#77   04-15-2012 4:40PM
Item(s) checked out to p18227442.

TITLE: Nicene Christianity : the future
BARCODE: 34213000265735
DUE DATE: 05-06-12

TITLE: Loving the questions : an explora
BARCODE: 441091000027145
DUE DATE: 05-06-12

TITLE: An aid to the Heidelberg Catechis
BARCODE: 441092000275855
DUE DATE: 05-06-12

TITLE: Reformed theology in America : a
BARCODE: 441092000180272
DUE DATE: 05-06-12

Clifton Fowler Library   303-963-3250
Renew at http://ccu.opac.marmot.org

The Folly of Practical Atheism. A Discourse Delivered in the Chapel of Yale College, on Lord's Day, November 23, 1794 (New-Haven, 1794).

7. Horace Bushnell, *Crisis in the Church* (Hartford, 1835).

8. Thomas Belsham, *American Unitarianism; or a Brief History of "the Progress and Present State of the Unitarian Churches in America," Compiled from Documents, and Information Communicated by the Rev. James Freeman, D. D. and William Wells Jun. Esq. of Boston, and From Other Unitarian Gentlemen in this Country, by Rev. Thomas Belsham. Extracted from His "Memories of the Life of the Reverend Theophilus Lindsey," Printed in London, 1812, and Now Published for the Benefit of the Christian Churches in this Country, without Note or Alteration* (Boston, 1815). Jedediah Morse and Jeremiah Evarts, "Review of American Unitarianism," *Panoplist* 11 (June 1815): 241-72.

9. William E. Channing, *A Letter to the Rev. Samuel C. Thatcher, on the Aspersions Contained in a Late Number of the Panoplist on the Ministers of Boston and the Vicinity* (Boston, 1815); Noah Worcester, *A Letter to the Rev. William E. Channing on the Subject of His Letter to the Rev. Samuel Thatcher* (Boston, 1815); William E. Channing, *Remarks on the Rev. Dr. Worcester's Letter to Mr. Channing, on the "Review of American Unitarianism"* (Boston, 1815); Noah Worcester, *A Second Letter to the Rev. William E. Channing on the Subject of Unitarianism* (Boston, 1815); William E. Channing, *Remarks on the Rev. Dr. Worcester's Second Letter to Mr. Channing on American Unitarianism* (Boston, 1815); Noah Worcester, *A Third Letter to the Rev. William E. Channing on the Subject of Unitarianism* (Boston, 1815).

10. [B. B. Wisner], *A Review of the Rev. Dr. Channing's Discourse, Preached at the Dedication of the Second Congregational Unitarian Church, New York, December 7, 1826* (Boston, 1827), 4.

11. William E. Channing, *A Sermon Delivered at the Ordination of the Rev. Jared Sparks, to the Pastoral Care of the First Independent Church in Baltimore, May 5, 1819* (Baltimore, 1819).

12. Moses Stuart, *Letters to the Rev. Wm. E. Channing, Containing Remarks on his Sermon, Recently Preached and Published at Baltimore* (Andover, 1819); [Andrews Norton], *A Statement of Reasons For Not Believing the Doctrines of Trinitarians Respecting the Nature of God, and the Person of Christ. Occasioned By Professor Stuart's Letters to Mr. Channing* (Boston, 1819); Leonard Woods, *Letters to Unitarians Occasioned by the Sermon of the Reverend William E. Channing at the Ordination of the Rev. J. Sparks* (Andover, 1820); Henry Ware, *Letters Addressed to Trinitarians and Calvinists, Occasioned by Dr. Woods' Letters to Unitarians* (Cambridge, 1820); Leonard Woods, *A Reply to Dr. Ware's Letters to Trinitarians and Calvinists* (Andover, 1821); Henry Ware, *Answer to Dr. Woods' Reply, In a Second Series of Letters Addressed to Trinitarians and Calvinists* (Cambridge, 1822); Leonard Woods, *Remarks on Dr. Ware's Answer* (Andover, 1822); Henry Ware, *A Postscript to the Second Series of Letters Addressed to Trinitarians and Calvinists, In Reply to the Remarks of Dr. Woods on those Letters* (Cambridge, 1823).

13. Samuel Miller, *Letters on Unitarianism; Addressed to the Members of the First Presbyterian Church, in the City of Baltimore* (Trenton, 1821). Cf. Moses Stuart, *Letters on the Eternal Generation of the Son of God, addressed to the Rev. Samuel Miller, D. D.* (Andover, 1822); Samuel Miller, *Letters on the Eternal Sonship of Christ: addressed to the Rev. Prof. Stuart, of Andover* (Philadelphia, 1823). Archibald Alexander, "Remarks on Correspondence between Prof. Stuart and Doc. Miller," MS, File D, Speer Memorial Library, Princeton Theological Seminary.

14. Lyman Beecher, *The Autobiography of Lyman Beecher*, ed. Barbara M. Cross, 2 vols. (Cambridge, 1961), 1:430.

15. Ibid., 1:400.

16. Ibid., 2:11.

17. Anon., Review of *The Atonement: Discourses and Treatises by Edwards, Smalley, Maxy, Emmons, Griffin, Burge, and Weeks. With an Introductory Essay by Edwards A. Park, The Congregational Quarterly* 1 (July 1859): 309.

18. An Edwardsean [Joseph Harvey?], *Letters, On the Present State and Probable Results of Theological Speculations in Connecticut* (no publication information), 27-28.

19. A Presbyterian, *A Critical, Philosophical, and Theological Review of A Dissertation on Native Depravity, by Gardiner Spring, D. D.* (New York, 1833), 9.

20. Charles Hodge, Review of *A Brief History and Vindication of the Doctrines received and established in the Churches of New England,* by Thomas Clap, *The Biblical Repertory and Princeton Review* 11 (July 1839): 369-404.

21. An Observer [N. Hewit?], *An Address, to the Congregational Churches in Connecticut, on the Present State of Their Religious Concerns* (Hartford, 1933), 17.

22. Charles Hodge, "Remarks on the Princeton Review," *The Biblical Repertory and Princeton Review* 23 (1851): 309.

23. Andrews Norton, "Thoughts on True and False Religion," *Christian Disciple* 2, new series (1820): 337-65; [Nathaniel Taylor], "Review of Eskine's Evidences, and Norton on True and False Religion," *The Quarterly Christian Spectator* 4 (1822): 249-64, 299-318, 445-48, 667-68; Andrews Norton, "Views of Calvinism," *Christian Disciple* 4, new series (1822): 244-80; [Nathaniel Taylor], "Review of Norton's Views of Calvinism," *The Quarterly Christian Spectator* 5 (1823): 196-224; Anon., "The State of the Calvinistic Controversy," *Christian Disciple* 5, new series (May and June 1823): 212-35; Anon. [Nathaniel Taylor], "Review Renewed," *The Quarterly Christian Spectator* 6 (1824): 310-37, 360-74.

24. Anon. [Nathaniel Taylor], "Review Renewed," 301.

25. Anon. [Nathaniel Taylor], "Review of Norton's . . . ," 217.

26. Ibid.

27. Leonard Bacon, "Future Punishment of Infants Not a Doctrine of Calvinism," *Spirit of the Pilgrims* 1 (January 1828): 45-52; "Future Punishment of Infants Not a Doctrine of Calvinism," *Spirit of the Pilgrims* 1 (February 1828): 78-95; and "Future State of Infants," *Spirit of the Pilgrims* 1 (March 1828): 149-64. Lyman Beecher, "To the Editor of the Christian Examiner and Theological Review," *Spirit of the Pilgrims* 3 (January 1830): 17-24; "To the Editor of the Christian Examiner and Theological Review," *Spirit of the Pilgrims* 3 (February 1830): 72-86; "To the Editor of the Christian Examiner and Theological Review," *Spirit of the Pilgrims* 3 (April 1830): 181-95. Cf. "Examination of a Note by Dr. Beecher," *The Christian Examiner* 4 (September and October 1827): 431-48; 5 (May and June 1828): 229-63.

28. Beecher, *Autobiography,* 1:410.

29. Ibid., 2:158.

30. Ibid., 2:159.

31. Anon., "Beecher's Sermon at Worcester," *The Christian Examiner* 1 (January and February 1824): 49-50.

32. Anon., "On the State of the Question Between the Orthodox and Liberal Parties in This Country," *The Christian Examiner* 5 (January and February 1828): 1.

33. Charles Hodge, "General Assembly of 1837," *The Biblical Repertory and Princeton Review* 9 (July 1837): 407-85. Cf. Charles Hodge, "Reunion of Old and

New-School Presbyterians," *The Biblical Repertory and Princeton Review* 37 (April 1865): 271-313.

34. Leonard Bacon, *Seven Letters to the Rev. George A. Calhoun, Concerning the Pastoral Union of Connecticut, and its Charges Against the Ministers and Churches* (New Haven, 1840), 20.

35. Charles Hodge, "The New Divinity Tried," in *Theological Essays: Reprinted from the Princeton Review* (New York, 1846), 12.

36. See Elwyn A. Smith, "The Doctrine of Imputation and the Presbyterian Schism of 1837-38," *Journal of the Presbyterian Historical Society* 38 (September 1960): 129-51.

37. Charles Hodge, "What is Christianity?" *The Biblical Repertory and Princeton Review* 32 (January 1860): 137.

38. Ibid.

39. See Peter Y. DeJong, *The Covenant Idea in New England Theology 1620-1847* (Grand Rapids, 1945).

40. Charles Hodge, "The First and Second Adam," *The Biblical Repertory and Princeton Review* 32 (April 1860): 340.

41. The Reformers included under the term *original sin* both what was inherited and what was imputed. The distinction between original sin and original damnation was to come later. Hodge's opponents saw in his position such a stress on imputation, hence on original damnation, that current corruption was not adequately affirmed. This objection took several forms. Goodrich in his debate with Hodge, carried in *The Christian Quarterly Spectator*, sought to embarrass Hodge on this point, arguing that "by insisting that *reatus* denotes mere *liability to punishment* rather than ill-desert (true guilt), [Hodge] has unwittingly espoused the position which Turretin ascribes to the Remonstrants, and which he attacks as really a denial of imputation" (Kennedy, "Charles Hodge's Doctrines of Sin and Particular Grace," 73). Later, Robert Dabney charged that Hodge's insistence on parallels in every detail between the representation of the two Adams led naturally to Arminianism and Romanism. On the latter point, justification would have to be seen as an infused righteousness to correspond to the infused corruption, and on the former point, faith must precede and not follow regeneration: "Every one who has a *modicum* of theological knowledge knows that this is precisely Arminianism" (Robert L. Dabney, "Hodge's Systematic Theology," *The Southern Presbyterian Review* 24 [1873]: 209). Along a slightly different line, Landis argued that Hodge undercut, with his insistence on this parallel between the Adams, an actual participation in Adam's sin. For Hodge, he thought, there was only imputed sin and not actual participation in Adam in his sinning (R. L. Landis, " 'Unthinkable' Propositions and Original Sin," *The Southern Presbyterian Review* 26 [April 1875]: 313-15). This charge was developed fully in his book *The Doctrine of Original Sin, as Received and Taught by the Churches of the Reformation, Stated and Defended, and the Error of Dr. Hodge in Claiming that this Doctrine Recognizes the Gratuitous Imputation of Sin, Pointed Out and Refuted* (Richmond, 1884).

42. Charles Hodge, *Commentary on the Epistle to the Romans* (Philadelphia, 1864), 176.

43. Ibid., 190.

44. Ibid., 185.

45. Charles Hodge, *Systematic Theology*, 3 vols. (New York, 1872), 2:203.

46. Hodge, "The First and Second Adam," 367.

47. Ibid., 340-41.

BENJAMIN B. WARFIELD

W. ANDREW HOFFECKER

When Benjamin B. Warfield was called from Western Seminary in Pittsburgh to Princeton Seminary in 1887, the Seminary had been an established and dominant force for over seventy years. He joined a succession of professors that included Archibald Alexander, Charles Hodge, and his son A. A. Hodge, who were influential in training over six thousand students in Christian theology.[1] Warfield occupied the chair of Didactic and Polemical Theology. His task at Princeton, like his predecessors', was to produce ministers who were so thoroughly trained in Reformed theology that they could effectively proclaim the gospel and refute any teaching that did not conform to the high standard of Calvinistic orthodoxy.

Warfield's legacy at Princeton was a proud tradition. As Archibald Alexander, Princeton's first president, approached death, he summoned Charles Hodge to his bedside and gave him a walking stick. This stick, explained Alexander, was handed down to Hodge "as a symbol of orthodoxy."[2] The elder Hodge fulfilled that theological mission by his dedicated leadership of Old School Presbyterians, his voluminous publications, and his diligent seminary teaching. Charles's son, A. A. Hodge, filled the chair of theology for only seven years after his father's death in 1878. Although the younger Hodge's premature death prevented him from attaining the stature of his father, his *Outlines of Theology* has been recognized by some followers of Princeton as a model of theological precision. Also, in his *Popular Lectures on Theological Themes*, published posthumously in 1887, Hodge articulated as forcefully as any of the other Princeton men a Calvinistic basis for the integration of Christianity with cultural activity. And when nineteenth-century secularists mounted campaigns for religious activity in American public life, Hodge urgently insisted that Calvinism was the only theological worldview from which Christians could defend traditional American values and institutions such as family, law, education, and economics.

Of course, in many academic circles today, theological wags would sarcastically whisper that Warfield's appointment perpetuated an already ingrown theological atmosphere. Their criticism would be that instead of adding diversity of opinion, the party line simply gained yet another advocate. But the Princetonians considered their tradition a sacred trust; they gloried in their Reformed heritage. And Warfield's appointment certainly enhanced their efforts through writing and lecturing to maintain orthodoxy's influence in American religious life. In a remark long remembered and often berated by Princeton's detractors, Charles Hodge twice publicly claimed that "a new idea never originated" at Princeton. Those sympathetic to Reformed theology echoed his words, interpreting them to mean that although scholarly research went forward, no modification of belief resulted. Not only did Princetonians deny adjusting their message to suit their times, but they also staunchly resisted any attempt to move Presbyterianism from its Calvinist moorings.

In fact, at the seminary's 1912 centennial celebration, Francis L. Patton proudly claimed that Princeton theology "is exactly the same as it was a hundred years ago." He added that while there has been a New Haven Theology and an Andover Theology, "there never was a distinctively Princeton Theology; Princeton's boast, if she has any reason to boast at all, is in her unwavering fidelity to the theology of the Reformation."[3] Hodge's and Patton's claims have been the object of much debate between old Princeton's friends and critics alike. Ned B. Stonehouse, as a sympathetic biographer of one of Princeton's revered professors, J. Gresham Machen, pointedly argues that Hodge's and Warfield's theologies were not "at every point as completely free of philosophical and speculative influences as they wanted to be and supposed they were—or as lacking in originality as they seemed to claim." Yet he qualified his remarks by saying that any noticeable change in emphasis was due to a "new note of militancy as the issues were drawn . . . in America and Europe."[4]

The purpose of this chapter is to evaluate several of Warfield's major contributions to the Princeton theology in light of discussions about continuity and discontinuity in thought among the various men. Even though Warfield produced no *magnum opus*, he wrote hundreds of articles and reviews that provide ample material by which both the broad outlines and the details of his views may be judged. This chapter will examine three areas that reflect concerns not only prominent in Warfield's work but stressed by his Princeton predecessors as well: religious experience, scholarly criticism in academic journals, and the use of Scottish Common Sense Philosophy. Warfield's predecessors had already articulated clear positions on each of these subjects. A commitment to preserve an established tradition was foremost in each of their minds, yet a changing historical context brought radical changes in the late nineteenth and early twentieth centuries. Liberal theological trends from Europe were threatening to dislodge not only Princeton's Reformed theology but evangelical theology as a whole.[5] Therefore, Warfield's views of the religious life, the theologian's academic task, and rational defense of the faith will be seen against the backdrop of a changing intellectual and cultural milieu.

Religious Experience: Private Piety and Cultural Transformation

Mark A. Noll has provided a revealing account of what concerns motivated Presbyterians to found a seminary in the opening years of the nineteenth century. In "The Founding of Princeton Seminary,"[6] he points out that Christian experience joined with sound theology was stressed at Princeton Seminary from its very inception in 1812. In fact, when Ashbel Green drafted his plan for the Seminary, he not only included a "plan of governance," but he also stipulated that academic study and spiritual nurture together were to form the foundation of ministerial training. Students were expected to explain and defend the Bible and to cultivate vital Christian piety. Princeton's founders wanted a learned clergy who could answer speculations posed by deism and unbelief and a respectable clergy who could bring stability to a newly formed and restless political order. But these founders also demanded a "pious clergy" whose spiritual influence could combat religion's loss of influence, which was threatening to engulf American society. In previous works I have attempted to show the Princetonians' desire and labors to fulfill this charge.[7] Not wanting merely to repeat conclusions of these studies, I believe that further clarification of what Warfield attempted is in order.

Writing in a popular journal, *The Presbyterian Messenger*, in 1896, Warfield explicitly stated his conception of how religious experience was to be related to theology. The conservative view that religion was the product of theology was being radically eclipsed among theological writers by liberals who reversed this relationship. By positing truth prior to both theology and experience, Warfield successfully sidestepped this recurring debate in which conservatives charged that liberals had subjectivized theology and liberals claimed that conservatives intellectualized religious experience. To Warfield, such disputation was fruitless. "Neither," he claimed, "is the product of the other, but both are products of religious truth, operative in the two spheres of life and thought."[8] Warfield's intention, however, was not to probe a dichotomous phenomenon—head versus heart, intellect versus feeling—as he was most wont to do in discussions of theology and religious experience. Instead he enumerated *three* "media" or "channels of communication"—authority, intellect, and heart—all three of which must relate harmoniously as the bases of both religion and theology. Each of these channels may plausibly be argued as the basis for the religious life and theological formulation. For example, he stated that by authority one knows "only what and as God tells." God's truth is also clearly "addressed to the intellect." Yet someone might contend that "our upward strivings, our feeling of dependence and responsibility supply the points of contact between us and God."[9]

But any simplified reduction of religion and theology ends in distortion. Exaggeration of authority yields traditionalistic dogmatism that renders mute the heart and intellect. Stressing intellect, on the other hand, results in rationalistic system building based on *"a priori* fancies" which system in turn precludes any authoritative claims of God's Word or of human conscience.[10] Finally, following only the heart renders one susceptible to mysticism that will bow to no authoritative word or rational thought, but only to "currents of feeling which flow up and down in our souls," giving birth to "competing revelations" and worshiping "the most morbid of human imaginations."[11] True to his Augustinian heritage, Warfield proposed that dangers can be avoided by following another great trinity similar to those enumerated by the famous early church father. Authority, intellect, and heart are the three sides of "the triangle of truth," which can be diagrammed as follows:

God's authoritative Word initiates both the religious life and theology.

Christian experience converts the soul and produces power for an obedient life.

CHRISTIAN THEOLOGY

Christian theology converts the soul and leads the renewed mind to receive spiritual things from the Spirit of God.

The unified triangle represents Warfield's belief that authority, intellect, and heart are unified under God's truth. He contended that Scripture is not, therefore, merely grist for the theologians' systematizing mill. It is also life-producing nourishment for the soul. To change the metaphor, it both "enlightens" the mind and "beautifies" the heart. God's truth reaches its final end not merely by being assembled and organized into a theological system. Scripture is only fully "understood," Warfield claimed, when it is "lived." Fittingly, he concluded with the Augustinian motto "Believe that you may understand," which is taken from Isaiah 9:7: "Unless you believe, you will not understand." An individual has intellectually apprehended the truth only when he displays a corresponding power in his religious experience. True theology, shaped by a sanctified intellect, is always inextricably united with vital religion motivated by an instructed heart. [12]

If this triangle of truth was the model for Reformed religion and theology, how consistently were religion and theology integrated by Warfield at Princeton Seminary? From its earliest days until its reorganization in 1929, weekly conferences were held on Sunday afternoons to discuss practical religion. In two of Warfield's most memorable conference talks, he spoke on seminarians' cultivation of the religious life. [13] Two points stand out in both addresses. First, Warfield admitted that at Princeton students could easily feel compelled to emphasize academics over piety. He cited an interesting story, however, related by the famous Episcopal clergyman Phillips Brooks of Trinity Church, Boston, that illustrated the opposite emphasis at another seminary. Because he had never attended a prayer meeting before, Brooks almost despaired during his first evening devotions at seminary when he could not pray with the fervent spirit of his peers. Yet the next day he was amazed that the same students who had prayed so piously the previous evening displayed a woeful lack of preparation for their first Greek class recitation. Warfield candidly commented: "Well, it was not at Princeton Seminary that Dr. Brooks saw these evils!" [14]

Since the Princeton ideal had always been scholarship accompanied by piety, the greatest danger confronting theological students was not the lack of religion or theology but the tendency to view the two as antithetical. [15] With the same deliberation used in discussing the "triangle of truth" (i.e., by refusing to give priority to authority, intellect, or heart) in "Spiritual Culture in the Seminary" Warfield ascribed equal importance to devotion, intellectual training, and practical experience. "If intellectual acuteness will not of itself make a man an acceptable minister of Christ, neither will facility and energy in practical affairs by themselves, nor yet piety and devotion alone. The three must be twisted together into a single three-ply cord." [16]

Second, Warfield exhorted students to cultivate both corporate and individual piety. By temperament Warfield was more inclined to stress the latter over the former; [17] therefore, his inclusion of an extended discussion on "public means of grace" is all the more significant. He emphasized that the seminary provided several opportunities for formal gatherings: weekly worship on Sunday, conferences on practical religion, and daily prayer at the conclusion of each day. In addition classes were opened by prayer and monthly prayer meetings were organized for missions.[18]

A second part of Warfield's emphasis on corporate religious life was his challenge for students to be motivated by a theology of organic church life while they were still students. Every group of seminarians, he explained:

> bound in as close and intimate association as we are, must have an organic life; and if the bonds that bind them together are fundamentally of a religious character, this organic life must be fundamentally a religious one. . . . No richness of private religious life, no abundance of voluntary religious services [i.e., in "voluntary" movements in society] on the part of members of the organism, can take the place of or supersede the necessity for the fullest, richest, and most fervent expression of this organic religious life through its appropriate channels. I exhort you, therefore, brethren . . . to utilize the public means of grace afforded by the seminary and to make them instruments for the cultivation and expression of the organic religious life of the institution.[19]

So important is participation in the seminary's public means of grace that Warfield said, "The entire work of the seminary deserves to be classed in the category of the means of grace,"[20] and he attributed to it the power of penetrating much more deeply into the foundation of their religious natures than activity in voluntary societies and other forms of public service. He also asked students quite pointedly: "Shall you have everything also [i.e., dormitory life, classroom studies, etc.] in common except worship?" If they had been separated from their normal family and church life, should they not form a "religious community, with its own organic religious life and religious expression?"[21] One might expect a proposal for a "religious order" to follow!

Using these probing questions, Warfield attempted to broaden the focus of Princeton piety, since its adherents usually viewed religon as a private, individualistic walk with God. In these two conference talks Warfield challenged seminarians to appreciate the significance of the visible church and participate in its life. Unfortunately, Warfield never explained in greater detail how to implement his vision of seminary corporate religion. How should students integrate community and private life beyond attending formal worship and maintaining individual devotions? What biblical materials as well as writings in church history stress public worship as a means of grace? And what role should the sacraments play in both corporate and private life? Of course these questions might be addressed by other seminary departments that dealt directly with practical theology, but Warfield's lack of attention to them is regrettable. Perhaps his own predisposition to private piety was too strong, and he could not ever fully overcome it. Nevertheless, the fact that Warfield mentioned these matters is significant in light of his prescient remarks about the future character of religious institutions: "Without at least this much common worship [i.e., common prayer in morning and evening and formal gatherings twice on every Sabbath] I do not think the institution can preserve its character as a distinctively religious institution."[22] Today Warfield's words are an appropriate warning for seminary trustees and administrators since one of their most difficult challenges at the end of the twentieth century is the recovery of spirituality. "Spiritual formation" has become a priority at many seminaries where leaders now perceive a danger in viewing ministerial training solely as an academic discipline.

Warfield's view of the religious life also affected how he viewed the believer's relation to the broader culture. But not all his predecessors agreed with his emphasis. Although Princeton Seminary was founded largely to stem the rising tide of unbelief in American culture, its founders and early leaders sought to combat these evils primarily through constructing and defending sound theology. Little stress was placed on cultural reformation.[23] Such a generalization was defensible in Princeton's founders and early leaders. However, it was least true of Warfield's immediate predecessor, A. A. Hodge. Among Princeton's theologians, the younger Hodge articulated most compellingly the Christian responsibility to implement cultural change. In one of his popular lectures Hodge took umbrage at secularists' campaigns to introduce religious neutrality into American public life and uttered a solemn pronouncement that intellectual and spiritual integrity requires Christians "to bring all the action of the political society to which they belong obedient to the revealed will of Christ the supreme King, the Ruler among the nations."[24] Hodge ended his lecture by surveying civilization from the Flood to his own day and concluding not only that America completes Christianity's westward expansion, but also that Christianity's phenomenal growth confirms its destiny to exercise moral and religious leadership in the world. God's challenge to this generation is to use its vantage point at "the pyramid top of opportunity on which God has set us [to view] forty centuries!" Christianity's commission is to "stretch our hand into the future with power to mould the destinies of millions."[25]

Despite the fact that Warfield succeeded Hodge at a time when secularization had infiltrated much of American life,[26] he did not emphasize Christian commitment to cultural renewal as strongly as the younger Hodge. But neither did he exclude it altogether. In fact, Christians' cultural responsibility appears more frequently in his writings than might be expected. His review of Herman Bavinck's *De Zekerheid des*

Geloofs recounts in some detail Bavinck's criticism of "pietistic legalism," Moravianism, and Methodism for their failure to acknowledge God's sovereign purpose in public as well as private life. Warfield quotes approvingly an extended passage that bears remarkable resemblance to Hodge's view of Christ's Kingdom:

> The earthly spheres of art and science, of literature and politics, of domestic and social economy are underestimated in value and significance by them, and are consequently not reformed and regenerated by the Christian principle. To "rest in the wounds of Jesus" or "to be converted and then go forth to convert others" seems to constitute the entire content of the Christian life.[27]

By limiting piety to "sentimentality and unhealthy emotion" and "excitement and zeal without knowledge" Moravians and Methodists avoid discharging their Christian vocation in everyday life. "The open eye, the wide outlook, the expanded heart—these things do not come to their rights."[28] In a word, he emphasized, Christianity so considered has lost its "leaven."[29] Warfield was not merely mouthing Bavinck's emphasis. His deep personal conviction is evident from his challenge reminiscent of Hodge's decades earlier: Reformed Christians call for "the reformation of the world after the plan of God and its gradual transmutation into his Kingdom in which his will shall be done even as in heaven."[30]

Warfield's advocacy of Christian cultural responsibility developed from his admiration of Calvin's broad influence in the Reformation. Frequently he linked Calvin's name to the growth of free institutions in the West. In *The Methodist Review* Warfield claims that by freeing the Genevan church Calvin created the Protestant Church and instilled a spirit in his followers "to the efflourescence of which this modern world of ours owes its free institutions."[31] But Calvin's foremost contribution to Western culture was education. Due to Calvin's influence three theological schools opened in France. Peasants in Scotland rose higher in their economic status than their counterparts in other countries. But the prime example of Calvinists' pervasive use of education to raise the general cultural level is Puritanism in America. The Puritan educational system "is opening up a new era of human history."[32] He also defends the Genevan Reformer against oft-repeated charges that Calvin depreciated art. Rather than condemning art, Warfield answered, Calvin argued for a "pure and reverent employment of art as a high gift of God, to be used like all others of God's gifts so as to profit man and glorify the Great Giver."[33]

Finally, he contrasted Calvin's holistic perspective on the Christian life with Martin Luther's tendency to limit the Christian vision to an individual sense of sin and justification. Calvin's interests were broader, resulting in a religious worldview encompassing all of life, public and private. Besides the redemption of individuals, Calvin envisioned in Geneva a redeemed social life. He summarizes the Reformed worldview as one that "begins . . . centers . . . and ends with the vision of God in His glory; and it sets itself before all things to render to God His rights in every sphere of life-activity."[34]

How seriously Warfield took the Reformed vision by attempting in his own calling as a Christian scholar to influence American culture is indicated by two essays published in 1888 and 1889. Because he was born and raised in Kentucky he wrote self-consciously as a southern Christian addressing the church's responsibility to recently freed American blacks. His proposals are quite striking considering Warfield's reputation as a conservative. Since Christians know "that God has made of one blood all the nations of the earth" and has invested them with "the missionary spirit," their task is to "serve as the hand of the Most High in elevating the lowly and rescuing the oppressed."[35] Warfield even asked whether it is "good public policy" to compact a lower class and thus continue a social system that allows a class to have heaped on it "year after year, petty injustices and insults."[36]

Convinced that secular training alone was insufficient to the task and that merely preaching a spiritual gospel that does not motivate concrete action in the public life is ineffectual, Warfield called for Christian schools staffed by teachers with missionary zeal to educate believers on how to heal this social evil. He closed with a question directed not at individuals but at his denomination: "Can the Presbyterian Church safely neglect to do her part in this great work?"[37]

His second essay, "Drawing the Color Line," challenged America's churches even more directly. In this essay he complains that so little has been accomplished for the blacks since the Civil War[38] and that even ecclesiastical bodies had succumbed to the political suggestion that only racial segregation would prevent future racial antipathy. He criticized denominations for debating about "drawing the color line" and creating separate white and black groups within their ecclesiastical bodies. Warfield argued against a proposal in the Presbyterian Church by which the General Assembly is "willing to buy reunion with its Southern brethren at the fearful cost of affixing an unjust stigma" on the blacks.[39] The results, he predicted, would only be future racial conflict. Although Warfield's unpopular proposals went unheeded, they clearly reflected his contention that Christian piety definitely should result both in changed individual attitudes toward blacks and in active efforts to integrate public life. Obviously some might argue that his support of blacks was out of character with his traditional private and individualistic piety. But Warfield's prophetic public rebuke of American Christians exemplified his own desire to use biblical principles to challenge trends in the culture and improve it by concerted Christian action.[40]

Conservative Reaction to Nineteenth-Century Scholarship

Contemporary historians of American religion have not recognized Warfield's substantial contributions in their surveys. Typically Hodge has received more attention than any of the other Princeton theologians. Sydney Ahlstrom in *A Religious History of the American People* mentions Hodge four times[41] and Warfield but once. In Ahlstrom's words, Warfield brought "great theological and historical prowess to the defense of the Reformed tradition." His interests in "Reformed doctrine and Biblical inerrancy provided a major theme in the 'Fundamentalist Controversy' that raged within Northern Presbyterianism."[42]

Summarizing Warfield's contribution simply in terms of defense and advocacy of Reformed theology and biblical authority has much in its favor. But those who notice only these two categories ignore the breadth of his interests and the sheer volume of his writings. Most scholars overlook his extensive reviews in various journals, primarily the *Princeton Theological Review*. No major movement or writer in Europe or in America escaped his notice. From the 1830s to the 1870s Old School Presbyterians faithfully read Charles Hodge's views of Charles Finney's revivalism and the theologies of New Haven and Mercersburg, and eagerly awaited the July issue of the *Biblical Repertory and Theological Review* to devour his carefully prepared assessment of business and debate at the General Assembly. Because Warfield was unable to leave the Princeton area due to his caring for his invalid wife, he could not continue Hodge's reportage of denominational affairs. Instead, he kept Americans abreast of contemporary liberal scholarship through his indefatigable writing of reviews in journals.[43]

Content to allow Hodge's voluminous *Systematic Theology* to remain as the fundamental statement of Princeton's views,[44] Warfield focused his energies on writing articles and reviews for periodicals, journals, dictionaries, and the popular press.[45] Warfield's numerous reviews testify to the tremendous pressure conservatives felt to respond to the flood of scholarly works written by liberals who advocated radical change in the study of religion and Christianity. His review articles show Warfield the scholar "in the trenches" fighting not only to fend off foes of his beloved Reformed theology but also to defend doctrines dear to conservatives of every theological stripe. Supernaturalism itself was being repudiated by scholars who believed that the academic study of religion should be treated just as "objectively" as any other academic discipline; that is, it should be subjected to accepted scholarly canons of "neutral" judgment. Radical critics denied the Western tradition of treating Christianity as the uniquely revealed religion. Instead it was just one religion among others, and scholars were to study its origins, doctrines, history, and influence with the same detached scientific method they used in examining the world's other major faiths.

Thus Warfield's struggles were with several factions: radical scholars who denied the supernatural and wanted to reinterpret Christianity on naturalistic terms, and liberals who wanted to alter basic Christian doctrines in less varying degrees. Since the former were making significant inroads in Germany, Warfield most frequently devoted his exceptional powers of analysis and erudition to prevent their ideas from gaining acceptance in America.

What immediately strikes the reader is Warfield's candid assessment of each work he reviewed. When confronting the most capable radical critics, he genuinely praised their intellectual gifts and scholarly acumen while he scorchingly derided the paucity of their radical presuppositions. For example, Warfield expressed sincere appreciation for the scholarship of the Tübingen School:

> There is no student of the New Testament who will not confess deep indebtedness to the work of [Ferdinand Christian] Baur, for example, both for facts in abundance and for generalizations and points of view of the most stimulating character.[46]

Critiquing the famous German church historian Adolf Harnack's *History of Dogma*, he said that it was "a great book, full not only of learning, but of genius and stimulus." Even though Harnack possessed "powers and learning second to no man's of our generation," his defective presuppositions made him "one of the most destructive forces" in Christendom.[47]

Warfield's candid respect for radical critics reflects that he was sufficiently secure in his own position that he could admire the talents and self-confidence of his opponents without fear that such admission might be interpreted as a concession. Warfield believed his own position was unassailable despite his opponents' assaults upon it. His predecessors also were confident that their theology could withstand all attacks. In the 1820s Charles Hodge had fearlessly gone to Europe to prepare himself more adequately in biblical languages and criticism for his teaching responsibilities at the seminary. In his journal and his correspondence with Archibald Alexander, Hodge reveals challenges to his faith posed by exposure to Friedrich Schleiermacher's pantheism and his liberal synthesis of Christianity and romanticism. But despite the threats of new criticism and Schleiermacher's innovations, Hodge returned with his faith intact.[48] At the end of the century Warfield, firmly grounded in the same self-assured tradition, believed that he could successfully meet whatever Europe could send in written form to America.

During the last decade of the nineteenth century Warfield penned several articles surveying the current theological scene—its trends, recent developments, net gains and losses for conservatism. His most positive assessment of nineteenth-century scholarship was "The Century's Progress in Biblical Knowledge" (1900), while other articles such as "The Rights of Criticism and of the Church" (1892), "Evading the Supernatural" (1894), "Heresy and Concession" (1896), and "Recent Reconstructions of Theology" (1898) indicate by their titles the battles that the Princetonians were fighting.

Warfield was pleased that the century's scholars had greatly expanded the store of biblical knowledge. They had advanced the fruits of preceding centuries' biblical study to a greater degree of completion than had been accomplished in any previous era.[49] And as biblical knowledge grew, conservatives successfully blunted critical attacks. Although the century had been filled with controversy, he believed the Bible emerged "without so much as the smell of smoke upon its very garments."[50] While these remarks suggest that orthodoxy remained victorious in the academic arena, Warfield had to concede that his opponents' ranks had increased in number. In "Evading the Supernatural" he admitted that at the thought of Strauss's and Baur's popularity in Europe "American cheeks used to burn in indignation. But now [in 1894] "we have grown used to something like them at home."[51]

In order to appreciate why Warfield claimed victory despite the increasing number of opponents, we must examine the claims of radical critics as well as Warfield's response to them. Warfield's most lasting contribution to late nineteenth- and early twentieth-century scholarship was his analysis and criticism of its worldview. In responding to one theologian's statement that "theologies change as doth a garment," Warfield said this represents the contemporary "despair of dogmatics,"[52] which must have motivated him all the more to show the inadequacies of their presuppositions, methods, and conclusions. He disarmed the radical critics' claim that Christianity was merely another natural religion by demonstrating that such assertions arose not from an examination of the Bible itself, but from the naturalistic presuppositions that critics brought to their study of Scripture. Under such rubrics as "modernizing the faith" or "thinking through Christianity in modern terms" biblical critics and theologians justified refashioning Christianity to suit their own philosophies. Warfield's most telling rejoinder was that because demands for updating the faith are based on the obvious truth that every age "has a language of its own and can speak no other," too frequently critics invert the relation between Christianity and its contextual expression: "Instead of stating Christian belief in terms of modern thought, an effort is made, rather, to state modern thought in terms of Christian belief."[53] Warfield had occasion to use this criticism in the opening paragraphs of his reviews more than any other single point.

Typical of Warfield's approach is his review of Wilhelm Bousset's *What is Religion?* (1907). Warfield first establishes that Bousset is not simply an advocate of "comparative religion" nor of the "history of religion" but of the "comparative" or "history-of-religion [*Religionsgeschichte*] school" (my emphasis). Warfield's careful distinction alerts the reader that Bousset's method of studying religion was based on a carefully developed school of thought. His method was an outgrowth of an underlying philosophy or worldview that explains Christianity "in its entirety, as a religion among religions, the product like other religions of the religious nature of man." Warfield argues convincingly that Bousset adopts naturalistic assumptions "practically as a postulate" in his introduction.[54] By presupposing historical evolution, the author considered "impossible, . . . irreligious, and Godless" any claim that Old and New Testament religions are revealed and that all others are the product of human imagination.[55]

In the remainder of his review Warfield shows how at every point Bousset's interpretation of Christianity is a function of his philosophical perspective. Christianity is presented as a product of "the universal evolution of civilization," a development that began with animism and continued as a function of social organization through a series of increasingly complex stages until universal religions developed. Bousset claimed that Christianity emerged out of "the soil of its own time," and Jesus' singular innovation was his simplification of Judaism. But Jesus' religion was not Christianity's final form, because Christianity continued to evolve up to the modern period. Liberal scholars now jettison Paul's, Augustine's, and Luther's ideas of redemption, Christ's deity and atoning sacrifice, and a revealed Bible by contending they are not compatible with modern thought. Bousset finally reduces Christianity's content to the parable of the Lost Son, the forgiveness of sins, obedience to God's will, and eternal hope. Warfield pointedly remarks that whenever Christianity is "reduced to a 'natural religion' in its origin, it is reduced also to a 'natural religion' in its contents: it shrinks at once to the meager contents of the familiar trilogy, of God, morality, and immortality."[56]

In addition to exposing Bousset's worldview Warfield demonstrated that his "primal assumption" of naturalism was then buttressed by a biblical critical method involving another "immense assumption, or rather a whole series of immense assumptions" that included the Graf-Wellhausen critical reconstruction of Old Testament religion and history and the results of the "history-of-religions" reconstruction of New Testament religion. And behind these is the assumption of the traditional view's invalidity.[57] In the final analysis, Bousset's and other recastings of Christianity are merely a thoroughly consistent hypothetical construction: Bousset says, in effect, "See, if this be conceived to be the way religion has come into existence and developed itself in the course of the ages, then Christianity may be conceived to be a growth of nature. The 'if' here is, however, a mighty one. . . ." In Warfield's opinion, Bousset's radical criticism has no "argumentative value" whatsoever. He has not demonstrated that Christianity is what he claims it to be. Bousset has merely shown "that a self-consistent scheme of the origins of Christianity as a natural religion can be constructed."[58]

In a similar manner Warfield evaluated Dr. William Mackintosh's denial of miracles in *The Natural History of the Christian Religion*. Mackintosh's refutation appears to succeed only because a "more or less clearly formulated assumption of the impossibility of miracles underlies the strenuous opposition to the admission of their reality."[59] A direct outcome of the critics' claim that Christianity is a natural religion is their reinterpretation of its central doctrines beginning with biblical revelation. Warfield's most frequent assertion was that critical scholars were preoccupied with separating the "kernel from the husk." He charged that a scheme which presupposes that divine revelation in Scripture is separable from the "husk" of its historical expression inevitably led to the weakening of biblical authority. Warfield stressed two tendencies in liberal views of Scripture: critics redefine revelation and question the Bible's reliability.

Warfield's review of Reinhold Seeberg's *Revelation and Inspiration* (1909) begins with a reminder that Seeberg's goal is to "modernize" these doctrines. Warfield characteristically takes great pains to explain—several pages containing many citations from the text—Seeberg's view of *Heilsgeschichte*, God's redemptive history, narrated in Scripture. Significantly, Seeberg contended that even though Scripture is a record of God's redemptive history, the Bible is not always trustworthy in what it affirms. It includes some statements that are "notoriously false," outdated cosmologies, and errors in both worldview and interpretation of prophecy.[60] Yet in contrast to naturalists such as Mackintosh and Bousset, who contend that errors only confirm Scripture's natural origins, Seeberg attempts to salvage Scripture's value as a record of revelation despite its errors. His purpose, states Warfield, is "Pragmatistic" because the redemptive record's purpose in Scripture is to work in us "a remarkable inward experience, in which we find ourselves in the presence of God."[61] Warfield's assessment is very astute. Seeberg's introduction of a distinction between historical facts and ideas of revelation—the husk that is irrelevant and sometimes wrong and the kernel that produces our experience of redemption—substantially changes our conception of the Bible's authority.

> The basis of confidence is shifted from the Bible to Christian experience, or to what we used to call "the Christian consciousness," and the Bible is made to play the role only of vehicle of transmission. The whole conception of an authoritative book is set aside and we are to accept in the Bible only what Christian experience validates.[62]

Warfield terms Seeberg's interpretation an example of "Modern-positive Theology," which in his opinion is not really new. It is merely the latest expression of subjectivism, which can be traced back to Schleiermacher.

A final emphasis in Warfield's reviews was his criticism of liberal Christologies. His efforts not only to expose what he believed to be false christological thinking but also to articulate the Reformed viewpoint were untiring.[63] The Princeton apologist was especially skillful in confronting christological studies constructed on naturalistic premises. In 1911 he reviewed a series of Johannes Weiss's works on Christ. Warfield declared Weiss to be "[Wilhelm] Wrede's successor as the *enfant terrible* of the 'liberal school.' "[64] His opening remarks conform to his usual pattern of establishing that the author's worldview is the most significant factor shaping his Christology. Weiss's works, though destructive to the faith, have this "virtue," that they disclose in no uncertain terms "the violence of the assumptions on which alone the naturalization of the origins of the Christian religion can be accomplished."[65]

Weiss discusses the doctrine of Christ through the New Testament from the history-of-religions perspective. He admits that his view of Jesus is not the same as the New Testament's—that Jesus was a "resurrected and exalted Christ." Instead of what he called "primitive Christianity," Weiss espouses a theology that "has its full satisfaction in permitting itself to be led to the Father by Jesus of Nazareth."[66] Warfield explained that basic to liberals' distinguishing various views of Christ even within the New Testament was their tendency to reject Pauls' view, which Weiss called "not a development but a transmutation of the religion of Jesus."[67]

What astounded Warfield, however, is that Weiss, against all reasonable expectation considering his radical bias, refuses to take the liberal critical method to its absurd conclusion and join the most radical scholars who denied that Jesus even existed. Instead, Weiss assumes the improbable mantle of a conservative apologist by arguing in favor of the historical Jesus.[68] But he retains his mediating position between orthodox affirmations of Jesus' true historical existence only by abandoning his usual naturalistic critical method. Warfield revels in Weiss's being caught between two worldviews:

> Either he must continue to use the methods common to him and his more radical opponents, and then he can scarcely escape their extremities of negation. Or else he must allow the sounder methods he tells them they ought to follow, and then he can surely not fail ultimately to reach "conservative" conclusions. It appears to be only a new instance of the old difficulty: "I see the good; the evil I pursue."[69]

Warfield frequently mentioned Ernst Troeltsch's assertion that even though many scholars in Germany were turning to "reduced Christianity" advocated by the most radical critics, the radical school was manifesting no productive power in German culture and showed little future promise. Warfield took great comfort in Troeltsch's judgment that "almost all the religiousness of today draws its life from modifications of the strong religious treasures propagated in the churches and in them alone." Interestingly, Warfield's warmest endorsement of Troeltsch was that his usually consistent naturalism did not prevent him from affirming that Jesus' historicity was essential for Christianity. Warfield never tired of citing passage after passage in which Troeltsch either affirms the historical Jesus or rails against those who made Jesus merely a symbol expressing their peculiar faith in God.[70]

Our survey of Warfield's reviews demonstrates that although he never constructed his own systematic theology, conservatives ever since have been greatly in his debt. While some may argue that conservatives could have rallied around a fresh restatement of orthodoxy to stem the liberal tide, others could justly counter that Warfield discharged his stewardship in forms most suited both to his gifts and to current needs. Through his reviews, Warfield not only kept his followers abreast of liberal scholarship, but he also disarmed the critics by disclosing how dependent their ideas were on their naturalistic philosophy.

Of course, Warfield did more than analyze critical scholarship. He carefully honed an apologetic system by which he believed the conservative position could be defended. Having discussed his evaluation of naturalistic criticism, we now turn our attention to how Warfield showed that positive use of reason can establish Christian truth.

Common Sense Philosophy and Its Appropriateness to Reformed Theology

Warfield was convinced that simply because radical critics misused criticism, that fact certainly did not negate conservatives' responsibility to carry out its proper function. Contrary to widespread belief that conservatives oppose criticism, Warfield answered in "The Rights of Criticism and of the Church" (1892) that the existence of truth demands criticisms for its vindication. Biblical scholars are just as obligated to test the claims of the Bible as classical scholars are to examine Aristotle's works.[71]

Crucial to any critical scrutiny is establishing what Warfield called "the pure facts."

Everyone of us exercises all the faculties God has given him and exhausts all the tests at his command to assure himself of the facts. . . . [Careful scrutiny of the facts] is good or bad in proportion to the accuracy and completeness with which the facts are apprehended and collected and the skill and soundness with which they are marshalled and their meaning read.[72]

A crisis has arisen, claims Warfield, not because of criticism itself but because of an "ineradicable tendency of man to confound the right of criticism with the rightness of his own criticism."[73] The Presbyterian Church must address modernism's proud claim to autonomy if it is to stand for the truth. Preserving revealed truth through apologetics has been vouchsafed to the church in the modern age just as it has been throughout history. Fundamental to Warfield's description of apologetics and his confidence that it would succeed in its task was his belief in Scottish Common Sense Philosophy (CSP). Philosophers in Scotland established commonsense principles in the eighteenth century to answer the skepticism of David Hume. Thomas Reid (1710-1796) argued that man's mind is so constituted by God as to know reality (not only the external world but also cause and effect and basic moral principles) directly by "common sense." John Witherspoon introduced Scottish philosophy in America when he became president of Princeton College in 1768. All the Princetonians learned it as the philosophical perspective by which they could not only achieve certainty in knowledge but also demonstrate fundamental apologetic truths. Princeton's dependence on this philosophy and particularly the question whether its use is consistent with Princeton's Reformed theology or whether it distorts their theology have stimulated heated debate between contemporary students and critics.[74] John Vander Stelt has written the most comprehensive, and critical, study of Scottish influence at Princeton in *Philosophy and Scripture: A Study of Old Princeton and Westminster Theology* (1978).[75] He explains how each of the Princeton thinkers was trained in Scottish philosophy and used its epistemological principles to ground his faith in rational certainty. Alexander used it to certify Scripture, Hodge developed it to construct an inductive method in theology, and Warfield carefully refined it into a rational apologetic system. Each development reflected the nature and intensity of opposition mounted against Princeton's position.

While he disagrees with all conservatives' use of Common Sense Philosophy, Vander Stelt is especially critical of Warfield's. Vander Stelt concedes that philosophical attacks increased after the Civil War and that Warfield believed that only a full-scale defense was capable of preserving Reformed thinking from crumbling. Nevertheless, he finds that Warfield's "entire framework of thought in his apologetics and Scripture is unmistakably intellectualistic" and has as its foundation a "dualism," an "ontological and religious distinction between the supernatural and the natural."[76] In one of his summary paragraphs on Warfield's thought, Vander Stelt explains this dualism:

> As to the structure of the natural world, Warfield found the basic assumptions of a philosophy of reality and truth that was greatly indebted to Scottish CSP acceptable and helpful in curtailing any threats upon certainty and security. By placing all of this within the larger context of the supernatural, Warfield tried to reinsure the former with the latter. Through a curious fusion of two basically conflicting worlds of thought, Warfield struggled to obtain theoretical and practical certainty for knowledge and faith by linking this certainty up with a *supra*-naturally qualified notion of infallibility and inerrancy that is supposed to be—but, in fact is not as the original autographs of the Bible are lost—within the reach of all rational men in this natural world.[77]

Thus Warfield took the Princeton faith in Common Sense to its furthest extreme without recognizing the vast internal tension it created within his system.[78]

In my previous work on Warfield I attempted to qualify some of the criticisms of Warfield's intellectualism and lack of emphasis on subjectivity that Vander Stelt has chosen to ignore.[79] While I agree with the central point of Warfield's critics, a defense can be made for his dependence on Common Sense principles. In a recent article Darryl Hart has defended Warfield's successor, J. Gresham Machen, on this point. His arguments apply with similar force to Warfield. Hart believes that Machen's continued adherence to Common Sense principles was a virtue despite its significant weaknesses. Without some of Common Sense Philosophy's principles epistemological skepticism might well have proven unavoidable. Its emphasis on universality, language, and history were not simply basic to knowledge but were also used in the defense of Christianity. All people are so constituted that they can know reality and communicate about it truthfully. Our knowledge of the past is something objective because memory is not just of an idea, but of the reality itself. These principles appeared fundamental as well to the biblical worldview, which holds man to be made in the image of God, recipient of a written revelation, and dependent on knowing certain objective redemptive historical events.[80] Long before Machen, Warfield used these principles repeatedly in his confrontations with liberal theology.

But an even more important factor in Warfield's retention of Scottish philosophy was his recognition of the bankruptcy in perspective of various philosophical systems that had replaced Common Sense. As we noted in the previous section, Warfield's skepticism of modern method was equally the match of modern thinkers' skepticism of traditional views of knowledge. Although he did not always refer to various philosophical systems, when he did, he barely concealed his contempt for them. Kantian epistemology, for example, in which the categories of the human mind take the place of God as the basis for knowing and in which God is reduced to a postulate of practical reason instead of its determining ground, represented "a veritable revolution by which God is dethroned and man elevated to His place as the center of the universe."[81] Kant's subjectivism was succeeded by Schleiermacher's, which ultimately gave way to Ritschlian thought. Frequently he attacked Albrecht Ritschl and his followers for their repudiation of metaphysics. Because the Ritschlites viewed revelation in purely personal terms and granted no place for propositions, they are unable to bequeath to the church anything more than "individualistic dogmatics."[82] In another summary for *The New York Observer* Warfield claimed that Ritschl's theology "was merely the old Socinianism in a new garment, cut from the cloth of Neo-Kantian speculation."[83] What Ritschl was attempting to do, Warfield continues, was to reduce Christianity's content to a nondogmatic faith. Thereby he hoped to save it from being ravaged by naturalistic philosophers, unbelieving scientists, and skeptical historians. While his motives may have been good, Ritschl made a common nineteenth-century error of gutting the Christian faith of its contents.[84]

Warfield's answer to modernist skepticism was that certainty is still achievable despite denials by contemporary philosophers and theologians. All that is required is a careful scrutiny of rational evidence. In an article written early in his career at Princeton, "Christian Evidences and Recent Criticism" (1888), Warfield claimed for rational apologetics virtually what he was to claim in 1900 about the Bible and criticism, that each had escaped from controversy without even the "smell of smoke" to suggest the battle. As we might expect, the method of proof for both was the same, examination of rational evidence—the facts.

Warfield's most memorable statement of Christianity's apologetic task was militant: "It is the distinction of Christianity that it has come into the world clothed with the mission to reason its way to dominion."[85]

The context of Warfield's remark is his rebuke of Abraham Kuyper's subordination of apologetics to the "narrow task of defending developed Christianity against philosophy, falsely so called."[86] One can sense Warfield's perplexity if not disdain as he claims that Kuyper's method of defending Christianity as only "the great assumption" bears all too much similarity to the hypothetical constructions of Bousset and Mackintosh. If Kuyper is correct, Christian scholars have been robbed of their incentives to validate Christian truth. The combined labors of exegetes, historians, and systematic theologians has "all hung, so to speak, in the air; not until all their labor is accomplished do they pause to wipe their streaming brows and ask whether they have been dealing with realities or perchance with fancies only."[87]

Several themes that we have examined so far coalesce in Warfield's repudiation of Kuyper's apologetics. Even more than he eschewed fancies in religious experience, Warfield despised them in theology and its preparatory discipline, apologetics. Conservatives, especially Reformed Christians in keeping with their holistic redemptive view, had a mandate not only to recapture Christian scholarship but also to regain the cultural mind.[88] These tasks in Warfield's opinion could never be accomplished by the Dutch apologetics of Kuyper and Bavinck. In his review of Bavinck's *De Zekerheid des Geloofs*, Warfield restates his commitment to evidentialist apologetics, which has the task among others of demonstrating God's existence and authenticating Scripture as God's Word. Christian faith, therefore, is a reasonable faith based on good and sufficient evidence, not a "blind and ungrounded faith."[89]

Warfield's frequent critique was that his opponents' theology was "Modern-Positive," as we saw above in his criticism of Seeburg. However, his own view of using "facts"—both rational facts to demonstrate God's existence and the authority of God's Word and biblical facts to arrive at a sound theology—sounds even more modern. His demand that critics ought to pay attention to facts carried the implication that liberals could be corrected if they would recognize the naturalism of their own position and scrutinize the evidence by virtually suspending their belief in naturalism just as phenomenologists advocate an epistemological epoche, "bracketing of existence," or suspension of belief in order to achieve greater accuracy in description of an object.[90]

Fortunately, in at least one significant writing, "The Right of Systematic Theology," Warfield discusses the influence of doctrine on facts. In the article Warfield challenged theologians and biblical scholars who were hostile to theology and saw in doctrine and propositional truth obstacles to religion. Some feared that doctrine would quench religious life and therefore they summarized Christianity as life, not doctrine. But the other group invented the watchword "Christianity consists of facts, not dogmas."[91]

Considering Warfield's predisposition to stress the objective or the factual basis of Christianity, we are not surprised that if given a choice between doctrine and facts, he would choose the facts. Nevertheless, consistent with many other instances in his writing he demands that neither can be relinquished; no antithesis is ever to be proposed which separates these two elements.

> What Christianity consists in is facts that are doctrines, and doctrines that are facts. Just because it is a true religion, which offers to man a real redemption that was really wrought out in history, its facts and doctrines entirely coalesce.[92]

All this we might have expected. But when Warfield discusses its implications he makes some strong statements that differ from his usually strict objective emphasis on facts.

> What is a fact that is wholly separated from what is here called "dogma"? If doctrines which stand entirely out of relation to facts are myths, lies [then] facts which have no connection with what we call doctrine could have no meaning to us whatsoever. It is what we call doctrine which gives all their significance to facts. A fact without doctrine is simply a fact not understood. That intellectual element brought by the mind to the contemplation of facts, which we call "doctrine," "theory," is the condition of any proper comprehension of facts.[93]

A few lines later, after quoting Dr. James Denney's statement that a fact without theory is a "blank unintelligibility, a rock in the sky, a mere irrelevance in the mind of man," Warfield adds that

> so closely welded are these intellectual elements—those elements of previous knowledge, or of knowledge derived from other sources —to facts as taken up into our minds in the complex act of apperception, that possibly we have ordinarily failed to separate them, and consequently, in our worship of what we call so fluently "the naked facts," have very little considered what a bare fact is, and what little meaning it could have for us.[94]

Certainly these few words do not make Warfield a presuppositionalist, just as Hart asserted that some of Machen's phrases did not make him one either. But Warfield never subjected facts to such searching criticism as he did in these words.

If the heirs of Warfield's evidentialist view and the advocates of Dr. Van Til's presuppositionalism are to make any progress in their internecine struggles, surely an item high on the agenda is a discussion of what constitutes a fact and how facts are to be used in both apologetic and theological disciplines. Was Warfield inconsistent in his apologetics, if only a few times? How are we to understand his use of Augustine's motto when we would have expected him to cite Thomas Aquinas' credo, "I understand in order that I might believe"? What is the significance of his basically presuppositionalist attack of his opponents in his reviews? What did he mean when he said that an "ineradicable tendency" in people makes them assert their own autonomy in critical studies? Has this any significance for discussions concerning the noetic effect of sin? How much effect, if any, do historical or contextual factors as well as individual subjective bias have on knowing, and can their effects be reduced or eliminated? Warfield's apologetic as a whole provides a vast storehouse of information for one side of the debate. But he was aware of other sides and established a precedent of interaction with them.

Conclusion

Benjamin B. Warfield's contributions to contemporary scholarship are more varied and complex than is immediately apparent. His scholarly production was voluminous and his range of interests spanned several theological disciplines. Even though his writing was often formal and his appeal was primarily to the scholarly community, he wrote on more than simply Reformed theology and the authority of Scripture where he left his considerable mark.

In the three areas that we have examined in this chapter we have noticed nuances and emphases that broaden our appreciation for Warfield's accomplishments. His piety was not exhausted by appeals to personal holiness and application of scriptural truth to one's private life. Even though his vision for a transformed American culture was cast in terms of his postmillennial faith, he challenges all followers of the Reformed tradition to rethink views of the visible church and of the leavening effect of the gospel in public life in order to extend what Warfield himself left unfinished.

Warfield's example in scholarly writing and particularly in the area of reviewing contemporary theology could hardly be more pertinent today. Reformed theologians need not only to continue to develop their theologies carefully in light of the Word of God but also to show how many contemporary theologians continue in the lines of their nineteenth-century counterparts by espousing twentieth-century presuppositions and proposals for action cloaked in terms borrowed from the Christian worldview.

Finally, Reformed theologians must continue to discuss how Christian truth can best be defended. The secularism that was building in

Warfield's day has become a dominant and established force at the end of the nineteenth century. Even though Warfield based his apologetic method on presuppositions that were more consistent with Scottish philosophy, he still possessed an essentially biblical vision of recapturing not only his church but also the wider culture with the gospel message.

Notes: Benjamin B. Warfield

1. Mark A. Noll, *Princeton Theology 1812-1921* (Grand Rapids: Baker Book House, 1983), 19.

2. A. A. Hodge, *Life of Charles Hodge* (New York: Charles Scribner's Sons, 1880), 382.

3. Ned B. Stonehouse, *J. Gresham Machen* (Grand Rapids: Wm. B. Eerdmans Publishing Company, 1954), 62.

4. Ibid., 63.

5. See Gary S. Smith, *The Seeds of Secularization* (Grand Rapids: Wm. B. Eerdmans Publishing Company, 1985), ch. 2.

6. Mark A. Noll, "The Founding of Princeton Seminary," *Westminster Theological Journal* 42 (1979): 72-110.

7. "The Relation between the Objective and Subjective Elements in Christian Religious Experience. A Study in the Systematic and Devotional Writings of Archibald Alexander, Charles Hodge, and Benjamin B. Warfield" (Ph.D. diss., Brown University, 1970) and *Piety and the Princeton Theologians* (Phillipsburg, NJ: Presbyterian and Reformed Publishing Company, 1981).

8. B. B. Warfield, "Authority, Intellect, Heart," in *Selected Shorter Writings of Benjamin B. Warfield*, ed. John E. Meeter, 2 vols. (Nutley, NJ: Presbyterian and Reformed Publishing Company, 1970), 1:668.

9. Ibid., 669.

10. Ibid.

11. Ibid., 670.

12. Ibid., 671.

13. "Spiritual Culture in the Theological Seminary," (1904), in ibid., 2:468-96 and "The Religious Life of Theological Students" (1911), in ibid., 1:411-22.

14. Ibid., 2:474.

15. Ibid., 412.

16. Ibid., 472.

17. He devoted more time to encouraging private piety, which he called "the center of our subject" (ibid., 481) and "the foundation stone of piety" (ibid., 1:422).

18. Ibid., 2:476.

19. Ibid., 477.

20. Ibid., 478.

21. Ibid., 1:418.

22. Ibid., 419.

23. In his excellent treatment of these issues Mark A. Noll probes Green's, Alexander's, and others' tendency to disparage active involvement in culture. They considered theological education to be the primary function of both the seminary and the college. Unfortunately, Princeton scholars were not devoted to

developing the Christian liberal arts. Noll also astutely argues that a symbiotic relationship should have existed between Princeton College and the seminary. The seminary should have provided the college "with the fruits of its labors from biblical study, theological reflection, and interaction with the Christian past," while on the other hand the college should have provided the seminary "with interpretations of modern learning and creative ventures of its own into the developing fields of nineteenth century thought." And both should have reflected "together on the foundational theological stances and philosophical presuppositions which shaped the inquiries of both bodies" (Noll, "Founding of Princeton Seminary," 105).

24. Hodge cited a list of corruptions in American society (divorce laws, desecration of the Sabbath, corrupt trade and commerce practices, and secularization of education) that needed to be redeemed by instituting Christian principles in public life. A series of impassioned questions revealed his concern over the dilution and elimination of Christian principles from American political, economic, and social institutions: "Whence come these portentous upheavals of the ancient primitive rock [Christianity] upon which society has always rested? Whence comes this socialistic earthquake, arraying capital and labor in irreconcilable conflict like oxygen and fire? Whence come these mad prehistoric anarchical ravings, the wild passages of a universal deluge which will blot out at once the family, the school, the church, the home, all civilization and religion in one sea of ruin?" (A. A. Hodge, *Popular Lectures on Theological Themes* [Philadelphia: Presbyterian Board of Publication and Sabbath School Work, 1887], 256).

25. Ibid., 334.

26. For a detailed view of the growth of secularization in American culture from the end of the Civil War to the beginning of World War I, see Smith, *Secularization*, ch. 2.

27. Warfield, *Shorter Writings*, 2:108.

28. Ibid., 108-09.

29. Ibid., 109.

30. Ibid., 110.

31. "John Calvin, the Man and His Word," in *Calvin and Calvinism* (New York: Oxford University Press, 1931), 20. In "Calvinism," an encyclopedia article originally written by Hodge but revised by Warfield, he narrates Calvin's effort to establish ecclesiastical freedom in Geneva. (See Warfield, *Shorter Writings*, 2:411.)

32. Warfield, *Shorter Writings*, 2:445.

33. Ibid., 184. He referred readers to Kuyper's Stone Lectures of 1898 at Princeton and to Emil Doumergue's "L'Art et le Sentiment dans l'oeuvre de Calvin" (1902) as correctives to the view that Calvin opposed artistic expression.

34. Ibid., 355.

35. "A Calm View of the Freedmen's Case," in ibid., 740. In words that might be labeled paternalistic today, Warfield calls on Christians to raise the blacks in their moral education. "The task before the American people in dealing with the blacks is nothing less . . . than the uprooting and expulsion of a settled and ingrained system of morality [which is the result of slavery itself] in order that a true morality may be substituted for it" (p. 737). Their social standing can only be compared to the caste system of India: "The harm that caste does toward those whom we would elevate cannot be overestimated. It kills hope; it paralyzes effort" (p. 741).

36. Ibid.

37. Ibid., 742.

38. Warfield quotes another commentator approvingly: "Emancipation has abolished only private but not public subjugation; has made the ex-slave not a free man but only a free Negro" (ibid., 744).

39. Ibid., 749.

40. Warfield's lack of comment on social issues is probably based on two factors: his temperament and his relatively secluded life. Unlike the Hodges who played significant roles in Presbyterianism, Warfield was confined to Princeton to care for his invalid wife. In his biography of Machen, Stonehouse said that Warfield rarely spent more than two hours away from her at a time and did not leave the town of Princeton between 1905 and 1915 (see Stonehouse, *Machen*, 220).

41. S. Ahlstrom, *A Religious History of the American People* (New Haven: Yale University Press, 1972). In each instance his discussion is inadequate considering Princeton's contribution to nineteenth- and twentieth-century theology and the depth of analysis Ahlstrom devoted to other movements such as Mormonism and Christian Science.

42. Ibid., 18. Winthrop Hudson in *Religion in America* (New York: Charles Scribner's Sons, 1965) discusses Warfield only briefly as a defender of the Westminster Confession and as instrumental with A. A. Hodge in forging the "Princeton doctrine of inspiration." Charles Hodge is discussed much more extensively. (Cf. pp. 167, 171, 180-81, 269, 284.)

43. For a cataloging of Warfield's articles and reviews see John E. Meeter and Roger Nicole, comps., *A Bibliography of Benjamin Breckinridge Warfield 1851-1921* (Nutley, NJ: Presbyterian and Reformed Publishing Company, 1974).

44. Cf. Patton's summary in his "Memorial Address," *Princeton Theological Review* 19 (1921): 387, explaining why Warfield never wrote his own systematics.

45. Due to limitations of space I will limit my remarks primarily to reviews collected in Vol. 10 of the Oxford series, *Critical Reviews* (New York: Oxford University Press, 1932), and to Warfield's *Shorter Writings*.

46. He credited Baur and his followers with pressing conservatives to increase their effort "to explore more deeply its record and to draw from them even more purely their treasures of truth" (Warfield, *Shorter Writings*, 2:9). In the very opening lines of one review of Ernst Troeltsch, Warfield said his "chief merit as a writer on theological themes lies in his straightforward downrightness" (*Critical Reviews*, 287).

47. Warfield, *Shorter Writings*, 2:451.

48. See my treatment of Hodge's trip in *Piety*, 48-52.

49. Throughout the article Warfield lists in detail major movements and publications in various areas of biblical scholarship, e.g., Old and New Testament, commentaries, textual aids, archeology, etc. Warfield was particularly gratified by exegetical gains.

50. Warfield, *Shorter Writings*, 2:13.

51. Ibid., 683.

52. *Critical Reviews*, 407.

53. Review of *Foundations. A Statement of Christian Belief in Terms of Modern Thought*, by Seven Oxford Men, *Critical Reviews*, 322.

54. *Critical Reviews*, 173.

55. Ibid.

56. Ibid., 177.

57. Ibid., 177-78.
58. Ibid., 178. I have included a detailed summary of Warfield's review of Bousset to indicate Warfield's careful and extensive treatment of the material and to show how radical Bousset's attack was.
59. "The Question of Miracles," in Warfield, *Shorter Writings*, 2:173. Later in the same essay Warfield evaluated David Hume's classic rebuttal of miracles. Hume's attack on the probability of miracles was based on the naturalistic assumption that our overwhelming experience of the uniformity of nature militates against their probability. But Hume's refutation is worthless as a rational argument. By affirming the absolute uniformity of nature, which renders miracles impossible, Hume is unable to answer the question of probability because probability "is the very thing in dispute" (p. 178).
60. *Critical Reviews*, 238.
61. *Critical Reviews*, 238.
62. *Critical Reviews*, 239.
63. Besides reviews, which are the focus of this paper, he produced numerous topical, exegetical, and historical studies. Cf. his *Christology and Criticism* (New York: Oxford University Press, 1929), and essays in *Shorter Writings*.
64. *Critical Reviews*, 266.
65. Ibid., 267.
66. Ibid., 286.
67. Ibid., 270.
68. Ibid., 273-74.
69. Ibid., 275.
70. Ibid., 294.
71. Warfield, *Shorter Writings*, 2:595.
72. Ibid., 596. Ascertaining the facts was as important in biblical study as it was in apologetics. In his review of Hastings' *Dictionary of the Bible*, Vol. 1, Warfield found it superior to other recently published works because of its greater reliability. But Warfield claimed that we still need a dictionary "which renounces speculation and sets out the facts" (*Critical Reviews*, 67). Warfield's remarks are reminiscent of Charles Hodge's statement on theological method in his *Systematic Theology*, that theologians use the facts of the Bible as a scientist uses the facts of nature. (See Vol. 1, pp. 1-17.)
73. Warfield, *Shorter Writings*, 2:596.
74. See Mark A. Noll's careful assessment of common sense as one of Princeton's "themes" in his excellent introductory chapter in *Princeton Theology*, 30-33, and George Marsden's assessments in *Fundamentalism and American Culture: The Shaping of Twentieth Century Evangelicalism, 1870-1925* (New York: Oxford University Press, 1980), 109-18.
75. Vander Stelt's notes and bibliography contain an extensive listing of scholarly works, including dissertations.
76. J. Vander Stelt, *Philosophy and Scripture: A Study of Old Princeton and Westminster Theology* (Marlburg, NJ: Mack Publishing Company, 1978), 182-83.
77. Ibid.
78. In the second part of his book Vander Stelt examines philosophy and Scripture at Westminster Seminary. He stresses the institutional shift away from Princeton Seminary led by Machen and the repudiation of Princeton's philosophical principles under Van Til's guidance. Perhaps Vander Stelt's sharp contrast between Princeton and Westminster might be seen as an attempt to win a hearing from Westminster for the Dutch tradition that he represents.

79. See Hoffecker, *Piety*, ch. 3. Vander Stelt refers to my work and uses some material on Hodge but does not concede that Warfield's work contained any subjective emphases.

80. D. Hart, "The Princeton Mind in the Modern World and the Common Sense of J. Gresham Machen," *Westminster Theological Journal* 45 (1984): 1-25. See also George Marsden's "J. Gresham Machen, History, and Truth," *Westminster Theological Journal* 42 (1979): 157-75.

81. *Critical Reviews*, 244.

82. *Critical Reviews*, 408.

83. Warfield, *Shorter Writings*, 2:449.

84. Ibid., 450.

85. Ibid., 99.

86. Ibid., 95.

87. Ibid., 96.

88. In "Christian Evidences and Recent Criticism" Warfield responded to Huxley's boast that "extinguished theologians lie about the cradle of every science as the strangled snakes beside that of Hercules." He retorted that "[theologians] keep company there with an interesting body of scientific lights"(!) (ibid., 129). Nevertheless, he continues, criticism such as Huxley's only spurs apologists to refine their arguments so that finally they may stand "easily victor against all modern assaults" (ibid., 131).

89. Ibid., 115. A rather significant historical irony is that while the Princetonians not only did not regain a hearing in American culture but also lost control of their Presbyterian denomination (see Lefferts Loetscher, *The Broadening Church* [Philadelphia: University of Pennsylvania Press, 1954]), the Dutch theologians continued to exercise significant cultural influence in their native Holland. See James Skillen and Stanley Carlson-Thies, "Religious and Political Development in Nineteenth Century Holland," *Publius* 12 (Summer 1982): 43-64.

90. Cf. "Phenomenology," in *Encyclopedia of Philosophy*, Vols. 5, 6 (New York: Macmillan Publishing Company, Inc., 1967), 140-44.

91. Warfield, *Shorter Writings*, 2:230.

92. Ibid., 234.

93. Ibid., 236.

94. Ibid.

II. THE WESTMINSTER SCHOOL

THE WESTMINSTER SCHOOL

W. ROBERT GODFREY

WESTMINSTER Theological Seminary was founded in the midst of the modernist-fundamentalist controversies of the 1920s. It purposed to carry on the Old School Presbyterian tradition of Princeton Theological Seminary. Its development was significantly shaped by theological reflection in the Netherlands. The result has been a distinctive influence on Reformed theology in America. Westminster's influence has not been the result of a vast number of graduates nor of connection with large denominations. Its influence has been significant because of the force of its ideas transmitted through the teaching and publications of its faculty, through its role in helping to educate a number of scholars and leaders in evangelical churches. This essay will seek to review the distinctive influence of the "Westminster School."

The Modernist-Fundamentalist Controversy

The confrontation between fundamentalism and modernism agitated many segments of American church life early in the twentieth century. In the Presbyterian Church in the United States of America the threat of modernism united conservatives in the early 1920s and for a time seemed likely to force liberals out of the denomination. The General Assembly of 1925 was the high point of conservative strength and influence.[1] The General Assembly determined to review the ordinations of men in New York Presbytery who had not affirmed the five points of doctrine declared essential for Presbyterian ministers by General Assemblies in 1910, 1916, and 1923.[2] New York Presbytery announced that the General Assembly's action was unconstitutional and that it would not comply. Rather than proceed to enforce discipline and risk a split in the denomination, conservatives agreed to establish a committee "to study the present condition of our Church and the causes making for unrest, and to report to the next General Assembly, to the end that the purity, peace, unity, and progress of the Church may be assured."[3] At this crucial juncture the majority of conservatives chose unity over purity. It was the last opportunity conservatives had to make a choice for purity as the majority in the church. By the next General Assembly conservative strength had waned dramatically. In the summer of 1925 the famous "Monkey Trial" was held in Tennessee with disastrous consequences for the image of fundamentalism. Conservatives in 1926 were a "much weakened" minority in the Presbyterian Church. "Perhaps members were simply tired of the acrimony of the debate, and the national fundamentalist fad had played itself out. There is no sure explanation for the decline. The simplest explanation lies in the sordid and reactionary cultural image it had acquired."[4] It certainly showed that the conservative strength was not built on profound theological convictions. The General Assembly of 1926 accepted the report of the committee appointed the previous year which emphasized that the church "flourished best . . . when it laid aside its tendencies to stress these differences [peripheral to a common core of faith] and put the emphasis on its unity of spirit."[5]

Contemporaries in 1925 did not realize that the best conservative opportunity had been lost. For more than a decade some conservatives would continue to maintain that the majority of the church was conservative.[6] But from 1926 on, the conservatives suffered a series of defeats that steadily diminished their influence in the church. The General Assembly of 1926 set in motion that series when it delayed the appointment of J. Gresham Machen as professor of apologetics and ethics at Princeton Theological Seminary. The majority of the faculty and Board of Directors recommended his appointment, but the president, J. Ross Stevenson, opposed the appointment. The Assembly, in delaying the appointment, established a committee to investigate the situation at Princeton.[7] The committee recommended that the Board of Directors (supervising educational matters) and the Board of Trustees (supervising financial matters) be merged. This apparently innocuous suggestion was seen by conservatives as threatening the entire character of Princeton. The majority of the faculty, supported by the Board of Directors, wanted to preserve the distinctive Old School theology that Princeton had always represented. During the time of the division of the Old School and New School Presbyterian churches (1836-1870) funds were given to Princeton on condition that the following be maintained:

> the leading doctrines declared in the Confession of Faith and Catechisms of the Presbyterian Church, such as the doctrine of universal and total depravity, the doctrine of election, the doctrine of the Atonement, the doctrine of the imputation of Adam's sin to all his posterity and the imputation of Christ's righteousness to all His people for their justification, the doctrine of human inability, the

doctrine of the necessity of the influences of the Holy Spirit in the regeneration, conversion and sanctification of sinners, as these doctrines are now understood and explained by the aforesaid Old School General Assembly.[8]

Most of the faculty wanted to preserve Princeton as a bastion in the church of that "unmodified Calvinism of the Westminster Confession."[9] President Stevenson defended a more inclusivist vision of the church. In 1920 he had supported the Plan of Union to merge the Presbyterian Church with several other denominations, including the Methodist. Stevenson wanted Princeton to represent all of the theological positions of the church. Stevenson supported the recommendation to merge the two Boards, confident that a single board would support his inclusivist position.

In 1929, over significant opposition (10,000 ministers and elders signed a petition), the General Assembly reorganized Princeton. Asserting that "Old Princeton" was destroyed, four Princeton faculty members—Robert Dick Wilson, O. T. Allis, J. Gresham Machen, and Cornelius Van Til—withdrew and led the creation of a new seminary. Westminster Theological Seminary began classes in September 1929 in Philadelphia, committed to continuing the traditions of old Princeton. The former Princeton faculty members were joined in that first year by R. B. Kuiper, Ned B. Stonehouse, Paul Woolley, and Allan MacRae. The new seminary received support from a variety of conservatives committed to opposing modernism in the church. Westminster supporters were united in hoping to have a seminary to provide orthodox ministers for the church.

J. Gresham Machen was clearly the leader of the movement to create a new seminary since he also led the conservative Presbyterian opposition to modernism. He was a renowned New Testament scholar, "who eventually assumed Warfield's mantle as chief intellectual spokesman for conservative Presbyterians."[10] He was a clear, effective communicator. His book *Christianity and Liberalism* (1923) was widely hailed as a brilliant presentation of the issues at stake in the debate between Christians and modernists.

The issue for Machen was simple. One had to choose between two mutually incompatible religions: "the Christian religion . . . is certainly not the religion of the modern liberal Church. . . ."[11] The issue was crucial for the church and for Western culture: "Seventy-five years ago, Western civilization, despite inconsistencies, was still predominantly Christian; today it is predominantly pagan."[12] For Machen the answer was to see clearly and to hold strongly to true Christianity focused in Jesus Christ: "Liberalism regards Him as an Example and Guide; Christianity, as a Savior: liberalism makes Him an example for faith; Christianity, the object of faith."[13] The struggle was for the gospel itself.

Machen was unlike many fundamentalist leaders in a number of ways. He had broad cultural interests. "Machen's family tradition was characterized by wealth, culture, marked intellectual ability and pronounced social influence."[14] As a part of the Princeton tradition, Machen saw the importance of vital piety in the Christian life,[15] but he insisted that Christian doctrine is the foundation of true piety. He shared the position that "Christian life is the fruit of Christian doctrine, not its root, and Christian experience must be tested by the Bible, not the Bible by Christian experience."[16] Machen feared that too many conservatives shared with modernists the idea that Christianity was at its deepest level a matter of subjective experience, that it was more love than truth.[17] Machen wanted to speak "the truth in love" (Eph. 4:15). The truth was biblical truth, best summarized in the Reformed theology of the Westminster Confession. He sought a disciplined church where people honestly subscribed to that creed. He spoke of the church as a voluntary association in relation to subscription. He believed that if one voluntarily subscribed to a confession, it should be done honestly. In this sense he was not "rigid" or inflexible. There were doctrines about which he tolerated differences. But he believed a Presbyterian Church ought to be genuinely Reformed.[18]

Machen's clear doctrinal commitments led him to a more radical strategy of confrontation than other conservatives could embrace. In response to modernism in the Foreign Missions Board, Machen led in 1933 the organization of the Independent Board for Presbyterian Foreign Missions. In 1934 the General Assembly issued a mandate ordering all Presbyterians to resign from the Independent Board and directing presbyteries to discipline those who would not resign. Some conservatives believed Machen had become too confrontational and did not support the Independent Board. But most of them believed that the Mandate of 1934 was unconstitutional and tyrannical. Machen defended himself but (eagerly) anticipated finally being out of "an apostate Church."[19]

In 1936 Machen led the formation of a new church, the Presbyterian Church of America. In the same year Clarence Macartney and others like him resigned from the Westminster Seminary Board of Trustees. O. T. Allis of the faculty joined them. Those who resigned were orthodox in theology but determined to remain in the Presbyterian Church in the U.S.A. They did not share Machen's pessimistic evaluation of the church and were determined to continue to work for reform from within. But they recognized that the majority of the faculty agreed with Machen and that Westminster Seminary was part of a militant Reformed movement that included the Independent Board and the Presbyterian Church of America.

Militant Presbyterian antimodernists formed the Presbyterian

Church of America.[20] Within a short time they found tensions among themselves. A minority in the new church, while Reformed, also shared views widely held in the Fundamentalist movement. The minority, including Allan MacRae, J. Oliver Buswell, and Carl McIntire, were premillennialists, strongly espoused total abstinence, and supported cooperation with non-Presbyterians in the Independent Board. The majority, including almost all of the Westminster faculty, were more distant from these fundamentalist characteristics. They were largely amillennial and sharply critical of dispensationalism although tolerant of premillennialism. They did not want to require total abstinence and sought to support distinctively Presbyterian agencies. The two factions each claimed, with some justification, to represent true, historic American Presbyterianism. The majority was more Old School, the minority more New School in orientation.[21] The majority tried to maintain the unity of the church, but the minority withdrew in 1937 to form the Bible Presbyterian Synod. Perhaps Machen could have prevented the split, but he had died early in 1937.

By 1937 the basic character and theological orientation of Westminster Seminary were formed. That character was shaped positively by the heritage of old Princeton and the influence of Dutch Calvinism. But its formation in the midst of the Presbyterian controversy was formation in the face of defeats and frustrations. On one level, the Westminster men were dispossessed. They lost their original seminary, their original denomination, much of their church property, many of their friends, and their great leader. In little more than a decade they had passed from being leaders in a culturally powerful institution (Machen was frequently quoted in *The New York Times*) to being a very small, often ignored movement. They felt betrayed by some of their conservative friends. Those experiences reinforced the militance of their Reformed orthodoxy and tempted them at times to angry or bitter reactions.

Continuing "Old Princeton"

Westminster Seminary continued the Old School theology of Princeton. It was also determined to defend that theology with the finest scholarship. In language borrowed from Princeton, Westminster declared that one of its goals was "to develop in those who shall aspire to the ministerial office, both that piety of the heart which is the fruit of the renewing and sanctifying grace of God and solid learning, believing that zeal without knowledge or knowledge without zeal, must ultimately prove injurious to the Church. . . ."[22] Westminster had the zeal of fundamentalism but utterly rejected its antiintellectual tendencies. Robert

Dick Wilson wrote, "We want to confound infidelity by laying the foundation of belief on a scientific basis of fact and knowledge."[23]

Westminster's commitment to scholarship was personified in Machen's work. Machen communicated effectively on the popular level but showed his scholarly abilities in his often reprinted *New Testament Greek for Beginners* (1923), *The Origin of Paul's Religion* (1921), and his masterful *The Virgin Birth of Christ* (1930). The young faculty members continued that scholarly tradition. The seminary began a scholarly periodical, *The Westminster Theological Journal*, in 1938 for the exposition and defense of the Reformed faith. Many faculty publications focused on the Bible. E. J. Young (1907-1968), who joined the faculty in 1936, became a noted Old Testament scholar. His knowledge of languages was phenomenal. Among his better known works were *An Introduction to the Old Testament* (1949); an introduction to the prophets, *My Servants the Prophets* (1952); commentaries including *The Prophecy of Daniel* (1949) and *The Book of Isaiah* (3 vols., 1965-1972); and his careful defense of the Bible's inerrancy, *Thy Word is Truth* (1957). In New Testament studies Ned Bernard Stonehouse (1902-1962) did pioneering work on the distinctive character of the Synoptic Gospels:[24] *The Witness of Matthew and Mark to Christ* (1944), *The Witness of Luke to Christ* (1951), and *Origins of the Synoptic Gospels* (1962). He published a collection of essays under the title *Paul Before the Areopagus* (1957) and wrote a fine biography, *J. Gresham Machen* (1954).

One of the major influences at Westminster was the Scot, John Murray. After teaching one year at Princeton, Murray came to Westminster in 1930 to teach systematic theology. His theological interests were expressed in a number of works: *The Free Offer of the Gospel* with N. B. Stonehouse (1948), *Christian Baptism* (1952), *The Covenant of Grace* (1954), *Redemption: Accomplished and Applied* (1955), and *The Imputation of Adam's Sin* (1959). His interests extended to ethics, as shown by his *Divorce* (1953) and *Principles of Conduct* (1957), as well as to biblical exposition in *The Epistle to the Romans* (Vol. I, 1959; Vol. 2, 1965).[25] He was an exponent of Old School Calvinism, yet he also sought to extend the received orthodoxy at some points. He developed the idea of definitive sanctification as a complement to progressive sanctification.[26] Murray also defined "covenant" exclusively in terms of grace. This led him to question the terminology of a "covenant of works" and to prefer "Adamic administration."[27]

As a teacher Murray influenced generations of Westminster students by his careful exhibition of the biblical foundations of the Reformed faith. He wrote that "Systematic theology is tied to exegesis. It coordinates and synthesizes the whole witness of Scripture on the various topics with which it deals. But systematic theology will fail of its task to the extent to which it discards its rootage in biblical theology as properly conceived and developed."[28] He taught systematic theology exegetically. Historical theology was not a prime element in his teaching. That was largely left to Paul Woolley and the Church History Department.

The division of exegetical theology from historical theology may well have been practical. Murray's approach certainly had the benefit of avoiding a dogmatic traditionalism divorced from the Bible. Students were attracted by the vital biblical character of Reformed theology as Murray presented it. The danger of this approach, especially in the Westminster context, however, was to leave the impression that exegetical theology presents the biblical truth and historical theology simply presents a variety of betrayals of that truth. Students could too easily miss the important contribution of historical theology as it clarified tolerable differences within the tradition of Reformed confessional theology. This problem may well have been reinforced by Woolley's reluctance to present his profound historical learning in publications. Militantly conservative students need a large dose of historical theology lest they too quickly identify their own views as the only possible biblical ones.

Murray's approach was influenced by Geerhardus Vos, the first professor of biblical theology at Princeton. Vos's work stressed the historical and eschatological character of revelation. His seminal work drew attention to the contours of the unfolding redemptive message of Scripture. His influence can be strongly seen in the work of later Westminster scholars Meredith G. Kline and Richard B. Gaffin, Jr.[29]

Vos's long career at Princeton from 1893 to his retirement in 1932 forged important links between Princeton and the revival of Calvinism in the Netherlands. Vos was born in the Netherlands in 1862 and came with his parents to the United States in 1881. He studied at Princeton and then returned to Europe for graduate study. There he came to know Abraham Kuyper and Herman Bavinck. Vos's influence may well have been a factor in the invitations to Kuyper (1898)[30] and Bavinck (1880-89)[31] to deliver the Stone Lectures at Princeton. It may be that Machen's knowledge of the Christian Reformed Church in America and the Gereformeerde Kerken in the Netherlands originated with Vos. Vos's significant presence at Princeton and Cornelius Van Til's one year of teaching at Princeton show the influence of Dutch theology at Princeton before the formation of Westminster.

The Dutch Influence

In 1937 the more fundamentalist element of Westminster Seminary and the Presbyterian Church of America withdrew. Allan MacRae, the only faculty member to leave, wrote in his letter of resignation: "Control of the faculty has passed into the hands of a small alien group without American Presbyterian background. . . . The major emphasis of the teaching of the Seminary . . . has now shifted so that it is no longer primarily against Modernism, but against Fundamentalism, so called."[32] MacRae's charge of an "alien group" points certainly to the Scot John Murray and the Dutch R. B. Kuiper,[33] Cornelius Van Til, and N. B. Stonehouse. Their influence was certainly great in shaping the future of Westminster and their background was not American Presbyterian. But does that mean their influence was contrary to the goals and ideals of Westminster Seminary, especially as envisioned by Machen?

Machen's attitudes to Dutch theology as expressed in the life of the Christian Reformed Church were positive. He lectured at Calvin Seminary in 1914[34] and wrote very positively of that church in 1925, commending especially its Christian school movement. He praised the piety of Calvin Professor Samuel Volbeda: "A piety rooted deep in the great historic Reformed Faith . . . very different from the shallow emotionalism that lacks a basis in the theology of the Word of God."[35] In 1930 Machen contrasted the sorry state of the Presbyterian Church with that of the Gereformeerde Kerken in the Netherlands: "It is simply that in Holland the issue was clearly faced, and faced in time . . . the Calvinists or evangelicals . . . separated from the state church and formed a truly Calvinistic church. They had the courage of their convictions; they set up and maintained a true church discipline. . . ." Machen also saw the health of the Dutch churches as supported by good doctrinal preaching and a good educational system. Machen wrote that the same strengths were to be found in "the noble Christian Reformed Church in America."[36]

Machen also sought out Kuiper, Van Til, and Stonehouse for the Westminster faculty. He clearly believed that they brought strength and stability to American Presbyterianism. Even when it became clear that Van Til was developing an apologetic approach quite different from that of Warfield and Machen, Machen supported him. Van Til offered to resign in 1934 because of those differences, but Machen urged him to stay.[37]

Van Til's influence on the shape of Westminster theology is surely the greatest of anyone except Machen. Van Til maintained the strong anti-Modernism and unmodified Calvinism of old Princeton. But he did decisively change the apologetic direction of the seminary. He built not on the evidentialism of Warfield, but on the work of Abraham Kuyper.

Kuyper's thought grew out of the cultural conflict in Europe epitomized by the French Revolution. For Kuyper the terror of the French Revolution represented the tyranny and destructiveness of unbelief. The alternative needed was a consistently Reformed world-and-life view. Kuyper developed such a Reformed outlook beginning with the conviction that the consequence of the Fall is a radically abnormal world. Only the sovereign, regenerating work of the Holy Spirit can overcome the rebellion of unbelief. An absolute antithesis exists in all of life (including all scholarly work) between believer and unbeliever. Christians must seek to give concrete cultural expression to their regeneration not only in personal ethics but also in institutions and scholarship. For Kuyper the antithesis was balanced by his idea of common grace. By the kindness of God unbelief is restrained from reaching its ultimate consequences. Therefore the unbeliever has insights from which the believer can profit. It is also proper for Christians to cooperate with unbelievers on projects where they have a common goal even though they come to that goal from antithetical motivations.

Van Til used Kuyper's notion of the antithesis to develop his presuppositional apologetics. For Van Til unregenerate man actively suppresses his knowledge of God. Man is not ignorant, he is rebellious. Man is never neutral or objective in his evaluation of evidence. Rather, in every act of interpretation and understanding man acts either as a servant of God or as an unbeliever asserting his autonomy. A key task of apologetics is to show the inadequacies of non-Christian or inconsistently Christian thought. This perspective led Van Til to analyze not only what a theologian or philosopher said, but also what he should have said according to the basic orientation of his views. Van Til pressed people to face the necessary extension of their views. Van Til's apologetic system gained the enthusiastic support of the Westminster faculty and has been so identified with the school as even to be called the Westminster apologetic.

Van Til's stress upon the antithesis in the context of militant conservatism could be distorted. Where the antithesis is not properly balanced with a recognition of common grace and of the problem of continuing sin in the regenerate, the antithesis can become an instrument of Anabaptist separatism.[38]

The Scottish and Dutch influences at Westminster were not alien. While they brought new emphases and a new apologetic to the seminary, they helped Westminster promote Reformed theology. In the twentieth century Westminster experienced something of the international character of Reformed theology that had made that theology so vital in the sixteenth and seventeenth centuries.

The Clowney Years

Westminster had a remarkably stable faculty for many years. With the exception of Wilson and Machen, the original appointments were rather young men and most spent their entire academic careers at Westminster. There were additions to the faculty over the years. Early appointments were John Skilton, Arthur Kuschke, Jr., and Leslie Sloat. In the 1950s Meredith G. Kline, Edmund Clowney, and Robert Knudsen joined the faculty.

The decade of the 1960s, however, brought dramatic changes at Westminster. In 1965 Clowney became the first president. An era in which the faculty had handled all administrative functions was coming to an end. In addition to structural changes there were dramatic changes in the faculty. In 1962 Stonehouse died, in 1968 Young died, and in 1966 Murray retired. In that decade Robert Strimple and Norman Shepherd joined the faculty in theology, John Frame in apologetics, Richard B. Gaffin, Jr. in biblical studies, Harvie Conn in missions, Jay Adams in practical theology, and D. Clair Davis in church history. Others have joined the faculty since. Although the changes in personnel were significant, the basic theological commitment of the seminary remained the same.

In recent decades an effort has been made to supplement the strengths of the seminary in theology and scholarship with more offerings in practical theology. The prolific work of Jay Adams may be taken as an example of that effort. Adams is best known for a distinctive approach to counseling in which he seeks to develop a biblical and Reformed alternative to much of modern psychology.[39] But he has also written on pastoral care and preaching.[40]

During the years of Clowney's presidency, Westminster's influence increased. The student body grew dramatically. Clowney personally sought to extend the influence of the Reformed faith through his involvement with a number of evangelical organizations such as Inter-Varsity Christian Fellowship and the International Council on Biblical Inerrancy. He led the seminary in opening two new campuses. The campus in Florida (1979-1983) offered a partial academic program linked to an internship program in local churches.

The campus in Escondido, California, now offers complete degree programs (M.A.R., M.Div., and D.Min.) and is fully accredited. Westminster Theological Seminary in California is now an independent institution but is still affiliated with the Philadelphia campus.

Westminster continues to face the problems that have beset American Presbyterianism throughout its history: discerning the boundary between confessionally legitimate and illegitimate theological formulations and determining how to promote the spread of Reformed Christianity without improper compromise. In all circumstances Westminster strives to be obedient to Christ and his written, inerrant Word and to apply "unmodified Calvinism" to the needs of the contemporary church and world.

Notes: The Westminster School

1. George M. Marsden, *Fundamentalism and American Culture* (New York: Oxford University Press, 1980), 175, 184.

2. The five essential doctrines were the infallibility of the Bible, the virgin birth of Jesus, the vicarious atonement, the bodily resurrection, and the reality of Jesus' miracles.

3. Minutes of the General Assembly of the Presbyterian Church in the U.S.A., 1925, 1:88, cited in C. Allyn Russell, "J. Gresham Machen, Scholarly Fundamentalist," *Journal of Presbyterian History* 51 (1973): 59-60.

4. Marsden, *Fundamentalism*, 191.

5. Minutes of the General Assembly of the Presbyterian Church in the U.S.A., 1926, 1:78, cited in Russell, "Machen," 60.

6. The conservative Presbyterians come to quite different views among themselves on the health of the Presbyterian Church. In 1927 Machen still thought it possible to appeal to a Christian majority in the church if one could circumvent the leadership (see David C. Jones, "Machen's Ecclesiology," *Presbyterian Guardian* 33 [October 1963]: 139). In 1930 his views are quite different. He argues that the church is not essentially sound although he recognizes that it is difficult to trace the decline: "Here as elsewhere the destructive forces have been content to labor for the most part in the dark" (Machen, "The Present Situation in the Presbyterian Church," *Christianity Today*, May 1930, 6). For other conservatives, however, even after the General Assembly ruled against Machen, it seemed the majority of the church was still conservative. This was the position of the Presbyterian League of Faith led by Dr. Clarence Macartney (see *The Presbyterian*, 9 July 1936, 1; and *Presbyterian Guardian*, 6 July 1936, 164).

7. Marsden, *Fundamentalism*, 192.

8. Quoted in "Minority Report of the Board of Directors of Princeton Theological Seminary" to the 1929 General Assembly, printed in *The Presbyterian*, 25 April 1929, 9.

9. These words are the often quoted expression of Dr. Francis L. Patton, ibid., 11.

10. Marsden, *Fundamentalism*, 137.

11. J. Gresham Machen, *Christianity and Liberalism* (Grand Rapids: Wm. B. Eerdmans Publishing Company, 1977), 15.

12. Ibid., 65.

13. Ibid., 96.

14. Russell, "Machen," 46.

15. Machen's piety was expressed in a number of ways including his preaching and his concern for seminary students and for missions.

16. *Westminster Theological Seminary Catalogue, 1929-1930*, p. 17. This statement is listed as one of three basic concerns of the seminary.

17. Marsden, *Fundamentalism*, 216-17.

18. For the genuinely Presbyterian nature of Machen's ecclesiology, see David C. Jones, "Machen's Ecclesiology," 134-43, and Dallas M. Roark, "J. Gresham Machen and His Desire To Maintain a Doctrinally True Presbyterian Church" (Ph.D. diss., State University of Iowa, 1963), summarized in Roark, "J. Gresham Machen: The Doctrinally True Presbyterian Church," *Journal of Presbyterian History* 43 (June 1965): 124-38 and 43 (September 1965): 174-81.

19. Shortly before the 1936 General Assembly Machen expressed his conviction about the Presbyterian Church in a letter to Clarence Macartney (see letter dated May 9, 1936, printed in *Presbyterian Guardian* 31 [January 1962]: 4-5). Machen

wrote, "I . . . am longing for a division, and hoping and praying with all my soul that the division may come soon. I am perfectly convinced that the Presbyterian Church in the U.S.A. is an apostate Church at its very heart. I do not think there is any blessing of God for us so long as we continue in such an apostate organization." Machen also expressed his strategy in relation to that church: "I think that the evil which this Permanent Judicial Commission is doing will result in the great good of a separation of evangelical forces in the Presbyterian Church in the U.S.A. from an apostate ecclesiastical machine. But I cannot acquiesce in that evil for one moment, and therefore I am adopting every legitimate means of presenting my case even before that Modernist Permanent Judicial Commission of the Presbyterian Church in the U.S.A. If that Permanent Judicial Commission should acquit me, I should adopt every means of forcing the issue immediately in some other way." Machen faithfully followed his principle that one must not do evil for the sake of good. In fact he structured his sermon at the concluding service of the first General Assembly of the Presbyterian Church of America on June 14, 1936, on that principle. He argued that any reason for staying in the Presbyterian Church in the U.S.A. ultimately comes down to doing evil that good may come. See Machen, "The Church of God," *Presbyterian Guardian* 2 (July 6, 1936): 152-56.

20. Ned B. Stonehouse, *J. Gresham Machen: A Biographical Memoir* (Grand Rapids: Wm. B. Eerdmans Publishing Company, 1954), 458.

21. For a careful examination of this division, see George M. Marsden, "Perspective on the Division of 1937," *Presbyterian Guardian* 33 (January-April 1964): 5-8, 21-29, 43-46, 54-56.

22. This statement in the original Westminster Theological Seminary Constitution was taken over from Princeton.

23. Robert Dick Wilson, "The Study and Defense of the Bible in Westminster Seminary," *Christianity Today*, June 1930, 6.

24. See Moises Silva, "Ned B. Stonehouse and Redaction Criticism," *Westminster Theological Journal* 40 (1977-78): 77-88, 281-303.

25. Many smaller works can be found in John Murray, *Collected Writings*, 4 vols. (Edinburgh: The Banner of Truth Trust, 1976-1982).

26. See ibid., 2:277-84.

27. See ibid., 2:47-59.

28. Murray, "Systematic Theology—Second Article," *Westminster Theological Journal* 26 (November 1963): 44, cited in *Redemptive History and Biblical Interpretation: The Shorter Writings of Geerhardus Vos*, ed. Richard B. Gaffin, Jr. (Phillipsburg, NJ: Presbyterian and Reformed Publishing Company, 1980), xxii.

29. For Vos's fullest exposition of his biblical theology, see G. Vos, *Biblical Theology* (Grand Rapids: Wm. B. Eerdmans Publishing Company, 1948). Meredith G. Kline taught full-time at Westminster from 1950 to 1965. He was an occasional visiting professor after 1965 and since 1981 has taught half-time at Westminster Theological Seminary in California. His biblical theology is expressed in *The Treaty of the Great King* (1963), *By Oath Consigned* (1968), *The Structure of Biblical Authority* (1972), and *Images of the Spirit* (1980).

Richard B. Gaffin, Jr. currently is professor of New Testament at Westminster in Philadelphia. He expressed his view of biblical theology in Gaffin, "Systematic Theology and Biblical Theology," *Westminster Theological Journal* 38 (Spring 1976): 281-99. See also Gaffin, *The Centrality of the Resurrection* (Grand Rapids: Baker Book House, 1978) and *Perspectives on Pentecost* (Phillipsburg, NJ: Presbyterian and Reformed Publishing Company, 1979).

30. Abraham Kuyper, *Lectures on Calvinism* (Grand Rapids: Wm. B. Eerdmans Publishing Company, 1931).

31. Herman Bavinck, *The Philosophy of Revelation* (New York: Longman, Inc., 1909).

32. Allan A. MacRae, Letter of Resignation from Westminster Seminary, April 26, 1937, printed in *Presbyterian Guardian* 4 (May 1937): 50; cited in Marsden, *Fundamentalism*, 44.

33. R. B. Kuiper taught systematic theology at Westminster from 1929 to 1930 and taught practical theology at Westminster from 1933 to 1952.

34. Stonehouse, *J. Gresham Machen*, 232.

35. Ibid., 438.

36. J. Gresham Machen, "The Present Situation in the Presbyterian Church," *Christianity Today*, May 1930, 5. See also Machen's strong words of praise for the Christian Reformed Church in his column "The Changing Scene and the Unchanging Word," *Presbyterian Guardian* 2 (July 20, 1936): 170.

37. John C. Vander Stelt, *Philosophy and Scripture: A Study in Old Princeton and Westminster Theology* (Marlton, NJ: Mack Publishing Company, 1978), 220, n. 153.

38. Some within the Westminster community feared that just such an excessive expression of the antithesis manifested itself in the "Clark case." In 1944 Gordon H. Clark was ordained to the ministry in the Orthodox Presbyterian Church (the new name of the Presbyterian Church of America). During his examination for ordination Clark made some statements on the incomprehensibility of God that led some members of his presbytery to protest his ordination. Most of those who complained were connected with Westminster Seminary (see Fred H. Klooster, *The Incomprehensibility of God in the Orthodox Presbyterian Conflict* (Franeker: T. Wever, 1951], 14). The precise issue in the controversy was whether God's knowledge is quantitatively or qualitatively different from man's knowledge. In the controversy, which lasted until 1948, two questions were debated: first, was Clark right or wrong, and second, even if he was wrong, were his views tolerable within the church? The theological and ecclesiastical intricacies of the controversy frustrated many who believed that the lines of orthodoxy were being drawn too narrowly. Others believed the issues were significant. (That is Klooster's conclusion [ibid., 129ff.].) Whoever was right, Westminster Seminary and the Orthodox Presbyterian Church lost support. One case in point may be Edwin H. Rian. Rian served as president of the Board of Trustees of Westminster from 1937 to 1946. In 1940 he published *The Presbyterian Conflict*, a passionate defense of Machen and the Orthodox Presbyterian Church. In 1944 he signed a statement supporting Clark. In 1947 he returned to the Presbyterian Church in the U.S.A. (See Rian, "Theological Conflicts of the 1920's and 1930's in the Presbyterian Church and on the Princeton Seminary Campus," *Princeton Seminary Bulletin*, 1984, 216-23.)

39. Jay Adams, *Competent to Counsel* (Nutley, NJ: Presbyterian and Reformed Publishing Company, 1970), and Adams, *Counseling and the Sovereignty of God* (Nutley, NJ: Presbyterian and Reformed Publishing Company, 1976).

40. Jay Adams, *Pulpit Speech* (Nutley, NJ: Presbyterian and Reformed Publishing Company, 1971); Adams, *Christian Living in the Home* (Grand Rapids: Baker Book House, 1972); Adams, *Shepherding God's Flock*, 3 vols. (Nutley, NJ: Presbyterian and Reformed Publishing Company, 1974-1975); Adams, *Studies in Preaching*, 3 vols. (Nutley, NJ: Presbyterian and Reformed Publishing Company, 1975); Adams, *Preaching with Purpose* (Phillipsburg, NJ: Presbyterian and Reformed Publishing Company, 1982).

J. GRESHAM MACHEN

W. STANFORD REID

J. Gresham Machen wielded a wide and important influence in his day, not only in Christian circles, but also on the entire American scene and beyond it. His fundamental motivation was his view of the Reformed theological position. He believed it was the most consistent and defensible expression of the Christian faith. A scholar, a leader, a powerful preacher, and at the same time a man of great charm, he was able to achieve much in his relatively short life. Caspar Wistar Hodge, who did not always agree with Machen, on hearing of his death stated that evangelical Christianity had lost its most outstanding leader and one of its greatest theologians. To understand Machen's importance on the American scene during the first third of this century we must understand his background, his theological development, and what he accomplished during his very active life.

Machen's Background and Development

In attempting to evaluate Machen's theological position and influence, we cannot avoid taking a quick glance at his background and development. But in so doing we have to keep in mind that the late nineteenth and early twentieth centuries were times of great upheaval in the Christian church, particularly in the Western world, with the rise of such phenomena as Higher Criticism, atheistic evolution, and the Marxist-socialist influences in government. The resulting conflicts in ecclesiastical circles in the Netherlands, the United Kingdom, and other countries spilled over into the American ecclesiastical situation with profound results. Consequently, to understand Machen's theological, apologetic, and social viewpoints we must look briefly at his personal experiences and background.

The home in which he was brought up was a Christian home, in which his ties with his mother were very close, and they remained so until the day of her death on October 13, 1931.[1] Educated first in a private school, he then attended Johns Hopkins University, from which he graduated in 1901 and went on to do a year's graduate work in classics under Basil L. Gildersleeve.[2] On his graduation he took his first of many trips to Europe, which whetted his appetite for further study in Germany. Before going to Europe for more academic work, however, he enrolled at Princeton Theological Seminary, although at this time he was by no means sure that he should enter the ministry. On the other hand, he seemed to feel that studying under such scholars as Francis Patton and Benjamin Breckinridge Warfield would be good training, no matter how he decided to spend his life.[3]

During his time at Princeton he had become very interested in the question of the virgin birth of Christ and had written a thesis on it, which was published in the *Princeton Theological Review* (1905-06). Even before this, however, he had left again for Europe to study at Marburg University, where he came under the influence of such Liberal theologians as Adolf Jülicher, Johannes Weiss, and Wilhelm Herrmann, all of whom caused him to have very serious doubts about the theological position that he had accepted at Princeton. From Marburg he went on to Göttingen where he studied under men such as W. Bousset who were as radically liberal as those at Marburg. Meanwhile some of his former professors had been pressing him to come back to Princeton to teach, an invitation that he finally accepted in 1906. He remained in the New Testament Department at Princeton until 1929.[4] But although he was an instructor in the seminary, he did not accept ordination until 1914. It took him eight years, with the help of W. P. Armstrong, Francis Patton, and others, to recover his faith after the experience in Germany.[5] In 1912 he really began his career as a writer with the publication of his address on "Christianity and Culture," and he followed that in 1915 with one on "History and Faith."[6] In both of these he laid down the foundation for most of his life's work, principles from which he never departed.

As he had gradually recovered his faith, Machen had become increasingly aware of the devastating effects of the Higher Criticism of the Scriptures and of the accompanying efforts to water down, if not to destroy entirely, its teachings.[7] As a result he felt convinced that the only answer to such attacks on the gospel was their refutation by an appeal to the historical sources and a proper "common sense" interpretation of their statements. The outcome of this conviction was a number of addresses dealing with such topics as the virgin birth and the resurrection of Christ, which were later published. In these he took a very definite stand on the historical reliability of the biblical record, and devoted considerable time to criticizing and refuting the modernist position. This, however, brought him into conflict with some of the seminary

authorities. Although in 1926 the Directors wanted him to become professor of apologetics, a move to which he was not much inclined, the
Trustees, led by the president, J. Ross Stevenson, were opposed. The
result was a battle that led to the reorganization of the administration:
the Board of Directors was abolished and full control of the school was
given to a single Board of Trustees to which two signers of the liberal
Auburn Affirmation were appointed. The resulting conflict between
Machen and the new administration led to his resignation from the seminary in June 1929, on the ground that Princeton had now left its historic
theological position.[8]

With the departure of Machen, some others connected with the
seminary felt they too should go. As a result they formed a committee
to establish a new seminary, Westminster, which opened in Philadelphia
as an independent educational institution in the autumn of 1929. In
his address at the opening of the new institution, Machen stressed two
articles of its constitution. One was the final authority of the Bible, which
he characterized as "a plain book addressed to plain men, and . . . it
means exactly what it says." The other was that since Princeton was now
"lost to the evangelical cause," the new seminary would stand firmly for
the Reformed theological position as expressed in the Westminster
Confession of Faith. Added to that, he warned that anyone coming to
Westminster would find that being a student would entail hard work![9]
Naturally Princeton was not pleased with this development, and when,
a few years later, the present writer visited Princeton to see some friends,
he was given a detailed diagnosis of "Dossie's" paranoia.

The establishment of Westminster, however, did not bring Machen
peace and ease of mind. He was also faced with the problem of what
would happen to the graduates of the seminary when they were prepared
to seek ordination. Some might, of course, go to denominations other
than the Presbyterian Church, U.S.A., but he was most anxious that
they should enter his church in the hopes of bringing about a true reformation. About this time the novelist Pearl Buck, serving as a missionary in China for the Presbyterian Church's Board of Missions, published
in *The Christian Century* an enthusiastic review of the radically liberal
Rethinking Missions, and followed that in January 1933 with an article in
Harper's Magazine on the propriety of Christian missions, in which she
virtually ruled out the New Testament message as a mystical concept of
Christianity, rejecting even the need for the historic person of Christ.
When the Board of Missions, while continuing to support Buck, then
turned down a Westminster graduate who applied for appointment, and
the General Assembly followed this with a vote of confidence for the
board, Machen and others felt that action had to be taken. The result
was the formation of the Independent Board for Presbyterian Foreign

Missions.[10] Against this move the Presbyterian Church took vigorous action, ordering that the Independent Board be dissolved. When that was not done, the judicial commission took action to discipline the participants, who either resigned or were defrocked. Among them was Machen.[11] Following this the only answer was the formation of a new Presbyterian church. The Presbyterian Church of America, later the Orthodox Presbyterian Church, was organized in 1936.[12]

Yet even the formation of a new church did not solve all problems. For one thing, some of Machen's supporters in the formation of Westminster Seminary, such as Professor Oswald T. Allis and Clarence Macartney, had not favored the formation of the Independent Board, and when plans were laid for the organization of a new Presbyterian church, they withdrew entirely along with some others. This was a great disappointment to Machen. But even more of a blow came when Carl McIntire and J. O. Buswell withdrew to form the Bible Presbyterian Church because of the new church's refusal, under Machen's guidance, to alter the Westminster Confession to make it more premillennial and to require total abstinence from alcoholic liquors a condition of church membership.[13] Added to all this the members of the Independent Board were now divided, for some were not particularly interested in establishing a new Presbyterian church, but instead favored independency.

At this point Machen was invited to go out to North Dakota for the Christmas holiday, which he did, but sadly while traveling around the state in the intense cold he contracted pneumonia and on January 1, 1937, died.[14] So ended the career of one of America's great defenders of the faith.

Machen's Theology

Machen's methodology is basic to an understanding of both his theology and his defense of it. He was not primarily a philosopher, which explains his reluctance to move from the New Testament department to become professor of apologetics at Princeton, and also his enthusiasm for the appointment of Cornelius Van Til to that position. Nor was he primarily a systematic theologian, although he knew his Reformed theology and was prepared to expound it whenever possible, as we can see from his *What is Faith?* and the two volumes of his radio addresses delivered just before his death.[15] Unfortunately he died before he could complete the radio series, but despite this misfortune, he clearly indicates his grasp of the system of Reformed theology. The fact is that he was a historian, as he indicated in the opening sentence of his 1915 essay "History and Faith" which stated that "the student of the New

Testament should be primarily an historian. The centre and core of all the Bible is history."[16]

Because of this historical orientation, he sought to prove the reliability of the biblical record by a sound historical investigation and analysis of the evidence provided by the documents. One only has to note the course he established on the introduction to the literature and history of the New Testament to realize this. Or what was even better, if one could attend his lectures on Apostolic History and listen to his enthusiastic presentation of the evidence for single authorship of the Gospel of Luke and the Acts of the Apostles, one would soon realize that he was indeed a sound and well-trained historian. His constant insistence in both his expository and his apologetic works on the validity of his historico-grammatical exegesis of the Bible was further evidence of his point of view. Some, even of his followers, however, have claimed that he followed too completely the Scottish Common Sense Philosophy of Thomas Reid, failing to take into consideration the question of the presuppositions of one's thinking. For this some have even declared him merely nineteenth century in his approach. It must be constantly kept in mind, however, that while he insisted that the validity of the historical analysis could lead one to accept facts as true, it did not then lead automatically to acceptance of the doctrine behind those facts. As he pointed out more than once, while one might acknowledge that history showed that Christ died, more was required for one to confess that he died for our sins. He could even state that a non-Christian might believe in Christ's resurrection, but it was only by the work of the Holy Spirit that that individual would believe that Christ rose victor over death for the sinner's justification. The presuppositions or faith of the Christian led to a very different understanding from that of the unbeliever, who began with very different presuppositions.[17]

As mentioned earlier, Machen had come to this specifically Reformed position only gradually. His home background seems to have been evangelical, but not strongly Reformed. During his time of study in Germany he undoubtedly had faced a large number of problems, particularly in dealing with the attacks of the various theological professors on the historical reliability of the New Testament, and had eventually come to realize that without the basic Christian faith, even historical evidence would not bring conviction of the truth of Christianity. This comes out very clearly in his lectures at the Grove City Bible School in 1925, which later appeared as the volume *What is Faith?* and his radio addresses over station WIP, Philadelphia, just shortly before his death. True, he did not work out the whole problem of presuppositions as did Cornelius Van Til, but he certainly never ignored them in favor of a positivistic view that held that the facts were all that were needed.

Because of his own presuppositions he followed the Reformed position that the Bible is the Word of God. But by doing so, he did not accept a mechanical type of dictation. He held the view that the writers of the Bible used the ordinary sources of information, that they as individuals had personal freedom but that they recorded the facts and their interpretation guided by the Holy Spirit, so that the Bible is truly infallible, the Word of God in the word of man.[18] Hence in order to gain a true and proper understanding of the divine revelation one must study the Bible by the grammatico-historical method. The trouble with so many of the so-called Liberals, he maintained, was that they refused to employ the proper historical method honestly and so twisted the meaning of the Scriptures.[19] A true evangelical and Reformed exegesis, on the other hand, employed the scientific historical method that is the true foundation and source of a sound Christian theology.

When one turns to a study of Machen's actual theology, one finds at its core a typically Reformed doctrine of God. God is triune: Father, Son, and Holy Spirit. This God is sovereign, a theme of which he never became tired. As one reads his various works, whether those primarily expository or primarily apologetic, the sovereignty of God is a constantly recurring note. But equally important in his thought was the fact that God is a gracious and loving God. As he pointed out in the second chapter of *What Is Faith?*, we can believe in God only as we know him, and this means that we must know him as he reveals himself to us in nature, in our own souls, and in the Scriptures of the Old and New Testaments. When we so know him we believe in him and trust ourselves to his sovereign grace.[20]

Only, however, as one comes to God through Jesus Christ, the incarnate Savior, does one truly know God. And Machen, as a New Testament scholar, was therefore very interested in setting forth evidence and arguments for the reliability of the New Testament's witness to Christ as the incarnate divine Savior. His first major work dealing with this matter appeared in 1921 under the title *The Origin of Paul's Religion*. In 1925 and 1926 he had two articles published on the virgin birth and resurrection of Christ, and another in the following year dealing directly with the apostolic witness to Christ.[21] But probably his most important work in this field was *The Virgin Birth of Christ*, published in 1930. In all of these writings he constantly insisted that the different writers of the New Testament books were united in their testimony to Christ.

This testimony was that he is the Son of God, the Savior of the world. In this testimony there was first the fact that he was conceived miraculously in the womb of Mary and thus was the son of a virgin. Machen also spends considerable time with Christ's divine powers and works. These he cites as witnesses to the fact that he was not merely a great and good mortal, but both God and man in one person. At the same time, Machen stresses Christ's teachings as being very relevant and applicable not only to the church, but also to society in our own day and age. Yet he was not prepared to accept the view that Christ's teachings were merely the setting forth of a moral code. They were far different, for Christ said very clearly and certainly that he was much more than merely a teacher. He was the Savior, the promised Messiah.

This stress on Christ as Savior was the expression of Machen's basic religious faith. Rejecting the view that he was merely a teacher and an example, Machen insisted that it is only as one places one's trust in Christ as his Savior who died on Calvary's cross and who rose the third day and ascended into heaven, that one may obtain the forgiveness of sins. Only then may one be truly called a Christian. In his chapter "Faith in Christ" in *What is Faith?* he constantly attacks and criticizes those who would dilute the New Testament message that Christ is the only Savior of men. And if one listened to his preaching one would very quickly realize that the preacher was in every respect an envangelist as well as a scholar. Machen's wholehearted conviction that Christ was *his* Savior is illustrated by his sending a telegram, one of the last acts before his death, to Professor John Murray, in which he said: "I'm so thankful for the active obedience of Christ. No hope without it."[22]

While Machen did not stress the work of the Holy Spirit as he did that of Christ, nevertheless the presence, power, and work of the Third Person of the Trinity is always taken into account when discussing the works of God. One only has to glance at the subject indices in his various works to see this statement borne out. Although he did not lay great stress upon it, Machen accepted the doctrine of Common Grace as part of the work of the Spirit. But even more important was his constant emphasis upon the work of the Spirit in the incarnation, in the writing of the biblical books, and in the regeneration and sanctification of the elect. In this he was following closely in the footsteps of Calvin. The application of Christ's saving work is the action of the Spirit, who in doing this bears witness to both the Father and the Son. In fact, that witness-bearing is what results in both regeneration and faith.[23]

Basic, however, to Machen's view of divine redemption was his insistence upon the doctrines of creation and providence. He emphasized the necessity of realizing that the triune God had created all things out of nothing and constantly sustained and ruled over them from moment to moment. He rejected all deistic or pantheistic attempts either to separate God from creation or to make him simply the essence of creation itself. And he insisted upon the necessity of recognizing the divine creatorship, because nature was the primary means of divine revelation since it was the "work of God's hand." Hence his great appreciation of the beauties of mountain climbing and natural scenery. But especially important was the necessity of recognizing that the creation of man was central to creation, and it was in creation that the drama of God's redemptive work was enacted.[24]

Machen's stress upon the saving work of Christ and the regenerating and sanctifying work of the Spirit arises out of his acceptance of what the Bible says about man. He accepted the doctrine of the Fall without any question, for he could see the sinfulness of man all around, and within. His introduction to *What is Faith?* as well as the chapter "Faith Born of Need" makes this only too clear. Because of man's sin he is alienated from God and has no desire to be reconciled to God, unless God takes the first step and draws the sinner to himself. This reconciliation is the only way in which man may inherit eternal life. Twelve years after he had stated the Reformed position in *What is Faith?* he dealt in his last radio addresses (published after his death under the title *The Christian View of Man*) with the subjects of the creation of man, the covenant of life, man's fall, and God's gift of grace. There he rings the changes on man's sinfulness, but also on God's sovereign predestination, and his working out of that predestination in history.

It is to be regretted that Machen did not live to present the third of his series of radio talks, which would have dealt with the subject of salvation. But the Lord saw fit to take him before that could happen. From his other writings, however, one can understand quite clearly that what he would have said would have been quite in accord with the Reformed tadition. One could quote many passages from his various writings, but perhaps one from *What is Faith?* brings out his views most clearly.

> Certainly, at bottom, faith is in one sense a very simple thing; it simply means that abandoning the vain effort of earning one's way into God's presence we accept the gift of salvation which Christ offers so full and free. Such is the "doctrine"—let us not be afraid of the word—such is the "doctrine" of justification through faith alone.[25]

"Justification by faith alone"—the words of Martin Luther, John Calvin, and the other Protestant Reformers looking back to the Apostle Paul and to Jesus Christ himself—was central to Machen's own Christian experience and so to his thought. Moreover, he knew that this faith was the gift of God through regeneration by the Holy Spirit.[26]

Faith, however, meant loving obedience. He did not hold, as do some modern theologians who claim to be Reformed, that obedience is part of faith, that one is justified by "obedient faith."[27] Works are the outgrowth, the result of faith, not part of it. This he reiterated repeatedly in his chapter "Faith and Works" in *What is Faith?* That one had faith in Christ as Savior resulted in a love for him and obedience to him. This means that the Christian is to obey Christ in all things, even in the ministry of the church. As he put it in a graduation address to the students of Westminster Seminary in 1934, in the midst of the conflict over the Independent Board:

> If you obtain your message from any other authority than the Word of God, if you obtain it from the pronouncements of presbyteries or General Assemblies, then you may wear the garb of ministers, but you are not ministers in the sight of God. You are disloyal to the Lord Jesus Christ: you have betrayed a precious trust.[28]

From this statement we can see that for Machen the central directory of the Christian life was the Scriptures, enlightened by the Holy Spirit in the hearts and minds of faithful Christians.[29]

Unfortunately Machen did not have much to say about eschatology. "Unfortunately" because a thorough study of New Testament teaching on this subject might have helped quite a number of people who were led to reject him as a teacher and a leader because he was not a premillennialist. That he held the amillennial position he stated on a few occasions. Furthermore, when an attempt was made in the early days of the Presbyterian Church of America to change the Westminster Confession to allow more room for premillennialism, he opposed it. He held strongly, however, to the view that God ruled over history and was leading it on to the consummation of all things. More important, apparently, in his thinking was the Christian hope of eternal life in the presence of God, where all things would be made new.[30] Again turning to *What is Faith?* this comes out very clearly in the last chapter "Faith and Hope." No doubt if he had lived to complete his series of radio addresses he would have dealt with this topic in more detail.[31]

In summing up Machen's theology one can only say that it was the theology of a typically Reformed scholar. He did not produce a systematic theology in the usual form, but sought to present doctrine in a popular manner that the ordinary layperson could understand. As he remarked when criticizing A. C. McGiffert's work *The God of the Early Christians*, although he did not agree with it, "it possesses at least one merit that is rare among contemporary religious literature—it is interesting."[32] Machen sought to write books with a similar popular appeal. At the same time, he was always ready to defend the faith, with the result that much of his work was taken up with apologetics. To this we now turn.

The Defense of the Faith

Although Machen's primary interest was the exposition of Christian doctrine, a very close second was his view that the Christian faith must be set forth as a valid system of thought. He believed that a radical change was needed in both the church and society in general. This would come only if there were a reformation similar to that which took place in the sixteenth century, and it would take place only if Christians were prepared to stand up and present the credentials of their beliefs, showing that they met all the requirements of sound thinking. While he acknowledged that ultimately man could not penetrate the mystery of God and the divine purpose or counsel, yet there was enough evidence in the Scriptures to show that what they said was true and historically verifiable.[33]

He felt the need for apologetics centered around the message of the gospel as set forth primarily in the four Gospels and in the writings of the Apostle Paul. Wherever he turned there seemed to be theologians, preachers, journalists, and others who were prepared to attack the Christian's faith and demonstrate that it had been misinterpreted or twisted to be something that was radically different from the historic doctrines. There were those in his own church, such as the signers of the Auburn Affirmation, who while not rejecting Christianity, at least officially, so undermined all basic doctrine that nothing was left. At the same time there were those who simply rejected the Christian teachings as completely wrong. In this class were people such as H. L. Mencken, Pearl Buck, and Albert C. Dieffenbach, who, while acknowledging Machen's strength of character and his loyalty to his position, yet rejected his ideas out of hand.[34]

In the face of dilutions of and direct attacks on the historic Reformed position Machen sought to put up a strong and effective defense. To do this, he insisted that it was possible to prove that the books of the New Testament were historically trustworthy. He maintained that the grammatico-historical approach to and interpretation of the documents, used with "common sense," would show that what they said was true. In this he was clearly following the line of thought of the Princeton school of apologetics, which in turn looked back to Thomas Reid's Scottish "Common Sense Philosophy." And whenever he had the opportunity he went after the Modernists who were attempting to undermine the Christian faith with their twisted and perverted interpretations. His first extensive work in this area was *Christianity and Liberalism*, first published by Macmillan in 1923, but republished seven times, the last printing being done in 1940, three years after his death.

Machen, however, did not believe that merely historical or rational arguments would convince an unbeliever and bring him to faith in Christ. As he pointed out more than once, while a person might know all the arguments for Christ's virgin birth or his resurrection, that person would come to faith only through the action of the Holy Spirit in regenerating the individual. Being very conscious of the noetic influence of sin, which effectively blocked man's spiritual vision, and also of the perversion of the human will, he recognized that even true "common sense" would ultimately make no sense to an individual unless the Holy Spirit opened that person's eyes and changed his or her will. Only then would the person believe.[35]

Having to depend upon the Holy Spirit to bring conviction to the unbeliever did not mean that Machen held to a kind of quietist position in which he waited passively until the Spirit moved. He maintained that the Christian, particularly the preacher, had the duty of proclaiming the gospel wherever and whenever he had the opportunity. Thus he was always ready to present his theological position and defend it even before quite skeptical audiences or in the secular press such as *The New York Times*, *Forum*, and *The Annals* of the American Academy of Political and Social Science. He did not doubt that he could prove his case if his critics and opponents would only stick to the facts and not attempt to circumvent them by irrational theories.[36] All this meant that the Christian must have freedom to proclaim the gospel and in so doing to evangelize. The gospel had to be carried to the far corners of the earth and it was not to be merely a gospel of feeling or sentiment, but was to have a sound intellectual basis, founded firmly on the revelation contained in the Scriptures.[37]

To carry out what he considered his God-given mandate to stand for the truth of the gospel necessarily involved Machen in controversy, particularly within the Presbyterian Church, U.S.A. He believed that it was the duty of all orthodox Christians to take their stand within the church against those who would pervert the gospel, thus depriving people of the knowledge of God's grace. He also felt that those who had signed the Westminster Confession and then proceeded to undermine its teachings by preaching and teaching doctrines and theories that were in conflict with it were dishonest and should be exposed for what they actually were doing. Since much of the administration of both Princeton Seminary and of the church as a whole seemed to be in the hands of such individuals, Machen was prepared to speak out no matter how unpopular such action would be, and he was maligned for so doing. He refused to modify his position, however, or give in to pressure.[38]

Machen, however, was no schismatic or secessionist. He did not follow the example of so many Christians who refuse "to get involved," and simply withdraw. He stayed in and fought until forced out. He left Princeton because he felt that the entire institution had given up its basic Reformed position, and helped to found Westminster to carry on the Princeton tradition.[39] But he did not leave the Presbyterian Church. Nor did he leave the church later when he helped to organize the Independent

Board, since the official board was accepting candidates who rejected the church's accepted doctrinal standards. Rather, he felt it necessary to organize a board that would maintain the church's professed theological position. The present writer can well remember a speech he made on "set-up" night to the Westminster Dining Club in 1936. After outlining the situation in the Presbyterian Church, U.S.A. at the time, he said forcefully: "But boys, I am not going to leave. This is my church, and I am staying in and fighting until they either change the Confession or throw me out." And they did the latter.[40]

Thus one may see that Machen's apologetic approach was no merely theoretical, classroom stance. It was a desire to defend and maintain the heart of the gospel. As he put it in his essay "Christianity and Liberty":

> Increasingly the great alternative is becoming clearer; give Jesus up, and confess that His portrait is forever hidden in the mists of legend; or else accept Him as a supernatural Person, as He is presented by all the four Gospels and by Paul.[41]

This was his position, and for it he was prepared to do battle both in the church courts and in the world at large.

The Application of the Faith

As we have endeavored to show, Machen was no ivory-tower scholar. One indication of this is his intense interest in the fortunes of the football teams of the area, and he frequently took interested students to see the Army-Navy game, which seems to have been his favorite sports spectacle. Also contrary to much popular opinion, especially at Princeton, he had a strong sense of humor. One who has attended his classes can vouch for that, for his humor appeared even in his lectures. But even more important was his insistence that a good minister must be a stunt man. As a result there was an annual Westminster stunt night at which he was frequently the star as he recited poetry satirizing the weaknesses and foibles of human nature. He was anything but the paranoid individual that many of his foes insisted upon picturing.

In the social field, Machen's primary interest was in the maintenance of freedom for the individual. He was strongly opposed to the increasing tendency toward collectivism in society that he saw growing on every hand. He felt that the civil government was forever attempting to regulate and control in order to make all citizens of the same pattern and so destroy the individual's wish to be an individual, different from others. He himself was no conformist, and he did not feel that others should be made to conform to the humors of a group of bureaucrats in Washington or in one of the state capitols. Therefore, he was constantly, and on every appropriate occasion, demanding that the individual should have liberty consonant with the liberty of his fellow citizens. Where true Christianity reigns liberty is the rule. "God is free, and where He is, there is liberty and life."[42]

Some of his opponents objected to his call for liberty at the same time that he demanded the disciplining of heretics within the church. Where was the freedom for which he fought? He pointed out, however, that there is a difference between voluntary and involuntary organizations. The state is an involuntary organization of which one is a member whether he wishes or not. The state that interferes with one's liberty must be restrained. In the case of a voluntary organization such as the church, no one is forced to enter. "Insistence on fundamental agreement within a voluntary organization is therefore not at all inconsistent with insistence upon the widest tolerance in the state."[43] He consequently insisted that the church not only had the right but also the duty to remove those who contravened the fundamental agreement. Thus he was prepared to battle for wide freedom under the state, but at the same time for close adherence to the constitution of voluntary bodies such as the church.

Machen's concept of state tolerance was not just centered on one or two things, but seems to have had a wide-angle lens. For instance, the story went the rounds at Westminster Seminary that at one point the city council of Philadelphia proposed enacting a law that would have forbidden jaywalking. An open session of the council was held to determine whether the people of the city wanted such a rule. Machen, who appeared at the council, voiced strong opposition to the rule as an infringement of the citizens' freedom and was to a considerable extent responsible for the proposal being dropped. Although he did not live to see it, he pointed out that the constant eroding of freedom would lead to national and international disasters throughout the world. He should have lived to 1984!

Liberty of action generally, however, was not the only aspect of Machen's concern. He was particularly interested in the matter of freedom of choice in education and backed the concept of the Christian school. He viewed the education of his own day as falling far short of what true education should be, pointing out that there was a tendency toward theory and not an emphasis upon learning the facts. He stressed the view that merely learning some techniques or methods of approaching facts was not really education. He felt that the whole idea of learning as a discipline involving the entire individual was being disregarded. In addition he insisted that while technical education was important, the study of broader subjects such as the humanities was being neglected, as were all attempts at moral education. "By this purely secular, non-moral and non-religious, training we produce not a real human being but a horrible Frankenstein. . . ." Furthermore, such education seeks to make everyone conform to one pattern or mold and teaches that all religious faiths are of the same value and that character must be built upon human experience, rather than upon the law of God.[44] It was these latter considerations that weighed so heavily in his mind in his opposition to the whole system of compulsory public education. But he also opposed any attempt to introduce Bible reading into the public schools, since that, too, could be dangerous, for without proper direction the Bible message could be distorted and changed. Furthermore, it would conflict with the whole concept of freedom of religion.[45]

The solution to this problem, as far as Machen was concerned, was the Christian school. True, he recognized that not every place had or could afford such a school. If that were the case, then there should be released-time instruction. If on the other hand it would be possible to have a Christian school that could teach from a truly Christian perspective, such a school should be established. However, and this was important to his thought, the parents must be able to determine. He pointed out that certain laws that had been proposed in Congress aimed at taking away the parents' right to determine their children's training, placing it instead in the hands of governmental bureaucrats. This he felt was definitely wrong and should be stopped.

The reason for Machen's preference for the Christian school was twofold. In the first place he believed that released time tended to give schoolchildren the idea that Christianity affected only a part of life, and a not very significant one at that. Most of life was dealt with in the secular-humanistic classrooms of the public school. Second, insisting that Christianity gave a world-and-life view that dealt with all aspects of human existence, he held that the entire curriculum of the Christian school should be taught from that point of view. At the same time, he stressed that the Christian school must do its job effectively so that even those who were not Christians would give it their backing, not only for its teaching but because "they really love freedom and the noble traditions of our people." Even more important was the need for the Christian part of the nation to give its support to the Christian school, not as a competitor of the Christian family, but as a support to what Christian parents were seeking to do in the home.[46]

Although Machen made no claim to be a prophet, nor the son of a prophet, many of the questions that he raised with regard not only to education, but to the whole structure of the Anglo-American cultural patterns seem to be moving toward a fulfillment that he foresaw. He was strongly oposed to the establishment of a federal Department of Education that would so regulate education that everything in that field would become monolithic and at the same time, in order to accommodate everybody, would maintain minimum standards. We are now beginning to see this in innovations such as "Process Writing," which are being introduced into schools, with the result that many college freshmen now have to take remedial English courses in order to be able to do their academic work. And much the same effect may be seen in other fields, even in automobile manufacture where thousands of cars have to be recalled each year in order to remedy mechanical defects of one kind or another. To Machen this would not be in any way surprising.[47]

The only solution to this problem would be a new Reformation. This would not be a harking back to the sixteenth century, but a new Reformation wrought by the Spirit of God in the contemporary Christian church. The result would be a restoration of true liberty to mankind in which "thinking [would] again come to its rights." Theological Modernism, which has led to much of the intellectual degradation of the day, would be pushed aside by those who were characterized by faith in Christ as Savior and Lord, and who, possessed "by an heroic honesty," would take their stand without any consideration of consequences. With such a movement, he believed, would come a new Renaissance that would encourage true originality, independence of mind, and "plain common sense."[48]

Such was the theological position of J. Gresham Machen and his application of it. Theologically he was not significantly different from his teacher B. B. Warfield, nor from John Calvin, nor even from the writers of the New Testament. His, however, was a different situation and set of circumstances from theirs. Faced with a decline in Reformed orthodoxy at Princeton and in the Presbyterian Church, U.S.A., and with the growing influence of godless, materialistic humanism in society as a whole, he was prepared to speak out. Believing in the objectivity of truth and employing a sound critical-historical approach to the Christian faith as set forth in the Bible, the Word of God, he attacked the growth of heresy within the Presbyterian Church, and also sought in very practical ways to offset and circumvent the forces that he believed were carrying it in a direction that would destroy it as a true Christian church. At the same time, he took his stand against the humanistic trends in society, calling for Christians to assert themselves as members of society, in order that they might be salt that has not lost its savor. He hoped and prayed for a new Reformation that would revive the church, and renew and reform the social structures.

In the introduction to this volume, George Marsden has delineated three types of Reformed theology: the doctrinal, the cultural, and the evangelistic. In a very real sense, Machen embraced all three. He represented the first in his strong defense of the doctrines of the faith; the second in his constant emphasis upon the Christian's responsibility to take social action; and the third in his willingness to proclaim the grace of God in Jesus Christ whenever he had an opportunity. For these reasons his influence went far beyond the confines of the Reformed community in America.

But how much influence did he have? This, of course, is hard to estimate. Undoubtedly he influenced many of his students at both Princeton and Westminster, but his sudden decease at a relatively early age appears to have cut back this influence, at least in the eyes of those who see such events only in their space-time context. It may well be, however, that in the purpose and plan of God he succeeded in sowing seed that may be part of the spiritual harvest that will bring to fruition the Reformation for which he longed.

Notes: J. Gresham Machen

1. Ned B. Stonehouse, *J. Gresham Machen: A Biographical Memoir* (Grand Rapids: Wm. B. Eerdmans Publishing Company, 1954), 564.

2. Ibid., 42, 47ff.

3. Ibid., ch. 3.

4. Ibid., chs. 5-6.

5. Ibid., 193ff.

6. Ibid., 205-06; J. G. Machen, *What Is Christianity? and Other Addresses*, ed. Ned B. Stonehouse (Grand Rapids: Wm. B. Eerdmans Publishing Company, 1951), 156-85.

7. D. G. Hart, "The Princeton Mind in the Modern World and the Common Sense of J. Gresham Machen," *Westminster Theological Journal* 45 (1984): 10ff.

8. Stonehouse, *J. Gresham Machen*, 441ff.

9. Machen, "Westminster Seminary: Its Plan and Purpose," in *What Is Christianity?* 224ff.

10. Cf. Machen, "The Christian View of Missions," in *What Is Christianity?* 148ff.; Stonehouse, *J. Gresham Machen*, 472ff.

11. Ibid., 491.

12. Ibid., 495ff.

13. Ibid., 504.

14. Ibid., 437.

15. J. Gresham Machen, *What Is Faith?* (New York: Macmillan Publishing Company, Inc., 1925); *The Christian Faith in the Modern World* (New York: Macmillan Publishing Company, 1936); *The Christian View of Man* (Grand Rapids: Wm. B. Eerdmans Publishing Company, 1937).

16. Machen, *What Is Christianity?* 170.

17. Ibid., 102-03; Machen, *What is Faith?* 47-48, 127-28, 151. Cf. *The New Testament: An Introduction to Its Literature and History* (Carlisle, PA: Banner of Truth, 1976) and also the discussions of this in Hart, "Princeton Mind"; Syd-

ney E. Ahlstrom, "The Scottish Philosophy and American Theology," *Church History* 24 (1955): 257ff.; George M. Marsden, "J. Gresham Machen, History, and Truth," *Westminster Theological Journal* 42 (1979-80): 157ff.

18. Machen, *Christian Faith in the Modern World*, 33ff.
19. Machen, *What Is Faith?* 23.
20. Ibid., 75ff.; Machen, *Christian Faith in the Modern World*, 117-18.
21. Machen, *What Is Christianity?* 24ff.
22. Stonehouse, *J. Gresham Machen*, 508.
23. Machen, *What Is Faith?* 171, 190ff., 207ff.; *The Christian Faith in the Modern World*, 152, 231ff.; *The Christian View of Man*, 164ff., 215-16, 289, 296.
24. Machen, *What Is Faith?* 59-60, 65-66; *The Christian View of Man*, 84ff.; *What Is Christianity?* 141, 304ff.
25. Ibid., 181, 190-91, 203, 209.
26. Ibid., 135ff., 190-91, 207-08; Machen, *Christian View of Man*, 175-76, 288, 291.
27. Cf. M. Karlberg, "Justification in Redemptive History," *Westminster Theological Journal* 43 (1981): 213-14.
28. Machen, *What Is Christianity?* 240.
29. Machen, *Christianity and Liberalism* (Philadelphia: Presbyterian Guardian, 1940), 136, 146-47.
30. Ibid., 147-48.
31. Machen, *Christian View of Man*, 84ff.
32. Machen, *What Is Faith?* 54.
33. Machen, "Christian Scholarship and the Defence of the Faith," in *What Is Christianity?* 126ff.; *Christianity and Liberalism*, Introduction.
34. Cf. his comments on McGiffert in *What Is Faith?* 54ff.; cf. also 210ff., 234ff., and Stonehouse, *J. Gresham Machen*, 473ff.
35. Cf. n. 23.
36. Cf. Machen, *What Is Christianity?* 126ff., 138ff.
37. Cf. Machen, "The Christian View of Missions," in *What Is Christianity?* 148ff.
38. Machen, *What is Faith?* 103; *Christian View of Man*, 131ff.
39. Machen, *What Is Christianity?* 224ff.; Stonehouse, *J. Gresham Machen*, chs. 22-23.
40. Ibid., chs. 40-41.
41. Machen, *What Is Christianity?* 271.
42. Ibid., 267ff.; Machen, *Christian View of Man*, 227ff.; *What Is Faith?* 181; *Christian View of Man*, 10.
43. Machen, "The Necessity of the Christian School," in *What Is Christianity?* 248ff.
44. Ibid., 296ff.; Machen, *What Is Faith?* 15ff.
45. Ibid., 15ff.
46. Ibid., 18ff., 103ff., 184.
47. Ibid., 15ff.
48. Ibid., 18ff., 103ff., 184.

CORNELIUS VAN TIL

WESLEY A. ROBERTS

R EFORMED theologians have been concerned not only with a correct understanding of the Christian faith but also with the rational defense and justification of Christianity's truth claims. The latter activity falls within the discipline of apologetics long regarded as a branch of theology. Reformed theologians, however, are not agreed on the relation of apologetics to the theological encyclopedia as a whole. B. B. Warfield, for example, argued that apologetics is the discipline that establishes the knowledge of God that theology explicates.[1] Dutch theologians like Abraham Kuyper and Herman Bavinck argued that apologetics should not precede but follow upon the work of systematic theology that determines the content of the Christian faith.

Cornelius Van Til, a student of both the old Princeton school of theologians and the great Dutch Reformed thinkers, sees a mutual dependence of apologetics and systematic theology.[2] Van Til is not a systematician but an apologist with a strong commitment to Reformed theology that permeates all his writings.

Van Til is regarded by many as one of the foremost Christian apologists of our time. He is perhaps the most controversial Reformed thinker of the twentieth century, the man responsible for initiating a new approach to apologetics. At Princeton Theological Seminary, Van Til was introduced to the traditional method of apologetics espoused by giants of the theological world such as Charles Hodge, B. B. Warfield, Francis L. Patton, William Brenton Greene, Jr., and J. Gresham Machen. This method "is to present evidence and arguments from all different lines of thought in an attempt to show that God exists and that the Bible is the Word of God, and that the burden of inferential proof is so great that there is no excuse for an unbeliever to reject Christianity."[3]

During the academic year 1928-1929, while serving as instructor in apologetics at Princeton, Van Til had an opportunity to assess the apologetic methodology he had received as a student and was using as a

119

teacher. He became convinced that this method was not consistent with the teachings of the Reformed faith. It was not, however, until he joined the faculty of the newly founded Westminster Theological Seminary in September of 1929 as Professor of Apologetics that he began to work out his new approach. Van Til's doctoral work in philosophy had made him aware of the insight of post-Kantian metaphysicians that "the given presuppositions of any philosophical position predetermined and governed much of its later outworkings."[4] When he applied this notion to the traditional apologetic method he saw that this method accepted the non-Christian presuppositions of its adversaries rather than challenged them. This led Van Til to his "pioneering insight" that in apologetics the presuppositions and not merely attendant arguments have to be biblical.[5] His reading of the writings of Abraham Kuyper and Herman Bavinck further strengthened his viewpoint that in apologetics one must not begin with human reason or some supposedly neutral position. Rather, one must begin with the presupposition that there is a God and that men are responsible to him. Information about this God is presented in the inspired Scriptures. This was the beginning of presuppositional apologetics with which Van Til's name has been identified for the past half century.

Van Til maintains an uncompromising commitment to Reformed theology. It is the Reformed expression of the Christian faith that he seeks to defend. He admits his indebtedness to the classic Reformed theologians and quotes freely from them. He is willing to go beyond them, however, in areas where he thinks they are weak. He thinks that he can best honor men such as Warfield and Kuyper by building on the main thrust of their thought rather than by carrying on what is inconsistent with their basic position.[6] Bernard Ramm has given a fine summary of Van Til's location within the Reformed faith:

> Van Til has made a sustained effort to have an apologetic system that grows naturally out of the reformed system of theology. The godfather of his system is certainly John Calvin, although he admits that Augustine was the first Christian theologian to try to work out a Christian metaphysics and epistemology. His more immediate apologetic relatives are such great Dutch thinkers as Kuyper and Bavinck and such outstanding Calvinists as Hodge and Warfield. He has had great sympathy with the Calvinistic philosophy as recently developed at the Free University of Amsterdam by Vollenhoven and Dooyeweerd.[7]

It is Van Til's conviction that in Calvinism more than any other form of Protestantism the message of Christianity is clearly presented as a challenge to the wisdom of the world.

Van Til's apologetic writings contain so much exposition of Reformed theology that critics have charged that he confuses apologetics with systematic theology.[8] This is a common misunderstanding of Van Til's position. Van Til does believe that "defense and positive statement go hand in hand" but he makes a distinction between the two.[9] The misunderstanding arises from Van Til's insistence that theology must have an apologetic thrust, and apologetics must expound theology. The difference in practice, as Frame points out, is a difference in emphasis rather than of subject matter.[10] To understand Van Til's apologetic is at the same time to understand his theology. For his epistemology is based on his metaphysics. Fundamental to his system is the Creator-creature distinction, which is kept in focus at all times. Without this basic distinction in mind one cannot grasp the significance of Van Til's position.

Christian Metaphysics

The doctrine of God is of fundamental importance to Van Til's apologetics. Everything in his system is made to turn on the existence of God. To him God is the absolute, self-conscious Being who is the source of all finite being and knowledge. Consequently, the "ontological" Trinity is made the category of interpretation for all things and the final reference point in all human thinking. The most basic fact of all facts is the existence of the triune God. Thus he asserts, "I hold that belief in God is not merely as reasonable as other belief, or even a little or infinitely more probably true than other belief; I hold rather that unless you believe in God you can logically believe in nothing else."[11]

Theologically, Van Til believes that every doctrine is bound to be false if the first and basic doctrine of God is false. "For apologetics it means that the non-Christian forms of metaphysics cannot be challenged in their basic assumptions."[12] The God of whom Van Til speaks is not one whose existence can be proved by philosophical arguments. He is the self-contained and self-sufficient God who has revealed himself in Scripture.

Unlike the old Princeton theologians who accepted the historically formulated theistic proofs, Van Til maintains that these arguments are invalid. If they were valid, he says, Christianity would not be true.[13] Van Til's point is that the non-Christian formulation of these "proofs" does not refer to the God of Scripture but to a finite god who is no God.[14] He does see value, however, in a Christian formulation of these proofs that rests on the ideas of creation and providence. As such, they appeal to what the natural man knows to be true because he is a creature of God.[15] He believes that the objective evidence for the existence of God and of the comprehensive governance of the world is so plain that men cannot get away from it. They see it about them and within them.[16]

God's existence therefore should be presented by the apologist not as "possible" or "probable," but as certain.

It is from his view of God that Van Til develops his view of reality. He believes Christianity is committed to a two-layer theory of reality or being. By this he means that God has one kind of being and the universe another kind, which is produced and sustained by God. God's being is infinite, eternal, and unchangeable; that of the universe is finite, temporal, and changeable.[17] This distinction allows him to address the philosophical problem of the one-and-many, the relation of unity to diversity. He distinguishes between the Eternal One-and-Many and the temporal one-and-many. In God unity and plurality are both ultimate and eternal. Unity is not sacrificed to plurality nor plurality to unity. The temporal one-and-many is the result of God's creation. Therefore the various aspects of created reality are made to sustain relations to one another according to the design of the Creator. He explains it as follows:

> All aspects being equally created, no one aspect of reality may be regarded as more ultimate than another. Thus the created *one and many* may in this respect be said to be *equal* to one another; they are equally derived and equally dependent upon God who sustains them both. The particulars or facts of the universe do and must act in accord with universals and laws. Thus there is order in the created universe. On the other hand, the laws may not and can never reduce the particulars to abstract particulars or reduce their individuality in any manner. The laws are but generalizations of God's method of working with particulars.[18]

Van Til seeks to be true to the Scriptures in his theory of reality. The triune God is placed at the center of his thinking and is brought to bear on every issue of philosophical importance.

Christian Epistemology

Van Til's theory of knowledge is based on his metaphysics. For there to be any validity to man's knowledge, Van Til believes we must presuppose the triune God revealed in the Bible. He believes that if the question of knowledge is made independent of the question of being, we are in effect excluding the Christian answer to the question of knowledge. Once we accept the biblical testimony with regard to God and man our knowledge will be true insofar as it corresponds with God's knowledge. The Christian, therefore, cannot be neutral to the nature of reality when he asks about the nature of knowledge.[19]

Starting with God's knowledge, Van Til argues that God's knowledge of himself and of the created universe is exhaustive. In other words, there can be no new knowledge for God about himself or the universe. God's knowledge is analytic in that he is himself the source of all that can be known. He does not add to his knowledge, which is eternal, analytic, comprehensive, and inexhaustible.[20]

From God's knowledge of himself, Van Til advances to God's knowledge of the universe. God's knowledge of the universe depends on his knowledge of himself.[21] He made the universe in accordance with his eternal plan, so its very existence depends on his knowledge. As a creature made in the image of God man can and does have true knowledge. God's knowledge is the standard of man's knowledge. "The one must be determinative and the other subordinate."[22] Van Til, however, is careful to point out that although man's knowledge of God must be true, it is not and cannot be exhaustive. Creatures cannot have comprehensive knowledge.[23]

Since man can know God truly it follows that he can also know the world truly. Van Til uses the doctrine of creation as the basis for his assertion. Since both the subject (man) and the object (created reality) of human knowledge are created by God, there must be objective knowledge. Subject and object are adapted to one another according to the plan of God. This is seen in the fact that man (subject) was given a mandate to interpret the world of objects under God. Without this interpretation of the universe by man, Van Til believes, the world would be meaningless.[24] The objectivity of knowledge, therefore, rests on the doctrine of creation. If this doctrine is relinquished, the particulars or facts of the universe would be unrelated and could not be in fruitful contact with one another.

Seeing, then, that the objects of knowledge are brought into relation with the human mind according to God's creative purpose, these objects will not be truly interpreted if they are not brought into relation with the divine mind. God being the ultimate category of interpretation, the things in the universe must be interpreted in relation to him.[25]

Van Til also points out that since God is incomprehensible to us, our knowledge, though true, is partial and always finds itself involved in paradox or seeming contradiction. "Our knowledge is analogical and therefore must be paradoxical."[26] To God there is no mystery, no paradox, but to finite man there is. God's comprehensive plan takes in all the facts but we do not need to know this plan; all we need to know is that reality is rationally controlled by God's plan.

The doctrine of revelation is important to Van Til's concept of epistemology. Since it is according to God's plan that finite things are made, Van Til insists that all knowledge that any finite creature would have must rest upon the revelation of God. Thus the knowledge that we have of the simplest objects of the physical universe is based upon the revelational activity of God.[27]

Van Til follows both Kuyper and Bavinck in stressing the fact that Scripture is *the* objective principle of knowledge for the Christian. This means that the truths of the Scriptures must be taken as the light in which all the facts of experience are to be interpreted. It follows necessarily that if Scripture holds such a crucial position its pronouncements about reality cannot be subject to the scrutiny of reason but must be taken on their own authority.[28] Van Til is aware that such a position will be criticized as authoritarian but he maintains that God's revelation is always authoritarian.[29]

> All the objections that are brought against such a position spring, in the last analysis, from the assumption that the human person is ultimate and as such should properly act as judge of all claims to authority that are made by anyone. But if man is not autonomous . . . then man should subordinate his reason to the Scriptures and seek in the light of it to interpret his experience.[30]

Van Til is opposed to both the rationalist and empiricist theories of knowledge. He criticizes Descartes for maintaining that man has knowledge within himself apart from God. Descartes's position does not recognize that all knowledge of man presupposes revelation. This also holds true for the empiricists. "Though they opposed the innate ideas of Descartes, they were no more ready to recognize the true place of revelation than was Descartes. For them the mind was a *tabula rasa*. But the mind of man as created by God cannot be a *tabula rasa*."[31] Van Til, of course, believes in innate knowledge but not in the Cartesian sense since it has no place for revelation. He sees innate knowledge as having a certain thought content, although it is involuntary and appears most clearly at the intuitional level of man's consciousness.[32] This innate knowledge does not work independently of acquired knowledge. They are correlative to one another.[33] Van Til's approach to epistemology, then, is neither inductive nor deductive, *a priori* nor *a posteriori*, as these terms have been historically understood.

Critics of Van Til have charged him with stripping men of sound intelligence. Clark Pinnock, for example, asserts that Van Til cannot escape the charge of fideism, the view that truth in religion is ultimately based on faith rather than on reasoning or evidence.[34] Pinnock, like most of his critics, misunderstands Van Til's view of the role of reason. Van Til does have a lofty concept of reason but he is careful to make reason function in total dependence on God. He believes reason is a gift given by God to man in order that he might order the revelation of God for himself. But it was never meant to function by itself without relationship to authoritative supernatural revelation.[35]

The law of contradiction is, for Van Til, the expression on a created level of the internal coherence of God's nature. He insists that the Christian should never appeal to this law as something capable of deciding what is possible or impossible. Rather,

> Christians should employ the law of contradiction, whether negatively or positively, as a means by which to systematize the facts of revelation; whether these facts are found in the universe at large or in the Scriptures. The law of contradiction cannot be thought of as operating anywhere except against the background of the nature of God.[36]

This position is set in sharp contrast to the position of the non-Christian that assumes that logic is a timeless, impersonal principle. Van Til points out that on the non-Christian assumptions no intelligible assertions can be made about the world of reality, which is really a world of chance. The non-Christian is bound to fall into self-contradictions since no assertions can be made about chance.[37]

In pointing out the dilemma of the natural man, Van Til does not intend to belittle the intellectual ability of the non-Christian. He wants merely to point out that non-Christian philosophy ought to admit that there is a dimension of reality that is beyond its reach and therefore it ought to listen to the voice of authority. Van Til admits that non-Christians often do have brilliant minds.

> We may greatly admire such a mind for what, in spite of its basic principle and because of the fact that God has released its powers in his restraining grace, it has done. For all that it must not be forgotten that this mind is still, be its name Aristotle, a covenant-breaker in Adam.[38]

However skillful the non-Christian may be in his use of logic, Van Til believes that once revelation is excluded he is bound to arrive at a conclusion contrary to the truth. He cites the example of Aristotle, who knew how to use logic. Aristotle, however, came to the conclusion that God is not the creator of man, knows nothing, and is not a person. "His conclusion was consistent with his premise. His logic was involved in his metaphysics as his metaphysics was involved in his logic."[39] It is Van Til's position therefore that revelation should not be presented for the judgment of the natural man, for every logical activity in which any man engages is in the service of his total vision.[40]

Starting Point and Methodology in Apologetics

The question of where one begins in presenting the claims of Christianity has been much debated since Van Til introduced his "new approach" to apologetics. It is Van Til's firm belief that the question of starting point is largely determined by one's theology. Thus he consistently sets the Reformed faith over against Roman Catholicism and Arminianism.

As a presuppositionalist, Van Til starts with the presupposition of the existence of God. His doctrine of God requires that it be made foundational to everything else as a principle of explanation. "If God is self-sufficient then he alone is self-explanatory. And if he alone is self-explanatory then he must be the final reference point in all human predication. He is like the sun from which all lights on earth derive their power of illumination."[41] The alternative to this, according to Van Til, would be to make man the final reference point, in which case he need not subject his mind to the revelation of God as absolutely authoritative for him. All that would be necessary is for man to refer to God as an expert who has had greater experience than he; but he need not make all thoughts captive to the obedience of Christ.[42]

Van Til maintains, therefore, that only on the presupposition of divine self-sufficiency and man's complete dependence can the difference between the Christian and the non-Christian points of view be clearly pointed out. The most basic difference between the two systems is to be found in their presuppositions. On the assumption of the non-Christian (that is, of human ultimacy), his system is one in which he himself occupies the place that God occupies in Christian theology.[43]

If, as Van Til points out, the Christian and non-Christian start from positions that are mutually exclusive, the question as to whether there is a point of contact for the presentation of the gospel to the non-Christian becomes one of tremendous importance. Stated differently, the issue has to do with whether there is a common point of agreement anywhere in the entire range of human discourse on which Christian and non-Christian can agree and argue their respective cases. If there is no common ground then there is no way of presenting the gospel to the mind and heart of man.

Van Til believes it is impossible to find a common area of knowledge between believers and nonbelievers unless there is agreement between them as to the nature of man himself. He bases this view on the fact that the human mind as the knowing subject makes its contribution to the knowledge it obtains. But since there is no agreement on the nature of man there can be no agreement on a common area of knowledge.[44] Therefore, epistemologically believers and nonbelievers are said to have nothing in common even though metaphysically they have all things in common.[45] Van Til admits that there is a sense in which all men have the facts "in common," since both saint and sinner are face to face with God and the universe of God. But because the sinner is like the man who wears colored glasses everything will be seen in a different light.[46]

Because Van Til refuses to compromise with the nonbeliever, he tells us that the only point of contact is that of head-on collision.[47] This does not mean that he has closed the door to the presentation of the gospel. The metaphysical point of contact is still open; it is to be found within the natural man. He tells us:

> With Calvin I find the point of contact for the presentation of the gospel to non-Christians in the fact that they are made in the image of God and as such have the ineradicable sense of deity within them. Their own consciousness is inherently and exclusively revelational of God to themselves. No one can help knowing God for in knowing himself he knows God. His self-consciousness is totally devoid of content, unless as Calvin puts it at the beginning of his *Institutes*, man knows himself as a creature before God. There are no atheistic men because no man can deny the revelational activity of the true God within him. . . . Every human being is by virtue of his being made in the image of God accessible to God. And as such he is accessible to one who without compromise presses upon him the claims of God.[48]

Van Til's position has not been without criticism. By stating in such an emphatic manner that the Christian and the non-Christian have nothing in common epistemologically, he has been accused of being confused on the question of common knowledge.[49] He is also accused of making unregenerate man totally devoid of knowledge.[50] These criticisms, however, are not valid, for Van Til does recognize the fact that the natural man is not always consistent with his antitheistic principle of interpretation. He constantly introduces the term "in principle" to qualify his statements about the natural man. He says very clearly that as long as the natural man *self-consciously* works from his satanic principle he can have no notion in common with the believer because the unbeliever's epistemology is informed by his ethical hostility to God.[51] Van Til, however, tells us that in the course of history the natural man is *not fully* self-conscious of his own position. Like the prodigal he cannot altogether stifle his father's voice. There is a conflict of notions within him of which he is not fully conscious. The principle of autonomy seeks to suppress his knowledge of God, and the restraining power of God's common grace seeks to suppress the principle of autonomy. This internal semiconscious conflict makes it impossible for him to proceed consistently from the one principle or the other.[52]

It is because of this situation, in which the natural man does not self-consciously work from his principles, that Van Til believes cooperation between believer and unbeliever in the field of science is possible.

Though all of the natural man's interpretations are from an ultimate point of view equally unsatisfactory, there is a sense in which he knows something about everything, about God as well as the world, and that in this sense he knows more about the world than about God. *This distinction is not only true, but important to make.* Many non-Christians have been great scientists. Often non-Christians have a better knowledge of the things of this world than Christians have.[53]

Van Til maintains this position on the ground that the world is not what non-Christians assume that it is, a world of chance, and is what Christians assume that it is, a world run by the counsel of God. It is for this reason that "even non-Christians have knowledge."[54]

Van Til's method of presenting Christianity is quite simple. Instead of trying to prove the truth of Christianity to the natural man, he assumes its truth at the outset and then challenges the presupposition of the natural man, pointing out that on his principles nothing is true, and nothing can be accounted for. Some critics view this approach as being too dogmatic. Van Til accepts this criticism because he believes God speaks to man in Scripture with absolute authority.

A Reformed method of apologetics must seek to vindicate the Reformed life and world view as Christianity come to its own. . . . This implies a refusal to grant that any area or aspect of reality, any fact or any law of nature or of history can be correctly interpreted except it be seen in the light of the main doctrines of Christianity.[55]

It is quite evident that Van Til does not present Christianity apologetically; neither does he admit that the natural man's interpretation of life is correct up to a point. Appeal to common facts is meaningless as far as he is concerned. This sets Van Til's approach at odds with the traditional method. He points out that the Romanist and Arminian views of Christianity force them to agree with the natural man in his principles of methodology to see whether or not Christian theism is true. This is due to the fact that they view the question of methodology, like that of starting point, as a neutral matter.[56] The Reformed apologist, however, cannot agree with the methodology of the natural man, which is tied up with his interpretation of himself as the ultimate reference point. Therefore, rather than utilizing the natural man's erroneous methodology in order to establish a point of contact with him for the gospel, the Reformed apologist finds his point of contact in the sense of deity that the natural man seeks to suppress. The point of contact is in the nature of a head-on collision—system with system.[57]

Van Til's method of reasoning by presupposition is controlled by his epistemological and metaphysical principles. The "ontological" Trinity is as basic to his methodology as it is to the doctrines of Christianity. Van Til's conclusion is just as fixed as his starting point. If Bertrand Russell could accuse Thomas Aquinas of possessing little of the true philosophic spirit because he knew his conclusion in advance,[58] Van Til, on this score, could be criticized for having none whatsoever. But the claim to neutrality in the investigation of truth by non-Christian thinkers is a delusion. It is this so-called neutrality, Van Til believes, that is used in an *a priori* manner to exclude the truth of Christianity before the outset of the investigation. Not to assume the truth of Christianity as a fundamental axiom in its defense would, for Van Til, be a denial of the very thing one is seeking to establish. Thus he offers no apology for his method of reasoning by presupposition.

This method of reasoning is seen by Van Til as indirect rather than direct.[59] By this he means that the issue between believers and nonbelievers relative to Christianity cannot be settled by a direct appeal to "facts" or "laws" whose nature and significance are already agreed upon by both parties in the debate. Since there is no agreement on the "facts" or "laws," the question must be settled indirectly.[60] That means the apologist is required to place himself on his opponent's position, assuming its correctness for argument's sake, in order to show him that on such a position the "facts" and the "laws" have no meaning. Conversely, the non-Christian will be asked to place himself upon the Christian position for argument's sake in order to be shown that only upon the Christian basis are "facts" and "laws" intelligible.[61] Van Til's aim is to challenge the knowledge of God that the natural man has but suppresses.

In contrast to his Reformed approach, Van Til sees the traditional method as being unable to challenge the presuppositions of the non-Christian at the outset of the argument. The reason is that "the Romanist and the evangelical are in some measure in agreement with the non-Christian on his presuppositions. They too attribute a measure of autonomy to man."[62] Van Til's conclusion is that the Romanist-evangelical method of defending Christianity has to compromise it while defending it. "As it cannot clearly show the difference between the Christian and non-Christian view of things, so it cannot present any clear-cut reason why the non-Christian should forsake his position."[63]

Even though Van Til is convinced that the non-Christian method is self-destructive, he does believe that the Reformed apologist should show interest in it. He believes the apologist should make a critical analysis of it, and even join his non-Christian friend in the use of it. "But he should do so self-consciously with the purpose of showing that its most consistent application not merely leads away from Christian theism but in leading away from Christian theism leads to destruction of reason as well as science."[64] Van Til's hope is that the non-Christian will see that Christianity is the only position that gives human reason a field for successful operation and a method of true progress in knowledge.[65]

From this one may be tempted to conclude that Van Til believes non-Christians cannot discover truth by the methods they employ, but that would be incorrect. He believes that because non-Christians are never able to employ their own methods consistently[66] they can discover truth. However, this is a discovery made

> in terms of principles that are borrowed wittingly or unwittingly from Christianity. The fact of science and its progress is inexplicable except upon the presupposition that the world is made and controlled by God through Christ and that man is made and renewed in the image of God through Christ.[67]

Throughout his career Van Til has been very critical of "the Arminian method" that has more or less characterized Protestant apologetics since the time of Bishop Joseph Butler. He believes Arminianism offers to the natural man a Christian theology with foreign elements in that it sees man as having ultimate ability to accept or reject salvation. "God has to await the election returns to see whether he is chosen as God or set aside."[68] This, Van Til believes, places the Arminian at the mercy of the natural man. For if the natural man is consistent he will tell the Arminian that "a little autonomy involves absolute autonomy, and a little reality set free from the plan of God involves all reality set free from the plan of God. After that the reduction process is simply a matter of time."[69] It should be noted here that what Van Til is criticizing is Arminianism as a system of theology and the method of apologetics employed to fit that system.

In contrast to Arminianism, Van Til believes that only in the Reformed faith can an uncompromising method of apologetics be found. "The Reformed apologist throws down the gauntlet and challenges his opponent to a duel of life and death from the start."[70] He does this because he knows that if the natural man is allowed to interpret any aspect of experience in terms of his principles without destroying the idea of intelligibility, then he has a right to claim that there is no reason why he cannot interpret the whole of experience in terms of his principles.[71] Only through reasoning by presupposition, Van Til believes, can one overcome the self-frustrating situation that the traditional method cannot avoid.

Cornelius Van Til has done a great service to apologetic methodology by seeking to develop a method that is consistent with the great doctrines of the Reformed faith. In his "epistemologically" self-conscious Calvinism he presents a consistent Christianity that effectively challenges any worldview that begins with any presupposition other than the triune God of Scripture. He boldly presents Christianity not as a worldview but as a divine system of truth that alone makes human experience intelligible and meaningful.

Notes: Cornelius Van Til

1. Benjamin B. Warfield, "Apologetics," in *The New Schaff-Herzog Encyclopedia of Religious Knowledge* (Grand Rapids: Baker Book House, 1951), 233.
2. Cornelius Van Til, *Apologetics* (Course syllabus, 1959), 3.
3. Floyd E. Hamilton, *The Basis of Christian Faith* (New York: Harper and Row, 1964), xiv.
4. William White, Jr., *Van Til: Defender of the Faith* (Nashville: Thomas Nelson, 1979), 74.
5. Ibid., 75.
6. Cornelius Van Til, *The Defense of the Faith* (Philadelphia: Presbyterian and Reformed Publishing Company, 1955), 397.
7. Bernard Ramm, *Types of Apologetic Systems* (Wheaton, IL: Van Kampen Press, 1953), 184-85.
8. In E. R. Geehan, ed., *Jerusalem and Athens* (Nutley, NJ: Presbyterian and Reformed Publishing Company, 1971), 349, 391-92.
9. Van Til, *Apologetics*, 3-4.
10. John Frame, *Van Til: The Theologian* (Phillipsburg, NJ: Pilgrim Publishing Company, 1976), 4.
11. Cornelius Van Til, *Why I Believe in God* (Philadelphia: Presbyterian and Reformed Publishing Company, n.d.), 20.
12. Van Til, *Apologetics*, 9.
13. Cornelius Van Til, *Introduction to Systematic Theology* (Course syllabus, 1961), 199.
14. Ibid., 198.
15. Van Til, *The Defense of the Faith*, 197.
16. Ibid., 254.
17. Van Til, *Apologetics*, 8.
18. Van Til, *The Defense of the Faith*, 42-44.
19. Ibid., 50.
20. Ibid., 51-52.
21. Ibid., 56.
22. Ibid.
23. Ibid., 57-58.
24. Ibid., 60.
25. Ibid., 61.
26. Ibid.
27. Ibid., 282-83.
28. Ibid., 125.
29. Ibid.
30. Ibid.
31. Van Til, *An Introduction to Systematic Theology*, 195.
32. Ibid.

33. Ibid., 197.
34. Geehan, ed., *Jerusalem and Athens*, 423.
35. Van Til, *An Introduction to Systematic Theology*, 189.
36. Ibid., 11.
37. Van Til, *The Defense of the Faith*, 143-44.
38. Ibid., 298.
39. Ibid.
40. Cornelius Van Til, *The Case for Calvinism* (Philadelphia: Presbyterian and Reformed Publishing Company, 1955), 137.
41. Cornelius Van Til, *A Christian Theory of Knowledge* (Course syllabus, 1954), 2.
42. Ibid.
43. Ibid., 4.
44. Van Til, *The Defense of the Faith*, 84.
45. Ibid., 260.
46. In B. B. Warfield, *The Inspiration and Authority of the Bible* (Philadelphia: Presbyterian and Reformed Publishing Company, 1948), 20.
47. Cornelius Van Til, *The Intellectual Challenge of the Gospel* (Phillipsburg, NJ: Lewis J. Grotennis, 1963), 19.
48. Van Til, *The Defense of the Faith*, 257.
49. Gordon H. Clark, "Apologetics," in *Contemporary Evangelical Thought*, ed. Carl F. H. Henry (New York: Channel Press, 1957), 155.
50. Ibid., 156.
51. Van Til, *The Defense of the Faith*, 189-90.
52. Ibid., 190.
53. Ibid., 286.
54. Ibid.
55. Ibid., 113.
56. Ibid., 113-14.
57. Ibid., 115-16.
58. Bertrand Russell, *A History of Western Philosophy* (New York: Simon and Schuster, 1945), 463.
59. Van Til, *Defense of the Faith*, 117.
60. Ibid.
61. Ibid., 117-18.
62. Van Til, *A Christian Theory of Knowledge*, 6.
63. Ibid.
64. Van Til, *The Defense of the Faith*, 119.
65. Ibid.
66. Ibid., 120.
67. Van Til, *The Case for Calvinism*, 106-07.
68. Van Til, *The Defense of the Faith*, 128-29.
69. Ibid., 129.
70. Ibid., 130.
71. Ibid., 198.

III. THE DUTCH SCHOOLS

THE DUTCH SCHOOLS

JAMES D. BRATT

In 1898 a Dutch Reformed minister recently arrived in the United States made his first contribution to that perennial topic of immigrant discussion, the contrast between Old World and New World cultures. For this observer, Foppe Ten Hoor, the difference appeared most clearly in work styles, which in turn reflected geographical constraints. In America, where land and resources existed in nearly absurd abundance, people who could work and move on quickly tended to stay on the surface of things, and regarded all affairs with pragmatic judgment. Netherlanders, however, with their limited terrain, had to be thorough and cautious, paying close heed to distinctions and boundaries, delving to the roots of things. The first group was enamored of results, action, and change; the second, with principle, theory, and tradition. The difference had consequences in all realms, Ten Hoor concluded, but most importantly in the theological.[1]

How his audience should negotiate the conflict that their mixed status (Dutch and American) entailed, Ten Hoor left to later occasions. More important for our purposes here is his delineation, on the verge of the twentieth century, of seminal "Dutch" characteristics; for the body of theological work the group would produce in that century bears out Ten Hoor's profile remarkably well. Most striking, perhaps, is Ten Hoor's very act of addressing such cultural concerns precisely in his role as professor of systematic theology at the Christian Reformed seminary in Grand Rapids. That the post brought with it this license, even mandate, to speak to any and all issues and that no office in the entire community held more prestige attest to the priority of place the Dutch Reformed have given theology.

Some of theology's function for this group is thus evident in Ten Hoor's decree. So is an uneasy duality at the heart of that function. On the one hand, as Ten Hoor insisted in hundreds of subsequent lectures and pages of commentary, Reformed doctrine was God's own truth, eternal, unchanging, fixed in his revelatory Word, the best interpretation of that Word. On the other hand, Dutch theology bore the stamp of a particular culture and was used by Ten Hoor and many others to differentiate "our people" from the "American world," even from other Reformed groups in that world. Quite simply, theology could not escape serving Dutch Americans as the medium of intellectual exchange, for their churches served as the center of their local communities and their denominations as the national networks binding these together. As all sorts of social dynamics and cultural issues—churchly or not, intraethnic or involving the outside world—registered in ecclesiastical terms, theology became the means of communal debate, confirmation, and resolution. Hence the theology professorship's broad portfolio and the community's doctrinal passion. Theology had to be but could not be left an eternal code of truth beyond the vagaries of interest and perception. Doctrine and life worked in a close and continuing dialectic, each speaking to the other as—and sometimes more—fully and directly as the fondest theorists of Calvinism might wish. Ten Hoor worked better than he knew in that quick, and quite typical, concluding leap from the earth to the religious.

Our analysis of this theology will move from the more common to the more particular; that is, first reviewing those elements that the Dutch share with other American Protestants, especially with evangelicals and other Reformed camps; then examining the features that have differentiated them from these; and finally tracing the issues of controversy within the community itself and the separate schools thereby produced. Put another way, we can describe Dutch-American distinctiveness and debates as functions of a particular selection and combination of elements from the general Reformed fund, and analyze that selection-combination process according to different trajectories of launch from the Netherlandic background, shifting patterns of consensus and tension within the community, and the ongoing dialectic between the community and the surrounding American world.

The Wider Context of Calvinism

The themes of commonality and particularity are prefigured in all three of Dutch Calvinism's confessional standards. That there were three suggests the motif of plurality as well. The Belgic Confession (1561), written in the fires of intense religious strife, gave primordial definition to the Dutch church, but also showed, in its anti-Catholic and anti-Anabaptist strains, how the Dutch could comport well with other Reformed movements whether on the continent or in America. The Heidelberg Catechism (1563), on the other hand, was famous for its pastoral, irenic nature. Written to promote unity between the Reformed and Lutherans in Germany, the document became as well a bridge between the Dutch and German Reformed, again on both sides of the Atlantic. Its practical piety also allowed its readers a way of negotiating the tension between orthodoxy and pietism that proved so disruptive elsewhere. Finally, the Canons of Dort (1619), forged in "a virtual ecumenical council of Reformed churches," buttressed the Dutch in their predestinarian, theocentric identity and in the scholastic methodology they would share for centuries with the decendants of Westminster.[2]

Since the proceedings at Dort coincided with the founding of New Netherland in the Hudson valley, the Dutch church in North America came into being with this full confessional structure at its disposal. It hardly made distinguished use of this resource or of any other, however, subserving rather the colony's economic purposes and suffering with its demographic, political, and diplomatic misfortunes.[3] The English conquest (1664) cost the Dutch church its preferred status, and for the next century it remained in a mixed state—an enclave for ethnocultural maintenance, yet a base of significant public power, uneasily housing both Jersey farmers and a Manhattan commercial elite. These divisions were to some extent mirrored in the controversy that ensued upon New Jersey pastor Theodore J. Frelinghuysen's use of "awakening" measures in the 1720s.[4] By the 1750s the church had divided into two camps, the "Coetus" (representing the Frelinghuysen line, with a platform of pietism and home rule), and the "Conferentie" (New York-based, holding more to the Amsterdam connection and confessional-liturgical traditions). Each group established connections with the respective "New" and "Old Light" factions in denominations around them. Yet rather than gravitating to these other orbits, the two sides were reunited with each other in the 1770s. The architect of the fusion, John H. Livingston, aptly represented the church's settled character: pious and intellectual, American (Yale) and Amsterdam educated, in contact with outsiders but first attentive to the home front.[5]

Signal features of this process, it should be noted, were no more "distinctively American" than characteristically "Dutch Reformed." The Netherlands was as central in the rise of evangelical pietism as pietism was in that nation's religious history in the century after 1650. Frelinghuysen himself was a child of the movement and brought it with him as an immigrant to America in 1720.[6] Moreover, in the Dutch case pietism generally had confessional orthodoxy as an ally, not—as often happened elsewhere—as an antagonist. This was the result of the long struggle within the Netherlandic church between the followers of Jacobus Arminius (and later, Descartes) and the strict Dortian party, which saw the former gradually gain tolerance, then dominance, so that orthodoxy became a minority view among the church elite. Over the same period, the more devout in hundreds of local congregations had been organizing conventicles to help prosecute a more rigorous type of religion than the established church could enforce. These found the themes of orthodoxy quite more to their taste than liberal esteem of reason and human nature; and the traditionalist theologians found in them a welcome base of support.[7] It was here, then, that pietism and confessionalism were married; that Gijsbert Voetius, champion of orthodoxy, and Willem à Brakel, exemplar of practical divinity, were bound together, to be venerated for generations as chief of "de oude schrijvers," "fathers" of the true faith.[8]

Such loyalties also figured prominently in the two developments of early nineteenth-century Dutch history most germane to our purposes. In the post-Napoleonic restructuring of the Reformed Church, local autonomy seemed threatened by an increasingly centralized administration, which had—even worse—opened the way for liturgical and doctrinal "corruption." The ensuing "secession" (in 1834) and formation of a network of "truly Reformed" churches essentially represented the old conventicle principles and clientele in more radical guise.[9] A decade later, the Seceder network provided key mechanisms of mobilization, transportation, and leadership for a new wave of Dutch emigration to America. Since this precedent was remembered for the whole second phase (1845-1920) of Dutch immigration, and since emigration and Secession appealed to the same strata of Dutch society, the orthodox made up a disproportionately high percentage of the nineteenth-century immigrants—and of the post-World War II migrants to Canada as well.[10] Hence the conservative branches of Dutch Calvinism took a central role in shaping the new ethnic subculture.

A pietist-confessionalist conjunction in the conventicle-Seceder mode thus forms the baseline of Dutch theology in America. It was also the source of the group's several similarities with its new Protestant neighbors. Like every strain in the American revivalist-evangelical tradition, Dutch pietism insisted that faith be deep, personal, and heartfelt, that it proceed from and through a bare confrontation with one's own unworthiness and the exclusive merits of Christ. Postconversion, the believer was to maintain the intimacy of this deliverance through daily introspection and devotions; was to "practice godliness," rejecting the "things of the flesh and the world"; and throughout, was to submit to the appraisal, admonition, and encouragement of the fellow "faithful."[11] Doctrinal comparisons, on the other hand, are more difficult since American evangelicals have hardly been of one mind on theological detail. But the Dutch have shared their characteristic, unifying insistence on a high view of scriptural veracity and authority, on Christianity's finality, and, in face of Enlightenment and Modernist critiques, on the plausibility and necessity of the supernatural, miraculous, and transcendent in religion and metaphysics. As one of their typical assessments concluded, the Fundamentalist "is our fellow believer," but the Modernist "is on the side of the anti-Christ and cannot be recognized as a believer at all."[12] So were the Dutch placed on the American spectrum.

The full extent of these congruences was best evident in the 1925-1950 era. Both the Dutch and the evangelicals entered the period lashed by the cultural crisis that had been precipitated by World War I. Both responded with a subcultural strategy—the Dutch reinforcing an inherited structure, the evangelicals building theirs new. Both took militant anti-Modernism as their overriding outlook, their prime motive force, for the entire era; and both moved toward strict, maximal claims as a result. On the side of ethics, the era began for the Dutch with their largest denomination officially (and unprecedentedly) proscribing three forms of "worldliness": dancing, gambling, and theater attendance.[13] An evangelical's list might have looked somewhat different (usually including smoking and drinking, which were still tolerated—if no longer virtually mandatory—among the Dutch), but the strategy of defensiveness, legalism, and symbolic repudiation of larger cultural trends was the same. As to theology, this was the clearest era of confessionalist hegemony in Dutch-American history. Appropriately, Louis Berkhof was its presiding figure; his *Reformed Dogmatics*, in three volumes, its definitive production. Though it became the best-known Dutch contribution to American theology, Berkhof's work had first of all an intracommunal intent. It was to be at once the *summa* of the inherited faith and the touchstone for measuring all other (read, "outside") opinion, an intellectual fortress amid "the widespread doctrinal indifference . . . superficiality and confusion . . . [and] insidious errors" of "the present day." Yet virtually any evangelical of the era, even those put off by Berkhof's Reformed insistencies, could cheer the priority (in logic, deference, and elaboration) he gave to Scripture, and relish his emphatic reassertion of every doctrinal construction offensive to liberalism.[14]

Dutch Distinctives

The very degree of similarity, however, prompted demonstrations of particularity. Not only did Berkhof's anti-Arminian strictures have this role vis-à-vis most revivalist and holiness movements; so did the confessional thoroughness and intensity, the systematization and doctrinalism evident in the Dutch tradition. If Berkhof's statement of purpose intended "insidious errors" for Modernists, "widespread doctrinal indifference, superficiality and confusion" covered large reaches of the evangelical complex. It was there (to conclude Berkhof's statement) that "sects . . . are springing up like mushrooms on every side." Nor was this Berkhof's complaint alone. From his predecessor, Foppe Ten Hoor, to his successors in the post-World War II era, from every Dutch-American denomination, from press as well as pulpit, the Dutch mounted a persistent critique of American Protestantism's creedal reductionism, and of the cultural spirit it evidenced. From this perspective, Fundamentalism with its "short list" and Modernism with its "no list" of "essential doctrines" looked oddly similar, and the "Bible alone" claims of small sects only echoed the doctrinal ignorance of big denominations. The phenomenon in general showed that the churches were mirroring all too faithfully the character of the society around them. The individualistic egotism and pragmatism of the second appeared as the characteristic "subjectivism" and "moralism" of the first—that is, the designation of personal experience or feelings on the one hand or practical action on the other as *the* core, and inevitably the extent, of Christianity.[15]

Confessional consciousness, expectably, offered several corrective counterpoints. For Foppe Ten Hoor, it presented a foil against Anglo-American—and not coincidentally, Arminian, subbiblical—ways.[16] For the more optimistic, it opened up the treasures, and the warning lessons, of the centuries of church history.

To turn one's back on the historic creeds is therefore to turn one's back on what God has given us through the struggle of centuries, and to run the risk of trying to build up once more what has already been tried and found wanting. . . . To preach a creed is one of the very best methods possible . . . of avoiding tangents and vagaries, of securing a balanced and full-orbed presentation of the Bible as a whole. . . .[17]

But for everyone, it forestalled the drift to liberalism on the left and pious self-absorption on the right to which the subjective impulse was particularly prone. The confessions alone had the resources equal to the challenges and temptations of modern culture. Moreover, this seemed the scripturally given psychology. True, one must experience salvation and prove it in action; but without recourse to the full body of biblical truth, to a holistic system mindful of first principles and aware of their logical implications and complications, these would prove fleeting, filled more with the spirit of the age than with that of the Word.[18]

Besides doctrinalism, several specific tenets worked to distinguish the Dutch among conservative Protestants. Persistently, discussions in this vein brought up the ideas of covenant and kingdom. The intertwining of the two and the vision they supported were best articulated by Abraham Kuyper (1837-1920), the eminent Netherlander whose Neo-Calvinistic movement did much to restore the concepts to the heart of Dutch

Reformed concern.[19] Of the dual goals that drove Kuyper throughout his staggeringly multifarious career, success in the first—combatting liberalism—required the second—awakening the devout from their pietistic slumbers. To be *Calvinists* again, Kuyper told his followers, they had to recognize the lordship of Christ over all areas of life, which meant that they could neither dismiss various fields (art, science, politics) as inherently "worldly" nor participate in these simply with and as non-Christians, but must bring into each a distinctively Christian commitment and program. The result would be an "organic church," working outside ecclesiastical institutional walls, but with a coherent plan and mutual discipline, living out the Word of God in "every sphere of life" and so building up the Kingdom of God in the midst of the world. Covenant figured centrally in this conception as the mechanism or ground of divine sovereignty (the "channel through which the waters of election flow"), just as kingdom denoted its scope or end.[20]

One measure of the Kuyperian presence among Dutch-Americans, their perennial efforts at Christian cultural action, has been much noted. It was from Kuyper that they got their early concern with "worldview," their habitual confidence in speaking to every phase of modern culture, from science to social theory, geopolitics to economics, and their determination to uncover philosophical preconceptions in every academic credo, every social program. But the covenant-kingdom conjunction itself played a major role in this project by shaping a Dutch-American church ethos that contrasted markedly, in their eyes, with that of the evangelical world. Put simply, covenant was arrayed against revivalism as a model of Christian initiation and against dispensationalism as a view of history; and kingdom stood over against individualism as the scope of God's purpose, and against mere soul-saving as the end. Against spiritual moods, the pressures of life, and faddish "winds of doctrine," the covenant rooted the believer firmly in social and historical context, and above all in the lasting will of God. He did not exist as a lonely individual but as part of a corporate body that supported him even as he contributed to its vitality. He did not have to extract the full message of faith from the Bible anew, nor alone puzzle out its complicated relationships with daily life, for he stood heir to the whole heritage of Christian history. Nor was the present era a parenthesis in the divine plan, allowing of only "spiritual" ends and means for Christian action. God's ages were an organic whole, as were his people, so a full-bodied, earthly witness to redemption was still the Christian mandate. Drawing off lifelong nurture, not just a single episode (periodically "renewed") of emotional "conversion," the life of faith would not be restricted to Sunday worship and special "spiritual" moments during the week but would involve everyday habits, customs, and work in home, shop, and school. More boldly, placed in the fabric of his peers and the order of generations past and present, believers could transcend the level of personal ethics alone and address collective structures, broad cultural movements, with the redemptive message.[21]

This vision manifests the basic axioms of Dutch Reformed thinking: the will of God, not the whims of man; organic connections, not fragments or individual parts. But the program's usual implementation shows the ethnic-communal factor in the group's life as well. "Kingdom-building" was too readily left at the construction of a cradle-to-grave institutional framework for the mutual association of Dutch-Americans; and the magisterial process of divine election through the corridors of time could devolve to just the baptism and indoctrination of the group's next generation. "God does not save people at random," said one commentator to this point, "but follows a certain order, and perpetuates his covenant from generation to generation through the families of believers"—Dutch-American believers, it turned out.[22] Grand visions and small achievements thus became the besetting paradox of this group. But perhaps that only manifested the dissonance it felt in the new land. With so few sharing their tastes, they worried with considerable realism that their salt liberally sprinkled might only lose its savor.

The "outsiders" with whom the Dutch felt most compatible were the "old Princeton" sector of American Presbyterianism. Confessionalism, theocentricity, and some of the same cultural vision the two shared. Just as important were the personal links between them: Geerhardus Vos, West Michigan's donation to the Princeton Seminary faculty in 1893, who drew a generation of future Dutch Reformed leaders there for graduate training; and J. Gresham Machen, who popularized the conservative Presbyterian cause among the Dutch in the great battles of the 1920s, winning funds and faculty for his new institutions.[23] But even here affinities were crossed by differences, the most obvious being epistemological. First, Princeton theology, deeply beholden to Scottish Common Sense Realism, tended to minimize the effect of sin upon human reason. Second, it posited that Christianity—and Christianity alone—was a rationally demonstrable and coherent system, that any fair-minded person could and would see the same and be brought to faith accordingly, and that apologetics was therefore the theologian's highest labor. Dutch Neo-Calvinism, in contrast, joined continental dialectical Idealism to a radical Augustinian psychology. There simply was no religiously neutral rational faculty or middle ground, Kuyper insisted again and again. Reason, like every other faculty, impulse, or activity, proceeded from and worked to serve one's fundamental commitment—in Kuyperian parlance, one's (necessarily religious) "life-principle." Accordingly, the world could contain any number of relatively coherent worldviews, none of which could finally convince another of its own superiority on strictly rational grounds. Apologetics would therefore be the last concern of the theologian, who should work instead to elaborate the full complex of faith on its own presuppositions for the battle of world systems.[24]

This disagreement hardly broke relations between the two schools. Benjamin B. Warfield, the lion of Princeton, praised Kuyper's work even though this part of it "utterly mystified" him.[25] But especially with J. Gresham Machen, Warfield's successor, further variances were shown that, added to the first, subtly complicated the connection. Machen's reformation of culture aimed at "all areas of thought," Kuyper's at "all areas of life." Machen had an individualistic, contractarian, and laissez-faire view of the state and society (and the first two also for the church), all of which were anathema to Kuyper. Kuyper's approach was intuitive, passionate, and populistic; Machen's intellectualist, controlled, aristocratic. Thus Machen's orthodox Presbyterians did not converge as steadily with the Dutch Reformed as might have been expected. The principal theological divergence over time involved the issue of biblical infallibility. The Kuyperian stress on the inner testimony of the Holy Spirit allowed an alternative to the Princetonian inerrancist-propositional model. Only some among the Dutch Reformed (and those the more identifiably Kuyperian) took that option, however; their opponents (perhaps the more traditionally confessional) preferred the more Princetonian conception. It might have been only appropriate, in turn, that the Presbyterian-based Rogers-McKim proposal showed considerable debts to Dutch Calvinist sources.[26]

Conflict Within Dutch Faith

This hint of intracommunal differences brings us to our third area of concern, the persistent presence of conflict within the Dutch Reformed circle itself. The most striking instance was its early division into two denominational camps: the Reformed Church in America (RCA), descended from the colonial era and attracting the early leadership and much of the rank and file of the post-1845 immigration; and the Christian Reformed Church (CRC), which emerged out of two breaks with that leadership, one in 1857, the other in 1880, and eventually garnered a majority of the later arrivals.[27] The CRC also inherited, therefore, virtually all of the Kuyperian influx into Dutch America and all of the tensions with the Seceder school that Neo-Calvinism induced. Thus, pietist-confessionalist vs. Neo-Calvinist is the second strain persisting throughout the group's history. Finally, both of these parties could divide within themselves as well, and forge coalitions across their earlier opposition. Thus, sometimes Kuyperians stood together against the pietists; other times some Kuyperians and pietists joined together against other kinds of Kuyperians and pietists; and throughout, the two denominations engaged each other variously in open warfare, armed peace, or cool suspicion.

The denominational divide did not simply reflect, as was long surmised, the Seceder–National Church rivalry from the Old World. The immigrant (Western) sector of the RCA and the CRC were equally beholden at their origins to Seceder clergy and clientele. Rather, the schism grew out of a tension within the Secession itself, which allowed two different perceptions of the Reformed heritage and the American situation. The RCA West represented that wing of the movement oriented toward experiential piety and practical morality—the very emphases, of course, of the antebellum American evangelicalism in which the RCA East participated. The affinity was reinforced by the correspondence between evangelicalism's favored-church status in the nineteenth century and the increasingly National Church background of the immigrants the RCA West attracted after 1880.[28] Thus the RCA became fixed on the relatively conservative side of mainstream Protestantism: generally orthodox but not overly concerned with Reformed confessional specifics; convinced of the Protestant character of the United States, and enthusiastic for the various early twentieth-century crusades designed to strengthen that character at home and spread it abroad. That stance persisted even after the crusades had failed. The RCA maintained in the post-Protestant ethos of mid-twentieth-century America the distinguishing marks of a mainstream affiliation: membership in the National and World Councils of Churches, wariness of anti-Modernist crusading, and entertainment of proposals for church union.[29]

That each of these was challenged from within the RCA West shows, however, the persistence there as well of the more cautious, confessionally emphatic Secessionist stream. That tradition was even stronger—we might say predominant—in the CRC, characterizing Ten Hoor and Berkhof on the seminary level and the majority of the denomination's clerical and editorial leaders through at least World War II. To this perspective, modern times constituted not an opportunity but a threat for faith, and the church was called not to move into the world but to attend to the loyal remnant. America's "Christian character" turned out to be a seductive veneer hiding a secular heart; and maximal Reformed consciousness—rather than ecumenical ventures in either the revivalist or social reform mode—seemed the only antidote sufficient to the threat. Yet befitting their common Seceder rootage, this was a defensive, as the RCA optimists' was an outgoing, pietism. Neither countenanced Kuyper's holistic, systemic approaches; both focused their energies within the institutional church, upon individual soul-saving and personal behavioral symbolics—we might say, upon missions and moralism.[30]

Neo-Calvinist discontent with this posture flared both in pointed disputes and in a persistent culturalist concern. The latter was clearly evident, for example, in the 1930-1950 era of Confessionalist hegemony when certain CRC ministers and academics, clustered around Calvin College and Seminary, sponsored conferences and a monthly journal dedicated to providing a comprehensive and distinctively Reformed interpretation of current philosophical, sociopolitical, and international affairs. Only such, this party claimed, was adequate to both the richness of the Christian heritage and the desperate needs of the modern era. Yet this project's anti-Modernist agenda comported well enough with the Confessionalists' to keep peace in the denominational house.[31] Such harmony did not always obtain. In fact, both the earliest and the latest theological battles in the CRC grew from the pietist–Neo-Calvinist tension, and both involved questions arising from that traditional seedbed of Reformed controversy, the doctrine of predestination.

In the first dispute (1890-1905), the timing of election itself opened the issue. The supralapsarians, representing the Neo-Calvinist line, placed election before the fall of man, indeed before creation itself, and correlatively placed regeneration virtually at birth, before baptism and "conversion experiences," which were taken as merely confirming what had already been effected by the will of God. This construction, the supras argued, best fit Calvinism's theocentricity, anchored the individual's salvation in the eternal will of God, and released the pulpit and pew from emotionalism and self-absorption for the comprehensive cultural witness that was the church's true business. The infralapsarians' reversals on all these points bespoke their Seceder heritage. So did their critique of the opposition's clientele. Abstract speculation might please the "dreaming philosophers," the arrogant elite, that comprised Kuyper's movement, Foppe Ten Hoor declared, but the health of the Reformed churches would lie always with the humble, who cherished the vital piety that Scripture and confession had ever mandated. Let "scientific" theologians have their worldly glory; the despised of the earth would inherit the Kingdom of Heaven. Happily for Ten Hoor, the infras' success in this case did not have to wait that long, as the Synod of Utrecht's (1905) decision for their side of the debate was accepted in Dutch America as well.[32]

The most recent controversy in the CRC involved similar hostilities but quickly moved from the nature of the will of God to the nature of his Word. Again the intelligentsia precipitated the conflict (in 1962), only this time arguing that election, as expressed in the Dortian statement on limited atonement, could be read as unduly restrictive. The Confessionalists saw this as an attack upon their hegemony, and the CRC Synod's somewhat tepid resolution of the matter in 1967 proved them right.[33] For the two sides almost immediately (1969-1972) clashed again over a more momentous issue, the nature and authority of Scripture. With this debate, denominational control shifted to the "progressives" who stood, albeit at some remove, in Kuyper's descent. The Confessionalists' inerrant-propositionalist constructs were demoted, though hardly excised, at crucial points. The Bible's authority, the Synod declared, lay not simply in divine inspiration but in its redemptive message; its meaning and veracity involved not so much empirical "facts" in various domains (geological, biological, historical) as its purpose of salvation and its focus in Christ.[34] A more clearly Neo-Calvinist formulation also entered the field at this juncture, reflecting the influence of Herman Dooyeweerd, one of Kuyper's successors at Amsterdam, among post-World War II immigrants to Canada. The Dooyeweerdians, as they became known, articulated a tripartite notion of revelation: besides (and perhaps through and before) the Inscripturated (Bible) and Incarnate (Christ) Word stood God's creation ordinances (the Law Word), by which the Christians' redemptive witness to all areas of society and culture could proceed. The Confessionalists could hardly decide which of these constructions troubled them more, and could draw little comfort from the rivalry between the two.[35] Indeed, one reason for the 1970s change in denominational power was the alliance of the two Neo-Calvinist parties, as opposed to the mutual recrimination and then coalescence, by one side or the other, with the Confessionalists that had occurred at two earlier crises.

That Kuyper spawned two schools instead of one owed largely to a basic ambiguity in his thought. On the one hand, Kuyper preached religious antithesis: the life-principles of Christians and unbelievers were diametrically opposed, the spiritual qualities of their respective actions were inevitably antagonistic, and Christians should therefore pursue their work in society from their own separate organizations. Later in his career, without diminishing this idea, Kuyper resurrected the doctrine of common grace: that God gave to humanity grace which, while not "saving," enabled them to attain much virtue and truth; that achievements in politics and scholarship, art and technology, which were not motivated by faith might still be cherished as gifts of God; and that cooperation between Christians and unbelievers was therefore possible and necessary.[36] Kuyper's American followers, unable to harness this paradox as had their master, diverged into schools that can be designated antithetical and positive. The first saw corruption (in principle and practice) present everywhere in the world, stressed the negative or condemnatory purpose of Christian sociocultural witness, and absolutized the need for separate organization. The second hoped to realize some of the improvements that the Christian critique offered society and sanctioned cooperation with people of different principles to this end.[37] That the Kuyperians thus divided along the same defensive-outgoing lines as had the pietists explains the types of interparty coalitions that were made. That the two fiercest conflicts in CRC history occurred between the two Calvinist factions, and both times in the wake of world wars, demonstrates the group's metaphorical use of theology. Common grace, as the doctrine relating the church to the world, cast in theological terms the question of Dutch America's relation to the outside world, exactly the issue that wartime nationalism had raised most intensely.

The first of these battles, like that of the early 1970s, took rise from the issue of Scripture. Drawing connections with the Modernist-Fundamentalist debate then reaching its zenith, a Confessionalist-Antithetical coalition in the early 1920s accused Roelof Janssen, chief positive Calvinist on the Grand Rapids faculty, of practicing higher criticism in his Old Testament instruction and of thereby partaking dangerously of the rationalistic and naturalistic spirit of the age. Janssen's reply, however appealed to Kuyper, Herman Bavinck, and other Reformed authorities, continental and American, to establish his orthodoxy and to turn the charges back on his critics. It was their denial of common grace, explicit among the Antitheticals, implicit among the Confessionalists, Janssen argued, that forced them to denigrate humanity's residual abilities, to eliminate God's grace from the natural realm, and to misconstrue the nature of miracles, revelation, and science. The debate's increasing focus on the relations between Old Testament Israel and surrounding nations hinted at the cultural issue involved: both sides saw the future of the Dutch "Israel" in America to be at stake. Enough of the community were suspicious of "progressive" adaptation to the nation that had, in World War I, so badly treated them that the tide swung against Janssen. He guaranteed the conclusion by refusing to testify before the 1922 Synod.[38] But then the tide swung against the Antithetical members of his prosecution, the CRC pastors Herman Hoeksema and Henry Danhof. Their absolutizing of the antithesis, and post-facto declaration that common grace had indeed been the root issue in the Janssen case, cost them their Confessionalist allies. These coalesced with positive Calvinists at the 1924 Synod to declare Hoeksema and Danhof in error. Common grace was Reformed orthodoxy, though more useful for evangelism than for cultural cooperation, and Hoeksema and Danhof were ordered to stop saying otherwise. They did not, and joined Janssen in the ranks of the demoted.[39]

The Confessionalist regime that this settlement installed lasted until after World War II. Then the drama was played out again, only with a less conclusive ending. Again, a "progressive" party arose at Calvin Seminary (George Stob and Harry Boer, with James Daane helping from the outside), eager to bear positive witness to the American world. Again, the Confessionalist majority brought accusations of the "heresy" currently in the air, i.e., "Barthianism"; and again they allied with Antithetical voices—Cornelius Van Til and H. Evan Runner—to quash the new school. The battle at the Seminary was dismissed (also the fate of the entire faculty) as a conflict of personalities, however, and the factions settled into uneasy coexistence.[40] Antitheticalism came to lodge chiefly among the Canadians in the CRC, positive Calvinism in the *Reformed Journal* and the denominational bureaucracy, and intelligentsia Confessionalism in *Torch and Trumpet* (later the *Outlook*), northwest Iowa, and assorted clergy who felt increasingly displaced, marginalized, in their own denomination.

Future Prospects

What will be the future course of Dutch-American theology depends much upon the future course of the community it has guided and served. Here signs are ambiguous. As to factional differentiation, each party now has connections with natural allies in the American Protestant world: the Confessionalists with conservative Presbyterians, Lutherans, and other battlers for the Bible; both types of Kuyperians with "progressive" elements in neo-evangelicalism; the RCA West with mainstream sociopolitical missions in the World Council of Churches. But each group has also returned to Netherlandic models for sustenance: Dort, Dooyeweerd, G. C. Berkouwer, and A. A. van Ruler, respectively.[41] As to communal persistence, the group's theological productivity has never been so high; neither, thanks to televised religion, has its rank and file ever been so open to non-Reformed pieties, programs, and personalities of every sort. As to past issues of debate, common grace—because it was so tied to the question of acculturation—will not likely cause uproar again, although its implications will be detectable. The question of hermeneutics will probably remain central, although less in itself than because of the clashing sociocultural agendas for which it has been both source and legitimation. The outcome of that struggle, finally, lies hidden in the oldest subject of dispute, the will of God, which for these Calvinists must always be the beginning of the matter, and the end.

Notes: The Dutch Schools

1. Foppe M. Ten Hoor, "De Amerikanisatie onzer Kerk," *Gereformeerde Amerikaan* 2 (May-June 1898): 180-87, 206-15. See similarly (all in *Gereformeerde*

Amerikaan) his "Het Engelsch Christendom," 5 (October 1901): 457-63; "Is het Christendom in Strijd met de Rede?" 18 (March 1914): 106-20; and a second series on Americanization, 13 (January-March, May, September 1909).

2. For the background of these documents, see Philip Schaff, ed., *The Creeds of Christendom* (New York: Harper, 1877), 1:502-23, 531-54. The quoted phrase is from Sydney E. Ahlstrom, *A Religious History of the American People* (New Haven: Yale University Press, 1972), 203.

3. For a capsule survey, see Ahlstrom, *Religious History*, 200-204; George L. Smith, *Religion and Trade in New Netherland* (Ithaca: Cornell University Press, 1973), is a detailed study.

4. The best biography is James Tanis, *Dutch Calvinistic Pietism in the Middle Colonies: A Study of the Life and Theology of Theodorus Jacobus Frelinghuysen* (The Hague: Martinus Nijhoff, 1967). See also Herman Harmelink III, "Another Look at Frelinghuysen and His 'Awakening,' " *Church History* 55 (1968): 423-38.

5. These events are presented in close detail in John P. Luidens, "The Americanization of the Dutch Reformed Church" (Ph.D. diss., University of Oklahoma, 1969).

6. Tanis, *Dutch Calvinistic Pietism*, 16-41.

7. F. Ernest Stoeffler, *The Rise of Evangelical Pietism* (Leiden: E. J. Brill, 1967), 116-17, 127-48.

8. On Brakel, ibid., 156-57; on Voetius, see Otto de Jong in A. G. Weiler et al., *Geschiedenis van der Kerk in Nederland* (Utrecht: Aula, 1963), 138-40. Dutch parishioners in America were reading these authorities in the pulpit and in private as final arbiters as late as 1900; see Henry Beets, *De Christelijke Gereformeerde Kerk in Noord Amerika* (Grand Rapids: Grand Rapids Printing Company, 1918), 22-27.

9. The best recent treatment of the Secession in Dutch is H. Algra, *Het Wonder van de 19e Eeuw* (Franeker: T. Wever, 1966). See also James D. Bratt, *Dutch Calvinism in Modern America: A History of a Conservative Subculture* (Grand Rapids: Wm. B. Eerdmans Publishing Company, 1984), 5-10.

10. The relevant data and bibliography on this much discussed issue are available in ibid., 7-10, 227-28. Hereafter, "Dutch" and "Dutch Reformed" have reference to the ethnoreligious community in North America, unless otherwise indicated.

11. Stoeffler gives great detail on the Dutch case vis-à-vis general pietist contours in his *Rise of Evangelical Pietism*, 109-79 and 6-23, respectively.

12. Clarence Bouma, "Ecumenism: Spurious and Genuine," *Calvin Forum* 15 (November 1949): 61-62. For the sources and contours of Dutch theological antiliberalism, see Bratt, *Dutch Calvinism*, 20-22, 127-31, 134.

13. See *Agenda of the Synod of the Christian Reformed Church, 1928*, 4-56.

14. Louis Berkhof, *Manual of Reformed Doctrine* (Grand Rapids: Wm. B. Eerdmans Publishing Company, 1933), 5; this was the one-volume distillation of *Reformed Dogmatics* (Grand Rapids: Wm. B. Eerdmans Publishing Company, 1932), intended for more popular use. For Berkhof's treatment of Scripture, see *Reformed Dogmatics*, 1:14-18, 24-30, 138-79. His broader critique of liberalism is evident in *Aspects of Liberalism* (Grand Rapids: Wm. B. Eerdmans Publishing Company, 1951).

15. Pre-World War I analyses of this sort, directed at "Methodism," are covered in Bratt, *Dutch Calvinism*, 58-60, 248-49; and Henry Zwaanstra, *Reformed Thought and Experience in a New World: A Study of the Christian Reformed Church*

and Its American Environment, 1890-1918 (Kampen: J. H. Kok, 1973), 43-49. For the interwar commentary, see Bratt, *Dutch Calvinism*, 132-34, 273-75.

16. Foppe M. Ten Hoor, "Het Engelsch Christendom," *Gereformeerde Amerikaan* 5 (October 1901): 457-63, and "Is het Christendom in Strijd met de Rede?" *Gereformeerde Amerikaan* 18 (March 1914): 106-20.

17. John E. Kuizenga, "Why We Need a Creed," *Leader*, 22 November 1922, 9.

18. Of very many statements on this point, a few succinct declarations are Clarence Bouma, "How Dead Is Calvinism?" *Calvin Forum* 1 (October 1935): 51-52; Ralph Stob, "Men of Principle," *Banner*, 29 November 1935, 1086; Lewis Smedes, "Evangelicals, What Next?" *Reformed Journal* 19 (November 1969): 4. Exemplary larger works are Bastian Kruithof, *The Christ of the Cosmic Road* (Grand Rapids: Wm. B. Eerdmans Publishing Company, 1937); and Henry Zylstra, *Testament of Vision* (Grand Rapids: Wm. B. Eerdmans Publishing Company, 1956).

19. A fine, brief introduction to Kuyper in English is Dirk Jellema, "Abraham Kuyper's Attack on Liberalism," *Review of Politics* 19 (October 1957): 472-85; see also Bratt, *Dutch Calvinism*, 14-33. An excellent sketch in Dutch is Jan Romein, "Abraham Kuyper: De Klokkenist der Kleine Luyden," in *Erflaters van onze Beschaving* (Amsterdam: Queridos, 1971). Three representative works of Kuyper in English translation are *Lectures on Calvinism* (Grand Rapids: Wm. B. Eerdmans Publishing Company, 1961 [1898]), *Christianity and the Class Struggle* (Grand Rapids: Piet Hein, 1950 [1891]), and *To Be Near Unto God* (Grand Rapids: Wm. B. Eerdmans Publishing Company, 1924).

20. See J. C. Rullman's precis of Kuyper's fullest elaboration of the doctrine of the covenant (*De Leer der Verbonden* [Amsterdam, 1885]), in *Kuyper-Bibliographie* (Kampen: J. H. Kok, 1940), 3:251.

21. This material is more fully elaborated in James D. Bratt, "The Covenant Traditions of Dutch Americans," in Daniel Elazar and John Kincaid, eds., *The Covenant Connection: Federal Theology and the Origins of Modern Politics* (Carolina Academic Press, forthcoming). Primary works from three different eras are John Van Lonkhuyzen, *Heilig Zaad* (Grand Rapids: n.p., 1916), 3; William Hendriksen, *The Covenant of Grace* (Grand Rapids: Wm. B. Eerdmans Publishing Company, 1932), 12-13; and Andrew Kuyvenhoven, *Partnership: A Study of the Covenant* (Grand Rapids: Board of Publications, CRC, 1974). Secondary analyses of these themes are conveniently available in Peter De Klerk and Richard R. De Ridder, eds., *Perspectives on the Christian Reformed Church* (Grand Rapids: Baker Book House, 1983): Anthony A. Hoekema, "The Christian Reformed Church and the Covenant," 185-201; and Fred H. Klooster, "The Kingdom of God in the History of the Christian Reformed Church," 203-24.

22. Hendriksen, *Covenant of Grace*, 65.

23. Bratt, *Dutch Calvinism*, 107, 128-29. Names and statistics of CRC leaders attending "old Princeton" are available on p. 270, n. 21. Dutch-related members of the Westminster Seminary faculty were R. B. Kuiper, Ned B. Stonehouse, and Cornelius Van Til.

24. George M. Marsden, *Fundamentalism and American Culture: The Shaping of Twentieth Century Evangelicalism, 1870-1925* (New York: Oxford University Press, 1980), 114-16, gives a succinct comparison. Much greater detail, from the Kuyperian point of view, is available in John Vander Stelt, *Philosophy and Scripture: A Study in Old Princeton and Westminster Theology* (Marlton, NJ: Mack Publishing Company, 1978).

25. Marsden, *Fundamentalism and American Culture*, 115.

26. Jack B. Rogers and Donald K. McKim, *The Authority and Interpretation of the Bible: An Historical Approach* (New York: Harper and Row, 1979); the Dutch theologians concerned are Gerrit C. Berkouwer and, through him, Herman Bavinck, Kuyper's contemporary in Amsterdam. A critical assessment of this connection is Richard B. Gaffin, Jr., "Old Amsterdam and Inerrancy?" *Westminster Theological Journal* 44 (1982): 250-89, and 45 (1983): 219-72.

27. A review from the RCA side is William Van Eyck, *Landmarks of the Reformed Fathers* (Grand Rapids: Wm. B. Eerdmans Publishing Company, 1922); from the CRC side, Henry Beets, *De Christelijke Gereformeerde Kerk in Noord Amerika*, 66-120. Valuable statistical and social scientific analyses of the first schism are available in Robert P. Swierenga, "Local-Cosmopolitan Theory and Immigrant Religion: The Social Bases of the Antebellum Dutch Reformed Schism," *Journal of Social History* 14 (Fall 1980): 113-35, esp. 123.

28. Swierenga, "Local-Cosmopolitan Theory," 123, 130.

29. Herman Harmelink III, *Ecumenism and the Reformed Church* (Grand Rapids: Wm. B. Eerdmans Publishing Company, 1968), illustrates, directly and indirectly, all three of these points.

30. This mentality in the CRC is presented in great detail for the 1890-1918 era in Zwaanstra, *Reformed Thought and Experience*, 70-95; over the longer run in Bratt, *Dutch Calvinism*, 47-50, 125-41, 190-95, 207-10. On the RCA side, ibid., 125, 135-37, 197-99, 205-06.

31. The journal was the *Calvin Forum*; for its views, see Bratt, *Dutch Calvinism*, 126, 142-56.

32. Ibid., 46-49. Exemplary statements on the infra side are Foppe M. Ten Hoor, "Principieele Bezwaren," *Gereformeerde Amerikaan* 9 (May and August 1905); Lammert J. Hulst and Gerrit K. Hemkes, *Oud- en Nieuwe-Calvinisme* (Grand Rapids: Eerdmans-Sevensma, 1913). On the supra side, John Van Lonkhuyzen, *Heilig Zaad*, and Richard Gaffin, ed., *Redemptive History and Biblical Interpretation: The Shorter Writings of Geerhardus Vos*, 231ff., 240-47, 263ff.

33. On this, the so-called "Dekker" case (after its protagonist, Harold Dekker, Professor of Missions at Calvin Seminary), see Dekker's articles in the *Reformed Journal*, December 1962-March 1963, and those of James Daane and Harry Boer in the same periodical, October 1964-March 1965. The opposition's case was best made by R. B. Kuiper in *God-Centered Evangelism* (Grand Rapids: Baker Book House, 1957), and "Professor Dekker on God's Universal Love," *Torch and Trumpet* 13 (March 1963): 4-9. For the Synodical debate, see *Acts of Synod of the CRC, 1967*, 486-607, 727-38.

34. For the final statement, known as "Report 44," see *Acts of Synod of the CRC, 1972*, 493-546.

35. This principle and its implications are dramatically presented in John A. Olthuis et al., *Out of Concern for the Church* (Toronto: Wedge Publishing Company, 1970). The Confessionalist response is John Vander Ploeg, "One 'Word of God' or Three?" *Outlook* 22 (February 1972): 5-8.

36. Bratt, *Dutch Calvinism*, 18-20; Simon J. Ridderbos, *De Theologische-Cultuurbeschouwing van Abraham Kuyper* (Kampen: J. H. Kok, 1947), 30-131, 233-57.

37. Bratt, *Dutch Calvinism*, 50-54; Zwaanstra, *Reformed Thought and Experience*, 95-131.

38. Bratt, *Dutch Calvinism*, 105-10, presents a review of the case and its literature.

39. Ibid., 110-15. Whereas Janssen went into exile as a broker in Chicago,

Hoeksema and Danhof started their own denomination, the Protestant Reformed Church.

40. Ibid., 190-96. The principals' major statements on the issue were: Cornelius Van Til, *Common Grace* (Philadelphia: Presbyterian and Reformed Publishing Company, 1947); H. Evan Runner, "Het Roer Om!" *Torch and Trumpet* 3 (April 1953): 1-4, and a series in the same journal, April-October 1955; William Masselink, *General Revelation and Common Grace* (Grand Rapids: Wm. B. Eerdmans Publishing Company, 1953); and James Daane, *A Theology of Grace* (Grand Rapids: Wm. B. Eerdmans Publishing Company, 1954).

To put all these debates in chronological order:

1) RCA-CRC split, 1857 and 1880-1882.
2) Supra-Infra debate, 1890-1905.
3) Common grace I (Janssen and Hoeksema cases), 1918-1924.
4) Common grace II, 1950-1960.
5) "Dekker case" (limited atonement), 1962-1967; leading on to "Report 44" debate (nature and authority of Scripture), 1969-1972.

41. On the role of Dooyeweerd and Berkouwer, see nn. 35 and 26 above, respectively. On the example of Dort, see, e.g., Peter Y. De Jong, ed., *Crisis in the Reformed Churches: Essays in Commemoration of the Great Synod of Dort, 1618-1619* (Grand Rapids: Reformed Fellowship, 1968). On A. A. van Ruler, see the special issue of *Reformed Review* devoted to him: 26 (Winter 1973).

LOUIS BERKHOF

HENRY ZWAANSTRA

DURING the period prior to the First World War, the Christian Reformed Church was self-consciously and openly Dutch-American. As hyphenated Americans, members and leaders in the Christian Reformed Church were preoccupied with Americanization. Being deeply committed to their Dutch Reformed theological and churchly heritage, they strenuously sought to resist the intrusion of American religious ideas and practices that would detract from or otherwise endanger their inherited tradition. Yet they were Americans convinced that they had a special task and calling in America. Louis Berkhof belonged to this generation. He was thoroughly bilingual, capable of expressing himself with equal facility in either Dutch or English. He was also deeply committed to preserving the Dutch Reformed theological tradition in the Christian Reformed Church. This tradition, properly preserved and represented, he believed was relevant for American thought and life.

Early in the twentieth century, the climate of theological opinion in America was not particularly conducive to dogmatic theology nor cordial to historic Reformed theology and Calvinism. The intellectual spirit of the age promoted the rise and progress of liberal theology and the Social Gospel. At the same time it provoked a conservative reaction that took the form of Fundamentalism. Louis Berkhof did his theological reflection and work in this environment. Before he concluded his career, Neoorthodoxy or Crisis Theology appeared on the American scene. He interacted with this theology, too, in its initial stages.

Louis Berkhof's life and work were immersed in the Christian Reformed Church. To it he devoted his time and energy. He served the Christian Reformed Church briefly as a pastor and preacher. For 38 years he was a professor of theology. During the last 13 of these years, he was also the president of Calvin Theological Seminary. He regularly served as an advisor to Christian Reformed Church synods. Being a gifted public speaker, Berkhof frequently addressed convocations and audiences.

It was, however, as a writer that he made his greatest and most enduring contribution to the Christian Reformed Church.

Being a person with broad interests, Berkhof wrote on many subjects. In addition to the theological works for which he is best known, he addressed social issues and problems, modern trends of thought, and such matters as Christian education, evangelism, missions, and the spiritual life. He was a contributor to periodicals widely read within the Christian Reformed Church such as *De Gereformeerde Amerikaan* (The Reformed American) and the *Calvin Forum*. He also regularly wrote series of articles in the denominational weeklies, *The Banner* and *De Wachter*. Berkhof's impact on the American theological world and the theological world at large was an uncalculated and unanticipated result of the favorable reception of his publications in systematic theology.

Formative Years: 1873-1906

Louis Berkhof was born on October 13, 1873, in Emmen, Drenthe, The Netherlands. His parents, Jan and Geesje (ter Poorten) Berkhof, were members of the Christelijke Gereformeerde Kerk (Christian Reformed Church). This church came into existence as a result of a secession from the Nederlands Hervormde Kerk (Netherlands Reformed Church) or state church in 1834. The Berkhofs' religious life, like that of most members of the churches of the Secession of 1834, consisted of deep and simple piety fused with devotion to the Reformed faith articulated in the historic confessions of the Reformed churches in The Netherlands. In 1882, when Louis was 8 years old, the Berkhof family emigrated to the United States, settling in Grand Rapids, Michigan.

At this time the Neo-Calvinist movement in The Netherlands under the leadership of Dr. Abraham Kuyper was already well underway. Kuyper was a man of extraordinary genius and deep personal piety. In addition to leading a second secession from The Netherlands Reformed Church in 1886 called the "Doleantie," Kuyper was the founder of the Free University of Amsterdam (1880) and its first professor in dogmatics. He was instrumental in bringing into existence a Christian school system from the elementary to the university level. He greatly advanced the cause of separate Christian labor organizations and succeeded in making the Anti-Revolutionary political party founded by Groen van Prinsterer into an effective Christian political force. For many years Kuyper served in the Dutch Parliament and was twice elected Prime Minister. The churches of the secessions of 1834 and 1886 united in 1892 to form De Gereformeerde Kerken in Nederland (The Reformed Churches in The Netherlands). The Neo-Calvinist movement, the Kuyperian ideas that inspired it, and the impact it made on social, political, and church life in The Netherlands all exercised considerable formative influence on the Christian Reformed Church in America and on the life and thought of Louis Berkhof.

When Louis was a teenager, he was an active member (secretary) of the first Reformed Young Men's Society organized in Grand Rapids, Michigan.[1] The society's purpose was to study Reformed doctrine and the principles of Calvinism for all areas of human life. Later Berkhof was reported to have said that he owed more to the young men's society than he would ever be able to repay. In that society he learned to study and express himself. There he also began to realize that God had given him some talents for labor in his kingdom. And there, he said, the desire to serve God in the ministry was awakened and began to ripen.[2] Berkhof was one of the first to urge the local society to organize on a denominational scale. The American Federation of Reformed Young Men's Societies soon came into existence. For many years Berkhof's book, *Subjects and Outlines*, specially prepared for the American Federation in 1918, was used as a study guide. The work covered a wide range of subjects: Bible History, Reformed Doctrine, General and American Church History, and various educational, social, and political issues. It concluded with a long list of resolutions for debate. After becoming a theological professor, Berkhof continued to show his loyalty to the organization and to repay the debt he owed to it by serving no less than 15 years on its Executive Board.[3]

Sometime in 1893 Berkhof publicly professed his faith in Christ in the Alpine Avenue Christian Reformed Church. In September of that year at the age of 19, he enrolled in the Theological School of the Christian Reformed Church. At the time the Theological School consisted of two parts, a literary department with a four-year course of study and a theological department with a three-year program of study. The literary department was gradually expanded into Calvin College and the theological department later became Calvin Theological Seminary.

In the spring of 1893 the Theological School sustained a severe loss when the youthful, brilliant, and much-loved professor of dogmatics and exegetical theology, Geerhardus Vos, accepted an appointment to teach biblical theology at Princeton Seminary.[4] Vos did, however, leave his reputation and unpublished lectures in dogmatics behind. Berkhof heard about the former; the latter he undoubtedly used.

Hendericus Beuker was Berkhof's teacher in dogmatics. Beuker was a graduate of the Theological School of the Christelijke Gereformeerde Kerk in Kampen, The Netherlands. After distinguishing himself as a capable pastor and churchman in The Netherlands, he emigrated to America in 1893. The following year he was appointed to teach dogmatics. Beuker's intellectual gifts were certainly adequate to the task. He was a severe critic of the German liberal theology and higher criticism of the day. Although himself an infralapsarian, he respected Kuyper for his scholarly work and appreciated the counterforce Kuyper posed to the "fearfully destructive hurricanes" coming out of the German universities.[5] Beuker was most favorably impressed with the theological thought and erudition of Herman Bavinck. When the first volume of Bavinck's *Gereformeerde Dogmatiek* (Reformed Dogmatics) appeared, Beuker judged it a fundamental contribution to theological science and a great blessing for the Reformed churches.[6] Early in 1900, the same year Berkhof graduated from the Theological School, Beuker died. Foppe M. Ten Hoor began teaching dogmatics in the fall of that year and continued to do so until retirement in 1924.

On September 16, 1900, Louis Berkhof was ordained to the ministry in the Christian Reformed Church in Allendale, Michigan. Less than two years later, his name was included in a list of potential candidates for appointment to a new chair in exegetical theology. The appointment, however, went to Roelof Janssen, a relatively unknown quantity in the Christian Reformed Church except for the fact that he held a Ph.D. degree from the University of Halle in Germany and was studying at Kampen. Janssen's advanced degree, even though it was not in theology, influenced the outcome of the synod's decision.[7] Berkhof decided to seek more formal education.

From 1902 to 1904 Berkhof studied at Princeton Seminary, a bastion of Reformed orthodoxy. There he came under the tutelage of Benjamin Warfield and Geerhardus Vos. Both men were staunch defenders of Reformed confessional orthodoxy and the authority of Holy Scripture, including verbal infallibility and inerrancy. H. Henry Meeter, professor of Bible at Calvin College and for many years a close personal friend of Berkhof, reported that Berkhof frequently said that he owed more to Vos than anyone else for his insights into Reformed theology.[8] Princeton awarded Berkhof the Bachelor of Divinity degree.

In August 1904, Berkhof was installed as minister of the Oakdale Park Christian Reformed Church in Grand Rapids, Michigan. There he quickly established a reputation for his insights into Scripture, carefully crafted sermons, and gifts in public speaking.[9] In addition to his work in the congregation, Berkhof promoted the cause of Christian education in the denomination with a pamphlet published in 1905, *Het Christelijk Onderwijs en Onze Kerkelijke Toekomst* (Christian Education and the Future of Our Church). While at Oakdale Park he also took some courses, chiefly in philosophy, by correspondence through the University of Chicago.

The Board of Trustees did not recommend Janssen for reappointment in 1906. Unresolved conflicts had arisen between him and Ten Hoor regarding the authority of the church in the study of theology. Furthermore, some members of the board were convinced that Janssen's teaching unmistakably leaned toward higher criticism.[10] In the absence of a recommendation from the board, the synod prepared a nomination for exegetical theology. Berkhof, the vice president of the synod, was included in the nomination and later chosen by a large majority to fill the vacant chair.[11]

Professor of Exegetical Theology and New Testament Studies: 1906-1924

On September 5, 1906, in the Commerce Street Christian Reformed Church, Louis Berkhof was installed as professor of exegetical theology. The same evening he delivered an inaugural address in the Dutch language entitled "De Verklaring der Heilige Schrift" (The Exposition of the Holy Scriptures). It was a noteworthy occasion and address. Berkhof argued that the correct interpretation of Scripture was contingent on a proper understanding of the Scriptures' peculiar character as the Word of God. He then proceeded to indicate how Scripture itself was threatened by many dangers such as higher criticism, liberal theology, modern biblical theology, and recent historical and archaeological discoveries. He concluded by emphasizing the great importance of the view of Scripture and its interpretation that he presented for ministers of the Word.[12]

From 1906 to 1914 Berkhof taught all the Old Testament and New Testament courses offered at Calvin Seminary: Hebrew, New Testament Greek, Old Testament and New Testament Exegesis, Introduction to the Old Testament and New Testament, and Old Testament and New Testament History.

In 1911 he published in the Dutch language a textbook on biblical hermeneutics.[13] In comparison with recent hermeneutical studies, Berkhof's treatment was simple and unsophisticated. In a manner that was to become characteristic of Berkhof, he first dealt with the task and history of the science of biblical interpretation, and then elaborated the essentials of the grammatical-historical theological method. In 1937, this work, only slightly edited, was published for the use of English-speaking students under the title *Principles of Biblical Interpretation*. During the time Berkhof taught both Old and New Testament he published only one special study, a pamphlet on the book of Joshua, *Life Under the Law in a Pure Theocracy* (1914).

In spite of his heavy teaching load and the breadth of his assignment, Berkhof did not neglect the pressing social issues and problems agitating the American church world and the Christian Reformed Church. For the benefit of the Dutch-American members of the Christian Reformed Church, Berkhof wrote *Christendom en Level* (Christianity and Life). As the title suggests, the work dealt with a wide range of issues pertaining to Christianity and culture. It also specifically addressed needs confronting Reformed people of Dutch ancestry as they faced the American world. Published in 1912, the book was described in *De Wachter* as one in which lines were drawn, fundamentals laid out, and valuable counsel given.[14]

The following year Berkhof wrote *The Church and Social Problems*. This was his first English-language publication. The pamphlet better than any other single source illustrates the breadth of Berkhof's interests and sympathies, his knowledge of contemporary American theological literature, his capacity for balanced judgment, and his ability to engage discursively and critically in theological issues and problems. In this work Berkhof gives a strikingly different impression from that presented in his textbooks on theology.

Berkhof proceeded on the assumption that the gospel of Jesus Christ was the greatest liberating force in the world, eminently applicable to the pressing social problems of the age. After briefly outlining the nature of the present social problem including quotations without additional critical comment from such works as Walter Rauschenbusch's *Christianity and the Social Crisis* and Josiah Strong's *The Challenge of the City*, Berkhof surveyed the history of the church's role in the existing social crisis. He acknowledged that the church itself contributed to the crisis and that many of the charges being brought against the church for social negligence, such as aiming at the salvation of the individual only while showing little concern for the regeneration of society, and preaching a one-sided "other-worldly" gospel that did not touch the realities of life, were true. The church definitely had social duties and responsibilities that were not being met.[15]

Berkhof thought the church, both as a spiritual fellowship of believers and as an organization, had a task in the movement for social reform. Natural and spiritual life could not be neatly compartmentalized, nor could the responsibilities for human life simply be parceled out so that the church as an institution found its duty only in the spiritual sphere. The church as an organization also had a role to play in social reforms. After emphasizing that the church should be a nursery for true, healthy, and vigorous spiritual life, Berkhof forthrightly asserted that the church should never forget the social message entrusted to it. The church was God's chosen instrument not only to save individuals and to prepare them for eternal life, but also to implement as much as possible the Kingdom of God on earth. The Bible contained many directives for social life, revealed principles that should control social reform, and offered the only final solution to social problems. Ministers of the gospel should fearlessly and clearly proclaim the broad principles underlying social life. The church also should exemplify in its own social life the social principles for which it stood in addition to bringing the gospel to the masses in the great cities of the nation. The church, he said, ought to make a thorough study of the present social problems and of the various movements working for social improvement. In conclusion Berkhof sounded the separatistic note characteristic of many Kuyperian Calvinists calling Christians to organize on a distinctively and positively Christian basis for social and philanthropic action.[16]

In 1914 the synod decided to divide exegetical theology into Old Testament and New Testament departments. Berkhof was given the assignment in New Testament. In spite of previous difficulties with Roelof Janssen, the synod by a sizable majority elected him to teach Old Testament.[17]

A reduced teaching load and a more narrowly circumscribed area of research enabled Berkhof to put his pen to work. In 1915 he wrote *Biblical Archaeology*, a study in the history and cultures of the Ancient Near East, and *Introduction to the New Testament*. *The Christian Laborer in the Industrial Struggle* appeared the following year. Although this pamphlet exhibited the same learned qualities as his earlier address on social issues, its focus was more limited and its purpose more parochial. Berkhof wrote to persuade the Christian Reformed Church of the incompatibility of membership in religiously neutral labor organizations and membership in the church of Christ.[18]

In the midst of the international turmoil and upheavals occasioned by the First World War, Henry Bultema, pastor of the First Christian Reformed Church in Muskegon, Michigan, published *Maranatha*.[19] The central thesis of Bultema's book was that the unfulfilled prophecies in the Bible should be interpreted literally just like those that have already been fulfilled. Bultema also attempted to defend chiliastic and premillennial views. *Maranatha* provoked an immediate response in the Christian Reformed Church. Berkhof was asked to speak on the subject. He did so in English. At the request of friends and because of the urgency of the matter, Berkhof had his address published in edited and expanded form in Dutch.[20] In April 1918 *Premillennialisme: Zijn Schrifttuurliche Basis en Enkele van Zijn Practische Gevolgtrekkingen* (Premillennialism: Its Scriptural Basis and Some of Its Practical Consequences) appeared. Berkhof cordially and judiciously refrained from mentioning Bultema in the text. In the notes Bultema and *Maranatha* appear along with other American premillennialists and their works.

After expressing great respect for the premillennialists' unconditional acceptance of the Bible as the Word of God and for the warmth of their devotion to Scripture, a striking contrast to the "icebergs of higher criticism," Berkhof proceeded to elaborate four objections to their views. Berkhof's first and most fundamental objection was to the premillennialists' mistaken insistence on a strictly literal interpretation of the prophetic writings. According to Berkhof the historic Christian church in its exegesis of prophecy self-consciously accepted and applied a different hermeneutical principle from that of the premillennialists. Those holding premillennial views did not deal adequately with the progressive and historical character of God's revelation. Berkhof insisted that the historical form in which a prophecy was given belonged to the essence of the prophecy and that it was proper to make a distinction between a literal historical explanation of a prophecy and its fulfillment. Berkhof also criticized the premillennialists for not interpreting Scripture according to the analogy of Scripture. In this respect they were following a practice wholly in agreement with modern, liberal exegetes. Berkhof further stated that Revelation 20:4-6 should also be interpreted according to the analogy of the New Testament. The Dutch theologians Kuyper, Bavinck, Greydanus, and Hoekstra so interpreted the text, as did Warfield, Vos, Milligan, and Eckman. And finally Berkhof asserted that by insisting on a literal fulfillment of prophecy the premillennialists got involved in all kinds of contradictions and bound God in fulfilling prophecies to conditions and situations that existed when the predictions were first given.[21]

Berkhof's second objection to premillennialism focused on the thousand-year kingdom of Christ and the doctrine of the second resurrection. After a rather extensive treatment of the texts appealed to in support of the doctrines, Berkhof concluded that the scriptural basis for both was very weak.[22]

Thirdly, Berkhof objected to the premillennialists' absolute separation of Israel and the church. The separation resulted in a denial of the spiritual unity between them. Berkhof argued that this separation and denial destroyed the unity of God's revelation, conflicted with the organic nature of his redemptive work, negated the salvation of humanity in Jesus Christ, and robbed the church of Christ of the blessings of the covenant.[23]

Finally, Berkhof objected to the premillennialists' customary use of the distinction between the Kingdom and the church in the New Testament. Again they separated the two so that Christ's present kingship was denied. Quoting Vos, Berkhof argued that the church is a form that the Kingdom takes after Christ's death and resurrection. He concluded by saying that the Kingdom is a present reality, its subjects are united with Christ in the church, and Christ is now really king.[24]

The synod agreed with Berkhof. Bultema and *Maranatha* were tested strictly by the standards of Reformed confessional orthodoxy and found wanting for separating Israel and the church, and the church and the

Kingdom, thus denying the spiritual unity between Israel and the church and the present kingship of Christ. Bultema was later deposed. He and his followers formed the Berean Church.[25]

In 1919 Louis Berkhof and three of his colleagues, William Heyns, Foppe Ten Hoor, and Samuel Volbeda, sent a letter to the Board of Trustees informing the board that student reactions to Janssen's teaching "irresistibly" raised the question whether or not Janssen was doing an injustice to the authority, infallibility, and trustworthiness of Holy Scripture.[26] The four professors did this without previously talking to Janssen. A bitter and heated controversy resulted. On the basis of student notes the four professors contended that Janssen denied the Mosaic authorship of the Pentateuch, the historicity of miracles recorded in the Bible, and the messianic significance of certain passages of the Old Testament. Janssen's explanation of many other Old Testament passages was also objectionable.[27] In the professors' judgment the Reformed doctrine of the inspiration, authority, infallibility, and trustworthiness of Scripture was threatened.[28] Given the rationalistic principles undergirding Janssen's approach, the professors predicted that his teaching, if allowed to continue, would certainly lead to a surrender of the authority of Scripture to modern critical science and a denial of Scripture as a divine redemptive revelation. It would also rob members of Christian Reformed congregations of their infallible rule for faith and life and the denomination of its Reformed distinctiveness, causing it to sink away into the watered-down Christianity so evident in the American world.[29]

Janssen replied to the four professors. In his reply he stated that all science including theology has for its aim the discovery of truth. In the quest for truth the empirical approach could not be avoided; thus all theological investigation, in the nature of the case, had to be critical. Janssen further affirmed that his scientific work rested on the presupposition that Scripture was God's infallible revelation. Nevertheless, in interpreting Scripture Scripture itself should be allowed to speak. The interpreter should not allow his presuppositions to determine the meaning of the text. Scripture stood above dogmatics and the latter should not be permitted to control the former. The meaning of Scripture, therefore, should not be a foregone conclusion. According to Janssen the Dutch Reformed theologians Kuyper, Bavinck, Aalders, and Grosheide agreed with this position.[30]

Janssen refused to appear at the synod where the matter was to be adjudicated because many of his accusers were also delegated to synod and in his judgment it was unfair for them to operate at the same time as plaintiffs and judges.[31] On the basis of the student notes, the synod found Janssen's point of view and method deficient because he did not give faith the role it deserved in theological science and because he did not allow the Bible as the divinely inspired Word of God to predetermine his conclusions. The synod also criticized him for subjectifying special revelation. Although the synod was careful not to charge Janssen with denying the inspiration of Scripture, it said that elements in his teaching could not be harmonized with the Reformed understanding of inspiration. The synod deposed Janssen from office.[32] Since Janssen had no following in the church, a schism did not result. A few younger ministers did, however, leave the church due to their unhappiness with the synodical procedures and the deposition.[33]

During the years of the Janssen controversy, Louis Berkhof's reputation as a theologian and churchman accelerated both inside and outside the Christian Reformed Church. In 1919 Berkhof was offered the presidency of Calvin College.[34] Three years later he was asked to become the editor of De Wachter.[35] Berkhof declined both appointments. During the 1920-21 academic year, Berkhof was invited to give the Stone Lectures at Princeton Seminary. He spoke on "The Kingdom of God in Modern Thought and Life."

In 1924 the Christian Reformed Church was again embroiled in theological controversy. The issue this time was common grace. Two capable and popular ministers, Herman Hoeksema and Henry Danhof, had written and spoken against the doctrine. Berkhof did not get directly involved in the dispute before the meeting of synod. In adjudicating the matter the synod officially declared three points: (1) the existence of a general or common grace of God shown to all men, (2) the restraint of sin by the general work of the Holy Spirit, and (3) the ability of the unregenerate to perform civic righteousness.[36] Disciplinary measures against the ministers who opposed the doctrine of common grace and the synodical decisions led to a schism of some proportion and to the formation of the Protestant Reformed Church. The following year, when protests and appeals were still pending, Berkhof entered the controversy with De Drie Punten in Alle Deelen Gereformeerd (The Three Points in All Parts Reformed). In 1926 the synod did not sustain the protests and appeals of the opponents of the three points.

Professor of Systematic Theology and President of Calvin Seminary: 1926-1944

After teaching dogmatics in the Dutch language for 24 years, Foppe Ten Hoor retired in 1924. Although the synod considered shifting Berkhof from New Testament studies to dogmatics, it decided instead to appoint Dr. Clarence Bouma as professor of dogmatics.[37] Two years later, the synod decided to separate apologetics and ethics from dogmatics. Bouma chose the former areas of theology, thus creating a vacancy in the latter. That Berkhof aspired to teach dogmatics was common knowledge in the church.[38] In the judgment of some his work on the "Three Points" clearly demonstrated an ability to do so.[39] Berkhof's interest went beyond a simple personal predilection. He considered biblical studies in some respects preparatory to the science of dogmatics, which made use of the fruits of biblical theology.[40] The synod complied with many interests and desires and appointed Louis Berkhof professor of dogmatic theology.[41]

After 1926 the turbulent storms of theological controversy in the Christian Reformed Church subsided never to return again with the same intensity during Berkhof's lifetime. The church had purged itself of premillennialism, the threat of free scientific inquiry and biblical criticism, and the danger of too narrow a conception of the operation of the Holy Spirit in human cultural life. With the retirement of Ten Hoor, the last vestige of enthusiastic infralapsarianism also disappeared.[42] An amazing theological consensus, basically conservative and deeply rooted in traditional Reformed confessional orthodoxy, resulted. In this general climate of theological opinion, and in harmony with it, Berkhof engaged in theological research, reflection, teaching, and writing.

During the first years that he taught dogmatics, Berkhof concentrated on research and teaching. He produced a special doctrinal study, *The Assurance of Faith*, in 1928. In 1931 the Board of Trustees decided to discontinue the annual rotating Rectorship at Calvin Seminary and to appoint a more permanent administrative head. Berkhof was a logical choice. He had frequently functioned as the spokesman for the faculty and had during the present academic year served very capably as Rector. Moreover, he enjoyed the confidence of the church and the respect of the students. The board elected Louis Berkhof the first President of Calvin Seminary, a position he held concomitantly with his professorship for 13 years.[43]

On September 9, 1931, a celebration was held commemorating Berkhof's 25th anniversary as professor of theology. On the same festive occasion he was installed as president of Calvin Seminary. Berkhof delivered an inaugural address entitled "Our Seminary and the Modern Spirit." The address is noteworthy in that it clearly indicated the content and direction of his thinking. In the speech Berkhof also commented on the specific purpose and task of Calvin Seminary. He began by putting the subject in historical perspective. During the previous century the modern scientific method and the theological thought of Schleiermacher made an impact on theological education. The Social Gospel also produced an increased emphasis on applied Christianity. As a result of these new directions seminaries were now breaking away from church control, and, under the banner of intellectual freedom, were loosing themselves from the authority of God's Word. A clearly discernible shift from dogmatics to practical theology and from church-centered to social-centered interests was also evident. Berkhof said that Calvin Seminary had not adapted itself in the past to these new directions and that it would not in the future accommodate itself to any changes that would compromise its stand on the Word of God and on the confessional standards of the church. Calvin Seminary did not recognize erring human reason as a source of divine truth and would not permit it to stand in judgment on the Word of God. The seminary would continue to honor the supernatural and would refuse to submit to present-day liberalism, which was bound to degenerate into pure naturalism. Speaking in the first person Berkhof said, "We accept the Reformed system of truth which was handed down to us by previous generations, attempt to exhibit it in all its comprehensiveness and in all its beauty and logical consistency, seek to defend it against all opposing systems, and endeavor to carry it forward to still greater perfection in harmony with the structural lines that were clearly indicated in its past development."[44]

As a professor of systematic theology, Berkhof believed his primary task was to present scriptural truth comprehensively and in logical order and to do so in a manner compatible with historical Reformed theology. He further sought to illuminate Reformed thought by contrasting it with what he considered aberrant doctrinal positions. In treating a doctrine, Berkhof ordinarily defined and presented the Reformed view, commented briefly on the history of the doctrine, then indicated the scriptural basis for the Reformed position, and finally discussed and critiqued alternative views. His basic criticism of Roman Catholic theology was that it made the hierarchical church the source of and authority for dogma. His sharpest barbs were, however, directed at modern liberal theology. This school of thought reduced theology to anthropology or to the mere study of religion. In Berkhof's judgment the modern psychological, sociological, and philosophical approaches to religion could never satisfy the demands for genuine theological inquiry and statement. Wherever appropriate he summarized and commented critically on the theologies of Schleiermacher and Ritschl. Berkhof's treatment of contemporary neoorthodoxy and neoorthodox theologians such as Barth, Brunner, and Niebuhr was brief, but not without penetrating insight. He appreciated their criticism of modern liberalism, their consciousness of the broken human condition, and their emphasis on the necessity of special revelation and the grace of God for salvation. He did not, however, agree with their basic theological position, and the strictures they placed on Reformation theology. Consequently he sincerely doubted that their thought represented historic Calvinism.[45]

According to Berkhof the object of investigation in theology was the knowledge of God as he revealed himself in Holy Scripture. Although it is impossible for man to know God as God knows himself, God could be known because and insofar as he revealed himself. In a somewhat Hegelian manner, Berkhof asserted that the knowledge of God formed the content of special revelation. Special revelation itself was an unfolding of the knowledge of God and the redemptive idea in Christ Jesus.[46] Although strictly speaking special revelation was broader than Holy Scripture, practically and concretely special revelation was synonymous with Scripture. Consequently Holy Scripture was the sole source for the subject matter of dogmatic theology. It was also the only authoritative norm or standard for judging the truth formulated and affirmed in theology.[47]

In Berkhof's judgment Reformed systematic theology was a scientific enterprise.[48] Holy Scripture contained truths in the form of facts and ideas, but it did not present a logical system that could simply be copied. The Bible, however, did itself suggest that the truths it presented were interrelated. God also saw truth as a unit and the truth revealed in the Word of God was an organic whole. Moreover, man as a rational creature had an irrepressible urge to comprehend truth in its unity. The peculiar task, therefore, of the systematic theologian was to think God's thoughts after him under the guidance of the Holy Spirit, to assimilate comprehensively the truth revealed in the Word of God, and to reproduce it logically in systematic form. Although Berkhof strenuously rejected the use of speculative reason as a source and norm of theological truth, he affirmed the proper and necessary function of reason for uniting the particular ideas and facts contained in the Word of God and for organizing them into a coherent system of truth. Reason should not, however, be permitted to function independently of faith. In theological science faith corresponded with the revealed knowledge of God and served as the necessary instrument within man for appropriating divine truth. In brief, faith appropriated revealed truth, reason organized and systematized it.[49]

And finally, according to Berkhof, Reformed dogmatic theology was an ecclesiastical affair. The church as a whole under the guidance of the Holy Spirit engages in the reflective activity that produces dogma. When the church collectively reflects on the truth of God's Word, this truth takes definite shape in the consciousness of the church and is formulated in clearly defined doctrines. Although Scripture always remains the source, norm, and final test for all dogmatic truth, the creeds and confessions of the church provide a nucleus of subject matter for dogmatic theology. Berkhof insisted that the theologian is always the theologian of a particular church. He receives the truth in the fellowship of the church, shares the church's convictions regarding it, and promises to teach in harmony with it as long as the church's understanding of the truth is not contrary to the Word of God.[50]

A surprising number of systematic theologians met Berkhof's basic criteria. He approved the works of the American theologians Robert Breckinridge, James H. Thornwell, Robert L. Dabney, Charles Hodge, Archibald A. Hodge, William G. Shedd, Henry B. Smith, Benjamin B. Warfield, and John L. Giradeau. He much preferred, however, the writings of the Dutch Reformed theologians Kuyper and Bavinck.[51]

Berkhof's major writings in systematic theology grew out of his classroom work and as textbooks were intended to meet the needs of students who could no longer read Kuyper and Bavinck. His *magnum opus, Systematic Theology,* was first published in two volumes in 1932 with the title *Reformed Dogmatics.* Later the same year the *Introductory Volume to Reformed Dogmatics* appeared in print. A revised and enlarged edition of *Reformed Dogmatics* was published in one volume in 1941 with the title *Systematic Theology.* Again, Berkhof revised the introductory volume and, in order to bring it in line with the major work, he renamed it *Introductory Volume to Systematic Theology.* Berkhof did not make a case for the change in titles except to say that it seemed better in America to use the title "Systematic Theology." He also called attention to the fact that even Warfield had defended the title.[52] To complete the textbook series in systematic theology, Berkhof in 1937 wrote a brief but comprehensive *History of Christian Doctrines.* Berkhof's book indicates that he was acquainted with a large body of literature on the subject including the works of Harnack, Loofs, Seeberg, and Newman. In it he descriptively presented the history of Christian doctrine in an orderly, nonjudgmental way. To assist students in their study of systematic theology, Berkhof's *Textual Aid to Systematic Theology* was published in 1942. In addition to these textbooks Berkhof wrote two special doctrinal studies, *The Vicarious Atonement through Christ* (1936) and *Recent Trends in Theology* (1944), before he retired.

Louis Berkhof was not a creative and imaginative theologian. Although he recognized that the systematic theologian had a critical as well as a constructive and defensive task,[53] he was not reflectively critical of the system he proposed nor aware of serious theological problems yet to be resolved. He believed that Reformed theology since Calvin had through the centuries assumed a more or less definite form.

In the Preface to his *Introductory Volume* published in 1932, Berkhof acknowledged that the general plan of his work was based on the first volume of Bavinck's *Gereformeerde Dogmatiek* and that in a few chapters he followed Bavinck's argumentation as well. In the revised edition, Berkhof included no such admission. Except for later additions, especially comments on neoorthodox theologians whom Bavinck antedated,

Berkhof, however, remained dependent on Bavinck for both the structure and content of his theology. In his *Systematic Theology*, Berkhof was only slightly less dependent on Bavinck. In this work Berkhof often rearranged materials taken from Bavinck's volumes and occasionally introduced a new division of the material. Berkhof's treatment of Barth and Brunner in the 1941 edition was original work. Nevertheless Berkhof's theology was essentially the theology of Herman Bavinck. Berkhof was also dependent on Bavinck for the names of most of the theologians he mentioned and on whose views he commented. The scriptural references Berkhof cited were for the most part taken from Bavinck's volumes. Bavinck, however, usually referred to many more texts than Berkhof, and occasionally Berkhof cited passages not found in Bavinck. Berkhof was, however, pervasively dependent on Bavinck, often to the point of literally reproducing Bavinck's words and phrases.[54]

Louis Berkhof possessed remarkable intellectual and personal gifts for doing systematic theology. A voracious reader and diligent scholar, Berkhof was theologically well informed. He had a unique capacity to assimilate a large body of material, to sort out its essential content, and reproduce it in condensed form. He was especially adept at defining theological terms and making theological distinctions. His clear, concise, coherent, and systematic lectures and writings bore the stamp of his penetrating and orderly mind. As a person he was reserved, dignified, gracious, humble, and thoroughly human. Berkhof was no fighter. He innately disliked controversy. These intellectual gifts and personal qualities combined in Berkhof to produce a theologian who knew how to present Reformed doctrine in a systematic way and who could at the same time accurately represent and fairly judge other theological positions.

Berkhof retired in 1944. At the time he retired, he was still physically and mentally vigorous. He later wrote *Aspects of Liberalism* (1951), *The Kingdom of God* (1951),[55] and *The Second Coming of Christ* (1953). When he died on May 18, 1957, he was still regularly contributing articles in the church periodicals on Christian doctrine.

No theologian or churchman has made a greater impact on the Christian Reformed Church than Professor Berkhof. During the 38 years of his professional career, he was directly involved in the instruction and training of over 300 Christian Reformed Church ministers. His textbooks in systematic theology became virtual standards of Reformed theological orthodoxy in the Christian Reformed Church. For many years candidates for the ministry were examined by the synod before being declared eligible for the ministry. In these examinations each candidate was questioned for twenty minutes on the introduction (prolegomena) to Reformed theology and for another twenty minutes on each of the six loci of systematic theology. After sustaining the synodical examination, a candidate had to submit to a similar examination in systematic theology at the classical level before being ordained to the ministry. In these examinations Berkhof's *Systematic Theology* provided both the basis for the questions and the content for the correct answers.

Reports on the celebrations honoring Berkhof when he became president of Calvin Seminary and when he retired as well as memorial articles that appeared in the church papers when he died indicate that he was greatly esteemed as a person and scholar and much trusted as a teacher and churchman. No one else in the history of the Christian Reformed Church has been so honored and respected.

Berkhof established a theological reputation in America almost exclusively through the publication of *Systematic Theology*. An Eerdmans advertisement stated that since the death of Warfield, Hodge, Kuyper, and Bavinck, Professor Louis Berkhof occupied a unique place in the world of Reformed dogmatics. His *Systematic Theology* was unequalled by any contemporary treatise in the English language. The advertisement further quoted Samuel G. Craig, who said that Berkhof's work was the most important work on systematic theology from an American source to appear in recent years.[56] In addition to Calvin Seminary many other conservative American theological schools and Bible colleges have used Berkhof's *Systematic Theology* as a textbook for instruction.[57]

Berkhof's *Systematic Theology* brought him international recognition as a Reformed theologian. English editions of his work have been sold in Australia, Canada, South Africa, England, and other European countries. This work has also been translated into Chinese, Japanese, Korean, Spanish, and Portuguese.

Recognizing Berkhof's administrative experience and his international reputation as an orthodox Reformed theologian, the delegates from conservative Reformed churches from many parts of the world chose Louis Berkhof to be the president of the first assembly of the Reformed Ecumenical Synod meeting in June 1946 in Grand Rapids, Michigan.

Notes: Louis Berkhof

1. *Young Calvinist*, October 1931, 3.
2. *Young Calvinist*, July 1957, 4.
3. Ibid.
4. Geerhardus Vos graduated from the Theological School in 1883. The same year Vos enrolled in a postgraduate course of studies at Princeton Seminary. From Princeton he went to the University of Berlin where he studied for one year. In 1888 Vos received a Ph.D. degree from the University of Strassburg. From 1888 to 1893 he taught at the Theological School where his work was highly

esteemed by his colleagues and students. Although no criticism was expressed regarding his teaching in biblical studies, opposition was raised to his dependence on Kuyper, especially Kuyper's supralapsarianism, in dogmatics. Vos's decision to go to Princeton was based on a variety of things, not the least of which was the attractiveness and challenge of the Princeton offer. The new chair of biblical theology at Princeton was very likely specially designed to offset the influence of Dr. Charles A. Briggs, who taught the same subject at Union Seminary in New York. Vos's first love was biblical theology, not dogmatics.

5. Address to the Synod of the Reformed Churches in The Netherlands in 1899, printed in *Acta der Synode, 1900*, 93.

6. *De Wachter*, 11 March 1896, 4. Herman Bavinck was also a son of the churches of the Secession of 1834 in The Netherlands. He first taught dogmatics in the Theological School at Kampen and then accepted an appointment to teach the same subject in 1902 at the Free University of Amsterdam.

7. *Acta der Synode, 1902*, 26; *De Wachter*, 25 July 1902, 1.

8. *De Wachter*, 11 June 1957, 5.

9. Ibid.

10. Cf. G. D. De Jong, "The History of the Development of the Theological School," in *Semi-Centennial Volume* (Grand Rapids: Published for the Semi-Centennial Committee of the Theological School and Calvin College, 1926), 37.

11. *Acta der Synode, 1906*, 34.

12. *The Banner*, 14 September 1906, 233.

13. Louis Berkhof, *Beknopte Bijbelsche Hermeneutiek* (Kampen: J. H. Kok, 1911), 1-209.

14. *De Wachter*, 10 December 1913, 5.

15. Louis Berkhof, *The Church and Social Problems* (Grand Rapids: Eerdmans-Sevensma, 1913), 3, 4, 9-12, 16-20.

16. Ibid., 16-20.

17. *Acta der Synode, 1914*, 27. After not being reappointed in 1906, Janssen studied in Germany, Scotland, and The Netherlands. He also completed a course of studies qualifying him for candidacy for the ministry at the Free University of Amsterdam. According to G. D. De Jong, the synod presumed that Dr. Janssen had "learned a great deal since 1906" (De Jong, "History," 41).

18. The synod did not completely agree with Berkhof. It advised Christian laborers, if they were compelled to join neutral unions in order to provide for themselves, powerfully to witness by word and deed within the unions to the fact that they belonged to Christ and sought his honor. *Acta der Synode, 1916*, 38-39. This was the only major issue in the Christian Reformed Church during Berkhof's life on which Berkhof and the synod differed.

19. Henry Bultema, *Maranatha: Eene Studie Over de Onvervulde Profetie* (Maranatha: A Study Concerning Unfulfilled Prophecy) (Grand Rapids: Eerdmans—Sevensma, 1917).

20. The reason is obvious. The synod was to meet in June and many synodical delegates could read and understand Dutch better than English.

21. Louis Berkhof, *Premillennialisme* (Grand Rapids: Eerdmans-Sevensma, 1918), 18-29.

22. Ibid., 30-40.

23. Ibid., 41-46.

24. Ibid., 52-53.

25. For a more complete history of the controversy, see John H. Krom-

minga, *The Christian Reformed Church: A Study in Orthodoxy* (Grand Rapids: Baker Book House, 1949), 72-74.

26. The letter is reproduced in F. M. Ten Hoor, W. Heyns, L. Berkhof, and S. Volbeda, *Nadere Toelichting omtrent De Zaak Janssen* (A Closer Look Concerning the Janssen Case) (Holland: Holland Printing Company, n.d.), 3.

27. Ibid., 34-63.

28. Ibid., 63-80.

29. Ibid., 82-83.

30. R. Janssen, *Voortzetting Van Den Strijd* (Continuing the Struggle) (Grand Rapids: n.p., 1922), 4-6.

31. Letter of Janssen to the synod, *Acta der Synode, 1922*, 27.

32. *Acta der Synode, 1922*, 270-78. For a more detailed history of the Janssen Case see Kromminga, *Christian Reformed Church*, 75-79.

33. The two most prominent were Quirinus Breen and R. B. Kuiper. Breen later was awarded a Ph.D. degree in church history from the University of Chicago and taught for many years at the University of Oregon. R. B. Kuiper, Janssen's brother-in-law, went to the Reformed Church in America. Without acknowledging he had made a mistake, Kuiper recanted positively and profusely in *As to Being Reformed* (Grand Rapids: Wm. B. Eerdmans Publishing Company, 1926). Kuiper later was appointed president of Calvin College (1930), professor of practical theology at Westminster Seminary (1933), and president of Calvin Seminary (1953).

34. *Minutes of the Board of Trustees*, June 1919.

35. *Acta der Synode, 1922*, 47.

36. *Acta der Synode, 1924*, 145-47. For a brief history of the controversy see Kromminga, *Christian Reformed Church*, 82-86.

37. *Acta der Synode, 1924*, 32.

38. Clarence Bouma, "Retirement," *Calvin Forum*, October 1944, 35.

39. *The Banner*, 23 October 1925, 676.

40. Louis Berkhof, *Introductory Volume to Systematic Theology*, rev. ed. (Grand Rapids: Wm. B. Eerdmans Publishing Company, 1941), 38, 60.

41. *Acta der Synode, 1926*, 107.

42. Ten Hoor was a vigorous proponent of the infralapsarian position and stridently opposed to Kuyper. Berkhof correctly represented the supra- and infralapsarian positions on the question of the logical order of the decrees. He did not consider the two views as absolutely antithetical and rendered the opinion that both were necessarily inconsistent yet compatible with Reformed confessional orthodoxy. He did not, however, indicate that historically the two positions came to represent very different systems of theology touching many doctrinal points. Cf. *Systematic Theology* (Grand Rapids: Wm. B. Eerdmans Publishing Company, 1941), 118-25.

43. Report of the Board of Trustees, *Acts of Synod, 1932*, 207-08.

44. *The Banner*, 11 September 1931, 791-92, 806.

45. Berkhof does not comment on Reinhold Niebuhr in his books on systematic theology. For his evaluation of Niebuhr's theology see his reviews of *The Nature and Destiny of Man*, in *The Banner*, 24 September 1943, 792, and of *Christianity and Power Politics*, in *The Banner*, 23 May 1941, 504.

46. Berkhof, *Introductory Volume*, 35-36, 61, 136, and his *History of Christian Doctrines* (Grand Rapids: Wm. B. Eerdmans Publishing Company, 1937), 25.

47. Berkhof, *Introductory Volume*, 58, 60.

48. Berkhof quite simply considered any systematized body of knowledge a science (ibid., 47).

49. Ibid., 61-62, 67-68, 72, 97, 181.

50. Ibid., 23, 37, 64.

51. Ibid., 89.

52. Ibid., 17. Berkhof's major theological works were published in condensed form for college students with the title *Manual of Reformed Doctrine* (1933). In 1938 the *Manual* was further reduced for use by high-school students. It carried the title *Summary of Christian Doctrine*.

53. Berkhof, *Introductory Volume*, 58-59.

54. For examples of the extent of Berkhof's dependence on Bavinck compare Bavinck's discussion of the nature of special revelation in *Gereformeerde Dogmatiek* (Kampen: J. H. Kok, 1918), 1:362, with Berkhof's treatment of the same subject in his *Introductory Volume*, 139-40, and Bavinck's view on the wisdom of God in 2:195-96 with Berkhof's view (*Systematic Theology*, 68-69).

55. Much of the material from Berkhof's unpublished Stone Lectures was presented in this work. Berkhof was still appreciative of the social conception of the Kingdom of God articulated in the Social Gospel for correcting the older one-sided individualism and one-sided eschatological understanding of the Kingdom. Now, however, he found serious fault with the modern theological underpinnings of the Social Gospel (Louis Berkhof, *The Kingdom of God* [Grand Rapids: Wm. B. Eerdmans Publishing Company, 1951], 73-85).

56. *The Banner*, 22 April 1949, 501.

57. H. Henry Meeter listed the following: Fuller Theological Seminary, Columbia Theological Seminary, Louisville Presbyterian Seminary, Southern Baptist Theological Seminary, Gordon Divinity School, Gordon College of Theology and Missions, Western Theological Seminary, Erskine College and Theological Seminary, Northeastern Bible Institute, Providence-Barrington Bible College, Bob Jones University, and Moody Bible Institute (*De Wachter*, 11 June 1957, 14).

HERMAN DOOYEWEERD IN NORTH AMERICA

C. T. McINTIRE

Dooyeweerd and the Institute for Christian Studies

When surveying the Reformed tradition in Christian thought, we quite naturally turn to theologians and theology. And, indeed, all the other thinkers treated in this volume are known for their theology. But, as in the Roman Catholic tradition, there is in Reformed thought a strong and vital tradition of Christian philosophy. It is here that we meet Herman Dooyeweerd (1894-1977) in North America.[1]

In this essay I shall first examine Dooyeweerd's thought as introduced in North America, and then see what happened to his thought in the next generation in North America, especially in a group of philosophers and philosophically minded scholars influenced by Dooyeweerd and associated in one way or another with what is now known as the Institute for Christian Studies in Toronto. Unlike some of the other essays in this volume, our survey will take us right up to the present day.

Dooyeweerd was a legal scholar and philosopher at the Free University of Amsterdam from 1926 until his retirement in 1965. His most significant work was *A New Critique of Theoretical Thought* (4 vols.), published in its definitive form in English in North America between 1953 and 1958.[2]

Immediately after the publication of this work he traveled twice to North America, once in the fall of 1958 and again in the spring of 1959. The 1959 visit included a lecture tour of several universities and colleges, beginning with Harvard, as well as some public lectures for general audiences. The result was the book based on his lectures, *In the Twilight of Western Thought* (1960), written in English. *Twilight* is probably Dooyeweerd's best introduction to his own thought.[3] The 1958 visit included a meeting with the board of the Institute's ancestor organization, then only recently established in Ontario, known as the Association for Re-

172

formed Scientific Studies (ARSS). The result there was Dooyeweerd's suggestion to the ARSS that they write a new creed, an educational creed, that would affirm Christian principles directly germane to scholarship and higher education.[4]

Dooyeweerd's thought had been known in North America before the mid-1950s. Notably, he had published a brief earlier work in English, *Transcendental Problems of Philosophic Thought* (1948),[5] and Cornelius Van Til of Westminster Theological Seminary had spoken of Dooyeweerd's work to his students in the 1930s. Eventually two North American philosophers, David Freeman and William S. Young, working with Dooyeweerd and an English teacher from The Netherlands, collaborated to produce the new English version we know as the *New Critique*.[6] This, together with his two visits, established Dooyeweerd's presence in North America from the 1950s onward.

His thought became a noticeable element in circles associated with the Christian Reformed Church (CRC). At Calvin College, the CRC's official college, Professor H. Evan Runner became the able advocate of Dooyeweerd's thought.[7] Runner had gone to Holland at Van Til's suggestion and studied with Dooyeweerd and his colleague (and brother-in-law), the philosopher D. H. T. Vollenhoven.[8] Runner's channels at Calvin were his lectures to large classes in the Philosophy Department and his charismatic leadership of a student club, the Groen van Prinsterer Society. Runner founded the club in 1953 and attracted mainly students whose families had recently immigrated to Canada from The Netherlands. Dooyeweerd's thought also had strong supporters in two new independent colleges in the CRC orbit, Dordt College in Iowa, established in 1955, and Trinity Christian College in Illinois, founded in 1959.[9] Periodicals associated with the CRC took notice of Dooyeweerd, including the *Calvin Forum* and the *Torch and Trumpet*. The Reformed Fellowship, a CRC laymen's group that published *Torch and Trumpet*, sponsored Dooyeweerd's 1959 lecture tour.

The chief focus of interest in Dooyeweerd's thought, however, was the new Association for Reformed Scientific Studies (ARSS). It had been founded in 1956 by a small group of Dutch immigrants, both lay and clergy, in the CRC for the purpose of establishing in Canada an institution of higher learning on the model of the Free University of Amsterdam. The educational creed that Dooyeweerd had suggested in 1958 appeared in 1961. It was written by Vollenhoven, Dooyeweerd's brother-in-law, together with Professor Runner. The ARSS sponsored student conferences starting in 1959 and published the lectures first in a series known as *Christian Perspectives*, and in later years in books. In 1967 the ARSS changed its name to the Association for the Advancement of Christian Scholarship (AACS) and founded the Institute for Christian Studies in Toronto (ICS). The Institute, modeled on the interdisciplinary Philosophical Institute of the Free University, offered seminars, gradually constructed a curriculum, gathered a small faculty of eight or nine members, named another seven nonresident fellows, and eventually awarded master's degrees in philosophy. In 1983 ICS received Royal Assent to a Charter from the Parliament of Ontario, and the AACS formally ceased to exist, leaving the ICS to carry on.[10]

Since 1956 scholars associated with the ICS and its antecedents have written a sizable body of books and articles for both scholarly and nonscholarly audiences. No one thinker has emerged as predominant. Instead, their writings might be called the workings of a community of scholars. These works comprise much of the scholarship of the next generation after Dooyeweerd in North America.[11]

This next generation has passed through three phases.[12] The first phase, during the 1950s and 1960s, consisted chiefly of translating Dutch scholarship into English, bringing Dutch scholars to North America, sending North American students to Amsterdam, and promoting Dooyeweerd's thought with the enthusiasm and aggressiveness that disciples have for their master. The second phase, from the late 1960s to the late 1970s, included converting the Institute into a serious academic community, taking the first important steps of independence from Dooyeweerd's thought yet continuing in the tradition of Dooyeweerd, and opening up differences between conservative and progressive emphases among the broad group of scholars who related to Dooyeweerd's thought. The third phase, since the late 1970s, has featured the production of new scholarship that in general continued the tradition of Christian thought identified with Dooyeweerd, while being fully involved in contemporary scholarship within the academic world at large. Often significant differences continued to appear among those who related to Dooyeweerd's tradition. Through this process of transmutation the scholars in this broad group sought to sift the enduring from the ephemeral.

Dooyeweerd's Thought

Dooyeweerd presented the primary elements of his thought in *A New Critique of Theoretical Thought*.[13] That work itself was a revised edition based on a translation of his three-volume *De Wijsbegeerte der Wetsidee (The Philosophy of the Law-Idea)* published in Holland in 1935-36. Altogether Dooyeweerd published more than 200 books and articles in the fields of law, political theory, and philosophy. His thought touched a wide range of areas—ontology, epistemology, social philosophy, philosophy of history, aesthetics, philosophy of science, legal theory, political philosophy, the history of law, theology, and the history of philosophy. He was a comprehensive thinker with an amazing versatility, and his ideas were capable of inspiring thought in almost any field of learning. As a system builder he may be compared with philosophers Jacques Maritain and Bernard Lonergan, theologian Paul Tillich, historian Arnold Toynbee, and social theorists Talcott Parsons and Pitrikim Sorokin. He sought to continue the Christian tradition of the great Dutch thinker and prime minister of the preceding generation, Abraham Kuyper (1901-1905).

Dooyeweerd claimed that he wrote, not theology, but philosophy informed by Christian insights. As such, he wrote not about God but about the general structure of the world and human existence. The characteristic elements of his thought may be grouped under the following themes: 1. religion; 2. creation, fall, and redemption; 3. modal theory; 4. individuality theory; and 5. the opening process of history.

1. Religion.[14] Dooyeweerd understood religion to be the supreme motive of human existence. He contended that we are related either to God in the totality of our being or to an idol, an alternative to God whether transcendent or this-worldly. Accordingly, religion is not a distinct department of life or something that we can do without if we so choose. Understood in this way, every human being is religious, and nothing that we do in life is separable from religion. All of life is from God, dependent upon God, and responsive to God.

According to Dooyeweerd, religion is integrative and central to life. Our religion is rooted in our hearts as the manifestation of our unity, what the Scriptures call our soul or spirit. He rejected all notions of a dualism between soul and body, and instead interpreted soul as the unifying totality of our being as related to God or a substitute.

Religion is the basic dynamic, the "ground motive," of our lives. God calls us and we respond, but not always in ways faithful to the will of God. Dooyeweerd, following St. Augustine, believed that there are two great types of this "ground motive"—the Spirit of God and the Spirit of the Evil One. He suggested that these have been translated into four specific ground motives—the Greek-Roman pagan motive of form and matter; the Christian motive of creation, fall, and redemption; the originally medieval motive of grace and nature that seeks a synthesis between pagan and Christian religion; and the secular humanist motive of freedom and nature. Thinkers empowered according to this modern secular motive, such as Immanuel Kant, are certain that "religion" is not relevant to theoretical thought and that reason is autonomous. The basic thesis of Dooyeweerd's "new critique" of theoretical thought is that belief in the autonomy of reason is a pretension that cannot hide the religious character of all thought.

2. Creation, Fall, and Redemption. This is the religious ground motive that is consonant with the Scriptures. Dooyeweerd explained its meaning in this way: *creation* denotes that all of reality is God's, a disclosure of his will, and good; *fall* indicates our radical resistance to the love of God and love of our neighbor, because of which our existence as God's creatures is filled with suffering and evil; *redemption* turns us to Jesus Christ by whom we may be radically restored to God and our neighbors, and the whole creation may become as it ought to be, the re-creation of God.

Dooyeweerd regarded his entire philosophy as an attempt to manifest the dynamic of this Christian religious motive in theoretical terms. He conceived of theory as an explication of the law-structure of creation. He emphasized the conflict among the fruits of the two Spirits—of God and of the Evil One—as the "antithesis" due to the Fall that divided thought from thought and persons from persons, even as it cut through the lives of Christians. He stressed that the structures of creation were norms by which God called us to do what is healthy and to work out by means of human action the redemption that Jesus Christ accomplished.

3. *Modal Theory.*[15] The first of two ways in which Dooyeweerd conceptualized reality was in his modal theory. In this he explicitly sought to expand upon the idea of "sphere sovereignty" put forward by Kuyper. Whereas in religion we tend toward the integration and unity of our lives, in the actual expression of our lives we manifest diversity. As Dooyeweerd depicted it, reality is temporal and cosmic time, like a prism, refracts the unity of the one light into many diverse modes of existence. The modes are aspects of reality, the many different ways in which an entity exists or an act occurs. The modal aspects are, on one side, structures or laws of creation; on the other, they are the various ways in which we exist historically, no one of which is reducible to any other.

Dooyeweerd provisionally identified fifteen modal aspects of reality, including the numerical, biotic, psychical, lingual, jural, and pistic (faith). Each aspect revealed a law or norm that characterized the aspect. For example, the biotic law is organic growth, the lingual norm is symbolic signification, and the jural norm is justice. Dooyeweerd worked out a very elaborate system by which he explained how each aspect referred by analogy to every other aspect, networking the aspects of reality in a complex but magnificent integration. He showed how each scholarly discipline pertained especially to a unique aspect, such as biology to the biotic, linguistics to the lingual, and theology to the pistic. Philosophy had the task of overall integration, such as by theorizing about the modes and their interrelations as a whole, while each science treated its own aspect within the context of philosophical interrelations.

4. *Individuality Theory.*[16] While his modal theory looked at *aspects* of reality—e.g., biotic, jural, pistic—his individuality theory analyzed

whole phenomena of reality—e.g., trees, states, and churches. Whereas by means of modality analysis he identified specific kinds of aspects of entities, by means of individuality analysis he identified kinds of entities. The important issue is to apprehend the unique and irreducible character of each modal aspect or each kind of entity. For example, in modal theory faith (pistic) manifests a unique character according to the norm of faith (transcendental certainty) and may not be reduced to the social or psychic aspects of faith. In individuality theory churches are communities properly characterized by faith and may not rightly be treated as merely social or economic in character, although those aspects are also present. Dooyeweerd was thus both a pluralist and an antireductionist; he accepted the diversity of created reality as basic.

His individuality theory enabled him to explain how there could be different kinds of entities, yet how each kind could exhibit every aspect of reality. For example, states such as France and Canada are characteristically jural communities united around the jural norm of justice. At the same time, states exhibit spatial, economic, social, and all the other modal aspects. They do so in ways that belong to a jurally qualified institution. Thus, states do not exist to make a profit or to create friendships, but to maintain justice. In this light, Dooyeweerd regards it as proper for states in the name of justice to redistribute wealth among the citizenry from the richer to the poorer members. Likewise, an industry such as General Motors Corporation rightly exists when it acts according to the characteristic norm of stewardly saving care for the human and natural resources of creation. While GM needs to match income with expenditure, even here the aim should not be to make profit, but act according to that norm of stewardship, in relation to all the other aspects of reality, including the aesthetic quality of the workplace and the equity of the decision-making process.

According to his theory, people express their religion directly by means of their response to the norm appropriate to each different kind of entity.

5. *History.* [17] Dooyeweerd's philosophy of history provided the invisible backbone of his whole system of thought. The elements of his philosophy of history were scattered, however. He regarded his theory of time as the basis of his system. It was an unusual notion of time. He called it cosmic time, and identified it as the pluriform diversity of the modal aspects. He contrasted it with the unity and coherence of reality as centered in the human heart, which he treated as supratemporal (beyond time). As a result there were different sorts of time, for example, linguistic time, astronomic time, or jural time.

What he called the historical aspect was merely one appearance of time as past, present, and future. The historical aspect he supposed was one mode among the fifteen he identified. It had to do with power, control, or mastery, and he sometimes called it the cultural mode. He believed that historical study specialized in analysis of the historical mode of any thing.

This historical mode served as the foundation or starting point for a very complicated process, called "the opening process," that swept through the modes in the actual course of any thing's history. By means of the opening process, static or closed cultures were made to develop by means of differentiation, individualization, and new integration. In this manner Dooyeweerd believed the world could unfold in fulfillment of the cultural mandate of Genesis 1. History would become a process of development initiated by faith. Dooyeweerd's vision of history was sweeping, and he linked it directly to St. Augustine's vision of the two cities in struggle for the course of history.

Many other elements of Dooyeweerd's thought, particularly in epistemology and philosophical anthropology, could be mentioned, but these five are both central and characteristic enough to indicate the thrust of his work.

The Generation after Dooyeweerd

When Dooyeweerd's work appeared in North America in the 1950s, a number of scholars took notice of it in books and articles. William S. Young, one of the translators of the *New Critique*, was the first, and he referred to it in his book *Towards a Reformed Philosophy* (1952). The second translator, David H. Freeman, completed a doctoral dissertation at the University of Pennsylvania, partly on Dooyeweerd (1958), and he published *Recent Studies in Philosophy and Theology* (1962) in which he compared Dooyeweerd with Étienne Gilson, Jacques Maritain, and Paul Tillich. Ronald Nash wrote *Dooyeweerd and the Amsterdam Philosophy* (1962), and Arthur Holmes included Dooyeweerd in *Christian Philosophy in the Twentieth Century* (1969). Rousas John Rushdoony discussed Dooyeweerd in several essays, including his Introduction to Dooyeweerd's *In The Twilight of Western Thought* (1960). [18]

These and many other writings contributed to an awareness of Dooyeweerd's thought. Evan Runner and the Association for Reformed Scientific Studies (ARSS) in Ontario, however, sought to go the next step and act on Dooyeweerd's thought. Runner and his Groen van Prinsterer Society at Calvin College inspired Hendrik Hart, Bernard Zylstra, James Olthuis, and Arnold De Graaff to go to the Free University of Amsterdam for their doctoral studies. Dooyeweerd supervised Zylstra's dissertation on Harold Laski's political theory. Hart went into general philosophy, writing on John Dewey's epistemology. Olthuis wrote on ethics and theology, and De Graaff wrote on psychology and education, Calvin Seerveld, only indirectly influenced by Runner at Calvin, went to Amsterdam earlier on his own to work under Vollenhoven, completing a dissertation on Benedetto Croce's aesthetics.[19] These five became the first members of the faculty of the Institute for Christian Studies after it opened in 1967.

The other avenue of Runner's influence was the series of annual student conferences begun by the ARSS in 1959 in Ontario. Runner's lectures at the first two were published separately by the ARSS in 1960 and 1961 and eventually put together as a book, *The Relation of the Bible to Learning* (1967).[20] Runner's themes were all Dooyeweerd's—religion, the ground-motives and the religious antithesis, sphere sovereignty and the modal theory, and the law of God in creation.

But some recognizably new emphases appeared in Runner's version of some of these themes. Chief of these was his stress on the Word of God, by which he meant the Bible. Dooyeweerd's emphasis, it may be said, was always on Creation-Order as a reality in the context of which the Scriptures were needed as a guide. Runner reversed the emphasis, in keeping with his North American Evangelical and Reformed experience, and made the Bible the centerpiece. Parallel with this, Runner stressed the religious character of everything under the new banner of "life is religion," and, in contrast with Dooyeweerd, put less emphasis on the theoretical analysis of reality. Thirdly, Runner accented the "religious antithesis," the utter opposition in thought and scholarship between the way of God and all other spirits. Dooyeweerd, by contrast, while working with the notion of religious antithesis in the sense of St. Augustine, had stressed creating his own system of thought in debate with other kinds of thought. Fourthly, Runner transformed the notion of working with Dooyeweerd's thought into a mission that Dutch Calvinistic youth in North America should especially undertake. With this he reversed the trend in Dooyeweerd from his accentuated Calvinism in the 1920s and 1930s to his ecumenical Christian thought based on the common scriptural message in the 1950s. (Dooyeweerd desired to change the name of his thought from Calvinistic philosophy to the more general term Christian philosophy.) By means of these four new emphases, Runner helped to create a small movement possessing an élan and a compelling purpose.

The founding of the Institute for Christian Studies in Toronto implemented Dooyeweerd's thought in a most tangible way. His thought was not made official, so to speak, but it did serve as the unwritten basis for interdisciplinary scholarly discourse within the Institute. It offered a model with two applications—first, for the intrinsic integration of Christian insight with scholarly thought, and second, for the identification and interrelation of all fields of scholarly study. The character and curriculum of the Institute reflected both applications at once.[21] The Institute regarded itself from the start as a *philosophical* rather than a theological school. Following Dooyeweerd, it regarded each field of academic study as resting upon a philosophical basis in which fundamental decisions were made about human nature, the purpose of life, and the character of reality. And such matters are the very ones that Christian insights directly illuminated. The Institute adopted Dooyeweerd's theory that philosophy by definition was an integrative endeavor, with respect to which Christian insights concerning the wholeness and integrity of reality were directly relevant.

By the early 1970s the Institute created two core courses—biblical foundations and philosophical foundations. In so doing it stressed that the Scriptures were not the special document of theology students and biblical scholars, but the integrative and directive religious source for the insights basic to any field of study. Thus philosophy, pursued according to biblical insights, served to ground and orient each academic field. For the rest, they added courses in the philosophy of as many fields as they could, given the limits of financial resources and personnel.

In the late 1970s the Institute faculty numbered nine scholars who taught in the areas of philosophy, history of philosophy, theology, philosophical theology, philosophy of history, political theory, economic and social philosophy, psychological theory, and philosophical aesthetics. The course of study was rounded out by a second-year interdisciplinary seminar that involved most fields, and by research on master's theses.

The Institute was founded with two clear mandates: to pursue the religious reformation of various scholarly fields, and to pursue academic research.[22] Both aims—reformation and research—were by definition inclined toward innovation. But both also required a stable institutional format and a stable relation with the supporting constituency. These needs for innovation and stabilization could—and did—often conflict. I have already referred to three phases in the Institute's history—the aggressive, the settling down, and the academically productive phases. These can now be paraphrased as the transition from being a movement to being a scholarly institution. Both founding mandates, actively pursued, were conducive to such a transition.

Included in the transition was a new relation to Dooyeweerd's thought. Whereas at the beginning the Institute depended on Dooyeweerd, by the late 1970s the faculty members had each moved to fresh terrain but always with Dooyeweerd's thought in the background. It is possible to review the five thematic elements of Dooyeweerd's thought surveyed earlier and observe what became of them in the teaching and writings of the Institute's faculty. The most important work for this comparison is a volume of essays entitled *The Legacy of Herman Dooyeweerd: Reflection on Critical Philosophy in the Christian Tradition* (1985).[23] The essays were written by six authors who were faculty members of the Institute. Of the many other writings by Institute scholars, especially notable are Hendrik Hart's *Understanding Our World: An Integral Ontology* (1984) and Calvin Seerveld's *Rainbows for the Fallen World: Aesthetic Life and Artistic Task* (1980).[24]

Two general observations may be made at the outset.[25] First, Dooyeweerd's system as a whole has not been taken over by the next generation. This may mean no more than observing that only Dooyeweerd could maintain Dooyeweerd's system, and that any subsequent thinkers who tried to do so would become scholastic disciples and not a group of scholars with their own contributions to make. Second, what did continue were some general orientations and some general themes and insights of a philosophically relevant kind concerning what was important and how to proceed in philosophy. These observations will become concrete as we review the five themes.

1. Religion. Institute members would agree that Dooyeweerd made his point about the religious basis of theoretical thought, indeed of all human activity. All humans are religious and as such their lives are oriented toward God or some substitute. Thus, the relation between religion and scholarship is intrinsic and integral.

They would grant, further, that religion is a motivating power, but it appears that no Institute scholar continues to work with the idea of religious ground-motives in Western civilization. None would carry on Dooyeweerd's extensive analysis of the polar tensions within the ground motives by which he interpreted the history of culture and philosophy. None would regard the heart as distinguishable from the whole of our person and our functioning; some have suggested that Dooyeweerd created a new dualistic view of our human make-up, in spite of his best intentions.

2. Creation, Fall, and Redemption. All the Institute scholars would regard this as an insightful summary of the central theme of the Scriptures concerning the world. But they would differ about whether it should be treated as a "ground motive" as did Dooyeweerd in the 1950s, or merely as a theme, or triad of themes, as Dooyeweerd did in the 1920s and 1930s. They all would regard an understanding of reality as creation, structured and good, as basic to Christian philosophizing. Likewise, they would understand the work of Jesus Christ as re-creation and in principle culturally pervasive in overcoming the effects of evil and suffering.

3. Modal Theory. All would agree that some sort of modal analysis is useful and valid to account for the constitutional diversity of reality.

Indeed, modal analysis would be taken as the chief means of identifying and interrelating the various distinct academic disciplines. But Institute scholars differ on what the modes may be, what their characterizing norms may be, and to what degree modal analysis is useful.

Some regard modal theory as useful first of all merely as an indicator of ontologically irreducible diversity. Others actively pursue modal analysis. For example, Olthuis stays fairly close to Dooyeweerd's version of the aspect of faith as transcendental certainty, calling it simply certitude. He agrees that theology is a special theoretical discipline focused on the mode of faith (certitude). Seerveld thinks Dooyeweerd is right about an aesthetic mode and aesthetics as a special science, but he rejects Dooyeweerd's understanding of aesthetics as having to do with harmony and beauty. He works instead with notions of allusiveness and imagination. Probably all would reject Dooyeweerd's proposal that there is a historical mode, and would work instead toward a more embracive understanding of history. Hart makes the move of conceiving of the modes, not as aspects, an idea that has static and spatial connotations, but as functions, calling up active and operational suggestions. All would agree that philosophy is best treated as an integrative as well as an analytic discipline, charged with conceptualizing the bases and interrelations of all the scholarly fields.

4. *Individuality Theory.* Probably all would think that theorizing about the structure of individual entities is important. Hart calls such phenomena "functors" and discusses functions (modal) as what functors do. But he does not pursue the theme of functors as fully as he does modal functions. Seerveld distinguishes art works as individual entities that are aesthetic in character from the aesthetic aspect of other nonaesthetic entities (such as someone's home).

On the whole, scholarly attention to individuality theory is slight compared with attention to modal theory. All would, however, stress the importance of a pluralist social theory that honored the distinctive yet interrelated character of each kind of social institution and relationship—churches, governments, colleges, neighborhoods, cities, labor unions, families, and so on.

5. *History.* I have already mentioned that all would reject the notion that history could be accounted for by means of Dooyeweerd's historical mode. All would also reject Dooyeweerd's theory of the heart as supratemporal, above and beyond time and history. They would disagree about whether time should be regarded as synonymous with ordered diversity (as in Dooyeweerd), or more pervasively identified as process and past-present-future relations. And they would disagree about the value of Dooyeweerd's theory of the opening process. The judgment

from the historian's angle has been that Dooyeweerd's theory wrongly elevates development above all other processes of history. What is needed is more theorizing about the great variety of temporal-historical processes, and this in a wide multi-cultural way. Dooyeweerd's relating of history to the cultural mandate of Genesis 1 would seem insightful as a way of identifying human responsibilities in history making, but more subtlety and actual historical analysis would be needed in order to create a more flexible philosophy of history influenced by Christian insights.

Conclusion

No doubt Herman Dooyeweerd has been the most creative philosopher in the Reformed tradition thus far in the twentieth century. However, the barriers to recognizing his creativity and transposing his philosophy to North America have not been small. His categories, special language, and method were shaped in a Dutch and European religious and philosophical milieu very different from that of his North American counterparts. The prevailing North American traditions of Reformed theology and analytic philosophy were unsympathetic to his thought. The Dutch Canadian community, which has been the chief transmitter of Dooyeweerd's thought, was separated from the mainstream of academic discourse like any immigrant group. The early aspirations to build a movement with a unique and exclusive salvific message needlessly impeded normal discourse about Dooyeweerd's thought.

Nonetheless, the presence of Dooyeweerd's thought in North America has been very beneficial. Once the effort is made to become acquainted with Dooyeweerd's work, the character of his creativity is evident.

The generation after Dooyeweerd has successfully made the transition to viable, innovative scholarship in full discourse with the North American academic community as a whole. Institute scholars have meaningfully relativized Dooyeweerd while seeking to distill the more enduring legacy he has to offer.

What may continue and be of value to others is not Dooyeweerd's system or his specific formulations, but a type of approach to scholarship. That approach may perhaps be summarized in this way: the impulse to explore reality empirically and theoretically, so that the irreducible diversity yet the coherent integration of reality is respected, that the insights of the Christian religion are intrinsic to scholarship in full discourse with the academic world, and that the results are of service to God and to all people.

Notes: Herman Dooyeweerd in North America

1. See "Christian Philosophy," *Encyclopedia Britannica* (15th edition, 1974), IV: 555-62; and *Philosophy in the 20th Century: Catholic and Christian,* ed. George F. McLean, 2 vols. (New York: Frederick Unger, 1967). We should note from the outset that there is another strong tradition of Reformed philosophy in North America that emphasizes philosophy of religion and rational discourse about claims concerning God, and that has associated with the tradition of Anglo-American thought known as analytic philosophy. In spite of differences, there are nonetheless strong affinities between philosophers in that Reformed line of thought and Dooyeweerd, chiefly by way of Dooyeweerd's predecessor Abraham Kuyper. See Hendrik Hart and Johan van der Hoeven, eds., *Rationality in the Calvinian Tradition* (Washington: University Press of America, 1983); and Alvin Plantinga and Nicholas Wolterstorff, eds., *Faith and Rationality: Reason and Belief in God* (Notre Dame: University of Notre Dame Press, 1983).

2. Dooyeweerd, *A New Critique of Theoretical Thought,* 4 vols. (Amsterdam: Paris; Philadelphia: Presbyterian and Reformed Publishing Company, 1953-1958). Hereafter *New Critique.*

3. Dooyeweerd, *In the Twilight of Western Thought* (Philadelphia: Presbyterian and Reformed Publishing Company, 1960). Hereafter *Twilight.*

4. The text of the educational creed is published in the *Academic Bulletin* of the Institute for Christian Studies.

5. Dooyeweerd, *Transcendental Problems of Philosophic Thought* (Grand Rapids: Wm. B. Eerdmans Publishing Company, 1948).

6. Freeman and Young collaborated on Volume 1, while Freeman and H. DeJongste collaborated on Volumes 2 and 3. Dooyeweerd went over the entire English version himself and revised and added sections.

7. On Runner, see John Kraay and Anthony Tol, eds., *Hearing and Doing: Philosophical Essays dedicated to H. Evan Runner* (Toronto: Wedge Publishing Company, 1979); and Henry Vander Goot, ed., *Life Is Religion: Essays in Honor of H. Evan Runner* (St. Catharines: Paideia Press, 1981).

8. On Vollenhoven, see *The Idea of Christian Philosophy: Essays in Honour of D. H. T. Vollenhoven* (Toronto: Wedge Publishing Company, 1973).

9. Two more Reformed colleges in CRC circles were founded in Canada, both with Dooyeweerd's thought as a factor, Redeemer College, Hamilton, Ontario (1982), and The King's College, Edmonton, Alberta (1979).

10. The history of the ARSS, AACS, and ICS has yet to be written. A special issue of the ICS Newsletter, *Perspective,* published in 1981 on the twenty-fifth anniversary of the founding of the ARSS, gives many interesting historical vignettes.

11. A partial list to 1975 is published in L. Kalsbeek, *Contours of a Christian Philosophy: An Introduction to Herman Dooyeweerd's Thought* (Toronto: Wedge Publishing Company, 1975), 313-39.

12. What follows is based on countless documents and personal observations over the years since 1960.

13. This treatment of Dooyeweerd's thought is based chiefly on the *New Critique,* his *magnum opus.* His published works through 1977 are listed in the back of a book that is an excellent scholarly introduction to his thought, Hendrik Van Eikema Hommes, *Inleiding tot de Wijsbegeerte van Herman Dooyeweerd* (The Hague: Martinus Nijhoff, 1982). The book by Kalsbeek, mentioned above, is also good and very readable. Other books to consult are Dooyeweerd's *Twilight,* and

his *Roots of Western Culture: Pagan, Secular, and Christian Options* (Toronto: Wedge Publishing Company, 1979).

14. Dooyeweerd treats religion, and creation, fall, redemption, in *New Critique*, Vol. 1.

15. He discusses modal theory in *New Critique*, Vol. 2.

16. Individuality theory is the subject of *New Critique*, Vol. 3.

17. Most of his philosophy of history is discussed in *New Critique*, Vol. 2, but much is scattered throughout the whole work.

18. Young, *Towards a Reformed Philosophy* (Franeker: T. Wever, 1952); Freeman, *Recent Studies in Philosophy and Theology* (Philadelphia: Presbyterian and Reformed Publishing Company, 1962); Nash, *Dooyeweerd and the Amsterdam Philosophy* (Grand Rapids: Zondervan Publishing House, 1962); Holmes, *Christian Philosophy in the Twentieth Century* (Nutley, NJ: Craig, 1969); Rushdoony, "Introduction," *Twilight*, vii-xvi.

19. Hart, *Communal Certainty and Authorized Truth* (Amsterdam: Swets and Zeitlinger, 1966); Zylstra, *From Pluralism to Collectivism* (Assen: Van Gorcum, 1968; New York: Humanities Press, 1970); Olthuis, *Facts, Values, and Ethics* (Assen: Van Gorcum, 1968; New York: Humanities Press, 1969); De Graaff, *The Educational Ministry of the Church* (Nutley, NJ: Craig, 1968); Seerveld, *Benedetto Croce's Earlier Aesthetic Theories and Literary Criticism* (Kampen: J. H. Kok, 1958).

20. Runner, *The Relation of the Bible to Learning* (Toronto: ARSS, 1967).

21. The Institute's statements of purpose and its curriculum have been presented in its *Academic Bulletin*, issued every year or two since 1967.

22. These mandates are presented in the Preamble and the Educational Creed of the ARSS (now ICS), which are printed in the ICS *Academic Bulletin*.

23. *The Legacy of Herman Dooyeweerd: Reflections on Critical Philosophy in the Christian Tradition* (Washington: University Press of America, 1985).

24. Hart, *Understanding Our World* (Washington: University Press of America, 1984); Seerveld, *Rainbows for the Fallen World* (Toronto: Tuppence Press, 1980). A full listing of publications by members of the Institute's faculty and associates may be obtained from the Institute, 229 College Street, Toronto, Ontario, M5T 1R4.

25. What follows is based on my reading of most of the publications by Institute scholars as well as firsthand knowledge of their teaching.

IV. THE SOUTHERN TRADITION

THE SOUTHERN TRADITION

MORTON SMITH

THERE are several distinctively southern developments of Reformed thought in America. The Reformed faith is found primarily in the mainline Presbyterian Church, though it should be recognized that other branches of the Church in the South have held to the Reformed Faith to a greater or lesser degree. The Associate Reformed Presbyterian Church, for example, still maintains the Reformed faith as set forth in the Westminster standards. The Cumberland Presbyterians have rejected the doctrines of full predestination, and thus hold only a corrupted form of them. Various Baptist groups hold to elements of the Reformed faith. Taking Warfield's basic premise, that all true Christians hold to Reformed faith wherever they are true to the Word, one could also say that all evangelical churches in the South hold elements of the Reformed faith.

The South was greatly affected by the revival movements of the past two centuries. One of the results of these revival movements was the development of the common consensus on the Christian religion that marked the "Bible belt." The basic elements of this consensus are an acceptance of the Bible as God's Holy Word, the recognition of our sinful and lost condition, and the conviction that the only way of salvation is to be found in Christ, who is to be received by faith. Insofar as these are all points that the Reformed faith teaches, it may be said that this much of the faith is held by the vast majority of all evangelical churches in the South. This same revivalism, on the other hand, with its strong emphasis on human ability to respond to gospel invitations, tended to minimize or even deny the Reformed distinctives, such as the doctrines of election, definite atonement, and efficacious grace.

Presbyterianism in the Colonial Period

Because the main developments in Reformed thought occurred in the Presbyterian Church, we shall concentrate on this church. The his-

189

tory of Presbyterianism in the South extends back to the first permanent settlement in Virginia in 1607. Ernest Trice Thompson in his *Presbyterians in the South* indicates that during the Colonial period there was no "South," but three different societies in the southern colonies: the Chesapeake society, based on tobacco; the Carolina society, built on rice and indigo; and finally the Back Country, still in the process of formation at the time of the Revolution.[1]

The Chesapeake society was the oldest. The Virginia Company's charter prescribed that "the word and services of God be preached, planted and used according to the rites and doctrines of the Church of England." The control of the Company was in the hands of the Puritans until the revocation of the charter in 1624. With the assumption of royal control of the colony in 1624, an act of conformity was passed. During the 1640s, despite Puritan control of Parliament in England, Governor William Berkeley continued to enforce conformity to the Church of England. This resulted in the departure of a number of colonists to Maryland at the invitation of Governor William Stone. They settled in Anne Arundel, Charles, and Prince George counties, near the present city of Annapolis. It is of interest that the ancestors of B. B. Warfield, one of America's greatest Presbyterian theologians, came to this region during this time.

During the period of the Commonwealth in England, the Puritans of Virginia were unmolested. A number of Scottish settlers arrived during the seventeenth century and settled along the Elizabeth River, near present-day Norfolk. Others settled along the Rappahannock, James, and Potomac Rivers.

Francis Makemie's main labors were on the eastern shore of Virginia and Maryland. He is sometimes known as the father of American Presbyterianism because of his leadership in organizing the first presbytery in the colonies. This was the Presbytery of Philadelphia, founded in 1705 or 1706. It had a very small beginning. There were four ministers from Maryland, two from Delaware, and one from Philadelphia.

Further South, there was a settlement of Presbyterians around Charleston, South Carolina, which had no relationship with the Presbytery of Philadelphia. The earliest records of Reformed worship in that area are of the French Huguenots. The last will and testament of a certain Caesar Mozé reveals that there must have been a French church in the Charleston area as early as 1687. There were also a goodly number of Scots, Dutch, and New England Puritans in South Carolina. An independent church, sometimes called Presbyterian, was formed in Charleston about 1690. It was composed of various peoples: French, Scots, Scotch-Irish, and New Englanders. A whole colony of New Englanders moved to South Carolina to found a Congregational church at Dorchester in

1696. Between 1752 and 1771 much of this group transplanted itself to Liberty County, Georgia, and established Midway Church there. From this Congregational church a large number of young men were fed into the ministry of various denominations. The Presbyterians received some 30, including Thomas Goulding, first professor at Columbia Seminary, and Daniel Baker, the great Presbyterian evangelist to the old Southwest. An independent Scottish Church was established in Savannah, Georgia, which still exists as the Independent Presbyterian Church of Savannah. Its grant of land from George II states that it is to be used for such "as are or shall be professors of the Doctrines of the Church of Scotland, agreeable to the Confession of Faith. . . ."[2]

An independent presbytery developed in the Charleston area, which George Howe, historian of the Presbyterian Church in South Carolina to 1850, dates from 1728. This presbytery required subscription to the *Westminster Confession of Faith*, as indicated in correspondence regarding the Rev. Josiah Smith, who was excluded in 1730 because of his refusal to subscribe. This presbytery passed out of existence at the time of the Revolution.

The independence of spirit reflected in the Charleston-Savannah area has been characteristic of much southern thought. No doubt it was forced on the early Presbyterians of this southern region simply by their distance from the rest of the American Presbyterians, but it was to leave a mark on the South Carolina Presbyterian mind. The people of this same area disagreed with their brethren in 1837-38 and formed the Independent Presbyterian denomination, which went its own way until the War between the States overshadowed their differences and brought about a union with other Southern Presbyterians.

The mainline Synod of the Presbyterian Church in 1729 adopted the *Westminster Confession* and *Catechisms* as the confession of faith of the Synod. Having thus declared herself, the Church might be assumed to have embarked on smooth sailing, but such was not the case. A controversy arose that was to divide the Church in 1741 between the Old Side Synod of Philadelphia and what later became the New Side Synod of New York. This division occurred in part as a result of the great revivals of George Whitefield and his followers and the development of the "log colleges" and academies for the training of ministers. The New Side, which espoused the revivals and the use of the academies, planted a number of churches in Virginia.

The Blairs maintained an Academy at Fagg's Manor, Chester County, Pennsylvania, at which Samuel Davies was to be educated. Davies may properly be called the "Father of Southern Presbyterianism" since his labors brought about the establishment of the Mother Presbytery of the South, namely, Hanover Presbytery. He labored off and on in Virginia from 1747 to 1759, and convened the first meeting of the Presbytery of Hanover on December 3, 1755, at the direction of the Synod of New York. The effects of his ministry were felt over all of Virginia and North Carolina. He held the *Westminster Confession* and *Catechisms* in the highest esteem. It was his regular practice to teach the *Shorter Catechism* to all of his members, and to have it recited at the worship service on Sunday.

William Henry Foote, writing a century later, in 1850, speaks of John Robinson and Samuel Davies and of their teachers, the Tennents and the Blairs, as laying a foundation that "had a controlling influence over Virginia Presbyterians in creed and practice" to his day. He says:

> From the time of these men, the Virginia ministers and people have believed in awakenings,—in spiritual exercises in religion,—in the power of godliness in men's hearts and lives. From deep conviction they have been believers in the depravity of human nature,—the sovereignty of God,—original sin,—and the absolute necessity of the new birth. Hoping for justification by the righteousness of Christ made theirs by faith, believing it would be safe to appear in it, in the judgment to come, ministers and people rejoiced in the unsearchable riches of Christ, through trials and difficulties that would make ordinary spirits tremble and quit the field. By the help of God they have left us a good report.[3]

In 1746 John Blair organized churches at North Mountain, New Providence, Timber Ridge, and the Fork of the James; these became the nucleus of Lexington Presbytery. It was out of the New Providence and Timber Ridge Churches that Liberty Hall Academy, the predecessor of Washington College (now Washington and Lee University), was to come. William Graham was the first teacher at the academy. He taught Archibald Alexander, the founding professor of Princeton Seminary. Others who came from this school were Moses Hoge, John Holt Rice, and George Addison Baxter. Hoge was the first professor of theology, appointed by the Synod of Virginia. Rice succeeded him, and founded Union Seminary. Baxter was professor of theology there at the time of the Old School–New School division of 1837.

Despite the fact that the Presbyterian Church of the South was marked with the revivalism of the New Side, there was a failure to follow up the gains of the first awakening. One of the major problems lay in the requirement of the Presbyterian Church for a highly educated ministry. There was a dearth of institutions in the South for such preparation. The Baptists and Methodists, on the other hand, had no such requirement. They used the itinerant system and the revivalism of Whitefield to reach the masses, and thus many who otherwise would have been Presbyterians were taken over into these groups. Even as

Presbyterians became established in the Southland and set up schools and academies, they were not able to keep pace with the demand for ministers during this period. It is hard to see how it would have been possible to have met the demands of the day with the limited resources that were available. Whether a plan could have been worked out and executed to meet the needs or not, it must be admitted that the Presbyterians failed to work out such a plan.

Presbyterianism After the Revolution

The period of the Revolution and following was marked by skepticism and widespread immorality. Especially was this true on the frontier. God graciously sent a revival of religion during this era, however. As early as 1787 an awakening began at Hampden-Sydney College in Prince Edward County, Virginia, that was to affect Presbyterianism for future generations because of those brought under its influence. It was a movement that enjoyed the participation of the President of the College, John Blair Smith. It spread to the sister institution of the Presbyterians across the Blue Ridge, Liberty Hall Academy, where William Graham participated in it. Through these two institutions the future leadership of the Presbyterian Church was affected. Archibald Alexander gave his heart to Christ under its influence. This young man was to become one of the country's greatest theologians. He received his theological education from William Graham. In 1812 he was called by the General Assembly to found Princeton Seminary. He was to serve there until his death in 1851. Charles Hodge was one of his students and became his colleague on the faculty. He taught a theology that was to become known as "Princeton Theology." Herman Bavinck described this theology thus: "The so-called Princeton Theology is chiefly a reproduction of the Calvinism of the seventeenth century, as it is formulated in the *Westminster Confession* and the *Consensus Helveticus*, and especially elucidated by F. Turretin in his *Theologia Elenctica*."[4] One may well question whether it should be called "Princeton" since it was taken from Virginia to Princeton by Alexander. Bavinck is correct in identifying this theology with that of Turretin. His work was used as the textbook on theology at both Princeton and Union Seminaries prior to the publication of Hodge's *Systematic Theology* at Princeton and Dabney's *Lectures in Systematic Theology* at Union.

Others to be affected by the revival in Virginia were Moses Hoge, John Holt Rice, George Addison Baxter, and Drury Lacy, all of whom helped to shape the theology of Virginia Presbyterianism. Moses Hoge was the President of Hampden-Sydney and the first officially appointed teacher of theology of the Synod of Virginia. John Holt Rice was to become the founder of Union Theological Seminary, and George Addison Baxter to succeed him there as Professor of Theology. Through these men the following generations received their training in the same sort of Presbyterianism that Alexander had carried to Princeton from Virginia. The affinity of Union and Princeton can be seen in a letter written by Rice to Alexander concerning his own hopes for his newly formed seminary:

> If, however, a Seminary can be established in the South, many will frequent it, who will not go to the North. . . . But my plan is, if we can succeed here, to take Princeton as our model, to hold constant correspondence with that great and most valuable institution, to get the most promising of our young men to finish off at Princeton; and, in a word, as far as possible, make this a sort of branch of that, so as to have your spirit diffused through us, and do all that can be done to bind the different parts of the Church together.[5]

That such a close relationship continued to exist is a matter of historical record. It may be seen in a number of ways. For one thing, both of these institutions were associated with the Old School branch of the Church in 1837 and following. Robert L. Dabney of Union Seminary received a call to Princeton in 1860. Again in 1915 Union Seminary sought to obtain the services of J. Gresham Machen of Princeton in New Testament. As recently as 1930-1940 Union Seminary had a Systematic Theology professor, James Porter Smith, who taught the same theology as that set forth at Princeton. The testimony of Smith's brother-in-law, the Rev. Gaston Boyle, is to this effect: "I am positive that he believed and taught the system of theology taught by Hodge and Dabney, including their beliefs concerning election, predestination and the inspiration of the Scriptures."[6] Thus the same theology that was taken by Alexander from Virginia and planted at Princeton continued to be the theology both of Princeton Seminary and of Union Seminary in Virginia for at least a century.

The Hampden-Sydney revival was to have far-reaching effects on the frontier, for through it James McGready was influenced to enter into evangelistic efforts in North Carolina. Thus the revival spread to Guilford and Orange Counties in 1791. McGready had a number of other ministers associated with him in his revival efforts, and moved into Kentucky. In 1798 McGready drew up a covenant with others to pray for one year for a revival. In answer to their prayer the revival began with the semi-annual sacramental service celebrated in July 1799 at Red River. The following year saw an increase of the revival in Cumberland County. McGready initiated the camp meeting that was to become characteristic of the Great Revival. He invited people to come prepared to camp for a sacramental season at Gasper River.

The Great Revival was a mixed blessing. On the one hand, many were brought to confess Christ as Savior. On the other hand, it led to the excesses for which the Kentucky revivals became known, namely, jerking, rolling, running, dancing, and barking. Not all the ministers countenanced such exercises, though some encouraged them and thus encouraged confusion. A worse side-effect of the revivals was the fact that there arose an uneducated ministry in Kentucky that, because of lack of training in the Scriptures and the standards of the church, began preaching and teaching something less than the full gospel of sovereign grace. A number of young men were licensed or ordained in the newly formed Cumberland Presbytery without having to subscribe to the *Confession of Faith*, except so far as they believed it to agree with the Word of God. Some rejected in particular the "alleged fatalism" of the Confession, which they thought the doctrines of predestination and reprobation implied. When, in response to complaint, the Synod of Kentucky investigated the irregularities and called for those licensed and ordained under such procedure to be reexamined, they refused to obey. The following year the Synod dissolved the Presbytery. Those who were unwilling to submit to the Synod withdrew and established a new and independent Cumberland Presbytery in 1810. Changes were made in the *Westminster Confession* by this group. Schaff summarizes the effect of their change: "The Cumberland Confession teaches on the one hand conditional election and unlimited atonement, and on the other, the final perseverance of the saints. It is an eclectic compromise between Calvinism and Arminianism; it is half Calvinistic and half Arminian, and makes no attempt to harmonize these antagonistic elements."[7]

In addition to the Cumberland Schism of 1810 there was another schism in the Upper Kentucky region led by Barton Stone. This movement was particularly anticonfessional. It arose because of the objection by more orthodox Presbyterians to the Arminianism of some of the revivalists. They in turn assumed that the creedal subscription of Presbyterianism was antievangelistic, and renounced creedal subscription. There was first an attempt to form an independent Presbytery of Springfield, which would be a part of the Presbyterian Church but not under the Synod of Kentucky. This Presbytery lasted just nine months during 1803-04. Some of its members were drawn away into the Shaker groups, while Barton Stone, rejecting all denominationalism, founded the so-called "Christian Church." In 1832 this body was to become associated with the group started by Thomas and Alexander Campbell under the name "Disciples of Christ." This movement continues in the South under the name "The Church of Christ" as well as the Christian Church. Sad to say, the "Church of Christ" has departed from the doctrine of justification by faith alone of the Protestant Reformation. They hold to a faith-plus-works doctrine, including the necessity of water baptism for salvation.

Despite the loss of the Cumberland and Disciples groups and the confusion caused by the excesses of the Great Revival, this movement did greatly affect the moral life of the country. Hays says, "Religion, from being a mere matter of contempt on the part of public men, became an essential and influential part of the general public sentiment of the Country."[8]

Generally speaking, only a few Presbyterian ministers were involved in these reactions to the full Calvinism of the Reformed faith. One of the basic problems in both the Cumberland and Disciples divisions was a lack of proper education of the revivalists and ministers ordained in Kentucky. This serves to confirm the historic position of the Presbyterian Church of insisting on a well-educated ministry, for it is all too easy to deviate from the full counsel of God if one has not been properly trained in handling the Word of Truth.

While the South was faced with the deviations brought on by revivalism, the Presbyterian Church in the North was involved in a plan to settle the newly opened Middle West that allowed New England Congregationalists to enter the Presbyterian Church without subscribing to the Westminster standards. Hopkinsian theology was on the rise in New England at this time. This meant that many of the Congregationalists who joined the Presbyterian Church came with a theology that was not Reformed. This became known as New School Theology.

By and large the Presbyterian Church in the South was not affected by New School Theology. There was a consciousness in the South of the fact that there was a difference between the Church North and South. This gave rise to the concept of "our Southern Zion" as early as the 1820s. The southern mind-set of simple trust in the Bible tended to cause a reaction against theological debate on matters that were not as clear as the basic evangelical tenets. The South remained generally aloof from the Old School–New School controversy. It was only with the clear deviation by the 1836 Assembly from the historic Reformed faith that Southerners became aroused.

Thompson says: "The Southern presbyteries, holding the balance of power in the Assembly, were generally in favor of ecclesiastical boards rather than the independent and co-operative Societies, and were overwhelmingly staunch in their adherence to the Westminster Standards and thus opposed to the New School 'heresies.' "[9]

Only in east Tennessee, where there was a breakdown of church discipline, was a college established where the Hopkinsian errors were taught. It is difficult to understand the failure of the Church to exercise discipline here, except that the founder of Abingdon Presbytery and the president of Greeneville College was the one who introduced these views. There was a natural hesitancy on the part of men more recently come to the presbytery and of some who had been educated under Mr. Balch to bring a charge against him. Also, the seriousness of Hopkinsian views was not fully recognized, especially in the light of the fact that Balch affirmed his belief in the *Confession* whenever brought before a court. A basic lesson to be learned is that personalities or position should not be allowed to prevent the proper exercise of discipline. Had the 1837 division not come when it did, a great deal more of the New School theology might have developed in the South than actually did develop.

It is interesting to observe that the few Southern Presbyterians who united with the New School Assembly did so for other than doctrinal reasons. Only in Tennessee, where, as we have already seen, the New School theology had a foothold, was there a majority of New School adherents. Even here it was not really because of theological agreement with the New School that these adhered to the New School Assembly. Rather, this may be accounted for by the influence of Hezekiah Balch, and by the fact that this area had been largely dependent on the American Home Missionary Society and the American Educational Society, both based in New England, for financial support. J. E. Alexander, historian of the Synod, says, "Though doctrinal differences constituted one of the causes of the division, it was evidently only a small portion of the Presbyterian ministers of the New School Body who held the doctrines of the New Divinity, at least in their full extent. The great majority of them were no doubt strictly orthodox and were influenced by the other considerations already mentioned."[10] The record of the Synod states the grounds as "the unconstitutional and unrighteous acts" of the two Reforming Assemblies, without mentioning doctrinal grounds.

In most of the other Synods minorities went independent, as in the case of the minority of the Presbytery of Charleston-Union and the Presbytery of Etowah in Georgia, which joined the New School Church. (The Charleston-Union Presbytery rejoined the Old School in 1852, and the Etowah Presbytery disappeared a few years after its formation.) In general, these defections from the Old School Church were not on theological grounds. The fear that the New School group would eventually denounce slavery as unchristian was appealed to by some as a ground for going with the Old School. On the other hand, the fear of centralization of power as represented by the 1837 exscinding action of the General Assembly was the motivation for some in Mississippi and South Carolina to withdraw from the Old School Assembly. Many felt that the actions of the 1837 Assembly had been unconstitutional, and thus allied themselves with the New School. Thompson concludes that "New School support in the South, with the possible exception of eastern Tennessee, was based overwhelmingly on opposition to what seemed unauthorized and unconstitutional authority exercised by the two Reforming Assemblies."[11]

Distinctive Theological Emphases

The Southern Presbyterian Church was essentially Old School in character. It is well to see what was peculiar to this brand of Presbyterianism. First, it was marked by strict subscription to the Westminster standards as the confession and constitution of the Church. Being thus committed to the Westminster standards, it was a Calvinistic church, embracing all of the tenets that go under that name.

The historic Puritan and Scottish doctrine of the sole headship of Christ over his church was maintained. Out of this came the high view of the church, that it is a positive institution of Christ and must do only what he teaches it to do in his Word. Thornwell of South Carolina was to carry out this principle with the greatest consistency, opposing at points such men as Charles Hodge of Princeton on certain matters of polity. Though Thornwell did not carry the day in the undivided church, his views were to prevail in the Southern Church after 1861.

Thornwell maintained that the church "is a positive institution, and therefore must show a definite warrant for everything that she does. It is not enough that her measures are not condemned, they must be sanctioned, positively sanctioned, by the power which ordains her, or they are null and void."[12] He opposed the use of boards to carry out the work of the church. Rather, the church courts ought to handle this directly. Instead of an independent, or semi-independent, board carrying on the work of missions the General Assembly should carry this work on through committees directly responsible to the Assembly. This position was adopted by the Southern Presbyterian Church, and though it abandoned it in the 1940s, the Presbyterian Church in America, which separated from the Southern Church in 1973, has returned to it.

A distinctively southern view of the office of the ruling elder arose. Following the 1837-38 division the practice of having the ruling elder lay hands on a man being ordained to the office of the ministry began in Kentucky. The General Assembly of 1843 declared that "neither the Constitution nor the practice of our Church authorizes Ruling Elders to impose hands in the ordination of ministers."[13] Drs. R. J. Breckinridge and J. H. Thornwell took issue with this double ruling of the Assembly. They maintained that the New Testament elder included both teaching and ruling elders, that as true elders they were an integral element of a presbytery and thus necessary to its regular constitution, and that they had a right to participate in all of the actions of presbytery including all steps to the ordination of ministers. The Assembly, however, in 1844 followed Hodge in denying the necessity of ruling elders in presbytery, and their right to participate in the ordination of ministers.With the division of 1861 the view of Thornwell became the accepted view of the Southern Presbyterian Church and continues to be one of the distinctives of this Church.[14] This has also been carried over into the Presbyterian Church in America.

Another southern development in church polity was the idea that the office of deacon is to handle all the temporal affairs of the church. This was first enunciated by Thomas Smythe of Charleston, South Carolina. The idea of systematic benevolences was also developed during this period, and had the support of such Southerners as Stuart Robinson and J. H. Thornwell. Generally speaking, the southern leaders of this period opposed instrumental music and liturgical elements in the worship service. This, of course, grows out of the *jure divino* view of church polity and worship that was held in the South.

This same view of the church was applied to the burning social issue of slavery:

> The Church of Christ is a spiritual body, whose jurisdiction extends only to the religious faith and moral conduct of her members. She cannot legislate where Christ has not legislated, nor make terms of membership which He has not made. . . .
>
> Since Christ and his inspired Apostles did not make the holding of slaves a bar to communion, we, as a court of Christ, have no authority to do so; since they did not attempt to remove it from the Church by legislation, we have no authority to legislate on the subject.[15]

This view of the church, which prevented the Assembly from legislating on the issue of slavery, kept the Old School body intact until 1861. Only then, under the heat of the circumstances of war, did the Assembly break with this principle and pass the Gardiner Spring Resolution. This resolution in effect decided the political issue between the North and South, and virtually exscinded all Southern Presbyterians from the Church. It said:

> Resolved, . . . that this General Assembly . . . do hereby acknowledge and declare our obligations to promote and perpetuate, so far as in us lies, the integrity of these United States, and to strengthen, uphold, and encourage the Federal Government in the exercise of all its functions under our noble Constitution; and to this Constitution in all its provisions, requirements, and principles, we profess our unabated loyalty. . . .[16]

Charles Hodge of Princeton, with 57 others, protested this action of the Assembly. This protest states in part: "The General Assembly in thus deciding a political question, and in making that decision practically a condition of membership to the Church, has, in our judgment, violated the Constitution of the Church, and usurped the prerogative of its Divine Master."[17]

B. M. Palmer, first Moderator of the Southern Assembly, declared:

> This question, lying wholly within the domain of politics, the General Assembly assumed the right to determine; so that, even if not ejected by what was equivalent to an act of expulsion, the Southern Presbyteries were compelled to separate themselves, in order to preserve the crown rights of the Redeemer and the spiritual independence of His kingdom and the Church. . . .[18]

The Presbyteries of the South dissolved their connection with the General Assembly of the Presbyterian Church in the United States of America. A total of 47 Presbyteries, making up 10 Synods, thus withdrew. On the 4th of December, 1861, at the First Presbyterian Church of Augusta, Georgia, the commissioners from these Presbyteries met and constituted the first General Assembly of the Presbyterian Church in the Confederate States of America. This meeting was opened with a stirring sermon on the Kingship of Christ over His Church by B. M. Palmer, pastor of the First Presbyterian Church of New Orleans. After adopting its official name, the Assembly then formally adopted the Westminster standards as its constitution, thus continuing the American Presbyterian tradition of commitment to these doctrinal standards. That the Southern Presbyterian Church saw itself as a distinctively Old School Presbyterian Church may be seen in the fact that she spoke out most clearly against the way in which the Old and New School branches of the Northern church reunited in 1869, which she judged to be a total abandonment of the Old School heritage.[19]

The Southern Presbyterian Church was marked by certain distinctive characteristics during the first 75 years of its life. They were a commitment to the Bible as the inspired and infallible Word of God; a thoroughgoing and enthusiastic Calvinism, regarded as a part of the gospel that was to be preached to the people; and a view of the mission of the church as spiritual, which was maintained both in theory and in practice. She developed an ecclesiastical polity that was distinguished for its constitutionality, particularly as seen in the complete parity of the ruling elders with the teaching elders, the carefully defined spheres and rights of the several courts, and its opposition to centralism. She stood for a strict construction of and adherence to the Westminster standards both in theory and in practice.

The newborn Church was especially interested in missions as the supreme work of the church. Among the resolutions of that first Assembly regarding missions is this classic statement regarding the place of missionary work in the life of the church:

> Finally, the General Assembly desires distinctly and deliberately to inscribe on our church's banner, as she now unfurls it to the world, in immediate connection with the headship of our Lord, his last command: "Go ye into all the world and preach the gospel to every creature"; regarding this as the great end of her organization, and obedience to it as the indispensable condition of her Lord's promised presence, and as one great comprehensive object, a proper conception of whose vast magnitude and grandeur is the only thing which, in connection with the love of Christ, can ever sufficiently arouse her energies and develop her resources so as to cause her to carry on, with the vigor and efficiency which true fealty to her Lord demands, those other agencies necessary to her internal growth and home prosperity.[20]

A particular development in Southern Presbyterian theological thought should be noted. It was the development of the doctrine of adoption as a separate *locus* in the Columbia Seminary school of thought. Hodge and Dabney had followed Turretin and dealt with adoption in connection with justification. The Columbia theologians followed the *Confession* and *Catechisms,* and thus developed the doctrine of adoption as a separate *locus.* This line of thinking began with John L. Girardeau of Columbia, and was continued by R. A. Webb, his son-in-law, who taught at Louisville Seminary. He produced a work entitled *The Reformed Doctrine of Adoption,* which was printed after his death.

Prior to the War between the States, the southern way of life allowed time for the development of a deep scholarship. Men such as Alexander, Thornwell, Dabney, Warfield, and Machen were all products of the South. They are among the most distinguished theologians America has produced. After the War, and during the long course of the slow recovery of the South from the cultural upheaval that her defeat brought, relatively few scholars arose from the South. The result is that though the seminaries of the South remained essentially sound up to the 1930s and 1940s, they were not really producing deep thinkers. Orthodoxy began to be looked upon as unscholarly. In the meantime Presbyterians of the North drifted into liberalism. Thus, when Southerners went north for theological training they were exposed to liberalism, even at Princeton after Machen's departure in 1929. These men came back to teach at the southern seminaries. Their appeal to the rising young generation was that scholarship was on the liberal side. The result was a rapid decline of the Southern Presbyterian Church into liberalism. The last

General Assembly controlled by the conservative element in the Southern Presbyterian Church was in 1939. Since that time the orthodox Christian has had a constant struggle to maintain his position in the Southern Presbyterian Church.

Recent Developments

There was a group that saw the necessity of reforming their Church. They developed several different means of reform. First, the *Southern Presbyterian Journal* (now the *Presbyterian Journal*) became a rallying point for conservatives in the Church. The *Journal* had its beginnings in the late 1940s. Unsuccessful efforts were launched by students of Columbia Theological Seminary during the early 1950s to have a liberal professor removed. A number of these men are now in the leadership of the Presbyterian Church in America. Successful efforts were launched to keep some of the presbyteries and synods of the deep South conservative. Belhaven College became a coeducational institution in 1954, and soon began training a stream of pre-ministerial students who became convinced of the Reformed faith and maintained their convictions even though many attended the liberal seminaries of the denomination. A number of these men now constitute a significant element of the ministers of the Presbyterian Church in America. In addition to this, the Pensacola Theological Institute began to bring in Reformed scholars and preachers from all over the world. They trained not only theological students, but also a large number of laymen from across the South.

One of the most encouraging occurrences was the increasing number of conservative young men who were getting advanced degrees and returning to the South as strongly committed and well-trained defenders of the historic faith. Though committed to the basic Reformed faith that they had learned in the South, they brought with them insights from their various schools of study, thus enriching the theological thought of the South.

The outside institution that had the greatest influence on the conservative Southern Presbyterians was Westminster Theological Seminary. There are several reasons for this. One that has already been noted is the affinity that the Southern Presbyterians had with the Old Princeton theology. Westminster was, of course, the successor of Old Princeton. Second, a fair number of Southern Presbyterian ministers were educated at Westminster. The influence of these became particularly evident in the movement toward a new Church, since a number of these individuals became teachers.

In 1964 the foundations of the Reformed Theological Seminary of Jackson, Mississippi, were laid, and this seminary opened its doors in

1966. Though there was no actual formal relationship between Reformed Seminary and Westminster, the original faculty of Reformed Seminary, of which the present writer was a member, viewed it as something of a daughter seminary to Westminster. Several members of that faculty had been trained at Westminster. They certainly felt that the theology they were teaching was the same as that of Westminster, and thus they looked to Westminster for encouragement and aid. Several of the Westminster faculty, including Dr. Cornelius Van Til, visited Reformed Seminary and gave special lectures. The relation seems to have been similar to that which Union Seminary of Virginia had with Princeton in its early history.

Reformed Seminary became one of the primary sources for conservative ministers serving Presbyterianism in the South. At the beginning most of the graduates of the Seminary were placed in the more conservative presbyteries of the Presbyterian Church in the United States. Many of these were to identify with the Presbyterian Church in America when it was founded in 1973. Others remained in the Presbyterian Church in the United States (now merged with the Northern Church to form the PCUSA). Since the founding of the Presbyterian Church in America, the majority of the graduates of the Seminary have entered its ranks as ministers.

Since its founding, Reformed Theological Seminary has become the primary source of Reformed theological developments in the South. In what follows we shall review some of these developments. The Seminary has witnessed an interesting melding of a number of streams of Reformed thought. The majority of the faculty have been drawn out of the Southern Presbyterian background. These have stood largely in the tradition of Thornwell and Dabney. They have sought to maintain the historic Reformed faith as developed in Southern Presbyterianism, coupling a warmhearted evangelism with full commitment to the Reformed faith. One of the early areas of discussion at the Seminary was the question of how evangelism is to be carried out. Many of the students came to the Seminary with evangelistic methods that reflected an Arminian approach to man and not the Reformed view. Efforts were made to encourage men to think through more consistently the implications of the Reformed faith in the area of evangelism. Generally speaking, the Seminary encouraged the Evangelism Explosion methods developed at the Coral Ridge Presbyterian Church, Fort Lauderdale, Florida, to get people involved in personal evangelism. The present writer has written a pamphlet entitled "Reformed Evangelism" that has had a good reception.

A particular area where the influence of Westminster is seen is in the field of apologetics. Westminster Seminary departed from the Old Princeton theology in the study of apologetics as developed under the tutelage of Cornelius Van Til. Had Westminster Seminary not been formed in 1929 under the leadership of J. Gresham Machen, Dr. Van Til no doubt would have developed his thinking at Princeton, since he was already on the faculty there before Westminster began. The apologetics of Dr. Van Til has come to be known as presuppositional apologetics, as opposed to the traditional evidential apologetics of Old Princeton. American Presbyterianism in general had uncritically accepted the evidential approach to apologetics in its conflict with the deism of the eighteenth century. The present writer, who had some of his theological training at Westminster Seminary, taught both Systematic Theology and Apologetics at Reformed Seminary during its first decade. In theology, he followed the exegetical, biblical theological method of Professor John Murray. In apologetics he taught the presuppositional approach. A large number of Reformed graduates are thus committed to this view of theology and apologetics.

One of the interesting developments that took place at Reformed Seminary during this period was the brief professorship of Dr. Gregg Bahnsen in the field of apologetics and ethics. It was during this time that he published his book *Theonomy in Christian Ethics*. A number of his students became committed to reconstructionist postmillennialism and to theonomy. Though Dr. Bahnsen is no longer at Reformed Seminary, the impact of his instruction there is still felt in the South in that a small number of his followers are now in the ministry of the Presbyterian Church in America. Though the question of whether theonomy is acceptable in the Presbyterian Church in America has been raised, the Church has declined to get into this matter. It has indicated that theonomy should not become a test of orthodoxy. Not all have been pleased with this position, but they have permitted the coexistence in the Presbyterian Church in America of theonomists and nontheonomists.

Two groups of theonomists have left the PCA in order to have what they consider greater freedom in the propagation of their views. The first of these is the Westminster Presbyterian Church of Tyler, Texas. This Church operates a small theological school called Geneva, and produces a number of publications. Some of this Tyler group have renounced the time-honored "regulative principle" of worship of the Westminster Catechism of the Presbyterian Church, which states that we are to include in worship only what the Bible teaches. This group also espouses paedocommunion.

The other group that left the PCA over theonomy is a small group of churches headed by the Chalcedon Presbyterian Church of the Atlanta area. These churches have formed a small Presbyterian denomination known as the Reformed Presbyterian Church in the United States. This group has not displayed the same kinds of deviations from historic Presbyterianism that the Tyler group has shown. Both groups hold to reconstructionist postmillennialism.

A revival of postmillennialism as an acceptable eschatological view has occurred in Southern Presbyterianism during the past two decades. Though the majority of the ministers in the South hold to amillennialism, there are a large number of pre- and postmillennialists. Not all of the postmillennialists hold to the reconstructionist view of R. J. Rushdoony, but many hold to a more traditional postmillennialism.

Still another stream of thought that has entered Southern Presbyterian circles, largely through Westminster and Reformed Theological Seminaries, is the concept of a Christian world-and-life view. Abraham Kuyper's Stone Lectures on *Calvinism*, delivered at Princeton Theological Seminary in 1898, introduced this broad concept to the American Presbyterian world. Earlier American Presbyterians had practiced the idea of living their faith out in various areas of life, as may be seen from the fact that many of them were influential in early American political life. In the South, however, there had been something of a drawing back from it, due to a misapplication of Thornwell's doctrine of the spirituality of the church. Many Southern Presbyterians applied this to their personal lives as well as to the church. With the carefully thought-out ideas of Kuyper and his development of "sphere sovereignty" a more balanced view of how we are to view the application of Christian principles to every area of life, and not just to the church, was found. The theonomists, of course, embrace this concept, but so do many others who are not fully identified with theonomy. For example, the Christian Studies Center of Memphis, Tennessee, has been seeking to propagate the Kuyperian world-and-life view for a number of years through publications and lectures. This organization has been established and kept alive through the untiring labors of Robert Metcalf, a ruling elder of the Second Presbyterian Church of Memphis. The Christian Studies Center has not met with great success, but is cited here as an illustration of the breadth of Reformed thought that now exists in the South.

With the recognition of the stranglehold that the liberals had on all of the institutions and agencies of the Presbyterian Church in the United States, and with the beginning of groups departing from that Church, the leadership of the conservatives in the PCUS determined that there should be a separation from that Church in 1973. Generally speaking, an effort was put forth to make this as peaceable as possible. Churches and individuals simply notified their presbyteries of their intention to leave. The first General Assembly of the Presbyterian Church in America was held at Birmingham on December 4, 1973.

This body saw itself as continuing the historic Presbyterian faith that the Southern Presbyterian Church had held during its early years, and which it had in turn received from the Old School Presbyterian Church prior to that. The PCA may be called an Old School Presbyterian Church, holding to the inerrancy of the Scripture in the original autographs, strict subscription to the *Westminster Confession* and *Catechisms*, and to Southern Presbyterian Church polity.

This Church has from its beginning seen as its mission to reach across the whole nation, and not to remain a regional church as the Southern Presbyterian Church had done. In 1982 the Reformed Presbyterian Church, Evangelical Synod joined the PCA, accepting its Southern Presbyterian polity. Thus, this polity is now being practiced across the entire nation in this new and growing Church. The roots of the RPCES went back largely to the Old School segment of the Northern Church. It held to the Old Princeton theology. Thus in this "joining and receiving" the streams of "Southern" and "Princeton" theology again merged.

The Southern Presbyterian Church (PCUS) has united with the Northern Church (UPCUSA) to form the Presbyterian Church in the United States of America. There remain those who are sound in the faith in this Church, but by and large the denomination must be characterized as liberal in persuasion and direction. The distinctives of the earlier Southern Presbyterians have been lost in this body. These distinctives are now carried on in the Presbyterian Church in America, which encompasses both Canada and the United States.

In this essay we have traced some of the distinctive developments of Southern Presbyterian thought on the American church scene. We have seen that there has been a separate development in the past, but we have also noted that in this century a good deal of broadening has taken place. This seems to be in accord with what is presently happening to the South. Increasingly the South is becoming amalgamated with the rest of the country in its thought and culture. One wonders whether there will continue to be a distinctively Southern Presbyterian strand of theology, or whether it will not eventually be merged into the broad stream of Reformed thought found both in America and abroad. Should the Southern distinctives gradually be lost, some of the South's contributions will no doubt become a part of the larger whole, while the South itself will benefit from the many advances in Reformed thought that are taking place in other parts of the Lord's vineyard.

Notes: The Southern Tradition

1. Ernest Trice Thompson, *Presbyterians in the South*, vol. 1, *1607-1861* (Richmond, VA: John Knox Press, 1963), 629.

2. *History of the Independent Church and Sunday School, Savannah, Ga.* (Savannah: George N. Nichols, 1882).

3. William Henry Foote, *Sketches of Virginia: Historical and Biographical* (Philadelphia: n.p., 1850), 1:146.

4. Herman Bavinck, *Gereformeerde Dogmatiek*, 4th ed. (Kampen, J. H. Kok, 1928), 1:177.

5. John Holt Rice, Letter to Archibald Alexander, dated Richmond, March 5th, 1823, in William Maxwell, *A Memoir of the Rev. John H. Rice, D.D.* (Philadelphia and Richmond, VA: n.p., 1835), 233.

6. Letter from Gaston Boyle to Morton H. Smith, November 1961, in Morton Howison Smith, *Studies in Southern Presbyterian Theology* (Amsterdam: Van Campen, 1962), 320.

7. Philip Schaff, *Creeds of Christendom*, 4th ed. (New York: Harper and Brothers, 1919), 1:815. Cf. 3:771-76 for the Cumberland Confession.

8. George P. Hays, *Presbyterians, a Popular Narrative of Their Origin, Progress, and Achievements* (New York: J. A. Hill and Company, 1892), 151.

9. Ibid., 384.

10. *A Brief History of the Synod of Tennessee from 1817 to 1887* (Philadelphia: MacCalla & Company, 1890), 32-33, cited by Thompson, *Presbyterians*, 409.

11. Ibid., 412.

12. James Henry Thornwell, *Collected Writings* (Richmond: Presbyterian Committee of Publication, 1881), 4:210.

13. Cited from *Minutes of the General Assembly (O.S.) 1843*, 183.

14. See Thornwell, *Collected Writings.*

15. *Minutes of the General Assembly (O.S.) 1845*, 16-17.

16. *Minutes of the General Assembly (O.S.) 1861*, 16-17.

17. Ibid., 340.

18. Thomas Carey Johnson, *The Life and Letters of Benjamin Morgan Palmer* (Richmond, VA: n.p., 1906), 502.

19. *Minutes, PCUS, 1870*, 529; also in *Alexander's Digest, 1888*, 451, and in *Digest 1861-1965*, 342.

20. *Minutes PCCSA, 1861*, 17.

ROBERT LEWIS DABNEY

DOUGLAS FLOYD KELLY

Robert Lewis Dabney was perhaps the greatest, and certainly the most prolific, Southern Presbyterian theologian of nineteenth-century America. Reformed theologians of Europe such as Lecerf, Bavinck, and Barth spoke of Dabney with appreciation and respect. The great Charles Hodge of Princeton so highly regarded Dabney that he repeatedly urged him to join the Princeton faculty in 1860. In later years, A. A. Hodge and W. G. T. Shedd considered Dabney to be the greatest teacher of theology in the United States. B. B. Warfield said: ". . . Dr. Dabney was not only an influential statesman and a powerful ecclesiastical force, not only an acute philosophiser and a profound theologian, but also a devoted Christian—which is best of all."[1]

Yet for all his massive abilities, voluminous writings, and widespread personal prestige, Dabney lived to see his own theological and ecclesiastical influence drastically wane, so that near the end of his life he could sadly say: "I have no audience."[2] From his death in 1898 until the early 1960s, Dabney's work was largely eclipsed in his own denomination, not to mention the wider church. The reasons for his rise to prominence and then his rather drastic decline are found primarily in his theological stance and secondarily in the events and attitudes of his own eventful life and times.

Dabney's Life

While much of Dabney's *Systematic Theology*, for instance, is in the standard Reformed idiom and thus speaks for itself, it would be very difficult—if not impossible—to understand his social, economic, and political philosophy as well as many of his more directly religious essays unless we took into account the cultural and historical context of his life in the Old South. Unlike many theologians who pass their lives in sequestered libraries and classrooms, Dabney, like Abraham Kuyper of Holland, lived much of his life in public positions during tumultuous times.

His biographer, Thomas Cary Johnson, wrote:

> The lives even of most great preachers pass in such quiet that the historian finds little to dwell upon. What he says of one day's labor and achievements may be said of almost every other day. Such was not the life of Dr. Dabney. His life touched so many points in the common history of church and state and touched them in a way so unusual that it is impossible to give an adequate sketch in a few pages.[3]

Dabney was born March 5, 1820, on South Anna River in Louisa County, Virginia, the fourth of six children. His parents, Charles and Elizabeth Dabney, were typical Virginia country gentry. Charles was Colonel of the county militia, as well as a magistrate and member of the county court. He owned a tobacco and grain plantation, two mills, and several slaves, and was an elder in the Presbyterian Church. The older Dabneys had been brought up during times of revival in Virginia (the latter years of the "Second Great Awakening"), and maintained a strict but warmly evangelical household. In this Calvinist home not only were the Bible and Westminster Shorter Catechism taught, but the children "caught" the principles of conservative, decentralized republican forms of government from frequent conversations between their parents and visitors. The Virginia of Washington, Madison, Jefferson, Henry, and Marshall had never ceased to be politically minded and intensely committed to the liberties guaranteed (to the property-holding classes) by constitutional, representative civil government.

In the Dabney home there was a mingling of Calvinist simplicity and Puritan hard work with an element of aristocratic leisure based on the "peculiarly southern" institution of domestic slavery. Dabney grew up deeply loving the life and institutions of his native Virginia and of the larger antebellum South. It was to him the ideal blending of plainness and modesty with the richness of genuine Christian culture. Dabney once wrote an entire letter describing the surprised reaction of a "proud New Yorker" to the unexpected gentility and culture of Richmond society.[4]

Life became much harder for the Dabney family when the father, Charles, died in early middle age in 1833. Robert, then age 13, had to take on a good deal of responsibility for the management of the plantation and the well-being of his brothers and sisters. His letters show that strong cords of mutual affection bound this family together to the last.

In the midst of all his responsibilities, young Robert Dabney received a very competent education for his time and place:

He received his preparatory training in country schools taught by his brother and other able men. The schedule of studies did not cover many lines, but very thorough work was done in Latin, Greek, Algebra, and Geometry. His zeal led him to ride once a week to get Dr. Thomas Wharey, his mother's pastor, to drill him in Mathematics.

He spent a short time at Hampden-Sydney College; it covered three sessions, as the course then ran . . . (in 1836 and 1837). . . . He finished Mathematics, Physics, Latin and Greek. When he left the college the faculty sent his mother a report and assigned him the most distinguished rank in behavior, and the most distinguished rank in industry. He was the only one of his class so highly ranked.[5]

Toward the end of his time at Hampden-Sydney "the college was visited by a powerful and genuine awakening." Dabney was converted during this revival in September of 1837, and many years later commented that "The most important event of this period to me was my profession of faith in Christ."[6]

Dabney left Hampden-Sydney without completing his course in order to come home and help his mother improve the precarious financial position of their plantation. For about two years Robert, though a slaveholder, worked with his hands quarrying stone, rebuilt one of the family mills, managed the fields, and in addition opened and taught a neighborhood school—all of this at age 18!

Dabney's education was not finished, however,

. . . because he found a way to enter the University of Virginia at Charlottesville. His uncle, Reuben Lewis, living near the University, had offered to give him board for himself and horse. The University offered fuller courses of study under more distinguished professors. . . . On July 5, 1842, he received his degree of Master of Arts. His study had made him a thinker.[7]

Robert returned to his mother's plantation for two more years of physical work, teaching of classes, and newspaper writing. He did so well as a writer that he was offered a job with one of the largest papers in the state—a forerunner of greater things to come. During this time he managed to save a few hundred dollars; this he was to spend on his subsequent education for the Presbyterian ministry.

In November, 1844, he entered Union Seminary at Hampden-Sydney, Va. This institution was under a cloud of depression. There were only three professors: Dr. Samuel B. Wilson was Professor of Systematic and Polemic Theology, Dr. Samuel L. Graham of Ecclesiastical History, Dr. Francis R. Sampson of Oriental Literature. There were only eighteen students. Some from Virginia and North Carolina were at Columbia and Princeton. Mr. Dabney chose the smaller Seminary, for he believed in building up home institutions.[8]

By this time American Presbyterianism had divided into two major streams: New School and Old School. New School Presbyterianism, largely—though not entirely—in the North, was more open to the spirit of the age, and accommodated itself theologically to some aspects of Arminianism and other elements of post-Enlightenment thought. The Old School, which comprised a slight majority in the North and a vast majority in the South, cordially and strictly held to the robust Calvinism of the Westminster standards, and consciously saw itself as challenging the errors of the age. The Presbyterian Church in America had split over this very issue in 1837. Union Seminary, like its more illustrious northern sister, Princeton Seminary, was solidly in the Old School camp.

Perhaps the greatest single influence on young Dabney at Union was the fine scholar and pious saint, Dr. Francis R. Sampson. One of Dabney's first major writings was to be the biography of Sampson in 1854. "In mature old age Dr. Dabney wrote: 'If I ever had any intellectual growth and vigor, I owed it to three things—first, the Master of Arts' Course in the University of Virginia; second, to Dr. F. R. Sampson, and third, to my subsequent mastery of Turretin.' "[9]

In the summer of 1846 Dabney finished his studies at Union and was licensed by West Hanover Presbytery. His Latin thesis was "Quomodo Homo Justificatus Sit?" and his Greek exegesis on Hebrews 6:4-6. Although Dabney was a tall, large-framed man, his health at this stage was rather poor and his life was not expected to be a long one. Thus the Presbytery assigned him to three small, remote congregations as a home missionary in his native Louisa County. In spite of his poor health, his ministrations here were very faithful and warmly appreciated.

In 1847 Dabney was called to be pastor of the Tinkling Spring Church in Augusta County, near Staunton, Virginia. He had an effective ministry here among the (at times) headstrong Scotch-Irish for over six years. During this time of hard study, continual pastoral work, and diligent exegetical preaching attended by deep and agonizing prayer, many blessings entered into the life of pastor and congregation. Dabney was the architect for a new church building (which still stands); he met Miss Lavinia Morrison, daughter of a neighboring minister, whom he loved at first sight and soon married; and to crown it all a revival broke out in the church in 1850, during which over 30 persons were brought to Christ.

Dabney demonstrated his practical bent and many-sided abilities by building his own house out of stone that he himself had cut. "He was a good practical farmer, a good teacher, a good pastor, a capital member of a military staff. He was a skillful mechanic and furniture maker. . . . He bound books well, drew maps and plans for buildings."[10]

In 1853, at the age of 33, Dabney was called to the Chair of Ecclesiastical History and Polity at Union Seminary in Hampden-Sydney. For the next thirty years this was to be the scene of his major life's work as teacher, writer, churchman, statesman, soldier, and—above all— theologian.

> With characteristic energy he prepared a course of study that made young men master the facts and principles of history. He impressed the importance of acquiring good habits of study, as a preparation for life. He made such a reputation that in a few years he was invited to teach at Princeton, but he declined it.
>
> He spent his vacations in traveling through Virginia and North Carolina seeking students, funds and the support of presbyteries and congregations. By 1859 the number of students had increased to fifty-nine, new professors had been secured. . . . Never again was the Seminary considered as a liability, but a great asset.
>
> He was called to the presidency of Hampden-Sydney College in 1858, to the Fifth Avenue Church of New York in 1860, and also to Princeton in 1860, but he remained at Union.[11]

In 1859 Dabney was transferred to the Chair of Theology, which he undertook with enthusiasm, immense competence, and fresh vitality. Dabney believed that Systematic Theology must be based fairly and squarely upon an exegesis of the Scriptures. In an article in 1856, Dabney described the work of both professors and students at Union Seminary:

> . . . each professor shall be required to expound some portion of the original Scriptures. This is important to the teacher himself, that he may be brought into immediate contact with the Word of God. . . . Exegetical study is the great means for cultivating a right literary spirit in the theologian.[12]
>
> The student begins with the great fact that the Word of God (in the originals) is the grand repository of all the *data* of the science of divinity. . . . the Professor of Systematic and Pastoral Theology . . . teaches him, with the Bible still in his hand to methodize and understand the mutual relations of the Scripture facts and doctrines that they may assume in his mind the strength of *a system*.[13]

Dabney taught by means of dialogue. Two days before he lectured on a subject he wrote on the board a series of questions for his students. (Many of these questions are preserved at the beginning of each of the chapters in his *Systematic Theology*.) Along with the questions Dabney gave the students specific readings in various theologians—especially

Turretin in Latin and Dick in English. The class had to answer the questions in writing, which Dabney corrected; then he lectured on the subject. During these years Dabney also served as copastor of the College Church, and was beginning to turn out a good deal of writing, especially in church periodicals. The pleasant though demanding routine of his scholarly life was soon to be interrupted by a momentous event that would change not only his own life, but that of the entire nation: the bitter and devastating War Between the States from 1861-1865.

The causes of this War are highly complex, but perhaps primarily revolved around the question of states' rights versus centralized national authority. Many in the South believed that the northern states were taking unfair advantage of the Union to advance their own economic interests (through tariffs, for instance), and that the various states had the constitutional right to withdraw from the Union; whereas many in the North felt that the states had no such rights, and that the power of the central government should be used to abolish southern slavery.

At first, Dabney—like most Virginians (and unlike most South Carolinians)—was a moderate on the question of both slavery and withdrawal.[14] Just before the outbreak of hostilities he joined with other evangelical ministers of both North and South in pleading with Christians in all parts of America to pray and do all they could to avoid fratricidal conflict.[15] In his earlier years he certainly favored the gradual emancipation of all slaves.[16] When the War did break out, however, Dabney committed himself wholeheartedly to the southern cause. His thinking became increasingly partisan and colored by all the emotion and vehemence of the "underdog" in this painful and deathly struggle. For the rest of his life he would believe that the southern cause was totally righteous and that "Yankeedom" was totally wicked.

Dabney firmly believed that the War was caused by the French Revolution "Jacobin" principles of New England Unitarian abolitionists and their liberal congressional "hacks," who wished to turn the original constitutional republic with its emphasis on state and local power into a secularized, centralized democratic power.[17] While a recent work by historian Otto Scott[18] indicates that there was at least an element of truth in this assessment, nonetheless Dabney's attitude was a gross oversimplification and in a sense ignored—or treated with contempt—the vital question of how the rest of the world felt about the morality of slavery.[19]

Not only was Dabney a literary apologist for the South and preacher to the troops, but for a while he served on the front lines as Chief of Staff to the famous Confederate general and pious Presbyterian deacon, Thomas J. "Stonewall" Jackson. Jackson said that Dabney was the most efficient officer he ever had.[20] Before the War ended, Dabney wrote a large and popular biography of Jackson. Not long after, he wrote *A De-*

fense of Virginia and Through Her of the South, which showed that slavery was not explicitly condemned by the Scriptures as sinful, and argued that it had been the most beneficial economic and moral system for all concerned in the South. From a strictly exegetical viewpoint, Dabney was right that the Scriptures never specifically condemned slavery, and yet in retrospect it seems strange and sad that he and the other southern defenders of slavery totally failed to come to terms with the implications of the biblical Jubilee—that a slave who became a brother in the faith must be given his freedom after seven years since he is now in the covenant[21]—and with the equally important fact that Christianity established new moral and social conditions that would render personal bondage unacceptable. Unlike Professor Frank Bell Lewis, who felt that Dabney's major failure at this point was his identification with the conservative Bibliocentrism of nineteenth-century Virginia rather than with the more liberal Jeffersonian tradition of eighteenth-century Virginia, we would suggest that Dabney was not overly biblical on this subject; on the contrary, he did not go as far as his Bible should have taken him.[22] Like all other fallen men, including theologians, he had blind spots where his devotion to the culture made it difficult for him to interpret the will of God.

After the bitter defeat of the South in 1865 and then the agony and humiliation of impoverishing Reconstruction, much of Dabney's life seemed to be lived under deepening shadows. He seriously considered emigrating from the United States, but decided to stay. As his biographer says, for the rest of his life "he was at war with much in his age."[23]

The eighteenth-century secularist Enlightenment and its nineteenth-century European developments were bringing vast changes in the Western world, and it seems clear that the War between the States hastened the breakdown of the relative isolation and conservative Christian consensus of the American South. "French" political radicalism, "German" Higher Criticism of the Scriptures, and "British" evolutionism were all influencing the intellectual classes of America, while a broad, basically Arminian type of evangelicalism with new methodologies (developed by evangelists Finney and Moody) was deeply influencing the popular classes. In the philosophical world, the very possibility of objective knowledge of reality—and specifically of any true knowledge of a personal God—was being radically questioned and excluded from consideration. Dabney waged vigorous and vehement war against all of these powerful, secularizing trends of the century.

Almost never an obscurantist, Dabney carefully read the works of the enemies of biblical Calvinism, and traced their errors down to their poisonous roots. He had a wide interest and a mind that could successfully grapple with complex issues in philosophy, logic, sociology, and economics. He brought vigorous, and at times caustic and scathing criticism to bear on humanistic and Arminian trends. He offered uncompromising, and sometimes painful, solutions from the Word of God to a remarkably broad variety of questions. While his analysis and solutions were generally well grounded biblically, and not infrequently manifested a radically brilliant insight, nevertheless his stringent tone, inflexibility, and on occasion lack of proper tact alienated many who otherwise might have fought on his side. On the other hand, a careful reading of his life and times will indicate that the basic reason for his increasing lack of popularity (even among his own Southern Presbyterians) was not his all too real failures of tone and tact, but his uncompromising, public insistence on total loyalty to the traditional biblical Calvinism that was becoming an embarrassment to the post-Enlightenment, broadening Evangelical mainstream that was inundating all of America's churches, the Reformed included.

Although he had had the honor of serving the (Southern) Presbyterian Church in the United States as Moderator in 1870, and had continued to publish widely read articles and significant books, still he was swimming against the mainstream as he opposed any sort of union with the Northern Presbyterian Church; as he opposed public education (as inherently secularist); as he opposed Moody/Sankey type "revivals"; and as he continued to oppose social and business accommodation of Southerners with the increasingly dominant "Yankee" capitalistic economy and culture.[24] By 1883 Dabney keenly felt "his loss of influence at the Seminary."[25] According to Frank B. Lewis, the Seminary authorities "had refused to accept his proposals for the future of that institution"; Dabney "felt himself isolated from the main currents of the life of the Southern Church," and "his long list of controversies had won him the reputation of being cantankerous."[26] In addition to this, his health was bad and his doctors advised a drier climate.

Thus (we can imagine with much sadness and frustration) he accepted a call to teach at the University of Texas in Austin, in the Chair of Moral and Mental Philosophy. While there in the final stage of his ever active life, he organized the Theological Seminary of Austin and wrote very widely in the fields of sociology, politics, philosophy, and economics.[27] In 1889 he became completely blind, but was able to continue teaching, preaching, and writing. As Dabney remained thoroughly conservative and Calvinist, however, the University of Texas was moving in a more liberal direction.[28] Because of this, in what was undoubtedly a parable of his life, Dabney was asked to resign in 1894. He continued to lecture and write, and two significant books came from his pen within a year of his death in 1898: *The Atonement* and *The Practical Philosophy*.

Dabney as a Theologian and Philosopher

Dabney's theological approach and methodology is remarkably similar to that of the Westminster standards: it is biblical (and to a degree exegetical), it is moderate and nonspeculative, and it faces the hardest questions while attempting to avoid harshness. If Dabney made extreme statements (and he did), these were made in the realm of politics and social philosophy, but almost never in theology. He wrote his theology the way standard church confessions are written—with the larger Reformed and Christian community in mind. Dabney certainly followed the advice of the Scottish Commissioner Henderson to the Westminster Assembly of the 1640s: "Let us avoid all scholastical disputes and unnecessary distinctions."

Dabney nobly exemplifies in his own theology what he says about the enduring quality of the Westminster standards:

> . . . The second marked trait of the Confession (is) its doctrinal moderation. . . . The Assembly . . . was too wise to attempt the conciliating of opposites by the surrendering of any essential member of the system of revealed truth. They present us the Pauline, Augustinian or Calvinist creed in its integrity. But on the other hand, they avoid every excess and every extreme statement. They refrained with a wise moderation from committing the Church of God on either side of those "isms" which agitated and perplexed the professors of the Reformed Theology.

Then Dabney illustrates the moderation of the Westminster Confession on the disputed questions of the Being and providence of God, supra- and infralapsarianism, mediate and immediate imputation, and general eschatology, which avoids commitment to either post- or premillennial theories.[29]

Dabney's lifelong insistence on balance, nonspeculation, and moderation in theological statement seems to come in part from his old Seminary predecessor, Baxter, in part from the Scottish theologian whose work he continually used, John Dick, and also from the Westminster standards themselves. Based on an analysis of his *Systematic Theology*, Lewis shows that of the more than 150 authors referred to by Dabney, those most frequently appealed to were—in this order—Turretin, Dick, Hill, Hodge, Knapp, Watson, Ridgeley, Calvin, Thornwell, and Witsius.[30] We note an absence of reference to his contemporary Dutch theologians, and very little direct interaction with any of the Fathers of the Greek or Latin Church (and in this, he and most other nineteenth-century American Reformed theologians were unlike Calvin). He does, however, make use of both Anselm and Thomas Aquinas in the original. Certainly Dabney did not mind differing from Calvin, Edwards, Dick, Hodge, and other respected Reformed scholars, although he did not seem to delight in differing, for instance, from Hodge in the way Thornwell appeared at times to do.

Another constituent element of Dabney's theological method was his adherence to the Scottish Common Sense Philosophy of Realism. He comments on this commitment extensively in his *Sensualistic Philosophy of the Nineteenth Century*, where he opposes the skeptical conclusions of the various forms of empirical and associational psychology and philosophy by means of the assumption of the original powers of the mind to form valid judgments that penetrate reality on the basis of data presented to the mind through the senses. Dabney saw the crux of the question as whether the mind can know objective truth:

> It is related that when the plan of Locke's Essay was first reported to his great contemporary, Leibniz, before the book had yet appeared in Germany, and the narrator stated that all was founded on a literal acceptance of the old scholastic law, *Nihil in intellectu quod non prius in sensu*, the great German replied, *Etiam, nisi intellectus ipse*. These words contain the key to the whole discussion. . . . In attempting to enumerate the affections of the mind, it overlooked the mind itself. . . .
>
> The *Ego* is a real existence. If our cognitions have any regular method, then it must be by virtue of some primary principles of cognition which are subjective to the mind. While we claim no "innate ideas", yet it is evident that the intelligence has some innate norms, which determine the nature of its processes, whenever the objective world presents the occasion of them. To deny this, we must not only believe the absurdity of regular series of effects without any regulative cause in their subject; but we must also deny totally the spontaneity of the mind.[31]

Thus, following Reid, Dabney presupposed the reality and validity of the mind, and the reality of cause and effect. Rather like Cornelius Van Til (who was born the decade Dabney died), Dabney showed that even to argue against these premises, one had to use them, and thus: "None but theists can consistently use induction."[32] Also like the later theologian Van Til, Dabney demonstrated that nontheists, too, reasoned on the basis of unproven, faith assumptions: "He who declares that science cannot have any *a priori* truths, virtually adopts as his *a priori* truth the ground maxim of that psychology. . . ."[33]

> These recent unbelievers admit the established facts; but, having approached them with the foregone conclusion that there can be no supernatural cause, they are reduced, for a pretended explanation, to a set of unproved hypotheses and fantastic guesses, which they offer us for verities, in most ludicrous contradiction to the very spirit of their "positive philosophy."[34]

Again he is like Van Til and Kuyper in showing the inevitable bias of the human mind against God's truth because of its commitment to a self-serving conceptual framework:

> . . . all who reason can see that no moral conclusion can be a pure intellection, but that some voluntary element must enter for good or for evil into the sources of every such judgment. No man on earth reasons towards objects which he either likes or dislikes strongly, with the same complete intellectual impartiality with which he reasons about pure mathematics. . . . . All people, while agreeing perfectly upon the truths of mathematics and numbers, differ more or less upon questions of property rights, law-suits, character, politics, medicine, and religion. It is because all these objects of thought involve elements which appeal to the feelings and the will.[35]

If Dabney had affinities with the presuppositional school of Kuyper and Van Til on the analysis of human reasoning, his views of natural theology and apologetics were certainly unlike theirs, and followed in the general line of Aquinas, Butler, Alexander, Chalmers, and Hodge. He followed the traditional Catholic and Reformed approach of first studying natural, and then revealed theology. It is perhaps here that his reliance upon Scottish Realism most shows through, when for example he establishes the traditional proofs for God's existence on the basis of cause and effect in the line of Thomas Reid against the arguments of Hume. Interestingly, Dabney, like Aquinas, did not favor the ontological argument for God's existence.

In his natural theology Dabney has very little, if anything, original or fresh to say, and like most natural theologians quietly imports a good deal of content from Scripture as to the Being and ways of God (which would be exceedingly difficult to see in nature unless one already knew the Scriptures). There are two areas, however, which stand on the border of natural and revealed theology, where he had some bright insights (which he did not develop systematically). These areas would later be developed in the twentieth century by thinkers such as Van Til and Francis Schaeffer on the one hand and Thomas F. Torrance on the other.[36]

As though he were anticipating Van Til, Schaeffer, and others, Dabney deals in a helpful way with the question of how a finite human mind can think and know the Infinite. This question was occasioned by Dabney's reaction to the Scottish philosopher Sir William Hamilton, who on this matter was influenced more by Kant than by Reid, and held that the limited mind cannot think "unconditioned" or infinite Being.[37] Dabney makes it clear that we can know truly that which is infinite without knowing completely or exhaustively.

> The finite mind would need to become infinite, in order to contain a complete and exhaustive conception of any infinite being. But we

do not claim such a conception. The finite mind may remain finite, and yet contain an incomplete, yet valid, apprehension of infinite being.[38]

The use of the word "apprehension" shows the deep insight of Dabney into the roots of this question (as opposed to the word "comprehension"). In his *Systematic Theology* Dabney explores in greater detail the important epistemological difference between apprehension (which finite minds can do of the infinite) and comprehension (which they cannot).[39] But even if the human mind only claims to apprehend God (rather than comprehend him), on what basis can one claim that even *that* is possible (as someone like Mansel, the follower of Hamilton and Kant, would have argued)?

Dabney clearly sees that the answer lies in the direction of man's creation in the image of God. God is infinite and personal, and man is finite but, because created in God's image, also personal. Thus, in spite of the difference between infinity and finitude, the personal can know the personal.[40] This would be developed more clearly in the next century by scholars such as Van Til and Schaeffer, but this insight was already an important element in the epistemology of Dabney.

Dabney also manifested penetrating insight into a second boundary area between natural and revealed theology, into what Thomas F. Torrance has called the necessary and irreducible "triadic structure of revelation" (i.e., God, man, *and* nature).[41] That is, Dabney clearly pointed out that any objectively valid revelation from God to man always involves the structures of created nature. Thus nature, far from being an embarrassment and hindrance to revelation, is its medium. Dabney deals with this important epistemological matter when he comments on the widespread biblical phenomenon of anthropomorphism, which was such an offense to the nineteenth-century idealism that depreciated nature as well as history ("the eternal truths of reason can never be expressed in the accidental facts of history"). The cutting off of Jesus and the church from their roots in Judaism, the desupernaturalizing of Christ and the Scriptures, and then the ultimate loss of "the historical Jesus" and consequent denial of the Incarnation were all part and parcel of the idealistic assumption that eternal reality and truth cannot be validly expressed and apprehended in the structures of nature and history.

In the course of his argumentation against Hume, Mill, and Spencer (on their denial of causation as a theistic proof), Dabney goes to the root of the matter of anthropomorphism and the very possibility of divine revelation in the created order:

> . . . if God has made the human mind "after His image, in His likeness," this would effectually guarantee all our legitimately ra-

tional processes of thought against vice from *anthropomorphism*. For, in thinking according to the natural laws of our minds, we would be thinking precisely as God bids us think. . . . The unreasonableness of the demand, that we shall reject any conception of the divine working, though reached by normal (human) inference, merely because it may be anthropomorphic, appears thus. It would equally forbid us to think or learn at all, either concerning God, or any other Being or concept different from man: for, if we are not allowed to think in the forms of thought natural and normal for us, we are forbidden to think at all. All man's cognition must be anthropomorphic, or nothing.[42]

He makes the same point, in a more directly theological way, in his *Systematic Theology:*

But when the inspired witness, the Bible, comes to us, with attestation, (by miracles, prophecies, &c.,) exactly suited to the forms of the human understanding, and assures us that our spirits are made in the likeness of God's, all fear of our theology, as made invalid by anthropomorphism, is removed. And especially when we are shown the Messiah, as the image of the invisible God, and hear Him reason, we have a complete verification.[43]

Dabney does not deal with some of the related philosophical problems involved in this concept of the essential triadic structure of revelation. Moreover, he does not even begin to develop in a systematic manner the epistemological and theological ramifications of it as T. F. Torrance does a century later, but his profound theological discernment certainly pointed him in the right direction.

In his voluminous work in the area of revealed theology, Dabney's approach may be consistently characterized as thoroughly conservative and displaying contempt for all innovation and speculation. Dabney adhered so closely in both letter and spirit to the Westminster standards that in a speech before the Southern Presbyterian General Assembly the last year of his life, he could seriously make this very strong assertion: ". . . the Confession will need no amendment until the Bible needs to be amended."[44] On the other hand, Dabney saw himself as above all a biblical and exegetical theologian. While he was not like a Geerhardus Vos, for example, who took into profound consideration the reality of progressive, historical development of revelation within the Scriptures themselves, he was in some respects a forerunner of great exegetical theologians such as B. B. Warfield and John Murray, who were prepared to question received Reformed terminology and concepts in light of careful word study and contextual opening of a passage. That is, on many occasions (though far from always) Dabney can be looked on as something of a bridge between the earlier traditional prooftexting of a Turretin and the later contextual, exegetical research of Warfield and Vos.[45] Many examples of the sort of faithful grappling with a text that yields sound exegetical theology can be pointed out in Dabney.[46] A model of his exegetical openness is his treatment of John 3:16, in which he differs with the traditional interpretation of such great Reformed theologians as John Owen in refusing to restrict the meaning of "world" to "all the elect."[47] Because of his careful exegetical study of some aspects of Bible covenants, Dabney in a certain sense seems to have anticipated the work of John Murray and others in stressing the very close relationship between the Mosaic and Abrahamic Covenants.[48] Granted Dabney's own consistent exegetical emphasis in theology, it is not surprising that he preferred, as Frank B. Lewis has pointed out, scriptural rather than speculative theologians.[49]

Closely related to Dabney's submission to the plain text of Scripture and his commitment to the sober and moderate Calvinism of the Westminster standards is his continual disavowal of all types of theological speculation—Reformed speculation included! Many are the places where Dabney says (over against the distinctions between infra- and supralapsarianism, mediate and immediate imputation, creationism and traducianism, etc.), ". . . this is a question which never ought to have been raised."[50] Here he follows the spirit of Calvin rather than of Beza and Gomarus.

In accordance with his moderate, non–"hyper"-Calvinism, and unlike the stringent spirit of some of his political and social statements, Dabney labors very hard to avoid all harshness as he faces the hard questions of theology. For instance, he definitely wishes to leave the door open to the possibility of the universal salvation of all who die in infancy.[51] He does not like the thought involved in the term "Limited" Atonement, and while he clearly affirms the "particular redemption" of the elect, still he prefers (against Dr. William Cunningham of Scotland) to hold to a certain "general design" in the atonement, a "sincere offer of mercy," and "a sense in which Christ 'died for' all those ends, and for the persons affected by them."[52]

Following John Dick of Scotland, Dabney attempts to describe the decree of reprobation in the mildest terms possible, omitting condemnation from the decree.[53] He criticizes his great contemporary, Charles Hodge of Princeton, for the undue harshness implied in his scheme of immediate imputation of the sin of Adam to his offspring.[54] Dabney dislikes any viewpoint of election that underrates or turns into a fiction the genuine pity and mercy of God for lost sinners.[55] Likewise he repudiates all "hyper-" systems that refrain from urging lost sinners to seek the face of God and pray.[56]

Apparently with no trepidation, Dabney enters the lists of the traditional argument (which ran through such varied schools as Plato, the New England Puritans, A. E. Taylor, and Van Til) over whether something is morally right because God commands it, or does he command it because it is right? Unlike most of the Puritans, and more in the line of Plato, Dabney thinks it sounds too harshly arbitrary to say that right is right because God wills it.[57] Of course he carefully states that he does not mean that there is a standard outside or above God. Still, Dabney seems to be lacking his usual penetration of the issues here, and out of fear of harsh overtones does not seem able to appreciate the important point being raised by the Puritans. Certainly his disagreement with the Puritans is merely terminological and not substantial, but he has not grasped, or simply dissents from, the propriety of their terminological concern.

As we would expect in a noninnovator, most of Dabney's work in the various topics of revealed theology is not notably different from the position of his scholastic Calvinist predecessors and his great conservative Reformed contemporaries. Some parts of his thought, nevertheless, do deserve comment. There are at least two areas of the theological curriculum where Dabney appears to have made some real contributions, especially in the sense of stating in a fresh, clear, and generally attractive way complex and difficult truths, and there is a third area where, in terms of the contribution of Calvin himself, Dabney's thought seems to miss the mark.

The late Professor John Murray of Westminster reportedly considered his own major contribution to Reformed theology to have been in the area of anthropology: especially the question of the Adamic Administration.[58] A careful reading of Dabney's *Systematic Theology, Sensualistic Philosophy of the Nineteenth Century*, and *Practical Philosophy* would seem to indicate that Dabney's fullest contribution to the development of the traditional Reformed theological curriculum also lies in the area of anthropology: particularly in his description of the *habitus* of the personality and also in his minute work on the place of the feelings in the human makeup.

Dabney's work on the *habitus* is usually in the context of such questions as free will, natural inability and moral responsibility, divine providence and human spontaneity, the influence of regeneration on the intellect and will, and the general causative effects of the character on human thought and action. In the course of these discussions, Dabney at times finds himself disagreeing with and correcting fellow Reformed scholars such as Hodge, Thornwell, and Dick.

By *habitus* Dabney essentially meant the basic dispositional and motivational complex at the roots of the human personality that determines what one's character is and thus what one's choices and actions are.[59] Dabney felt that he was being more consistently clear than Dick, Thornwell, or Hodge in showing that the entire soul is a unity (or "monad") both in its unregenerate and regenerate states,[60] and that if this unity is not kept in the forefront of a Christian anthropology, then confusion will result in several areas. Therefore, Dabney clarifies or corrects confused thinking in some areas of the theology of Dick (on the inability of the natural man to understand Scripture), of Thornwell (on the will's natural inability and the righteousness of God), of Hodge (on the illumination of the mind and depravity of the whole soul), and of the controversial southern minister and writer Bledsoe in dialogue with Jonathan Edwards (on the freedom and spontaneity of the will).[61] Dabney's writings on the effects of regeneration on the whole character (based on the change of dispositional *habitus*) are marked by a lucidity and pungency in the line of the old Scottish divine, Thomas Boston.[62]

Given Dabney's interest in and study of human psychology (especially in his *Practical Philosophy* and *Sensualistic Philosophy*), it comes as no surprise that he has much clarity and several insights to contribute to Reformed theological anthropology in the area of the feelings. Unlike those forms of rationalistic theology (whether of the liberal or fundamentalist variety) that tend to treat the human mind as though it were in neutral abstraction from the complex motivations and feelings of the moral character, Dabney perceives the immense moral, epistemological, and theological importance and influence of man's subjective emotions. Dabney knew that feelings were important and required careful analysis and consideration as a part of the theological curriculum because:

> Essentially, feelings are man's motive power. Intellect is the cold and latent magnetism which directs the ship's compass. . . . Feeling is that elastic energy which throbs within the machinery, and gives propulsion to its wheels. . . . The vigor of the functions of cognition itself depends, in every man, more on the force of the incentive energizing the faculty, than on the native strength or clearness of the intellect. . . . It is chiefly the feelings which make the man.[63]

Dabney carefully examines and categorizes the feelings and judges them to be expressions of man's basic character disposition (or *habitus*).[64] These basic motivational expressions are then related to man's moral obligation or conscience. The relationships and inner workings of basic character, feelings, and conscience are made central to Dabney's system of ethics, and his insights into these interconnections seem often to enable him to "get inside" the motivations, problems, and responsibilities of human beings individually and socially.[65]

Dabney's close study of the feelings, for instance, enables him to give a penetrating analysis of "spurious religious feelings" in which he sheds burning light on carnal, selfish feelings in religion.[66] Dabney's work at this point should be studied by all who have to deal with the "prosperity teaching" of some segments of the "Electronic Church" in America. He offers interesting thoughts on how immersion in emotional novels (today we might substitute "soap operas") can degenerate genuine sentiment into cheap sentimentality, which weakens the vigor of the moral resolve when one goes back into the real world.[67]

In addition to his contribution in the realm of Reformed anthropology, Dabney also clarifies, and in that sense develops, another topic of classical theology: providence. His basic area of concern is the *concursus* between God's sovereign, primary control of all things, and the reality and validity of human and natural secondary causation. In his *Systematic Theology* he deals with the question "How God's effective providence can intervene consistently with the uniformity of natural laws"[68] in a way that he believes is clearer than the expositions of Dick, Hodge, and McCosh.[69] He also corrects what he feels are defects in the doctrine of the physical *concursus* of God in evil as well as in good acts and physical causes, which was held by his great mentor Turretin of seventeenth-century Geneva, and by the Dutch Calvinist Witsius (who followed a false lead from Aquinas at this point).[70]

As we see from his *Sensualistic Philosophy*, Dabney wishes to avoid a hypersupernaturalism that short-circuits moral effort and responsibility, while at the same time strongly affirming the traditional Calvinist doctrine of God's total sovereign control.[71] Dabney prefers not to speak of providence as "the supernatural violating of natural laws," but rather as God's perpetual superintendence of the "regular" law of nature.[72]

A third area of Dabney's work in the traditional theological curriculum deserves comment: his view of the sacraments. Here, in terms of Calvin's sacramental understanding, Dabney seems to take a step backward, giving future generations of Southern Presbyterians a generally weak or low view of the sacraments. Dabney finds Calvin's profound teaching on the powerful and gracious reality of the Holy Spirit's work in effectuating a sacramental union between the physical elements in the sacrament and the blessings of union with Christ's glorified human nature to be ". . . not only incomprehensible, but impossible."[73] Here, perhaps, his commitment to the categories of Scottish Common Sense Realism has restricted the usual depth and richness of his theological discernment. In his own day, a contemporary theologian from South Carolina, John B. Adger, answered this critique of Calvin's view of the sacraments, but still Dabney's viewpoint has predominated in the church.[74]

Dabney as Prophet and Social Critic

Dabney manifests a wider and deeper cultural, social, and political interest than any other theologian of nineteenth-century America. He was in a sense ahead of his time in spanning the fields of both sociology and religion. His penetrating theological critique of culture is at times like that of E. Rosenstock-Huessy and R. J. Rushdoony. While Thornwell and Shedd were more eloquent than Dabney, Hodge more influential, and B. M. Palmer a greater preacher, Dabney excels them all as a prophet. In a very limited yet real sense, Dabney was like Ezekiel and Jeremiah in that the development of his prophetic gift was very costly to himself: he passed through the fires of experiencing the bitter defeat of his homeland and the resultant breakup of the southern culture that was the pride and joy of his heart. This was both his strength and his weakness: the defeat of the South served to give him uncanny insight into the future problems of American culture, and at the same time tended so to wrench his emotions that his thought became prejudiced and his moral vision blinded in some very important areas of human life and endeavor.

Dabney's open hatred of the post-Civil War industrialization of American society made him an outsider to the developing cultural consensus, and strengthened the vision of his ever keen moral eye to penetrate the weaknesses of America's increasingly secularist materialism and industrialism. Dabney utilizes a strong, largely correct, and far from comforting critique of the evils of debt capitalism,[75] of the immoral use of the civil government by the industrial plutocracy to enforce monopolies that crushed smaller competitors,[76] of the dishonesty of monetary inflation,[77] of the treatment of man as a machine,[78] and of the certainty of the eventual de-Christianization and secularization of public school education.[79] Most sobering of all, he foresaw the coming, twentieth-century struggle in America for religious and civil liberties between a powerful centralized state with totalitarian temptations and a broad and shallow church that had forgotten the theological and constitutional basis of liberty.[80]

Dabney also had valid insights into the general weakening of Reformed theology and practice in the Calvinist churches of late nineteenth-century America. He foresaw impending problems with the weakening of Christian intellectual resistance to evolutionary speculation[81] and to higher criticism of the Scriptures,[82] the decline toward liberalism in the theological seminaries,[83] the decline of serious church discipline,[84] the growth of human inventions and the loss of real unction in worship,[85] and the bitter harvest to be reaped from humanly induced methods of more rapid and successful evangelism,[86] and he even discussed the development of the false split between Christ as Savior and Christ as Lord.[87] Dabney apparently offended many as he deplored the growing tendency of Christians to indulge themselves in luxury and to be forgetful of the poor.[88]

Much less happy in biblical insight was the deeply jaundiced viewpoint that Dabney turned upon the situation of the black people. In addition to supporting slavery before the War, he vehemently protested the ecclesiastical equality of black people as potential officers in white churches and presbyteries after the War.[89] He opposed tax-paid education for blacks in Virginia (but he opposed it for poor whites as well).[90] He held that the blacks were culturally inferior[91] (he seems to leave the question of whether they were personally inferior an open one), and hence he theorized that it would take untold generations before blacks could be raised to cultural equality with whites. This sort of attitude of course helped drive the black freedmen from white churches to the detriment of the unity of the body of Christ and healing of the nation.

In retrospect, it seems sadly shortsighted that Dabney could offer the people of the Reconstruction South such a clear solution from degeneracy in times of oppression, and yet fail to see that the very same solution should hold true of the blacks, who were also created in the image of God. In "The Duty of the Hour" Dabney advises:

> The correlated duty is that of anxiously preserving our integrity and self-respect. . . . The victims of unrighteous oppression, are usually degraded by their unavenged wrongs. . . . The man who has ceased to feel moral indignation for wrong has ceased to feel the claims of virtue. Nor is there a valid reason for your insensibility to evil, in the fact that you yourself are the object of it.[92]

Undoubtedly Dabney's greatest blind spot in this whole matter was, as Terry Johnson has pointed out, his underestimation of the power of the gospel in the life and culture of blacks (which can make saints, leaders, and heroes of them as well as of any other people).[93]

Dabney's prophecy, then, was both remarkably right and grievously wrong. As his close friend and biographer, T. C. Johnson, has pointed out, Dabney was often too pessimistic about the future of the church.[94] And as Charles R. Wilson has noted, Dabney failed to see that "a separate southern religion [would] survive in the postwar South, as a foundation for a distinctive southern culture."[95]

We whose unperceived blind spots will be deplored by future Christian generations will not speak too harshly of Dabney, who was marked by the fallenness of his own time and culture, as we are by ours. The way forward is to see beyond him by standing on his shoulders— and on those of all the saints and doctors of the church in all ages.

It is interesting to note that Dabney, who said "I have no audience" and described himself as "the Cassandra of Yankeedom,"[96] now, in the 1980s, has a larger audience than any time during his life. Indeed, since the mid-1960s nearly all of his works have been reprinted (in some cases, several times) on both sides of the Atlantic. Perhaps T. C. Johnson was right when he wrote some eighty years ago:

Dr. Dabney was a great man. We cannot tell just how great yet. One cannot see how great Mt. Blanc is while standing at its foot. One hundred years from now men will be able to see him better.[97]

Notes: Robert Lewis Dabney

1. B. B. Warfield in *The Princeton Theological Review* (1905).
2. R. L. Dabney, *Discussions: Evangelical and Theological*, 2 vols. (London: The Banner of Truth Trust, 1962), 2:558.
3. Thomas Cary Johnson, *In Memoriam: R. L. Dabney* (Knoxville: University of Tennessee Press, 1898), 7.
4. Thomas Cary Johnson, *The Life and Letters of Robert Lewis Dabney* (Edinburgh: The Banner of Truth Trust, 1977 [1903]), 192.
5. C. T. Thompson, "Robert Lewis Dabney—The Conservative," *The Union Seminary Review* 35 (January 1924), 155-56.
6. Johnson, *Life and Letters*, 42-43.
7. Thompson, "R. L. Dabney," 156.
8. Ibid., 157.
9. Ibid.
10. Johnson, *Life and Letters*, 551.
11. Thompson, "R. L. Dabney," 159-60.
12. Johnson, *Life and Letters*, 153.
13. Ibid., 151-52.
14. Ibid., 210-34.
15. See "Christians, Pray for Your Country," in R. L. Dabney, *Discussions*, 2:393-400.
16. James H. Smylie, "The Burden of Southern Church Historians: World Mission, Regional Captivity, Reconciliation," *Journal of Presbyterian History* 46 (December 1968), 295.
17. Dabney regularly criticizes "Jacobinism," e.g., in *Discussions by Robert L. Dabney*, 4 vols. (Harrisonburg: Sprinkle Publications, 1979-1980), 4:542; 3:498ff.; *A Defence of Virginia and through Her the South* (Harrisonburg: Sprinkle Publications, 1977), 254; *Life and Campaigns of Lieut.-Gen. Thomas J. Jackson* (Harrisonburg: Sprinkle Publications, 1976), 162-69, 159-61; *The Sensualistic Philosophy of the Nineteenth Century* (Anson D. F. Randolph, 1887), 58.
18. Otto J. Scott, *The Secret Six: John Brown and the Abolitionist Movement* (New York: Times Books, 1979). Of course, some in the North saw the War as a southern, slaveholders' conspiracy; see William A. Clebsch, *Christian Interpretations of the Civil War* (Philadelphia: Fortress Press, 1969), 2, 6.
19. This is not to imply that Dabney does not deal openly and boldly with slavery, for he does in *Defence of Virginia* and elsewhere, but rather that he could not take seriously the moral challenge raised by nearly all other Christians throughout the Western world. Instead, he tended to discount the challenge as motivated by "Jacobinism" (or as we would say, "radical secular humanism").
20. Johnson, *Life and Letters*, 272.
21. Lev. 25:39-55. See also Exod. 21:2.
22. Frank Bell Lewis, *Robert Lewis Dabney: Southern Presbyterian Apologist* (Ph.D. diss., Duke University, 1946), 213-14.

23. Johnson, *Life and Letters*, 568.

24. See "The New South," in Dabney, *Discussions*, 4:1-24.

25. Smylie, "The Burden of Southern Church Historians," 292.

26. Lewis, *Robert Lewis Dabney*, 30.

27. See Dabney, *Discussions*, Vols. 3 and 4, and *Practical Philosophy*.

28. David H. Overy, *Robert Lewis Dabney: Apostle of the Old South* (Ph.D. diss., University of Wisconsin, 1967), 292-98.

29. Dabney, "The Doctrinal Contents of the Confession of Faith," in *Memorial Volume of the Westminster Assembly, 1647-1897* (Richmond, VA: The Presbyterian Committee of Publication, 1897), 95.

30. Lewis, *Robert Lewis Dabney*, 161.

31. Dabney, *Sensualistic Philosophy*, 248-49.

32. Ibid., 412.

33. Ibid., 97; see also p. 54 on J. S. Mill's circular reasoning.

34. Ibid., 100.

35. Dabney, *Discussions*, 4:512-13.

36. There is no line of direct thought from Dabney to these scholars. Their insights were not developed in dialogue with his writings.

37. See Dabney, *Sensualistic Philosophy*, ch. 10, esp. 216-17.

38. Ibid., 223.

39. Dabney, *Systematic Theology*, 149, also 138-39. Saint Hilary works with this distinction as early as the fourth century in the first two books of his *De Trinitate*, but it is highly unlikely that Dabney had read this. Hilary of course influenced Calvin, whom Dabney had read.

40. Dabney, *Sensualistic Philosophy*, 138-39, 230-31, 237-38, etc.

41. See, e.g., Thomas F. Torrance, *Reality and Evangelical Theology* (Philadelphia: The Westminster Press, 1982) and *God and Rationality* (London: Oxford University Press, 1971), ch. 4.

42. Dabney, *Sensualistic Philosophy*, 405-06. Again, early fathers such as Novatian of Rome in the third century had dealt very clearly with anthropomorphisms in terms of God's accommodation to man's littleness, and this had influenced Calvin, whom Dabney knew, if not Novatian.

43. Dabney, *Systematic Theology*, 295; see also his *Discussions*, 1:297.

44. Dabney, "Doctrinal Contents of the Confession of Faith," 94.

45. Probably Joseph Addison Alexander of Princeton, had he lived longer, would have been even more of a bridge in this direction than Dabney; but of course Alexander was not primarily a systematic theologian.

46. See, e.g., Dabney, *Discussions*, 1:238 (on repentance); ibid., 262-63 (on Rom. 5); ibid., 271 (on "sinned in Adam"); ibid., 312 (on John 3:16); ibid., 555ff. (an exposition of I Cor. 3:10-15); *Systematic Theology*, 34 (original sin); ibid., 35 (imputation of Adam's guilt); ibid., 207-08 (on the eternal generation of the Son); ibid., 386 (on Col. 2:16-17); ibid., 573-77 (on the "understanding" and the "heart"); ibid., 619ff. (good exegetical work on justification).

47. Dabney, *Systematic Theology*, 527-28, 535; *Discussions*, 1:311-13.

48. *Systematic Theology*, 454-55. Cf. John Murray, *The Covenant of Grace* (London: The Tyndale Press, 1956).

49. Lewis, *Robert Lewis Dabney*, 164.

50. *Systematic Theology*, 233 (on the order of the decrees). Note also his refusal to speculate in other areas of theology: ibid., 317, 320, 338-39, 340-41; *Discussions*, 1:290. Dabney explains well why he dislikes theological speculation in his critique of Hodge and Turretin on "immediate imputation" in ibid., 1:165-66:

Nearly all Dr. Hodge's positions may be found in the ninth chapter of Turretin's Locus on Original Sin. The true verdict on this history of opinion seems to us this: that a few of the more acute and forward of the Calvinistic divines were tempted, by their love of system and symmetry of statement and over-confidence in their own logic, to excogitate the ill-starred distinction of the antecedent and gratuitous imputation. Their error here was exactly like that of the supralapsarians, who thought they could throw light and symmetry on the doctrine of the decree by assigning what they thought was the logical order of sequence to its parts. But they became "wise above that which was written." They added no light to the mystery of the decree, but they misrepresented the moral attributes of God, and provoked a crowd of natural cavils and objections. The distinction of supralapsarians and infralapsarians ought never to have been heard of. . . . So, say we, this distinction of the antecedent imputation ought never to have been drawn. . . . But the difference with Dr. Hodge seems to have been this: his love of systematizing enticed him to adopt the extreme points of his great teacher, Turretin.

51. See Dabney, *Discussions*, 3:193-94, 200-05; also his *Review of Theodosia Ernest; Or, the Heroine of Faith* (Richmond: Shepperson and Graves, 1869).

52. *Systematic Theology*, 529.

53. Ibid., 239. Dr. Morton Smith suggests with insight that Dabney's refusal to parallel the decrees of election and reprobation is like that of G. C. Berkouwer, who says, "The Gospel can be understood and preached only if balance, symmetry, and parallelism are excluded" (*Divine Election*, 202); quoted in Morton Smith, *Studies in Southern Presbyterian Theology* (Amsterdam: Jacob Van Campen, 1962), 214.

54. Dabney, *Discussions*, 1:144-45, 166-67; *Systematic Theology*, 342.

55. See Dabney, *Discussions*, 1:285-86, 307; *Systematic Theology*, 532-33, 559.

56. Ibid., 609.

57. Ibid., 163-64; also *Sensualistic Philosophy*, 324. Terrill Elniff explains the significance of this debate among the New England Puritans in *The Guise of Every Graceless Heart* (Vallectio, CA: Ross House Books, 1981).

58. Iain H. Murray, "Preface," in *Collected Writings of John Murray* (Edinburgh: The Banner of Truth Trust, 1977), 2:vii-viii.

59. See Dabney, *Discussions*, 3:240-41, where Dabney says:

. . . this law of free volitions is the soul's own rational and appetitive nature—its *habitus*. Hence the rational free volition is not an uncaused phenomenon in the world of mind; it only arises by reason of its regular efficient, which is the subjective motive. By subjective motive is meant that complex of mental judgment as to the preferable, and subjective appetency for the object which arise together in the mind, on presentation of the object, according to the mind's own native disposition. In a word, the free volition will arise according to and because of the soul's own strongest motive; and that is the reason why it is a rational, a free, and a responsible volition. Hence we believe that such volitions are attended with full certainty—which is what we mean by moral necessity—and also with full freedom.

See also Dabney, *Systematic Theology*, 578:

The will has its own *habitus*, regulative of all its fundamental acts, which is not a mere modification of the intelligence, but its own co-ordinate, original character; a simple, ultimate fact of the moral constitution. Hence an interaction of will and intellect. On moral and spiritual subjects the practical generalisations of the intellect are founded on the dictates of the disposition of the will.

60. See ibid., 323:

But when we thus discriminate the faculties, we must not forget the unity and simplicity of the spirit of man. It is a monad. And, as we do not conceive of it as regenerated or sanctified by patches; so neither do we regard it as specifically depraved by patches. Original corruption is not, specifically, the perversion of a faculty in the soul, but of the soul itself.

61. On Dick see Dabney, *Systematic Theology*, 578; on Thornwell, ibid., 298; on Hodge, ibid., 570-71 and *Discussions*, 1:232-34; on Bledsoe, *Discussions*, 3:181ff. and 211ff.

62. See *Systematic Theology*, Lecture XLVII, esp. 561-62. Cf. Thomas Boston, *Human Nature in its Fourfold State* (London: The Banner of Truth Trust, 1964), part III, "Regeneration."

63. Dabney, *Discussions*, 3:274-75.

64. In his *Practical Philosophy*, Dabney arranged the feelings in terms of pairs under nine "sensibilities." Each pair is bounded at opposite ends by desire and aversion. In light of subsequent developments in psychology before and after, pro and con Freud, Dabney's work is somewhat dated and limited in scope. Yet as ethics it still deserves a serious reading.

65. His "Love of Applause" and "Duties of the Family" are models of penetrating ethical insight, and his "Civic Duties" raises many of the most difficult critical questions that face Christians today who live under hostile regimes (see his *Practical Philosophy*).

66. See Dabney, *Discussions*, 3:456-61.

67. See ibid., 2:161-62.

68. Dabney, *Systematic Theology*, 281.

69. Ibid., 279-80.

70. Ibid., 286-91.

71. See Dabney, *Sensualistic Philosophy*, 352-69.

72. Cf. ibid., 353, 359-60. By this superintendence, God "guides with His skillful but invisible hand to just those combinations which release the powers of the second causes He needs for His purpose, and reduce to potentiality those whose tasks are for the time completed" (359-60).

73. *Systematic Theology*, 811. See also on the question of the nature of our union with Christ, 616-17, 730. Dabney wishes to refute Calvin's *Institutes*, IV, ch. 17 (*Institutes of the Christian Religion*, 2 vols., ed. John T. McNeill, trans. Ford Lewis Battles [Philadelphia: The Westminster Press, 1977]). Ronald S. Wallace's important study *Calvin's Doctrine of Word and Sacrament* (Tyler, TX: Geneva Divinity School Press, 1982, rpt.).

74. See John B. Adger, *My Life and Times, 1810-1899* (Richmond, VA: The Presbyterian Committee of Publication, 1899), 310-26.

75. See esp. David H. Overy, "When the Wicked Beareth Rule: A Southern Critique of Industrial America," *Journal of Presbyterian History* (Summer 1970), esp. 132, 135. See also David H. Overy, *Dabney: Apostle*, 290; also Dabney, *Discussions*, 4:1-24.

76. See Smylie, "The Burden of Southern Church Historians," 291; also Dabney, *The Practical Philosophy*, 476; *Discussions*, 4:53-70 and 321-40; and David H. Overy, *Dabney: Apostle*, 285-88.

77. Dabney, *Discussions*, 4:341-53.

78. Dabney, *Defence of Virginia*, 15; also Overy, "When the Wicked Beareth Rule," 135.

79. See his various articles against the Virginia state school system in *Discussions*, 4:176-247, 260-80. See also E. T. Thompson, *Presbyterians in the South*, 3 vols. (Richmond: John Knox Press, 1963-73), 2:341-49.

80. Dabney predicts in his *Practical Philosophy*, 394:

> The history of human rights is, that their intelligent assertors usually learn the true grounds of them "in the furnace of affliction"; that the posterity who inherit

these rights hold them for awhile, in pride and ignorant prescription; that after a while, when the true logic of the rights has been forgotten, and when some plausible temptation presses them to do so, the next generation discards the precious rights bodily, and goes back to the practice of the old tyranny. . . .

You may deem it a strange prophecy, but I predict that the time will come in this once free America when the battle for religious liberty will have to be fought over again, and will probably be lost, because the people are already ignorant of its true basis and conditions.

See also his *Discussions*, 3:321, 503.

81. See, e.g., his controversy with Professor Woodrow of Columbia Seminary, who came to accept organic evolution, in *Discussions*, 3:91-181; also *Sensualistic Philosophy*, ch. 6.

82. See Dabney, *Discussions*, 1:350-439.

83. T. C. Johnson, *Life and Letters*, 532.

84. Dabney, *Discussions*, 4:545, 3:564. In an undated letter to the Rev. R. H. Fleming of Woodstock, Virginia, Dabney speaks of the refusal of the Presbyterian General Assembly to speak against current sins, which undercuts sessional discipline, which in turn—Dabney feared—would lead "to the death of the church." This letter is in the collection of the Presbyterian Historical Foundation, Montreat, North Carolina.

85. See R. L. Dabney, *Sacred Rhetoric* (Carlisle, PA: The Banner of Truth Trust, 1979), 115-17 on unction; and Thompson, *Presbyterians in the South*, 2:429-35 on changes in worship.

86. See Dabney, *Discussions*, 2:76-95 and 551-74.

87. Dabney, *Systematic Theology*, 601.

88. See Dabney, *Discussions*, 1:1-28, 4:528; T. C. Johnson, *Life and Letters*, 408.

89. See Dabney, *Discussions*, 2:199-217; Johnson, *Life and Letters*, 319-22.

90. See Dabney, *Discussions*, 4:176-90.

91. See ibid., 25-45.

92. Ibid., 109-12.

93. Terry Johnson, "Gone with the Wind: R. L. Dabney and the Evangelical Defense of Slavery" (Paper written at Gordon-Conwell Theological Seminary), 38.

94. Johnson, *Life and Letters*, 325-26.

95. Charles R. Wilson, "Robert Lewis Dabney: Religion and the Southern Holocaust," *The Virginia Magazine of History and Biography*, 89 (January 1981), 89.

96. Overy, "When the Wicked Beareth Rule," 131.

97. Johnson, *Life and Letters*, p. 569.

JAMES HENLEY THORNWELL

LUDER G. WHITLOCK, JR.

JAMES Henley Thornwell once expressed a desire "to be regarded as the greatest scholar and most talented man that ever lived."[1] Although he failed to achieve that distinction, Thornwell did become one of the outstanding Presbyterian leaders of the nineteenth century, rising rapidly in the esteem of his colleagues, so that in 1847 at the age of 35 he became the youngest moderator of the General Assembly in the history of the Presbyterian Church in the United States. This son of a plantation overseer, as a result of a discussion about Aristotle at a dinner party in New York in 1856, received a copy of Aristotle from Harvard professor George Bancroft, who was sufficiently impressed to inscribe on the flyleaf the following words: "A testimonial of regard to the Rev. Dr. J. H. Thornwell, the most learned of the learned."[2] Daniel Webster, after hearing Thornwell speak at a South Carolina college, was reported to have remarked that he was the greatest pulpit orator he had ever heard.[3] And Henry Ward Beecher referred to him as the most brilliant minister in the Old School Presbyterian Church and the most brilliant debater in the General Assembly.[4] He was selected by the Board of Commissioners on World Missions to preach the anniversary sermon at the General Assembly in New York City in 1856. It is said that Thornwell would have been the first man pointed out to a stranger arriving at his first General Assembly. Moreover, the stranger probably would have been surprised to discover that this small, stooped gentleman so unimpressive in physical appearance was the acclaimed J. H. Thornwell.

In 1837 he was elected to the professorship of Logic and Belles Lettres at South Carolina College where he had graduated first in his class in 1831. He spent the greater part of his professional years at the college, remaining there until 1855 except for one year, 1840-41, during which period he served as the pastor of the First Presbyterian Church in Columbia, South Carolina. Thornwell had a significant influence on the college as professor, chaplain, and president. As the sixth president,

232

he was perhaps the most important person connected with the college until that time, for in him the institution possessed the outstanding religious personality in the state and perhaps the outstanding Presbyterian in the South.[5] In 1855 his tenure as president of the college was terminated in order for him to become Professor of Didactic and Polemic Theology in the theological seminary at Columbia. This he did for the benefit of the seminary, which was at this time in a precarious position insofar as the strength of its faculty was concerned. His presence assured confidence and support for the seminary from the church.

It is not surprising to discover that when the Southern Presbyterian churches withdrew from the Presbyterian Church in the USA in 1861, Thornwell became the principal spokesman for the Presbyterian Church in the Confederate States of America. His "Address to All the Churches of Jesus Christ Throughout the Earth" was unanimously adopted by that body at its initial General Assembly at Augusta, Georgia, in December 1861.[6] It was in the Presbyterian churches of the southern states that he left his lasting mark, and that influence was strongest in the area of ecclesiology.[7] His views essentially became the position of the Presbyterian Church, U.S. for about a century and are to a large degree embodied in the recently formed Presbyterian Church in America.[8]

Ecclesiastical Debate

Thornwell's contribution must be evaluated in the light of the period in which he lived. During the first half of the nineteenth century American Presbyterians became embroiled in heated debate and serious reflection regarding their theology and church government. A primary cause of this intensive discussion was the Plan of Union of 1801, designed to bring Presbyterians and Congregationalists into close cooperation. Their common Calvinistic heritage and regular correspondence dating back to 1766 made the arrangement seem most reasonable.[9] The Plan of Union allowed new congregations to choose a minister from either denomination, to rule themselves according to Presbyterian or Congregational government, and to send official representatives to meetings of either denomination. In addition, voluntary benevolent societies were formed as a joint venture by individuals from both denominations.[10]

This period of cooperation was halted abruptly by the rupture of Presbyterians into Old and New Schools in 1837. The Old School Presbyterians had become convinced that the New England theology was diluting the confessional stance of the Westminster Confession of Faith and that the future of Presbyterianism was in jeopardy. They were evidently even more upset by their inability to control the situation.[11] Therefore, when the Old School Presbyterians found themselves holding the majority of commissioners at the 1837 General Assembly they proceeded to excise the New School Presbyterians, including all churches, presbyteries, and synods received during the period in which the Plan of Union had been in effect.[12] The same General Assembly passed a resolution declaring that the American Home Missionary Society and the American Education Society were exceedingly injurious to the peace and purity of the Presbyterian Church and urged that they no longer be allowed to operate within any of the churches in the denomination.[13]

The aftermath of the division found Old School Presbyterians seeking to identify themselves as Presbyterians in contrast to Congregationalists and other denominations. Consequently, in the year subsequent to the division and until 1860, there were prolonged, often heated, debates regarding the nature of Presbyterian polity. These debates revealed that significant matters of polity had not been thoroughly worked out by the denomination previously. While revolving around topics such as church boards, the status of the ruling elder, and related matters, these debates all centered on the location and exercise of power as that related to the genius of Presbyterianism. They should probably be seen as an expression of a desire to perpetuate the Presbyterian form of government.

Exactly what was the nature and mission of the church and what would that mean for the structure of the church?[14] If various tasks such as evangelism and ministries of mercy were eventually assumed by the voluntary societies, would this mean that the church would ultimately be left with very few functions, perhaps only worship and the administration of the sacraments? Apparently concerns of this nature troubled many Presbyterians, including Charles Hodge, who argued that Thornwell's position would compel the church to divest itself not only of boards, but seminaries, colleges, and similar institutions.[15] On the other hand, if the church were to assume responsibility for the various tasks being addressed at that time by the voluntary Christian organizations, then what organizational changes would be required in order to accomplish that effectively? That question bothered Thornwell and many of his colleagues.

Thornwell harbored intense convictions regarding the distinctiveness of Presbyterian doctrine and polity. He was convinced that the principles involved in the discussions affected the heart and soul of Presbyterianism. For these reasons he entered vigorously into the debates— debates that stretched across a span of more than twenty years and culminated with his famous encounter with Charles Hodge on the issue of the administration of missions at the 1860 General Assembly in Rochester, New York.[16]

The real issue of that debate, as Hodge himself observed, was not merely the propriety of church boards, but "what is Presbyterianism?"[17]

Thornwell claimed that the central question was the organization of the church itself.[18] He insisted that "God gave us our church government, as truly as he gave us our doctrines; and we have no more right to add to the church government, than to add to the doctrine."[19] He visualized the alternatives in this way:

> Thus, one party amongst us holds that Christ gave us the materials and principles of church-government, and has left us to shape them pretty much as we please. But the other holds that God gave us *a Church*, a constitution, laws, Presbyterys, Assemblies, Presbyters, and all the functionaries necessary to a complete organization of his kingdom upon the earth and to its effective operation; that he has revealed an order as well as a *faith*, and that as our attitude in the one case is to hear and *believe*, in the other it is hear and obey. Of one of these parties the motto is, "you may do all that the Scriptures do not forbid"; of the other, "you can do only what the Scriptures command."[20]

The Presbyterianism that Thornwell espoused reserved all power for the church courts. That power belonged to the elders or presbyters who were the rulers of the church. It was not to be vested in voluntary societies or boards that could act independent of the church in its ecclesiastical capacity. If committees or boards existed, they must be directly accountable to the General Assembly of the church.[21]

Another matter of great importance to Thornwell in regard to church government was the status of the ruling elder. Some controversy had occurred during the General Assemblies of 1842-1844 regarding whether or not ruling elders had the right to lay on hands at the ordination of ministers. The 1843 General Assembly concluded that ruling elders did not have that right.[22] The 1843 General Assembly also dealt with another pertinent matter when it ruled that a presbytery meeting could be convened and a quorum could be declared present without the presence of a ruling elder.[23]

Thornwell was convinced that if the rights of the ruling elder were slighted a "sacred hierarchy" would result in the church, and the concentration of power in the hands of the clergy occurring thereby would spell doom for Presbyterianism. He was convinced that the delicate balance of power effected through two classes of presbyters, teaching and ruling elders, could not be dispensed with without serious results for Presbyterianism as a system of government. Moreover, presbyters could not be limited to the clergy, for that would be prelacy. Rather, presbyters were both ruling elders and teaching elders, that is, both laymen and clergy. "Presbyterianism stands or falls with a distinction between ruling and teaching elders," he maintained.[24] In this way the balance of power was maintained within the church courts, and this power was representative, not by proxy, which would be Congregationalism. So power was reserved for the church "in its ecclesiastical capacity," and yet that power was carefully distributed between clergy and laity acting in a representative capacity. In that way he distinguished Presbyterianism from every other form of church government:

> The government of the Church by parliamentary assemblies, composed of two classes of Elders, and of Elders only and so arranged to realize the visible unity of the whole church—this is Presbyterianism.[25]

Since differing views on theology and church government were the principal issues leading to the division of 1837 and, with the slavery issue, continued to dominate the attention of Presbyterians during the remainder of Thornwell's life, it is not surprising that a major portion of his energies was directed to these matters.[26]

Invariably, his immediate recourse for the resolution of the matter was to the authoritative Scriptures. In this respect he found company with Old School Presbyterians and other evangelical Christians of his era. His basic assumption in developing his arguments was the hermeneutical principle that whatever is not commanded in the Bible is forbidden. There would have been a consensus among many of his colleagues in regard to this principle as well. Thornwell is open to criticism, however, for his failure to justify this hermeneutical principle so crucial to the development of his argument. Thornwell's difficulty lay not in the persuasive power of his vigorous logical mind, but rather in a failure to plumb carefully and vigorously the assumptions on which he built his telling arguments.

Another question that comes to mind as one assesses his involvement in the discussions on church government is the degree to which the secular political situation may have influenced Thornwell and his contemporaries in the divergent approaches toward the polity that they adopted. For example, the states'-rights principles that became important factors in southern sectionalism appear to be reflected somewhat in the Thornwellian polity. Perhaps this is the explanation for Thornwell's desire to retain as much authority as possible for presbyteries, especially if it is kept in mind that Thornwell was from South Carolina where southern sentiments were most pronounced and which was also the home state of John C. Calhoun, formulator of the doctrine of nullification. This might also partially explain the keen interest of Southern Presbyterians to maintain a balance of power though the parity of elders since Southerners were sensitive to such matters because of their efforts to maintain a balance of power in Congress as more states were added, both slave and free, and as the population of the northern states swelled more rapidly, yielding them an edge in the House of Representatives. The question is not one of Thornwell's theological integrity, nor that of Southern Presbyterians in general; rather, it is the question to what degree one remains captive to his culture while attempting to understand and apply the truth of the Bible.

Similar questions may be raised regarding Thornwell's position on slavery. He was well aware of the magnitude and pervasiveness of this issue. In his opinion, the Bible did not condemn slavery and so the church should not do so either. Actually, Thronwell concluded,

> The Scriptures not only fail to condemn slavery, they as distinctly sanction it as any other social condition of man. The Church was formally organized in the family of a slaveholder; the relation was divinely regulated among the chosen people of God; and the peculiar duties of the parties are inculcated under the Christian economy. These are facts which cannot be denied.[27]

If that was the case, then Christians needed to the fullest extent possible to bring biblical principles to bear on all aspects of the current practice of slavery. So Thornwell developed a position for a Christian doctrine of slavery that included a careful delineation of the status of the slave as a person made in the image of God and therefore as one who should be regarded as a brother.[28] The master did not have a right to unlimited control, but only a right to his labor.[29] On the other hand, Thornwell argued that if a master should emancipate his slave, then operating on the same benevolent principle a rich man should share all of his estate with his poor neighbors. If such ideas were implemented it would, he warned, bring disaster to all institutions of civilized society.[30]

Scripture and Philosophy

A more reasonable explanation for Thornwell's positions than the influence of the political situation seems to be the influence of Scottish Common Sense Philosophy, resulting in a cultural and social conservatism that typified the views of James Henley Thornwell and Old School Presbyterians.[31] Scottish Common Sense Philosophy dominated Princetonian thought from Witherspoon on and Old School Presbyterianism throughout the first half of the nineteenth century. Princeton was by far the most influential of the northern colleges on southern education.[32] Therefore, it is relatively easy to see how Common Sense Philosophy would have become pervasive in the South. Southern colleges offered courses in moral philosophy, required of all students, introducing Scottish Common Sense Philosophy to them in this manner.[33] This school of philosophy not only became dominant in Old School Presbyterianism, but became "The Reliable Handmaiden of Southern Theology,"[34] and Thornwell was no exception to the rule. There is the specific reason that Robert Henry, Professor of Logic and Ethics at South Carolina College, had studied at Edinburgh. It was said of him that he was the man who had taught South Carolinians to think. Henry, Thornwell's professor, introduced him to Dugald Stuart's writings, and Thornwell read them before moving on to the study of William Hamilton.[35]

Thornwell warmly embraced this mode of thinking, as can be seen from his writings.[36] In his inaugural address as professor at Columbia Theological Seminary, he noted that the task of theological scholarship was to show the complete harmony of sound philosophy and theology.[37] He saw the truth of nature and Scripture in harmony, and he saw them as one system of truth. Since grace presupposed nature, there was a need to lay the natural foundation for an examination of the Scriptures. To begin abruptly with the doctrine of redemption with no connection to natural religion did not appeal to him at all.[38] Thornwell saw moral philosophy as a form of natural theology and the ground of moral obligation to be through philosophical description. Although ethics was based on biblical precept, actually the Scriptures were a validation of the conclusions of Common Sense Philosophy.[39]

That this should be the case seems incongruous with Thornwell's insistence on the final, determinative authority of the Scriptures for faith and practice. His statements regarding this matter are unequivocal:

> Christianity in its living principles and its outward forms is purely a matter of Divine revelation. The great error of the Church in all ages, the fruitful source of her apostasy and crime, has been a presumptuous reliance upon her own understanding. Her own inventions have seduced her from her loyalty to God, and filled her sanctuary with idols and the hearts of her children with vain imaginations. The Bible cuts at the very root of this evil by affording us a perfect and infallible rule of faith and practice. The absolute perfection of the Scriptures as a directory to man was a cardinal principle of the Reformation, and whatever could not be traced to them either directly or by necessary inference was denounced as a human invention—as mere will-worship, which God abhors so deeply that an inspired Apostle has connected it with idolatry or the worshipping of angels.[40]

Of course, there is no question about his desire to be faithful to the Scriptures and for them to serve as his ultimate authority. The question is rather to what degree he was able to achieve this objective as a theologian. In answering this question, the influence of Common Sense Philosophy on his theology must be measured carefully. An evaluation of Old School Presbyterianism and Princeton theology appears to be equally applicable to Thornwell:

> In short, what is praiseworthy in this Presbyterian theology is its eagerness to be confessionally scriptural, scientifically respectable, and culturally relevant. It made a valiant attempt to retain its theological orthodoxy while it was constantly surrounded, and at times subtly tempted, by formidable philosophical movements that seemed, outwardly, at least, to be congenial to a biblical stance.
>
> This desire to be fully biblical was so strong that these Presbyterian theologians soon developed the conviction that all their ideas, including the philosophical, were of a thoroughly scriptural character, as well as the belief that their reading and understanding of Scripture was not in any way blurred by superimposed philosophical constructs.
>
> It could be maintained that the scriptural intent of Presbyterian theology has actually been undermined by the attempts of this theology, particularly during the nineteenth century, to adapt itself to certain philosophical thought-patterns that were then culturally in vogue. In fact, these philosophical ideas were generally neither expressive of, nor congenial to, a full-orbed, scriptural ontology, anthropology, and epistemology.[41]

Thornwell's affirmation of Common Sense Philosophy invariably led him to a particular view of the sinful world in which he lived and how that world could best be brought into conformity to the Bible. In the first place, he accepted society with all its imperfections as the consequence of God's providential ordering of things.[42] He viewed society and nature as joint aspects of a whole—one unified scheme. Society involved a system of relationships rooted in natural law. Therefore, just as growth and development were slow, gradual processes in nature, in similar fashion one would anticipate that that would be the case with God's design for progress and reform in society; one would not expect it to involve "sudden changes or violent revolutions."[43] The influence of believing individuals would be an appropriate catalyst for salutary change.

This attitude toward social change sounds somewhat similar to but is different from Thornwell's view of the "spirituality of the church."[44] Attributed to Thornwell, this position was a distinctive of Southern Presbyterianism for many years. Essentially, he delineated two separate spheres of authority and function: the church and the state were "as planets moving in different orbits."[45] The church, he said,

> is exclusively a spiritual organization, . . . she has nothing to do with the voluntary associations of men for various social and civic purposes. . . . Her mission is to bring men to the cross, to reconcile them to God . . . imbue them with the spirit of the Divine Master

and then send them forth to perform their social duties, to manage society, and perform the functions that pertain to their social and civic relations.[46]

The church was limited in the scope of its activity. It was not to interfere with the state and its decisions. But the individual Christian experienced no such restriction. He was expected to be active, and the more Christians who participated in government, the more Thornwell would have been pleased. He was active himself, drafting a paper on slavery, advocating support of public schools and the inclusion of religious instruction in the curriculum, and shaping a General Assembly statement regarding peace in Mexico. Occasionally the relationships appear to be blurred as, for example, when he joined the Synod of South Carolina in urging the people of South Carolina "to imitate their revolutionary forefathers and stand up for their rights."[47] In holding this position regarding church and state, Thornwell placed himself in the tradition of the Westminster Confession of Faith.

Conclusion

Thornwell must be viewed as a champion of his Old School Presbyterian theological heritage. His forceful, eloquent leadership contributed substantially toward assuring a legacy of orthodoxy for later generations of Southern Presbyterians. His desire to understand the Scriptures and to seek obedient conformity to them in church and society is the essence of what it means to be Reformed. His weakness lay in assuming that his understanding of the Scriptures was not distorted by his philosophical frame of reference, which was weak in regard to the relationship between natural and revealed theology. Thus his remarkable contribution bears the theological and philosophical marks of the nineteenth-century Old School Presbyterian mold in which it was cast.

James Henley Thornwell still casts a long shadow in Southern Presbyterianism, particularly in the nascent Presbyterian Church in America and in the Reformed Theological Seminary in Jackson, Mississippi.

Notes: James Henley Thornwell

1. Benjamin Morgan Palmer, *Life and Letters of James Henley Thornwell* (Richmond: Whittet and Shepperson, 1875), 397.

2. Ibid., 537.

3. Paul L. Garber, "James Henley Thornwell: Presbyterian Defender of the Old South," *Union Seminary Review* 54 (February 1943): 99.

4. Ibid.

5. Daniel W. Hollis, *The University of South Carolina*, 2 vols. (Columbia, SC: University of South Carolina Press, 1951), 1:161.

6. The address provided the rationale for the establishment of the Presbyterian Church in the Confederate States of America.

7. Thomas Peck, a contemporary, thought Thornwell's great contribution was in ecclesiology (Thomas E. Peck, *Miscellanies of Rev. Thomas E. Peck*, ed. T. C. Johnson, 3 vols. [Richmond: The Presbyterian Committee of Publication, 1895], 1:434). Garber, "In whatever manner the Southern Presbyterian church may have departed from the ideals he defined for its establishment in 1861, that denomination remains to an extent the lengthened shadow of James Henley Thornwell as the Scottish church is of John Knox" (Garber, "Thornwell," 99). H. Sheldon Smith concluded that Thornwell's theological thought dominated most of the history of Southern Presbyterianism ("The Church and the Social Order in the Old South as Interpreted by James H. Thornwell," *Church History* 7 [June 1938]: 115ff.).

8. The First General Assembly of the Presbyterian Church in America met in Birmingham, Alabama, on December 4, 1973. The name National Presbyterian Church was selected at this initial assembly, but changed at the 1974 General Assembly.

9. William O. Bracket, Jr., "The Rise and Development of the New School in the Presbyterian Church in the USA to the Reunion of 1869," *The Journal of the Presbyterian Historical Society* 13:121.

10. The American Home Missionary Society and the American Board of Commissioners for Foreign Missions were two of the societies that functioned under the Plan of Union. Tension soon began to rise, however, because of increasing denominational interests in the official boards and agencies of the Presbyterian Church. Cf. Clifford S. Griffin, "Cooperation in Conflict: The Schism in the American Home Missionary Society, 1837-1861," *Journal of the Presbyterian Historical Society* 28 (1960): 213-233.

11. George M. Marsden, *The Evangelical Mind and the New School Presbyterian Experience* (New Haven: Yale University Press, 1970), 59.

12. Approximately half of the denomination was ejected by this action, which eliminated about 100,000 members.

13. This development was not peculiar to Presbyterians alone. Similar efforts emphasizing denominational distinctives were occurring in several major ecclesiastical bodies during the first half of the nineteenth century. This would be expected in the light of the numerical and geographical expansion that was occurring.

14. For samples of recent literature that has grappled with the relationship of church and parachurch groups as well as the structure of the church itself, see Richard G. Hutchenson, Jr., *Mainline Churches and the Evangelicals: A Challenging Crisis* (Atlanta: John Knox Press, 1981); also Hutchenson, *Wheel Within the Wheel: Confronting the Management Crisis of the Pluralistic Church* (Atlanta: John Knox Press, 1979); Howard A. Snyder, *The Problem of Wineskins: Church Structure in a Technological Age* (Downers Grove: InterVarsity Press, 1975); Ralph D. Winter, "The Two Structures of God's Redemptive Mission," in *American Society of Missiology* (1974).

15. *The Collected Writings of James Henley Thornwell* ed. John B. Adger and John L. Girardeau, 4 vols. (Richmond, VA: Presbyterian Committee of Publication, 1871-1881), 1:230-31.

16. For a more detailed account of Thornwell's views on this subject see

Kenneth J. Foreman, Jr., "The Debate on the Administration of Missions by James Henley Thornwell in the Presbyterian Church 1839-1861" (Ph.D. diss., Princeton University, 1977). For a more comprehensive analysis of Thornwell's views see Morton H. Smith, *Studies in Southern Presbyterian Theology* (Jackson, MS: Presbyterian Reformation Society, 1962), 121-82.

17. Charles Hodge, "Presbyterianism," *Biblical Repertory and Princeton Review* 32 (October 8, 1860): 546.

18. Adger and Girardeau, eds., *Collected Writings*, 4:218.

19. Ibid.

20. Ibid.

21. Ibid., 230.

22. *Minutes of a General Assembly of the Presbyterian Church in the USA, 1838-1847* (Philadelphia: Presbyterian Board of Publication and Sabbath School work, n.d.), 276-77.

23. Ibid.

24. Adger and Girardeau, eds., *Collected Writings*, 125.

25. Ibid., 267. It is interesting to note that in the infant Presbyterian Church in the Confederate States of America, Thornwell's position was adopted and the parity of ruling elders and teaching elders was closely guarded. See Ernest T. Thompson, *Presbyterians in the South*, 3 vols. (Richmond: John Knox Press, 1963), 1:516. For an analysis of Thornwell's position on the parity of elders see Luder G. Whitlock, Jr., "Elders and Ecclesiology in the Thought of James Henley Thornwell," *Westminster Theological Journal* 38 (Fall 1974): 44.

26. Lefferts Loetscher, *The Broadening Church* (Philadelphia: University of Pennsylvania Press, 1957), 5; Marsden, *The Evangelical Mind and the New School Presbyterian Experience*, 67.

27. Adger and Girardeau, eds., *Collected Writings*, 4:386-87.

28. Ibid., 403.

29. Thornwell, "The State of the Country," *Southern Presbyterian Review* 13:874.

30. Ibid., 391, 432. Also see H. Shelton Smith, "The Church and the Social Order in the Old South as Interpreted by James H. Thornwell," *Church History* 7 (June 1938): 115-24.

31. An excellent presentation of this point of view is found in Theodore Dwight Bozeman, "Science, Nature, and Society: A New Approach to James Henley Thornwell," *Journal of Presbyterian History* 50 (1972): 307-25; see also Bozeman, *Protestants in an Age of Science: The Baconian Ideal and Antebellum American Religious Thought* (Chapel Hill, NC: University of North Carolina Press, 1977); Loetscher, *The Broadening Church*, 6; V. L. Parrington, *Main Currents in American Thought*, 2 (New York: Harcourt Brace Jovanovich, 1955); D. H. Meyer, *The Instructed Conscience: The Shaping of the American National Ethic* (Philadelphia: University of Pennsylvania Press, 1972); E. Brooks Holifield, *The Gentleman Theologians: American Theology and Southern Culture, 1795-1860* (Durham, NC: Duke University Press, 1978), 110-54.

32. Donald R. Come, "The Influence of Princeton on Higher Education in the South before 1825," *William and Mary Quarterly*, third series, 2 (1945). Therefore, it is easy to see how this particular way of thinking would have become pervasive in the South.

33. Holifield, *Gentleman Theologians*, 119.

34. Ibid., 126.

35. Dugald Stuart was a disciple of Thomas Reid at Edinburgh. This phil-

osophical frame of reference was Thornwell's heritage and milieu. Thornwell became, as might be expected, an enthusiastic advocate of the Common Sense Philosophy.

36. For a good synopsis see Bozeman, "Science, Nature, and Society"; also Holifield, *Gentleman Theologians*, 110, 126.

37. Adger and Girardeau, eds., *Collected Writings*, 1:580.

38. Ibid.

39. Holifield, *Gentleman Theologians*, 127.

40. Adger and Girardeau, eds., *Collected Writings*, 4:163-64.

41. John C. Vander Stelt, *Philosophy and Scripture: A Study in Old Princeton and Westminster Theology* (Marlton, NJ: Mack Publishing Company, 1978), 304-05, provides a very helpful survey and extensive critique.

42. Adger and Girardeau, eds., *Collected Writings*, 4:404, 421, 430.

43. Ibid., 428, 431-32.

44. See Ernest Trice Thompson, *The Spirituality of the Church* (Richmond: John Knox Press, 1961); also his *Presbyterians in the South*, Vol. 1; Bozeman, in "Science, Nature, and Society," explains his view in the light of Common Sense Philosophy, which would have disdained meddling with God's providentially ordered affairs. Adam Smith developed his *laissez-faire* economic policy out of similar philosophical principles, Bozeman notes. Is it possible that Thornwell has developed a theological equivalent? Bozeman observes that McCosh in his *Divine Government* adopts a similar pattern of reasoning. Challenging these points of view is Jack P. Maddex, "From Theocracy to Spirituality: The Southern Presbyterian Reversal on Church and State," *Journal of Presbyterian History* 54 (Winter 1976): 438-57. Maddex contends that antebellum Southern Presbyterians did not teach absolute separation of church and state.

45. Adger and Girardeau, eds., *Collected Writings*, 4:177.

46. Ibid., 473.

47. Thompson, *Presbyterians in the South*, 1:558. Thompson notes that the synod, after careful study by some of its members, concluded that a sacred inheritance of rights, as in their case, could not be surrendered without sinning against God. Therefore, this particular action must be evaluated in that light.

V. NEOORTHODOXY

NEOORTHODOXY

DENNIS VOSKUIL

THE 1930s was a decade of transition in America. Under the sway of a devastating Depression, the nation moved through a decisive era of social upheaval, economic adjustment, and political realignment. This was also a decade of religious transition as liberal Protestantism, the most vital theological force of the previous quarter-century, underwent a process of decline and was challenged by a movement that has come to be known as American neoorthodoxy. During three succeeding decades neoorthodoxy was at the cutting edge of theological development.

When it is taken at face value the term "neoorthodoxy" can, for various reasons, be somewhat misleading. First, the term suggests a wholesale return to orthodoxy. Actually, the early formulators of neoorthodoxy—most notably Reinhold and H. Richard Niebuhr, Walter Marshall Horton, Walter Lowrie, Wilhelm Pauck, Elmer G. Homrighausen, and Edwin Lewis—were all former liberals who "converted" to the new movement as they became increasingly disenchanted with the reigning assumptions of liberalism. While they did adopt a number of preliberal motifs, these thinkers did not really advocate an uncritical appropriation of Protestant orthodoxy. From a certain perspective, then, "neoliberalism" would have been an apt label, for it was as much a revamped liberalism as it was a repristination of orthodoxy. Second, "neoorthodoxy" is so closely identified with the continental movement known as Barthianism that the American version is often subsumed under the European original. This is unfortunate, for while the exponents of the American movement appreciated Karl Barth's critique of liberalism, they did not generally appropriate his radical methodology or propositions. Third, those who have come to be identified as proponents of the American movement did not generally describe themselves as neoorthodox; it was originally a term of abuse employed by disapproving liberals. Moreover, those who were labeled "neoorthodox" adhered to such diverse expressions of thought that no school or coterie of theologians

247

emerged to claim and give precise distinction to the term. Even the Nie-buhr brothers were such independent thinkers that it cannot be said that there was a coterie of Niebuhrians.

However unsatisfactory, the term "neoorthodoxy" has persisted and given title to the postliberal theological movement that burgeoned during the 1930s. There were many other name tags for "neoorthodoxy," of course, and if they failed to gain wide currency, all tell us something about the character of the movement. Among those most often employed were "Neo-Supernaturalism," "Theological Realism," "Neo-Protestant-ism," and "New-Reformation Theology."[1] Each of these appellations underscores the Reformed temper of American neoorthodoxy. The ex-ponents of the movement sought to move beyond fundamentalism and modernism by reaching back for the major themes of faith enunciated by the great Reformers of the sixteenth century. Neoorthodox writings were laced with Reformation mottoes: God as sovereign and transcen-dent, humans as sinners, salvation by grace, the primacy of Christ, and the importance of Scripture.

Neoorthodoxy reiterated major motifs of Reformed thought and in the process stirred not only a renaissance in the study of Calvin and Luther, but also interest in the biblical foundations of their thought. Their embrace of the Reformation, however, was cautious and selective. Nurtured in the liberal system, the neoorthodox disdained the creedal-ism and biblical fundamentalism that characterized much of Reformed orthodoxy in this country. While many moderates within Reformed com-munities in America became full participants in the new movement, most conservatives came to reject neoorthodoxy as a deceptive and dan-gerous ideology. It was considered deceptive because it employed or-thodox terminology that was not anchored to orthodox epistemology; it was considered dangerous because it deceitfully lured the orthodox away from secure foundations of faith. Those who stood within the Reformed tradition, then, were faced with this question: Were the neoorthodox Reformed sheep, or were they wolves in sheep's clothing?

The Revolt against Liberalism

American neoorthodoxy was a postliberal movement. Unlike most of the Reformed theologians who so vigorously assailed liberalism at the turn of the century, the neoorthodox were disenchanted liberals whose initial challenges to liberal thought came from within the liberal camp. While this internal critique quickly burgeoned into a full-scale revolt, its points of departure continued to be framed in liberal terms.

American religious liberalism took hold during the last quarter of the nineteenth century when the evangelical consensus began to crack under the intellectual pressures of Darwinism, Freudianism, historicism, and higher criticism. While those who came to be identified as fundamentalists shored up their theological barricades and prepared to do battle with the modern world, the liberals were eager to forge a truce with the new sciences and worked at mediating the modern worldview and the Christian faith. By nature inclusive and comprehensive, liberalism naturally gave birth to divergent theologies, but all were undergirded by what William R. Hutchison has called "the modernist impulse"—a willingness not only to embrace modern culture but also to accommodate the Christian faith to it.[2] Nurtured during an era of national well-being, and building on a base of philosophical idealism, the liberals developed a theological system that breathed optimism and progressivism. It generally assumed the immanence or indwelling of God in nature and humanity, expressed confidence in the goodness and improvability of human nature, stressed the person of Jesus as a universal moral model, embraced higher-critical study of the Bible, and adopted evolutionary theories of human development. Although it sustained constant attacks from humanists on the left and Christian fundamentalists on the right, liberalism was certainly the most compelling theological movement in America through the early quarter of the twentieth century.

Liberalism appeared to survive the shocks of the First World War as it continued to dominate American theology through the 1920s, but it was surely drained of much of its prewar idealism and optimism. God no longer seemed so immanent, humans no longer seemed so altruistic, and modern culture no longer seemed so attractive. By the late 1920s the liberal movement, which had warded off external attacks, began to fracture as it absorbed stinging blows of self-criticism. While few of the self-critics were emotionally or intellectually prepared to abandon the liberal banner, those who did became the standard-bearers of neoorthodoxy.

Certainly the most devastating internal critic of this period was Reinhold Niebuhr, an activist pastor of Bethel Evangelical Church in Detroit for thirteen years before his appointment to the faculty of New York's Union Seminary in 1928. A prolific writer and popular conference speaker, young Niebuhr had a decisive impact upon postwar American Protestantism. A somewhat doctrinaire liberal during the early years of his pastorate, Niebuhr became disturbed by liberalism's inability to sustain moral potency during times of trial and tragedy. His first book, *Does Civilization Need Religion?* (1927), already castigated the liberals for a facile analysis of human nature, for identifying God too closely with contemporary culture, and for easy optimism regarding the social efficacy of the Christian faith.[3]

While he was liberalism's most persistent critic during the late 1920s, Niebuhr was certainly no lonely prophet of religious realism.

Among the many liberals who joined the chorus of self-criticism were Walter Marshall Horton, a young Oberlin theologian who complained that the liberal doctrine of God had failed the test of reality because it was "emotionally sterile and practically impotent," and Edwin Lewis, a Drew University theologian and one-time spokesperson for liberal Methodists, who lamented the fact that liberal preaching was impotent because liberal theology had sacrificed the essentials of the faith upon the altar of modernity.[4]

As the internal critique of liberalism continued to gain strength during the crisis-ridden era of the early 1930s, it became apparent that liberal theology was terminally ill. Most of the doomsayers were themselves liberals who genuinely mourned the passing of a theological system that had nurtured them during a happier era. In 1931, for instance, Henry P. Van Dusen submitted an article to the *World Tomorrow* that was ominously titled "The Sickness of Liberal Religion." To support his diagnosis that the "ill-health of liberal Christianity" was the most certain fact in the "baffling religious situation" of that time, Van Dusen cited numerous symptoms: the falling off of missionary support, decline of church enrollment, loss of religious certainty among the laity, and a mood of desperation in the liberal ministry.[5] Numerous announcements of the imminent demise of liberalism were to follow. John C. Bennett asked "After Liberalism—What?"; Wilhelm Pauck pondered "What is Wrong with Liberalism?"; Henry Sloane Coffin wondered "Can Liberalism Survive?"; and Arthur Cushman McGiffert proposed "The Future of Liberalism in America."[6] In the same vein Gaius Glenn Atkins, a venerable Chicago-school liberal, posed an uncomfortable question, "Whither Liberalism?" for the readers of *Religion in Life* in 1934. He too perceived that liberalism was in a state of distress and that a number of younger religious readers had moved into something ("they have not yet found a name") of a far more radical character. In his survey of the decline and fall of the liberal movement, Atkins admitted that liberalism had been unjustifiably idealistic and optimistic about the human situation. Hitting upon a theme that the neoorthodox would repeat again and again, Atkins concluded that many liberals, in their desire to adapt the gospel to modern culture, had "surrendered the central position around which religion had always been organized."[7]

The Barthian Influence

Throughout 1939 *The Christian Century* published an extensive series of autobiographical articles in which contributing theologians and prominent church leaders took note of the changes that had taken place in their thinking during the previous decade. Titled "How My Mind Has

Changed in the Past Decade," the series demonstrates quite conclusively that American liberal thought went through a period of profound transition during the 1930s. In a summary assessment, the Editor of the liberal weekly, Charles Clayton Morrison, estimated that more than three-fourths of the contributors experienced a "considerable change in their thinking" and that one-fourth experienced a "radical change." As Morrison read the situation, liberalism had been put on the defensive by "a highly sophisticated attack on the foundations of liberal theology." America had just passed through a crucial decade in its religious development. Liberalism had waned while "a whole new theological outlook had emerged."[8]

A survey of the mind-change articles reveals that the transition from liberalism to neoorthodoxy had been stimulated, at least in part, by the sobering events of the 1930s. Nearly all the contributors took note of "the multiplying social catastrophes"[9] that had driven them toward a more "realistic" faith. These, of course, included the economic depression, the rise of totalitarian regimes in Europe, and the failure of efforts to achieve international disarmament.

If the theological transition was encouraged by crisis events, it was also influenced by European crisis theologies, especially those that were most closely associated with the thought of Karl Barth. Of the various European religious movements that have impacted America since the First World War—the renaissance of Kierkegaard, Luther studies, Lundensian thought from Sweden, new directions in biblical studies[10]—the most important has been Barthian theology (also identified as European neoorthodoxy, dialectical theology, the theology of the word, and the theology of crisis). European neoorthodoxy was a broad-based movement that incorporated the thought of many prominent thinkers in America, but it was almost exclusively identified in this country with those great Swiss theologians, Emil Brunner and Karl Barth. And while Brunner was widely read, it was Barth who proved to be the lightning rod of the movement.

In 1918 Barth produced Europe's first great postliberal work, a strange commentary on Paul's letter to the Romans. To those accustomed to liberal refrains, Barth's message was jarring: the utter transcendence of God; the utter feebleness of humanity; the utter discontinuity between time and eternity. Unleashing the thunder and lightning of God's eternal absolutes, *Der Römerbrief*, in the words of Karl Adam, "fell like a bomb on the playground of the theologians."[11]

If Barth's commentary had an explosive impact on European theology, it took nearly a decade for the shockwaves to reach America. By 1926 some articles on Barth began to appear, but Barth's own thought was not actually available until 1928 when Pilgrim Press of Boston published *The Word of God and the Word of Man,* an important edition of early essays translated by Douglas Horton. Not until 1933 did presses in England make available an English translation of *Der Römerbrief.*[12]

The first book-length interpretation of Barth's thought was produced by an orthodox Calvinist, Alvin Sylvester Zerbe, professor emeritus of Central Theological Seminary in Dayton, Ohio. In 1930 Zerbe produced *The Karl Barth Theology, or, The New Transcendentalism,* an extremely acerbic assessment that concluded that Barth's theology was "but a cosmic philosophy in which the fundamental doctrines of God, man, sin, redemption, the Bible, time and eternity are in a new setting and have a meaning entirely different from the old creeds and confessions."[13] While Zerbe's book seems to have gone unnoticed by mainstream theologians, Wilhelm Pauck's *Karl Barth: Prophet of a New Christianity,* published during the following year, became the standard treatment of Barth during the 1930s. A church historian at Chicago Theological Seminary, Pauck had recently emigrated to America, taking with him a certain ambivalence about the Barthian movement. In the end Pauck criticized Barth's radical dualism and his doctrine of Scripture as evidence of an unhealthy return to "the barren, exhausted field of ecclesiastical scholasticism."[14] In 1932 Walter Lowrie produced a favorable assessment, *Our Concern with the Theology of Crisis.* An Episcopal layperson who would become best known as a translator of Kierkegaard, Lowrie served as an unabashed apologist for the Barthian gospel.

By the end of the 1930s Barth's theology had been introduced in America, at least in theological circles. It is significant that thirty-two out of the thirty-four contributors to the *Christian Century* mind-change series took note of the Barthian movement. It is equally significant that most were unimpressed by Barth's methodology and message. To the liberal mind the philosophical constructs of paradox and dialectic made Barth's writings seem opaque, convoluted, and irrational. One frustrated and disapproving contributor sniffed that most of Barth's writings were nothing more than "exaggerated piffle."[15]

Predictably those who might be considered "converts" to American neoorthodoxy found Barth less objectionable than the stalwart liberals did. In fact, the Niebuhrs, Edwin Lewis, George Richards, and Elmer Homrighausen have paid rather high tributes to Barth.[16] Still, even these proponents of American neoorthodoxy have remained cautious in their embrace of Barthianism. While influenced by Barth, they maintained a "yes . . . but" attitude with respect to his thought. Yes, there is much to be learned from Barth's critique of liberal Protestantism, but his radical dualism and obscure dialectics cannot be fully embraced. The American movement was influenced but not definitely shaped by Barthianism. It was not simply a backwoods variety of the European movement, but a genuinely indigenous form of religious thought.

The Neoorthodox Alternative

The core of neoorthodox theology was already being laid bare during the late 1920s when liberal self-criticism intensified. Certainly young scholars like Reinhold Niebuhr were in the process of announcing neoorthodox alternatives to certain liberal positions. Their persistent attacks upon liberal doctrines of divine immanence, human efficacy, and cultural accommodation were certainly predicated upon the incipient doctrines of divine transcendence, human sinfulness, and culture resistance. Still, neoorthodoxy did not cohere as a theological movement until the early 1930s when a series of significant neoorthodox treatises were published.

The early translations and assessments of European neoorthodoxy helped to condition the theological transition in America, but the most important early treatise was Reinhold Niebuhr's *Moral Man and Immoral Society*, released by Scribner's in 1932. Described by Sydney Ahlstrom as the "most disruptive religio-ethical bombshell of domestic construction to be dropped during the entire interwar period,"[17] the treatise blasted those liberals who failed to come to grips with the inherent immorality of "collective egoism." Disdaining the ameliorative prescriptions of liberal moralists who believed that social injustice could be resolved through moral or rational suasion, Niebuhr adumbrated a system of ethical realism that was informed by a biblical view of sin and a Marxian analysis of Western culture.

Niebuhr's book struck a liberal nerve. While agitated liberal reviewers complained that the author was a prophet of disillusionment, despair, and pessimism, they seemed to agree that this strong dose of religious realism was necessary theological medicine.[18] Medicine of a similar sort was dispensed by German émigré Paul Tillich in his *Religious Situation*, another sober Marxian analysis of bourgeois Western culture. Translated and introduced by H. Richard Niebuhr, this short work did not become an American classic, but it certainly matched the tone and temper of *Moral Man and Immoral Society*.

The transition from liberalism to neoorthodoxy became especially evident in 1934, when a raft of neoorthodox works were published. Reinhold Niebuhr issued his *Reflections on the End of an Era*, but it broke little new ground and was overshadowed by the bombshell hurled two years before. More important were Walter Marshall Horton's *Realistic Theology* and Edwin Lewis's *Christian Manifesto*, books that signaled theological about-faces for these young former liberals. Horton's brilliant work insisted that liberalism had been rendered outmoded and impotent because it had become aligned with the presuppositions, prejudices, and illusions of contemporary Western culture, and in a counterpose introduced a realistic theological system that would be based upon the recognition of deeply rooted human sin. Lewis blasted the liberals for rejecting or eviscerating essential Christian doctrines and proposed a theological corrective founded upon revitalized doctrines of divine transcendence and human sin. The other important neoorthodox book to appear in 1934 was George W. Richards's *Beyond Fundamentalism and Modernism: The Doctrine of God.* A church historian who served as President of Lancaster Seminary (Reformed Church in the United States), Richards was obviously uncomfortable with the theological assumptions of both liberals and fundamentalists. What he offered was a Barthian-flavored alternative that seemed congenial to his confessional Reformed heritage.

In 1935 two more significant books strengthened the neoorthodox critique. Reinhold Niebuhr published his Rauschenbusch Lectures as *An Interpretation of Christian Ethics,* a work that sought to anchor his ethical system to a distinctly Christian assessment of social systems, and a distinctly Christian remedy for social sin. In the same year H. Richard Niebuhr, Wilhelm Pauck, and Francis P. Miller collaborated to produce *The Church Against the World,* a neoorthodox manifesto to the churches. As the title suggests, each of the contributors warned the church to avoid corrupting alliances with contemporary culture, be they naturalism, nationalism, capitalism, or any competing forms of idolatrous anthropocentrism.

By the 1930s, then, the essential themes of American neoorthodoxy had been introduced. During the next two decades this compelling movement would set the theological agenda in this country. The early exponents were joined by a diverse group of thinkers who would make significant contributions to the corpus of neoorthodox writings even while they were often uncomfortable with the neoorthodox label. A list of such persons would include John C. Bennett, Paul Lehman, John MacKay, Paul Minear, W. Norman Pittenger, and William Hordern. The most important representatives of American neoorthodoxy, however, continued to be two of its early formulators, Reinhold and H. Richard Niebuhr. A careful scholar and penetrating observer of the relationship between religious ideas and contemporary culture, H. Richard has left us with some of the religious classics of the twentieth century, all of which reflect at least some of the basic motifs of neoorthodoxy. Besides *The Church Against the World* he produced *The Social Sources of Denominationalism* (1929), *The Kingdom of God in America* (1937), *The Meaning of Revelation* (1941), *Christ and Culture* (1951), *Radical Monotheism and*

Western Culture (1960), and *The Responsible Self* (1963). By nature a polemicist, Reinhold produced the important neoorthodox tracts for the
times. His important later writings include *The Nature and Destiny of
Man* (1941), *The Children of Light and the Children of Darkness* (1944), *Faith
and History* (1949), and *The Irony of American History* (1952). Certainly
his most significant theological contribution was the two-volume study
of human nature and human destiny. By 1939 when he delivered these
as the Gifford Lectures at Edinburgh University, Niebuhr had become
interested in delineating a theological system that was faithful to the
essential themes of the Bible and of the Reformers. It was, of course, a
work in apologetics, as Niebuhr sought to interpret traditional doctrines
such as creation, the Fall, original sin, and grace in terms that would be
understandable and compelling to the modern mind. In this respect, *The
Nature and Destiny of Man* is the most important theological treatise to
be produced in America during the twentieth century.

Essential Neoorthodoxy

American neoorthodoxy began as a theological corrective, but its
critique of liberalism eventually developed into a constructive and self-
sustaining theological program. First, over against a liberal doctrine that
seemed naively to assume the essential goodness of individuals and the
essential altruism of social groups, the exponents of neoorthodoxy reap-
propriated a doctrine of sin that they believed to be consistent with the
teachings of Paul, Augustine, Luther, and Calvin. Second, disturbed by
the liberal stress upon divine immanence, the neoorthodox emphasized
the transcendent and sovereign nature of God. Third, convinced that the
liberals had anthropomorphized the Scriptures, the neoorthodox showed
renewed interest in the Bible as revelation, and while they were open
to modern forms of biblical scholarship, exponents of the new movement
emphasized the role of faith in understanding biblical truths. Fourth,
concerned that liberal attempts to Christianize culture had been far too
idealistic and individualistic, the neoorthodox posited a social gospel
that rested upon a realistic analysis of individual and collective egoisms,
a commitment to serving both within the context of justice, and an acute
awareness that perfection will never be attained in a finite world. And
fifth, having condemned the liberals for wholesale accommodation of
the gospel to the thought-forms of modern culture, neoorthodoxy insisted that the church must stand against culture.

To understand "essential neoorthodoxy" it is helpful to identify the
philosophical approaches that most influenced the movement. Certainly
neoorthodoxy should be identified as a variant religious strain of the
movement of philosophical realism that began to dominate American

thought during the early decades of the twentieth century. Associated with the likes of William James, George Santayana, George Herbert Mead, Douglas Clyde MacIntosh, and Henry Nelson Wieman, philosophical realism was characterized by objectivism, behaviorism, and anti-idealism.[19] While some of the neoorthodox figures found philosophical realism a congenial counterbalance to forms of liberalism, they normally identified themselves as realists with respect to their sober analysis of the human condition. Hence the Christian realism of neoorthodoxy drew more from Paul and Augustine than from William James and George Herbert Mead.

Neoorthodoxy was also influenced by existentialism,[20] a movement in Western thought associated with Nietzsche, Camus, Sartre, and Heidegger, but which in its Christian form owes most to the tormented but brilliant mind of Soren Kierkegaard. Kierkegaard's emphasis upon the leap of faith, his insistence upon personal and responsible decision, and his formulation of the qualitative distinction between the divine and the human impacted American as well as European forms of neoorthodoxy.

Finally, neoorthodoxy was pervaded by the dialectical mood. The modern dialectical movement was informed by Hegel and Marx, but was put to Christian use by Kierkegaard and Barth. American thinking tended to resist wholesale retreats into dialectics, but in coming to grips with the poignant issues of existence and faith Reinhold Niebuhr and others would speak of paradoxes, antinomies, contradictions, and impossible possibilities.

The Reformed Response

The Reformed tradition has had such a pervasive impact upon American thought that nearly all forms of theology could plausibly claim the lineage of John Calvin and the other Reformers. However diffused and diluted it may have become, Reformed thought has served as something of a theological common denominator, one that has affected liberals and conservatives alike.

In many respects, neoorthodoxy should be interpreted as a Reformed movement. Not only were nearly all of its early exponents drawn from denominations that cherished Reformed confessions of faith, but they also emphasized many of the central themes of Reformed thought: divine transcendence, human sinfulness, and the Bible as revelation. Certainly, over against liberalism the new orthodoxy appeared to be the new Reformation.

What, then, was the response to neoorthodoxy of those who claimed to be the keepers of the Reformed tradition? First, it can be said that those theologians who were most self-consciously Reformed showed early and sustained interest in both European and American forms of neoorthodoxy. A review of publications related to the movement reveals that those connected to Reformed and Presbyterian colleges and seminaries generally were more concerned with neoorthodoxy than those related to other theological traditions. Moreover, Reformed-oriented schools such as Lancaster Seminary, Union Seminary in New York, and Princeton Seminary tended to serve as centers of neoorthodox influence.

Second, those who were most receptive to neoorthodox thought tended to be moderates on the theological spectrum. While most liberals and fundamentalists assailed neoorthodoxy for opposite reasons, the moderates tentatively embraced it as a viable theological alternative. The moderate Reformed response was delineated by George Richards in his book *Beyond Fundamentalism and Modernism*. Written in a similar vein is Holmes Rolston's *A Conservative Looks to Barth and Brunner*, published in 1933. While he was not wholly uncritical of neoorthodox categories, the Southern Presbyterian invited fellow conservatives to embrace Barth and Brunner as genuine exponents of Reformed faith. Rolston represents the response of irenic orthodoxy.

The response of those who could be identified as staunchly orthodox or fundamentalist tended to be much more suspicious of neoorthodoxy. While Donald Grey Barnhouse, the prominent Presbyterian premillennialist from Philadelphia, became convinced through an interview with Barth in 1933 that the Swiss flamethrower was "not only a great theologian, but a great Christian" who was "taking off the grave clothes of modernism,"[21] most of the orthodox who made the effort to read and understand neoorthodoxy concluded that it was a new form of liberalism disguised in orthodox terminology. And it was precisely because the neoorthodox were considered wolves in sheep's clothing[22] that they were deemed dangerous to the flock of the faithful.

Many of the best and brightest among the orthodox attempted to expose the wolves of neoorthodoxy. Zerbe's early assessment of Barth was superseded by numerous others, especially after the Second World War. The orthodox generally concentrated upon Barth and Brunner rather than the American exponents of neoorthodoxy. In part this was due to the fact that the Swiss giants seemed to position themselves closer to traditional interpretations than Americans such as Niebuhr and hence posed a greater threat to orthodoxy. Moreover, the Europeans were much more systematic in their theological enterprises, and therefore addressed directly those issues that most exercised the conservative Reformed community.

Recognizing emphases that seemed to square with those of Reformed orthodoxy, the harshest critics of neoorthodoxy took pains to identify the real intellectual roots of the new movement. Beneath every neoorthodox doctrine was located the corrupted stain of liberalism. Representatives from competing segments of the Reformed community contributed to the systematic exposé of neoorthodox thought. Fred Klooster, a Dutch-American Calvinist, concluded from an extensive study of Barth's doctrine of reconciliation that while employing the terminology of traditional Reformed theology Barth "has not really regarded sin seriously" and that he "almost completely ignores the traditional theories of the atonement."[23] The same conclusions were reached by Louis Berkhof, who complained that the neoorthodox doctrines of sin, election, atonement, and sanctification were not in harmony with the teachings of Scripture and the Reformers.[24] In a review of Reinhold Niebuhr's *Interpretation of Christian Ethics* that appeared in the *Westminster Theological Journal* during the late 1950s, William Young reiterated the most common fundamentalist concern about neoorthodoxy: its failure to accept "an inerrant or infallible Bible." The hydra of all neoorthodox heresies was an approach to Scripture that accepted higher criticism, "sometimes in its most radical and destructive forms."[25] With a system of interpretation based upon an inerrant Scripture, premillennialists were generally opposed to neoorthodoxy. In a review of Edward Carnell's rather irenic treatment of Reinhold Niebuhr's theology, John F. Walvoord of Dallas Theological Seminary concluded that neoorthodoxy differed from the orthodoxy of the Reformed tradition in that "it denies such essentials as the infallible inspiration of the Scriptures, the deity of Jesus Christ, the efficacy of blood atonement, in particular the cross of Christ, and the doctrine of a bodily second advent of Christ."[26]

The most incisive orthodox assessments of neoorthodoxy were written by Carl F. H. Henry and Cornelius Van Til. Baptist by denominational affiliation, Henry was deeply influenced by Reformed doctrine and was widely read in Reformed communities. In his erudite treatment of twentieth-century theology, *The Protestant Dilemma* (1949), Henry, then of Fuller Seminary, delineated and dismantled the ideological foundations of neoorthodoxy. While he was able to acknowledge certain salutary features of the movement, he concluded that it was too laden with liberal presuppositions to serve as a faithful theological standard. The holdover of liberal views included, according to Henry, "an evolutionary view of origins, a higher critical view of the Scriptures, and a reluctance to define revelation in propositional terms."[27]

Van Til, a professor of theology at Westminster Seminary, was the most persistent conservative critic of neoorthodoxy. Over the years he produced numerous articles and two comprehensive books, *The New Modernism* (1946) and *Christianity and Barthianism* (1962), in what has become a lifelong passion to unmask the liberalism of neoorthodoxy.

Like Henry, Van Til was eager to prove that the dialectical theologians were actually so dependent upon post-Kantian critical methodologies that they had become thoroughly enmeshed in the historical relativism and psychological subjectivism they had sought to escape. Convinced that "the presupposition of the self-contained God of Scripture" was the only sure foundation for Christian theology, Van Til painstakingly argued that the neoorthodox had built their systems upon the sand of antimetaphysical and phenomenalistic modern philosophies. Burdened with an antipropositional epistemology, they were incapable of constructing a truly biblical and Reformed doctrinal system. To the skeptical eye of Van Til neoorthodox doctrine was fool's gold, for while its formulators clutched in vain for the solidity of traditional Reformed faith "they were able to use only its form of words, without the context that gives them meaning and content." Van Til implored fellow orthodox to see crisis theology for what it really was: "a friend of modernism and a foe of historic Christianity." The danger of this new modernism, according to Van Til, was that orthodox Christians, "in spite of much experience with camouflage, will once more permit the wolf to enter their home and that to their own destruction."[28]

It is ironic that many liberals tended to agree with Van Til that the new orthodoxy was actually a new modernism. In 1950 Charles Clayton Morrison, still the editor of *The Christian Century*, wrote a remarkable three-part article titled "The Liberalism of Neo-orthodoxy." It was Morrison's thesis that neoorthodoxy rightly rejected "an arrested liberalism" during the 1930s, but that in essential ways it was simply following the liberal agenda. As examples of the liberalism of neoorthodoxy Morrison cited views of Scripture, sin, and eschatology, as well as methodological approaches.[29]

It is certainly true that neoorthodoxy bore some of the traits of liberalism. Especially with respect to an openness to critical approaches to Scripture, the new movement betrayed its liberal heritage. It is also true that the exponents of neoorthodoxy, seeking to preserve the values of intellectual freedom, rigorous inquiry, and the spirit of tolerance, generally resisted a return to narrow traditionalism. "When I find neo-orthodoxy turning into sterile orthodoxy or a new Scholasticism," confessed Reinhold Niebuhr late in his career, "I find that I am a liberal at heart and that many of my broadsides against liberalism were indiscriminate."[30] Yet, all of this should not obscure the fact that neoorthodoxy developed as a theological counterweight to liberalism. Regardless of the mutual contentions of Van Til and Morrison, neoorthodoxy proposed a distinctive postliberal faith-and-life perspective. It was a separate and self-generated theological movement, one that grew out of a liberal context but that rejected the very ideological pinions upon which liberalism rested. Quite obviously the neoorthodox did not adopt all the presuppositions of fundamentalism and orthodoxy, but does that mean that it was therefore a disguised form of modernism? Does that mean that neoorthodoxy could lay no claim to biblical and Reformed traditions? One's conclusion about the Christian orthodoxy of neoorthodoxy depends to a great degree upon one's own philosophical presuppositions. The conservative response to neoorthodoxy tells us as much about American fundamentalism and Reformed orthodoxy as it does about neoorthodoxy itself.

What Happened to Neoorthodoxy?

Neoorthodoxy captured the pulse of American theology during the 1930s and penetrated the seminaries and universities during the next two decades. While its emphases did reach the grass roots of church life indirectly, through preaching, biblical studies, liturgies, and curriculum materials, it remained an intellectual movement that to a large degree was never truly popularized. By the late 1950s even the intellectual ethos of neoorthodoxy had become so diluted that it ceased to exist as a coherent or compelling theological system. A transitory movement, neoorthodoxy was stimulated by and best sustained during an era of social and intellectual crisis.

It is ironic that neoorthodoxy, which lampooned liberalism for capitulating to bourgeois Western culture, should itself experience a similar fate. Such a sentence of doom was pronounced already during the mid-1930s by Edward Scribner Ames, a wily Chicago-school liberal. In a review of Walter Marshall Horton's *Realistic Theology*, Ames complained that the new approach "appears as a backwash from the tragedy of the war and a 'failure of nerve' in times of Depression." According to Ames, pessimistic neoorthodoxy was periodized and culture-bound, "a passing episode, salutary in certain of its criticisms and emphases, but yet only an eddy in the mainstream" of American theology.[31]

Ames was certainly perceptive and prophetic. Indeed, while the proponents of neoorthodoxy were castigating the liberals for capitulating to an Age of Optimism, they were themselves formulating a theology for an Age of Crisis, or, in the words of H. Richard Niebuhr, "Theology in a Time of Disillusionment."[32] Following the Second World War when America entered another era of progress and prosperity neoorthodoxy began to disintegrate. Like all religious movements, it was at least in part a reflection of the times. Whatever its contributions to American religious thought, it proved to be "a passing episode . . . only an eddy in the mainstream."

Notes: Neoorthodoxy

1. William Hordern stresses the continuities between neoorthodoxy and Reformation theology. See Hordern, *The Case for a New Reformation Theology* (Philadelphia: Westminster Press, 1959), esp. 11-30.

2. See William R. Hutchison, *The Modernist Impulse in American Protestantism* (Cambridge, MA: Harvard University Press, 1976).

3. Reinhold Niebuhr, *Does Civilization Need Religion?* (New York: The Macmillan Company, 1928), 1-18.

4. Walter Marshall Horton, "The Impotence of God," *The Christian Century*, 18 March 1931, 370-73; and Edwin Lewis, "The Fatal Apostasy of the Modern Church," *Religion in Life* 2 (Autumn 1933): 483-89.

5. Henry Pitney Van Dusen, "The Sickness of Liberal Religion," *The World Tomorrow* 14 (August 1931): 256-59.

6. John C. Bennett, "After Liberalism—What?" *The Christian Century*, 8 November 1933, 1403-06; Wilhelm Pauck, "What is Wrong with Liberalism?" *The Journal of Religion* 15 (April 1935): 146-60; Henry Sloane Coffin, "Can Liberalism Survive?" *Religion in Life* 4 (Spring 1935): 194-203; and Arthur Cushman McGiffert, "The Future of Liberal Christianity in America," *The Journal of Religion* 15 (April 1935): 165-75.

7. Gaius Glenn Atkins, "Whither Liberalism?" *Religion in Life* 3 (Summer 1934): 335-39.

8. See Morrison, "How Their Minds have Changed," *The Christian Century*, 4, 11, 18, 25 October 1939 and 11 November 1939, 1194-98, 1237-40, 1271-75, 1300-03, and 1332-35. The quotation is taken from p. 1194. The fascinating group of contributors was dominated by liberals and former liberals. It included one full-blooded conservative, Clarence Edward McCartney, minister of the first Presbyterian Church, Pittsburgh, and one simon-pure Barthian, Karl Barth, the only non-American.

9. Quoted from Horton's contribution to the mind-change series, "Between Liberalism and New-orthodoxy," *The Christian Century*, 17 May 1939, 639-40.

10. For a fine survey of European influences, see Sydney E. Ahlstrom, "Continental Influences on American Christian Thought Since World War I," *Church History* 27 (September 1958): 256-72.

11. Karl Adam, quoted from John McConnachie, "The Teaching of Karl Barth: A New Positive Movement in German Theology," *The Hibbert Journal* 25 (April 1927): 385-86. McConnachie gleaned Adam's famous metaphor from a June 1926 number of *Hochland*, "the leading Catholic monthly in Germany" (p. 385).

12. The first English edition was *The Epistle to the Romans*, trans. Edwyn C. Hoskyns (London: Oxford University Press, 1933). For a treatment of Barth's early impact upon American theology, see Dennis N. Voskuil, "America Encounters Karl Barth, 1919-1939," *Fides et Historia* 12 (Spring 1980): 61-74.

13. Alvin Sylvester Zerbe, *The Karl Barth Theology, or, The New Transcendentalism* (Cleveland, OH: Central Publishing House, 1930), 270.

14. Wilhelm Pauck, *Karl Barth: Prophet of a New Christianity?* (New York: Harper and Brothers, 1931), 62.

15. Frederick D. Kershner, "Realities and Visions," *The Christian Century*, 1 February 1939, 149.

16. See Horton, "Between Liberalism and the New Orthodoxy" and "How Barth Has Influenced Me," *Theology Today* 13 (October 1936): 359-60; Lewis, "How Barth Has Influenced Me," *Theology Today* 13 (October 1936): 358-59; Hom-

righausen, "Calm After Storm," *The Christian Century*, 12 April 1939, 477-79; Reinhold Niebuhr, "The Quality of Our Lives," *The Christian Century*, 11 May 1960, 570; and H. Richard Niebuhr, "Reformation: Continuing Imperative," *The Christian Century*, 2 March 1960, 248-51.

17. Sydney Ahlstrom, *A Religious History of the American People* (New Haven: Yale University Press, 1972), 941.

18. For an assessment of the reviews of *Moral Man and Immoral Society*, see James H. Smylie, "Reinhold Niebuhr: Quadragesimo Anno," *Religion in Life* 42 (Spring 1973): 25-36.

19. For a survey of philosophical realism, see Herbert W. Schneider, *Sources of Contemporary Philosophical Realism in America* (Indianapolis: Bobbs-Merrill Company, Inc., 1964).

20. For philosophical roots, see Walter Kaufmann, "The Reception of Existentialism in the United States," *Midway* 9 (Summer 1968): 97-126.

21. See Barnhouse, "An Interview with Karl Barth," *Revelation* 4 (January 1934): 5, 30-33.

22. In a review of Van Til's *The New Modernism*, John F. Walvoord wrote that the author points to Barth as "a wolf in sheep's clothing" (*Bibliotheca Sacra* 103 [October-December 1946]: 489).

23. Fred H. Klooster, "Barth's Doctrine of Reconciliation," *Westminster Theological Journal* 20 (May 1958): 180-83. See also Klooster, "Barth's Doctrine of the Resurrection of Jesus Christ," *Westminster Theological Journal* 24 (May 1962): 137-72.

24. Louis Berkhof, "Is Neo-orthodoxy Tainted By Liberalism?" *The Banner*, 3 November 1950, 1353.

25. William Young, review of *Interpretation of Christian Ethics*, by Reinhold Niebuhr, *Westminster Theological Journal* 19 (May 1957): 231.

26. John F. Walvoord, review of *The Theology of Reinhold Niebuhr*, by E. J. Carnell, *Bibliotheca Sacra* 109 (October-December 1952): 374.

27. Carl F. H. Henry, *The Protestant Dilemma* (Grand Rapids: Wm. B. Eerdmans Publishing Company, 1949), 53.

28. Cornelius Van Til, *The New Modernism: An Appraisal of the Theology of Barth and Brunner* (Philadelphia: The Presbyterian and Reformed Publishing Company, 1946), xx, 1-8, 364-79.

29. Charles Clayton Morrison, "The Liberalism of Neo-orthodoxy," *The Christian Century*, 7, 14, and 21 June 1950, 697-99, 731-33, and 760-63.

30. Reinhold Niebuhr, "The Quality of Our Lives," *The Christian Century*, 11 May 1960, 568.

31. Edward Scribner Ames, "The Human Predicament," *Christendom* 1 (October 1935): 179-81.

32. This was the title of Niebuhr's 1931 Yale Alumni Lecture.

REINHOLD NIEBUHR

GABRIEL FACKRE

REINHOLD Niebuhr is spoken of in many ways—Christian realist, champion of neoorthodoxy, polemicist, social ethicist, political activist, ecumenical pioneer—but rarely if ever as "Reformed theologian." Indeed, on occasion he was very critical of features of Calvin's thought and Calvinism.[1] And the exposition of Reformed doctrine as such was not a concern of his, although he often busied himself with the moral and political exegesis of "Reformation of faith." Yet the inclusion of Niebuhr in this volume is fitting. A fundamental Reformed theme is an abiding characteristic of his theology. Further, he has shown the importance of this perception and commitment for public affairs more astutely than anyone else in this century. We shall call this motif "the Reformed vision" (with no apologies for that metaphor, given Calvin's discerning use of light imagery).[2]

The Reformed Vision

"In the year that King Uzziah died I saw the LORD sitting upon a throne, high and lifted up; and his train filled the temple. . . . 'Holy, holy, holy is the LORD of hosts' " (Isa. 6:1). Reformed faith stands with Isaiah, awestruck before the majesty of God. Reformed theology begins and ends with divine sovereignty: *finitum non capax infiniti* and its outworking in debate with the Lutheran *finitum capax infiniti* on subjects that run from Christology to sacramentology; election in all forms of Calvinist thought to the specifics of predestination in orthodox Calvinism; the freedom of God that eludes our efforts to bind the infinite to our finite plans.

Inextricable from the divine glory is awareness of our misery, as the second question of the Heidelberg Catechism makes clear.[3] Before the God who is high and lifted up, we cannot help but confess, " 'Woe is me! For I am lost; for I am a man of unclean lips, and I dwell in the midst of a people of unclean lips; for my eyes have seen the King, the LORD of hosts' " (Isa. 6:5). Yet for Reformed piety and doctrine the divine majesty establishes itself as just that by confuting all our human notions of a retributive sovereignty. The freedom of the high God suffuses the fires of judgment with the light of forgiveness: " 'Your guilt is taken away, and your sin forgiven' " (Isa. 6:7).

Reformed *behavior* is shaped accordingly by the vision of transcendence. Thus the request: " 'Whom shall I send, and who will go for us?' " and the response, " 'Here am I! Send me' " (Isa. 6:8). This tradition is known for its ethics of grateful obedience, the determined pursuit of righteousness as envisioned by the awesome and gracious Sovereign. Indeed, the world acknowledges Reformed piety and theology most often from the signs of this commitment. Hence the comments of a seventeenth-century observer: "I had rather see coming toward me a whole regiment with drawn swords, than one lone Calvinist convinced that he is doing the will of God."[4] Here is the "world-formative" faith (Nicholas Wolterstorff) that has taken the divine rule learned in the Temple to precincts far from it, seeking to shape a Genevan city, an ancient society, a new land, and even an epoch—all by the vision of the glory of God.

Reformed allegiance to the divine majesty and Reformed sobriety about human sin should make for a self-critical spirit strong enough to acknowledge the very hazards that attend its own insights. The vision of divine sovereignty can produce a South African Calvinism that endorses apartheid and at the same time a World Alliance of Reformed Churches that stingingly indicts that view.[5] Loyalty to the rule of God alone will drive some to defend Reformed tradition with exclusivist passion. Yet the same faithfulness to the freedom and majesty of God will press other Calvinists beyond Calvinism to speak of a faith that is "evangelical, catholic, and reformed." For all its susceptibility to distortion, the Reformed vision is a gift to the whole church. And Reinhold Niebuhr is one of those through whom the Giver gives it.

Divine Sovereignty as Mercy and Judgment

"The whole Christian enterprise must regard itself as witness of the ultimate majesty, which is sovereign over the whole of history. . . . The servants of faith must not confuse this witness with their own puny interpretations of the divine sovereignty, which presides mysteriously over the drama of history."[6] The Reformed vision of "God's ultimate majesty" is there at the center of Niebuhr's theology.

While the accent on sovereignty is often construed in the imperative rather than the indicative, we begin with the affirmations. Foundational here is the assurance that God rules and that this "framework of meaning" provides the warrants for justice and the ways to pursue it. Sovereignty so understood is the declaration that all of history is the workshop for "perfectly wise and loving ends" (General Assembly, Church of Scotland). Time is in holy keeping, moving through ambiguity and mystery toward a fulfillment of the divine purpose. To trust that these things are so breeds a serenity in the believer that transcends his defeats in history with their predictable invitations to despair and flight. That same confidence in God's rule secures the faithful as well against the temptations of complacency or self-righteousness in our own fragmentary achievements. The confidence that it is God with whom we have to do, One who shall be "all in all," is a confidence in the divine sovereignty in its future manifestation. God's power to fulfill the divine purpose is expressed both in the providential working of a "rough justice" in history, and the completing of our incompleteness here through God's eschatological work at the end of history.[7]

Witness to God's majesty is no abstract theism for Niebuhr. The trust in the divine regency that leads history toward its goal is grounded in the knowledge of the One who has disclosed this power and purpose in particular mighty acts among a special people. In the election of Israel, and in the work accomplished by God incarnate in its chief prophet, priest, and king, the divine sovereignty is made known and made effective. The powers of sin and death meet their match in the life, death, and resurrection of Jesus Christ, enabling the eye of faith to see the end toward which we move, a destiny that the eye of sight perceives of as ambiguous at best and disastrous at worst.[8]

The God high and lifted up abases as well as abounds. Exalting the believing heart, God humbles it as well. Without this awareness of an ultimate accountability, the self knows nothing against itself. "With me it is a very small thing that I should be judged by you. . . . I do not even judge myself. . . . It is the Lord who judges me" (I Cor. 4:3-4). The confessor knows the universal bondage of sin, grasping this misery by perceiving the grandeur of God revealed in the radical love of Christ. Measured by this scale, "There is none righteous, no, not one" (Rom. 3:10). The penitent learns at the foot of the cross that the final power of divine sovereignty is the power of powerlessness, the crucified Lord whose suffering at our hands drives us to confess our rebellion. Yet here is the power to heal as well as to shame; sovereignty manifests itself in God's capacity to take into the divine heart, in the vicarious act of Jesus Christ, the judgment we so much deserve. "With his stripes we are healed" (Isa. 53:5).[9]

At work here in Niebuhr's theology and piety are both the Reformed and the Lutheran readings of the biblical understanding of the self *coram Deo*: the Calvinist awe of the divine righteousness and its exacting measure, and Lutheran honesty about the wiles of sin that persist even in the life of the redeemed. We also meet Calvin's firm grasp of Christ's priestly work, and Luther's searching probe of its source in the blessing that receives into itself the curse, the divine love that overcomes the divine wrath.[10]

To grasp the self as all known and all forgiven is to read our larger history in an unconventional way. For Niebuhr the ultimate standard of public as well as private conduct is the majesty of the Lord. When this standard of accountability is brought to bear on the affairs of nations and institutions, "collective egotism" is exposed for what it is. As in the self, so in society, the will to power is unmasked in all its ugliness. Indeed, its character as megalomania is better understood, as is its inclination to hide its imperial drives in self-justification. Thus the human condition in macrocosm is read by Niebuhr in the dynamics of sin and judgment known in microcosm.[11]

Here too the Reformed sense of misery—sin as well as finitude—before the divine grandeur is joined to a Lutheran sensibility—the distinction between private and public expectation—"moral man" and "immoral society," later reformulated by Niebuhr as "the not so moral man in his less moral communities."[12] Niebuhr's keen eye for the intractability of collective sin, and the naiveté of trust in moral suasion to deal with it, is an adaptation of the two-kingdom theme familiar in Lutheran theology.[13] What appears to be within reach in personal morality to some extent, and qualifiedly effective in interpersonal relationships, cannot be transposed into a moral posture for macroinstitutions. Given collective intransigence, another set of norms must be brought into play, one that settles for the restraint of the destructive tendencies of political and economic power—indeed, by the responsible use of countervailing power—rather than trusting to the conversion of institutions by moral exhortation or spiritual overture.[14]

Niebuhr's adaptation of the two-realm view, however, was always qualified by a Reformed sense of the overarching divine sovereignty, a note regularly missed by Niebuhr's critics, especially those who in his later days accused him of settling too quickly for conservative political options.[15] His realism about the limits of moral suasion in the public sphere was always held in tension with a vision of Christ's kingly rule over that terrain. One can never accept undialectically, or impenitently, the compromises of absolute love required by actions for justice amidst the relativities of the public arena. The divine majesty still calls us toward "the impossible possibility" and the "relevance of an impossible ideal."[16] What is necessary in a fallen world is a necessary *evil*, an action that cannot be conceived as good, even while it might be fitting. And that action is itself always called beyond itself toward higher approximations by virtue of the divine transcendence. The pressure of a more ultimate vision never lets one rest content with the lower duties of a too rigid double-kingdom concept, as for example the "law and order" premises of a simplistically interpreted Romans 13. Revelation 13 is always to be held in tension with Romans 13, a restless critical principle based finally on the divine sovereignty.

Yet another implication of the Reformed vision is the knowledge that because the sinner is always judged by the absolute rule of sovereign love, humility is appropriate in confrontation with the most demonic of foes. Even the best actions of the just are tainted with sin. There can, therefore, be no simple division between the moral and the immoral; all stand judged before the majesty of God. Thus the Manichaean politics of the religious right and the religious left are called into question. A self-critical Reformed spirit knows itself judged by the Lord and therefore warned against dividing the world up into the dualism of the armies of light and night, empires evil and empires good.[17]

The majesty of God functions in Niebuhr's reading of history also in the transposition of the *way* sin functions before God's majesty in the self into a wider social context. The self aware of its ultimate destiny, yet tied to the facts of finitude, lives in anxiety at the "juncture of nature and spirit."[18] Our flight from the ambiguity of this condition is the occasion of our pretension to be more than we are. Nations and collectivities live with the same ambiguity and also fall prey to playing God and lording it over others. Further, the sense of a higher destiny and accountability prompts collectivities to surround their pretension with moral justifications. Thus the Russian bear attacks its foes, it alleges, because it strives to protect the oppressed cubs from their enemies. And the American eagle swoops on its prey fighting for the freedom of its young. Yet, "He who sits in the heavens laughs" (Ps. 2:4). The majesty of God cannot be challenged by the royal illusions of nations, and their pious cover-ups are exposed by the all-seeing Eye.[19]

While institutions and societies stand judged before the divine glory, that same ultimacy calls us to make discriminating judgments between the less and more of collective egotism. As traditional Lutheranism fails to apply the rigors of this rule to the political realm, settling too easily for the way things are, an extremist form of Reformed judgment on all corporate expressions of pride so concentrates on this universality of sin that it is no longer able to discriminate between the lesser and the greater of two evils. Thus it paralyzes political judgment and action and denies necessary support to the less destructive human options. Niebuhr's intense exchange with Karl Barth at the first assembly of the World Council of Churches at Amsterdam, and his challenge to him to make relative judgments between a Western democracy and its manifest hypocrisies on the one hand, and more destructive Stalinist utopianism on the other, is a case in point.[20]

The sovereignty of God is not only for the eye of faith, but also for the eye of sight. Judgment descends upon history as well as presiding over it, and that punishment can be discerned empirically. The One who sits in the heavens and laughs also "has put down the mighty from their thrones" (Luke 1:52). As Israel understood the rule God exercised in history over national pretension, its own and others, so the interpreters of secular history can perceive the limits set by the divine hand to the imperial agenda of nations and institutions. The divine sovereignty has written a law into the nature of things that cannot be violated without self-destructive consequences.[21]

Punishment, however, never corresponds exactly to our historical crimes. In this world there is only "rough justice." For society as well as the self, the final majesty of God must complete this incompleteness. Thus Christian faith expresses its final confidence in God in eschatological symbols. The last judgment, the resurrection of the dead, and the coming of the Kingdom of God are affirmations that justice shall be rendered to the oppressor and the oppressed, and the divine rule vindicated in God's own time and way.[22]

The Divine Sovereignty as Moral Imperative

"If the realization of the tragedy of sin merely busies the sensitive soul with efforts to find theological, metaphysical, and mystical solutions for the problem of our mortality, the poor devils who bear in their bodies the agony of social injustice may be pardoned if they regard religion with indifference and contempt."[23] So thought Niebuhr about an early Barthianism on the eve of the Depression. Throughout his life he was wary of any emphasis on the holiness of God that did not issue in moral passion and practical action. How could it be otherwise with a Reformed theologian? Indeed, how could it be otherwise with Karl Barth himself, as his challenge to Nazism later demonstrated, and as current research on his ethics in early years and throughout his life has further illuminated. Niebuhr later came to acknowledge to some extent the radical implications of Barth's Reformed commitments, but remained uneasy about sweeping assertions of the sovereignty that did not recognize the "nicely calculated less and more" choices that must be made in the midst of history's ambiguities.[24] Behind this determination lay the Reformed zeal to serve the sovereign God at all cost in the world.

The social mandates of God's majesty made their presence felt in Niebuhr's own career. His prophetic witness began with his challenge of Ford's industrial practices during his Detroit ministry, and continued through subsequent periods of his life with his participation in the founding of various political and parapolitical organizations such as the Union for Democratic Action, the Liberal Party, and Americans for Democratic Action, the launching of Christian "middle organizations" such as the Fellowship of Christian Socialists, and his editorship of the related journals *Radical Religion, Christianity and Society,* and *Christianity and Crisis.* The acknowledgment by one or another formative figure of his prophetic role in American life is a tribute to his influence, as with Adlai Stevenson, Walter Reuther, Arthur Schlesinger, Jr., and Martin Luther King, Jr. His chair of Professor of Applied Christianity at Union Theological Seminary, the stream of volumes that came from his pen relating faith to political, social, and economic issues—*Moral Man and Immoral Society, The Interpretation of Christian Ethics, Reflections on the End of an Era, Christianity and Power Politics, The Children of Light and the Children of Darkness, The Structure of Nations and Empires, Faith and Politics, Man's Nature and His Communities*—all testify to the ethical fervor and insight that rose out of his Reformed vision. So too did the regular flow of commentary on the passing political scene that appeared in his editorials in *Christianity and Crisis* and his frequent contributions to *The Christian Century, Atlantic Monthly, The New Republic, World Tomorrow, The Nation,* and *The New Leader.* The founding of a chair in social ethics in his name at Union Seminary is evidence of his impact on issues of justice and peace, especially so when the list of luminaries that supported that venture is reviewed, an array that includes Eleanor Roosevelt, Hubert Humphrey, Henry Luce, Ralph Bunche, W. G. Auden, Robert Hutchins, Robert Oppenheimer, Herbert Lehman, Norman Thomas, Barbara Ward, Sir Sarvepalli Radhakrishnan, and Charles Malik. Niebuhr was such an influential voice for Christian faith because, as a British social reformer put it, he wrote "theology straight from the furnace of social contact and tragedy."[25]

Niebuhr was found in the thick of the social struggle because he believed that the sovereign God claimed that terrain for his purposes and called those who professed allegiance to its Lord to be there living out a grateful obedience. Indeed, for him doctrine was regularly tested in this furnace. "By their fruits you shall know them" is constantly on his lips and in his methodology. Not only did this judgment test faithful behavior but it also cast light on responsible doctrine. Does an interpretation of Christian faith lead its exponents to or away from the struggle for a righteous society? Does a theological assertion produce attitudes and actions that prompt despair and retreat from social conflict (such as naive views of human goodness that are shattered by the intransigency of sin)? Is a moral posture or political program held with such fervor that it produces a fanatic intolerance of criticism and/or denies adverse facts (optimistic views of history that ignore the persistence of sin that parasitizes every social advance)? An apologetic is at work here that argues the invalidity of alternative perspectives to the Christian faith on the basis of their moral inadequacy, and that contends for the viability of Christian teaching on the basis of its undiminished moral passion.[26]

The ground for this moral passion in the face of human perversity is finally traceable to the divine sovereignty. What sustained moral urgency for Reinhold Niebuhr was the Reformed vision. The believer cannot turn from the claims of that sovereignty, for the eye of faith is set relentlessly on its goal, the Kingdom of God. Thus the One high and lifted up becomes a pillar of fire going before the pilgrim, a futuring of transcendence that anticipates in many respects the subsequent theology of hope.[27] "The Christian is taught to pray constantly, 'Thy Kingdom come.' The hope of this prayer, when vital, is a constant pressure upon the conscience of man in every action. . . . He can never rest complacently in the sinful standards which are normative in the world."[28] We are deprived, thereby, of the false security of having arrived, and exposed as having fallen short of the glory of God. While coming under this judgment of the not yet, the believer is also assured, as we noted earlier, that moral commitment is not an exercise in futility. It is rendered valid by virtue of a continuity between the justice sought here and the justice finally established by the sovereign God in the end time. "The vindication of Christ and his triumphant return is therefore an expression of faith and the sufficiency of God's sovereignty over the world in history, and in the final supremacy of love over all the forces of self-love which defy, for the moment, the inclusive harmony of all things under the will of God."[29]

Other aspects of the imperatives that rise from the indicatives of sovereignty have been mentioned earlier in our discussion of the divine judgment on sin and the moral impetus that continues in the face of the ambiguities of moral choice. We shall pursue some of these themes further as they touch on self-criticism in the succeeding section.

Sovereignty as Institutional, Spiritual, and Intellectual Self-Criticism

To believe God is "high and lifted up" is to be alert to the human inclination to usurp the divine sovereignty by claiming too much for expressions of finitude. The sovereignty of God, in this connection, means a pressure to delegitimate, relativize, and demythologize the Godlike pretensions of our plans and programs. Discernible in Niebuhr's thought are three variations of this theme.

1. Niebuhr's sharp eye for violations of God's majesty is fixed regularly upon religious and moral presumption. The brightest and the best, achievers and achievements with the highest credentials, he saw to be the most likely candidates for self-glorification.

In his long struggle with a too-simple reading of moral dilemmas, he frequently attacked "perfectionism."[30] Pacifists and purists who assume that human beings are capable of untainted attitudes and acts of love, alleging that conflicts and questions of social justice can be resolved by this kind of moral posture and political policy, came sharply under fire. Niebuhr appealed to historical evidence to demonstrate that moral counsel of this sort did not bring the desired results in social change. Nor did an honest look at the self's own ambiguous motivations give one much confidence in this advice. While Niebuhr pointed to empirical and introspective evidence, the real source of his judgment is to be found elsewhere. Formally it is grounded in his doctrine of sin. But that recognition of the universal bias in the self toward the self's own interest, the bondage of the will, is related to the heights of the divine transcendence, which claims us for indeterminate possibilities. The awareness of the majesty of God's Agape warns off those who would claim a too-simple application of these final norms. As God is God and we are human, there is no simple exporting of the divine will from heaven to earth. Our finitude as well as our sin, and behind that God's sovereignty, calls into question easy solutions to moral quandaries.

Modesty about moral judgments is matched by wariness of claims that God is intimately bound up with one or another phenomenon of finitude, including those in which Niebuhr himself discerned a divine relationship. A case in point is the church. Niebuhr believed that the Roman Catholic Church in its medieval expression and pre-Vatican II posture drew too straight a line between Christ and ecclesiastical structures. The reason, however he may have expressed it in a given critique—for example, questioning the theory of the church as a "continuation of the Incarnation"—finally roots in the distancing principle we have identified here as the Reformed vision. The majesty and mystery of God cannot be domesticated in any finite form. Niebuhr believed firmly that Pentecost is a deed of God, the bringing to be in God's holy history of the community that knows the Good News. Indeed, a later Niebuhr increasingly found a place for the sacramental and liturgical graces associated with a high ecclesiology. But he always understood the special relation of God to this people dialectically. To whom much was given, from the same much was expected. And that expectation included the humility of not claiming intimacy with the divine plan, or the assurance of divine privilege.[31]

If the temptation of ecclesiasticism came in for a challenge by the

Reformed vision, so too did the temptation of Protestant biblicism. Niebuhr viewed the sacred book of the latter as the occasion for the same kind of understanding as the holy church of the former. His frequent allusions to "a moribund biblicism" suggest that an Enlightenment premise informs his critique of fundamentalism.[32] The parallel between Roman Catholic and Protestant hazards, however, indicates deeper warrants. For Niebuhr the divine sovereignty stands beyond all human expressions, including those specially graced. A theory or usage of Scripture that so fuses the divine Word with human words denies the critical distance between creature and Creator. While Niebuhr tended to see a monolithic biblicism in the evangelical constituencies developing in his time, and thus failed to discern significant differences between dictation and inerrancy views, or between inerrancy and infallibility views, he sought to guard the divine ineffability wherever he felt it imperiled by inordinate claims for Book or Church.[33]

Divine sovereignty also stands beyond the structures and processes of the common life, and stands firmly against claims for ultimacy by any such penultimate reality. Strident voices could be heard on every side in Niebuhr's time making such claims for race, class, and nation. The blood and soil posturing of Hitler and Nazism; declamations about the role and destiny of the proletariat, and the rhetoric of Western nationalism filled the air with sound and the future with peril. The Reformed impulse in the neoorthodoxies of the hour shaped the church's response, especially so when religious justification cloaked the megalomania of race, nation, or class. The most dramatic example of this confrontation was the Barmen Declaration of 1934, bearing the imprint of Karl Barth's Reformed thought (and also Lutheran sobriety about sin by way of the co-drafter with Barth, Hans Asmussen). Here Reformed transcendence took christological form as Barmen called Christian believers to disavow the idolatry of nation and race before the majesty of God who cannot be confused with our intentions and institutions:

> Jesus Christ, as he is attested for us in Holy Scripture, is the one Word of God which we have to hear and which we have to trust and obey in life and in death. We reject the false doctrines, as though the Church could and would have to acknowledge as a source of its proclamation, apart from and beside this one Word of God, still other events and powers, figures and truths, as God's revelation.[34]

Niebuhr mounted the same kind of attack on Aryan ideology, more in a theocentric vein than a Christocentric one (similar to brother Richard Niebuhr's "radical monotheism," and influenced as well by colleague Paul Tillich's "Protestant principle"). Other imperial claims that came under judgment were North American evidences of racism, superpatriotism, industrial barony, and later technocratic hegemony. On the world scene Marxist utopianism and Stalinist tyranny received the same fire. The divine majesty cannot be transferred to either the organisms or the artifacts of modern culture. The Reformed vision sees such illusion and pretension as idolatry to be determinedly resisted in both proclamation and politics.

2. Niebuhr applied the Reformed vision that relativizes false absolutes to intellectual formulations as well as social forms. As in the earlier mentioned case, so here extrabiblical as well as biblical factors were at work, bringing together Renaissance and Reformation influences.

The historical conditioning of truth claims, and thus the relativity of all human formulations, is a widespread assumption of modernity, manifest in historical inquiry, the sociology of knowledge, psychological investigations and theories, and the laboratories and conceptualities of physics and chemistry (a doctrinal absolute that itself presupposes what it seeks to deny, as critics have regularly pointed out). The impact of Marx and Freud on Niebuhr propelled him toward the historicity of propositions, including theological ones. More significantly, however, the Reformed vision is operative in this area, both in why Niebuhr holds to the conditioned nature of theological affirmations and how he does it.

While Marx's theory of ideology and Freud's notion of rationalization contribute to Niebuhr's realism, the Reformed vision, insisting as it does on the inexhaustible reaches of divine mystery, most decisively establishes us as finite, and judges our efforts to deny this as sinful. But to know that "we are men and not God" does not deny meaning in the midst of the mystery, "truth in the myth," continuity with truth in the discontinuity of our formations of it. While theological assertions do not exhaust the reality to which they point, they are trustworthy indicators of it, necessary though not sufficient statements of the way things ultimately are. Thus to acknowledge the finitude of our formulas does not preclude their reliability in our language world. To assert that God is personal is to declare that God is at least that, whatever more the divine reaches of ineffability might be. This intellectual humility is very different from questioning all objective truth claims because of their historicity.[35]

Contributing also to the way Niebuhr construed the limits of intellectual formulation is the world-oriented nature of the Reformed vision. As the theater of divine glory, the world is the arena of God's action, moving forever forward toward the divine destination. Theological affirmations and interpretations must keep pace with the providential working. Out of this understanding comes the Reformed commitment to "the ever new light and truth that breaks from God's holy Word."

Pastor Robinson's declamation was of a piece with a vision that propelled the Reformed people to a new land. This "Semper Reformanda!" is an imperative for both the intellectual and the geographic journey. But as with the issues of vertical continuity within the discontinuities, so too with this horizontal continuum. While doctrine does develop, being subject to correction and enrichment over time, sound teaching is always convergent with ancient truth, a new phase in the trajectory that comes from the biblical source.

The practical result of Niebuhr's belief that we honor the God of history when we acknowledge our own fallibility is his "courage to change," as June Bingham expresses it in the title of her biography of Niebuhr.[36] On the one hand, he was willing to abandon ideas that proved to be in error (by Niebuhr's norms of revelation and reason), as in such major transitions as from cynic to "tamed cynic," from a modified utopianism to realism, from political ideology to pragmatism, from uncritical acceptance of Enlightenment premises to biblical faith. On the other, he sought to refine and enrich long-standing commitments in the light of new learnings, as in his attempt to find apologetically effective language for his doctrine of sin ("self-regarding impulses").[37]

3. Yet another implication of Niebuhr's belief in the distance between human proposals and divine disposals is the freedom with which he dealt with his own Reformation heritage, and, on occasion, even his Christian moorings. The electing love of God really means God will choose whom God will choose.

This wideness in God's mercy is reflected in Niebuhr's openness to learning from a variety of Christian sources. While we have tried to make a case here for the adjective Reformed as befitting Niebuhr, this commitment never exhausts the factors in his spiritual formation. He has been identified, with some reason, as an Augustinian, a Paulinist, a Pascalian, a Kierkegaardian, and even "a Lutheran Voltaire without a periwig."[38] Further, his openness to Anglican liturgy and "catholic substance," his acknowledgment of the critic-in-residence role of the peace churches, his appreciation for the vitalities of Black Baptist piety, etc., represent this freedom from particularity that goes with a loyalty to the transcendence of God over our partial perspectives. Niebuhr's vigorous participation in the ecumenical movement, including his significant role in the theological development of the World Council of Churches, is an expression of this human resiliency-cum-divine majesty. The pilgrimage of Niebuhr's own church from the Evangelical Synod of North America to the Evangelical and Reformed Church to the United Church of Christ, and his own modest but important role in these changes, is yet another evidence of this.[39]

Niebuhr's relation to Judaism can be understood in the context of his effort to be faithful to divine transcendence. Toward the end of his career he disavowed Christian efforts to convert Jews, implying a relativity of Christian truth claims. His experience of Jews as allies in various political and social struggles (in contrast to the ambiguous record of his Christian compatriots), and his appreciation for Jewish theologians like Abraham Heschel and Martin Buber, had something to do with this. But also at work here is a sense of defending the divine prerogative, especially when the record of Jewish suffering and of our complicity in it is so manifest. There are other ways of being in solidarity with Israel's struggle and showing penitence for our complicity in anti-Semitism that preserve Christian particularity and the evangelical mandate better than Niebuhr's succeeded in doing. But the witness to the freedom of God can be heard in his effort to distinguish our too-simple theories and unreflective practices of the relationship of Christianity and Judaism.

Also derivative from the assertion of the freedom of God is the frequent allusion by Niebuhr to the divine use of "an Assyrian rod," and the capacity of God "from these stones to raise up children to Abraham" (Matt. 3:9). Here Niebuhr is honoring the uncovenanted mercies of God, and in particular the secular vehicles of grace. The divine chastisement may be rendered by an enemy nation (Russia) or a heretical movement (Marxism) that is employed by God to awaken us to the condition of the exploited. The raising up of children to Abraham may entail whole epochs and their witness such as the Renaissance and Enlightenment that, for all their illusions, may be carriers of wisdom that is neglected by more orthodox stewards of the divine working.[40] In these extracovenantal affirmations Niebuhr assumes and develops a doctrine of general revelation, acknowledging the range of reality beyond holy history. Here is a common grace that the Reformed tradition has always affirmed, one that is related to the larger vision of the freedom of God to be where God chooses to be, as well as where God promises to be in the life and history of a particular people.

Conclusion

Does the Reformed vision in Niebuhrian form have any bearing on another generation, with its own religious and political questions and currents? D. R. Davies, writing at the end of World War II, was prescient:

> All revolutionaries can sense this element [of corruption] in the movements which they oppose. The greatness of Niebuhr is that he senses it in the movements which he champions. . . . Revolutions, of which there's going to be a rich crop in the post-war world, will be less likely to stultify their historic mission if the revolutionaries who engineer and guide them will be men labour-

ing under a sense of guilt for their extravagance and intolerance. Europe will suffer less if its future explosions are in the hands of Cromwells rather than Lenins and Stalins. Can anyone imagine Stalin, for instance, saying "I beseech you, comrades, in the bowels of The Dialectic, think it possible you may be mistaken"? Given this insight, which is characteristic of Niebuhr's whole attitude, revolutionaries would acquire a sense of guilt—to the infinite blessing of a tortured humanity.[41]

Niebuhr's sharp eye for self-deception, given acuity by the light of the God high and lifted up, has profound implications for today. One example is its import for political questions. Revolutionaries, reformers, restorationists, and all those who are quite sure they have the formula for a righteous society need to see the flaws in themselves and their designs with the eyes of a Reformed vision of God's majesty and human frailty.[42] The closer these movements are to the ways of justice the more they need this astringent realism about themselves, or else their victories portend the fanaticism or despair that Niebuhr saw to be the result of self-righteousness.

In special need of this sobriety-born-of-sovereignty are those religio-political movements of both left and right that give unabashed theological justification to their crusades. Where a too-simple equation is made between finite and self-interested political programs and the will and way of God, the vision of the God high and lifted up has been lost. The corruption in the causes that we oppose is easily seen, but not so easily perceived is the corruption in the causes that we champion. "We know nothing against ourselves," dividing the world up into the moral and the immoral, the armies of light and the armies of night, we and they. The God before whom we must give our final accounting will not tolerate this pretension here or hereafter. May those who are stewards of the Reformed vision help us to see with Isaiah the "LORD sitting upon a throne, high and lifted up," and with the seraphim exult, " 'Holy, holy, holy is the LORD of hosts; the whole earth is full of his glory.' "

Notes: Reinhold Niebuhr

1. Niebuhr criticized Calvinism for its tendencies toward self-righteousness, legalism, biblicism, economic individualism, and determinism, and Calvin for uncritical respect for government. See, for example, Reinhold Niebuhr, *The Nature and Destiny of Man* (New York: Charles Scribner's Sons, 1945), 1:221-22 and 2:116-17, 201-04; Reinhold Niebuhr, *Man's Nature and His Communities* (New York: Charles Scribner's Sons, 1964), 17, 64; Reinhold Niebuhr, *Faith and Politics*, ed. Ronald H. Stone (New York: George Braziller, Inc., 1968), 60-61, 91-94.

But at the same time Niebuhr could say, "In its final form, Calvinistic theory probably came closest to a full comprehension of all the complexities of political justice" (*Nature and Destiny*, 2:281). He had reference here to a "later Calvinism," or "left-wing Calvinism," as in the constituencies of Cromwell's army that carried through the Reformed principle of "the authority of God beyond all human and historical authorities, enabling us to defy those authorities with a resolute 'We must obey God rather than man' " (*Faith and Politics*, 60-61). John Milton came in for special praise, especially so in his resistance to authority grounded in his declaration, "My conscience I have from God, and I cannot give it to Caesar" (*Man's Nature*, 26). See also *Nature and Destiny*, 2:223ff., 234ff., and 282; and *Faith and Politics*, 191-92.

More often than in these explicit affirmations of certain forms of Calvinism, Niebuhr's allusion to the Reformed vision came in his references to "prophetic faith," "Hebraic faith," and "biblical religion."

2. On the Reformed character of Niebuhr's views Langdon Gilkey has this to say:

The synthesis he achieved was one which combined a Calvinistic (rather than a Lutheran) form of the Reformation with the modern sense of unlimited possibility—which should surprise no one familiar with Niebuhr's overwhelmingly moral and political interpretation of existence. As with Calvin, justification in Niebuhr is teleological, leading to a more fruitful moral and political existence, and so in relation to history to a more creative and human social order in the future. Because it was in a humanistic, moralistic, and optimistic culture that Niebuhr emphasized sin and justification, he was mistaken as 'merely a Lutheran' who separated law and Gospel so far as to be unable to bring them together again. No interpretation of Niebuhr could be further from the truth, I think; all of the Calvinistic moral passion and implicit moral and political teleology in time was in him. However, this 'Calvinism' was now set within the new atmosphere created by the Enlightenment and the nineteenth century . . . (Langdon Gilkey, "Reinhold Niebuhr's Theology of History," *The Journal of Religion* 54 (1974): 384.

3. Thus following the famous answer to the first question, which speaks of the gospel of the triune God, the answer to the second question concerning the first of three things to be known in order to "live and die in the blessedness of this comfort" is "the greatness of my sin and wretchedness."

4. Quoted in Nicholas Wolterstorff, *Until Justice and Peace Embrace* (Grand Rapids: Wm. B. Eerdmans Publishing Company, 1983), 9.

5. On the suspension of the Nederduitse Gereformeerde Kerk (in the Republic of South Africa) and the Nederduitse Hervormde Kerk van Afrika from the privileges of membership in the World Alliance of Reformed Churches by its General Council, see *Called to Witness to the Gospel Today: Studies from the World Alliance of Reformed Churches* (Geneva: WARC, 1983), 26-30.

6. Reinhold Niebuhr, "The Test of the Christian Faith Today," *The Christian Century*, 28 October 1959, 1243. See also Reinhold Niebuhr, *Discerning the Signs of the Times* (New York: Charles Scribner's Sons, 1946), 3-13; *Nature and Destiny*, 1:125, 137, and 204.

7. Ibid., 1:90-91, 2:33-34; Niebuhr, *Discerning*, 57-72.

8. Niebuhr, *Nature and Destiny*, 2:1-97.

9. Reinhold Niebuhr, *The Self and the Dramas of History* (New York: Charles Scribner's Sons, 1955), 3-72; (*Nature and Destiny*, 2:22, 25-26, 71-72, 107, 126, 192-95; *Discerning*, 134.

Thus Niebuhr: "The sinner who justifies himself does not know God as judge and does not need God as Saviour" (*Nature and Destiny*, 1:20).

10. Ibid., 1:138-42, 2:35-56; *Discerning*, 14.

11. Niebuhr, *Nature and Destiny*, 1:208, 2:29, 246-47; *Discerning*, 137.

12. Reinhold Niebuhr, *Moral Man and Immoral Society* (New York: Charles Scribner's Sons, 1932); *Man's Nature*, 22.

13. Niebuhr, *Nature and Destiny*, 2:187-89; "The Test of the Christian Faith Today," 1240-41.

14. Reinhold Niebuhr, *An Interpretation of Christian Ethics* (New York: Harper & Brothers, 1935).

15. See especially the critical comments of Richard Shaull and Harvey Cox in the symposium on Niebuhr's work, *Christianity and Crisis* 27 (August 1968): 175-90. The writer's response appears in "Realism and Vision," *Christianity and Crisis* 30 (April 1970): 72-77, and in Gabriel Fackre, *The Promise of Reinhold Niebuhr* (New York: J. B. Lippincott Company, 1970), 65-80 and passim.

16. Niebuhr, *Nature and Destiny*, 1:223, 298, 2:76ff.; *Interpretation*, 101-36.

17. This writer has sought to develop this point in detail with respect to political fundamentalism in *The Religious Right and Christian Faith* (Grand Rapids: Wm. B. Eerdmans Publishing Company, 1982).

18. Niebuhr, *Nature and Destiny*, 1:12-18.

19. Reinhold Niebuhr, *Love and Justice*, ed. D. B. Robertson (Cleveland: World Publishing Company, 1967), 57-240; *Faith and Politics*, 185-268.

20. Niebuhr, "We Are Men and Not God," in *Applied Christianity*, ed. D. B. Robertson (New York: Meridian Books, 1959), 168-74. See Niebuhr on Barth, also in *Applied Christianity*, 147-67, 175-96.

21. Reinhold Niebuhr, *Reflections on the End of an Era* (New York: Charles Scribner's Sons, 1934), 139-62; Reinhold Niebuhr, *Faith and History* (New York: Charles Scribner's Sons, 1949), 102-70; *Nature and Destiny*, 1:4.

22. Niebuhr, *Nature and Destiny*, 2:94-95, 287, 321; *Faith and History*, 214-43.

23. *Applied Christianity*, 145; see also *Nature and Destiny*, 2:96, 121, 244, 247. So too Niebuhr's oft-quoted testimony in his first years of ministry: "I am really beginning to like the ministry. I think since I have stopped worrying so much about the intellectual problems of religion and have begun to explore some of its ethical problems there is more of a thrill in preaching." (Reinhold Niebuhr, *Leaves from the Notebook of the Tamed Cynic* [Chicago: Willet, Clark & Colby, 1929], 27).

24. Niebuhr, *Nature and Destiny*, 1:220.

25. D. R. Davies, *Reinhold Niebuhr: Prophet from America* (London: James Clark, Ltd., n.d.), 22.

26. Niebuhr, *Nature and Destiny*, 1:95-96, 123-25, 137; *Discerning*, 17, 87ff., 188, 194; *Faith and Politics*, 30-31, 66; *Man's Nature*, 21, 27. Niebuhr concludes his Gifford Lectures with this observation:

> Thus wisdom about our destiny is dependent upon a humble recognition of the limits of our knowledge and our power. Our most reliable understanding is the fruit of "grace" in which faith completes our ignorance without pretending to possess its certainties as knowledge; and in which contrition mitigates our pride without destroying our hope (*Nature and Destiny*, 2:321).

27. For example, *Discerning*, 74ff., 94-110. When Richard Neuhaus introduced Wolfhart Pannenberg, a figure closely associated with this movement, to Niebuhr in 1967, however, "theologically the conversation was disappointing." Richard Neuhaus, "Wolfhart Pannenberg: Profile of a Theologian," in Wolfhart Pannenberg, *Theology and the Kingdom of God* (Philadelphia: Westminster Press, 1969), 32.

28. Reinhold Niebuhr, *Beyond Tragedy* (New York: Charles Scribner's Sons, 1937), 278.

29. Niebuhr, *Nature and Destiny*, 2:290.

30. Niebuhr, *Love and Justice*, 241-302; *Interpretation*, 169-98; Reinhold Niebuhr, *Christianity and Power Politics* (New York: Charles Scribner's Sons, 1946), 1-32.

31. Niebuhr, *Applied Christianity*, 197-264.

32. Niebuhr, *Nature and Destiny*, 2:202-04; *Applied Christianity*, 125-27.

33. Niebuhr, *Nature and Destiny*, 2:152, 229.

34. Declaration, Synod of Barmen, 1934.

35. Niebuhr, *Faith and Politics*, 15-32. The writer struggled with the puzzling use by Niebuhr of symbol in some dissertation research, and came to the conclusion that truth claims were being made in the employment of figural language, a position comparable to that of Wilbur Urban's distinction between the "truth of the symbol" and "symbolic truth." See *Religious Representation and Reality in the Thought of Reinhold Niebuhr* (B.D. thesis, University of Chicago, 1948).

36. June Bingham, *The Courage to Change* (New York: Charles Scribner's Sons, 1961).

37. Niebuhr, *Man's Nature*, 23-24.

38. David Wesley Soper, cited by Robert Fitch in "Reinhold Niebuhr's Philosophy of History," in *Reinhold Niebuhr: His Religious, Social and Political Thought*, ed. Charles Kegley (New York: Pilgrim Press, 1984), 386.

39. On Niebuhr and ecumenism, see *Faith and Politics*, 164-81, and *Applied Christianity*, 265-344.

40. Niebuhr, *Nature and Destiny*, 2:157-69, 203.

41. Davies, *Prophet*, 61, 63.

42. Current works that continue this tradition are Wolterstorff, *Until Justice and Peace Embrace*; Max L. Stackhouse, *Creeds, Society, and Human Rights* (Grand Rapids: Wm. B. Eerdmans Publishing Company, 1984); and Lesslie Newbigin, *The Other Side of 1984* (Geneva: World Council of Churches, 1983).

H. RICHARD NIEBUHR

MALCOLM REID

Hᴇʟᴍᴜᴛ Richard Niebuhr (1894-1962) was a self-consciously Protestant moral theologian. Within Protestantism his thought shows the
closest affinity to the Reformed tradition in theology and ethics. All of
his work was sustained by a deep personal faith in the sovereignty of
God and was motivated by a corresponding concern for a radical and
continuous reformation of the faith and action of the Christian church.
The continuing significance of his thought lies, I believe, in the original
and disciplined way in which he combined clearly articulated theological
convictions with a comprehensive and incisive understanding of the
motivation and actions of selves and the dynamics, history, and structure
of the social order.

The Sovereignty of God and the Reformation of Culture

At various points in his writings Niebuhr has given brief summary
statements of those convictions that formed the essential core of his own
personal religious faith and theology.[1] In his retrospective essay "Reformation: Continuing Imperative" (1960) he pointed to three convictions
that had been and remained fundamental to all his theological thinking
since he first adopted them as a young theologian seeking more substantial theological roots than religious liberalism had, in his judgment,
been able to provide.[2]

Theologically, his basic convictions were, first, the being and value
of God are ontologically prior to, and transcendent over, all other being
and values; second, man is a sinner insofar as he denies the sovereignty
of God and idolatrously regards some other being(s) as a "center of
value" and ultimate object of trust. All selves live by faith in some "center
of value" that functions to give existential meaning to their lives. Finally,
to live by faith in the ultimate trustworthiness of that "God" who is the

ground of all being, value, and personhood is a miraculous gift mediated effectively, if not exclusively, through the ministry of Jesus Christ.

Ethically, the question of a person's ultimate trust was also the central issue. Before all inquiry about the appropriate rules for guiding human behavior; beyond all investigation into the virtues and vices that form or deform a person's character; behind all of our natural faith in the efficacy and sufficiency of democratic institutions, science, and technology or the conventional piety of organized religion is the fundamental ethical question about that "center of value" in relation to which or to whom good and evil, right and wrong are defined. Those who "incarnate" this radical faith in all their roles and relations, in all their dispositions and actions, live as truly "responsible selves." They will experience the freedom and joy of living a fully human life. He acknowledged that "experience and study" had produced some changes in the formulation of these convictions but together they remained the essential core of his theology.[3]

Niebuhr's early study *The Kingdom of God in America* (1937) fostered in him a new and enduring awareness of the normative importance of just these convictions for understanding the Protestant movement in America. This did not mean that the sociological point of view he had taken in his previous study *The Social Sources of Denominationalism* (1929) was invalidated, but it did mean that that approach could account neither for the origin nor for the effect of those convictions that were independent of culture. When he turned his attention to the two fountainheads of Protestant Reformation, Luther and Calvin, he was convinced that these same three themes were central to their thinking also. Again, a careful reading of his most influential book, *Christ and Culture* (1951), reveals that it is precisely these three theological convictions that are present in the mediating positions of the "synthesist" (best represented by St. Thomas), the "dualist" (especially Luther), and the "conversionist" (St. Augustine) in a way that they are not in the two extreme positions mentioned in the book, that is, in those views that either reject culture in the name of Christ or identify culture with the cause of Christ.

Translated into the context of "the culture problem" this means first that the "median" theologians were agreed that to affirm the sovereignty of God as Creator, Judge, and Redeemer means that the spheres of nature and culture can be neither wholly rejected as the exclusive Christian does (for God not only judges their sinfulness but he has created and redeemed them), nor simply accepted as they are as the culture-Christian tends to do (for God does judge the fallenness of man and all his works). Further, these centrist Christians all believe that man's sinfulness is universal and irradicable by his own efforts. The idea that sin is universal both in the sense that it is true of all men and in the sense that it penetrates the totality of human personality is, for different reasons, rejected by both extreme positions. Unlike the median views they each tend "to posit a realm free from sin; in the one case the holy community (the exclusive Christian), in the other a citadel of righteousness in the high place of the personal spirit (the culture Christian)."[4] Finally, this mediating group affirms both the primacy of God's grace and the need to enter upon cultural activity in gratitude to God and in service to the neighbor. The Kingdom of God is both a gift and a task. The two extreme groups tend (again for different reasons) to posit the primacy of law over grace. The exclusive Christian tends to interpret the gospel as a "new law" to be obeyed for the sake of attaining ethical purity while the culture Christian fashions spiritual ideals or categorical imperatives from the gospel to which the angels of his better nature are, with effort, well able to conform.[5]

Given the fact that the theological basis of these three types of Christian social ethics are identical with his own theological convictions, which of them did he himself support? If this question had to be answered solely from a reading of *Christ and Culture*, only a tentative answer could be given. On the one hand, consistent with his emphasis on historical and theocentric relativism, Niebuhr argues that no one of these answers can be named *the* Christian answer. Any attempt to do so would, he believed, be "an act of usurpation of the Lordship of Christ which at the same time would involve doing violence to the liberty of Christian men and to the unconcluded history of the Church in culture."[6] A radical monotheist must restrain himself and simply confess "that Christ as living Lord is answering the question in the totality of history and life in a fashion which transcends the wisdom of all his interpreters yet employs their *partial insights and their necessary conflicts.*"[7] On the other hand, in his treatment of the final median position, "Christ the transformer of culture," the reader could not fail to note the absence of any criticism of its theological or strategic adequacy comparable to that offered of each of the other four views. When the rest of Niebuhr's work is taken into account, however, there can be no doubt that he consistently championed the "conversionist" or "transformist" position. It is, for example, a particularly important theme in *The Meaning of Revelation* (1941). There he argued that natural and revealed religion entail "neither mutually exclusive principles" (thus dualism is rejected); "nor yet distinct stages in a continuous development" (thus the synthesist view is set aside); "but rather a transformation or conversion in which the latter is less the product than the transformer of the previous state."[8]

Conversionism, in Niebuhr's judgment, has much in common with the dualist position. It is closer to the dualist than to the synthesist view with respect to its understanding of man's sin and God's grace. The conversionist position accredits itself as a "distinct motif" from that of the dualist by its "more positive and hopeful attitude toward culture."[9] This attitude is not a simple human optimism. It arises as a consequence of the conviction that God is now active in all the events of history and culture, bringing human life to fulfillment to the glory of God. Conversionism is nourished by certain theological convictions about creation, the fall of man, and history that taken together, in Niebuhr's view, mark it off as a type of approach to the Christ-culture problem distinct from that of the dualist position with which it otherwise has much in common.

The conversionist places greater emphasis on the *present* creative and ordering activity of God in the totality of nature and culture than does the dualist, who tends, Niebuhr believes, to regard creation as simply a necessary prelude to the supreme deed of atonement. As a result the dualist tends to see the wrath of God as particularly manifest in the physical world and culture at the expense of his creative and ordering activity. For the conversionist the activity of God is at every moment a creative, ordering, and redemptive activity.[10] Niebuhr also argues that the dualist tends to blur the distinction between man's created goodness as a finite being and his fall into sin. The conversionist on the other hand distinguishes sharply between creation and fall; the first is entirely a good work of God, the latter is wholly a moral and personal action of man. All the good gifts of love, aspiration, and reason he retains as a fallen creature but in his exercise of each he violates, corrupts, and perverts every object and every relationship he engages. These differences have consequences for the attitude shown by the conversionist and the dualist toward culture. For the conversionist

> culture is all corrupted order rather than order for corruption, as it is for dualists. It is perverted good, not evil; or it is evil as perversion, and not as badness of being. The problem of culture is therefore the problem of its conversion, not of its replacement by a new creation; though the conversion is so radical that it amounts to a kind of rebirth.[11]

Finally, although the conversionist agrees with the dualist that this transformation awaits a final fulfillment that lies beyond history, nevertheless he looks more to the present than to the future, as much to man's cultural activity as to the life of the Christian community for the manifestation of God's presence and transforming power.[12] It is precisely this conviction of the direct presence of God to man in every historical event that is the theological foundation of Niebuhr's ethic of responsibility. A radically monotheistic ethic of responsibility affirms: "God is acting in all actions upon you. So respond to all actions upon you as you respond to his action."[13] The conversionist lives in eschatological hope of the divine rather than human possibility that all creation and culture is *now* being transformed into a kingdom of God in which all the activities of all men will be directed toward and so reflect the love and glory of God.

Radical Monotheism and the Responsible Self

The just concluded account of Niebuhr's central theological convictions has not done justice to the power or the subtlety of his expression of them. But it does suggest the possibility of identifying two concepts or principles that provide a rudimentary structure for understanding his moral theology. The technical term employed by Niebuhr to refer to the first was *radical monotheism*. This is another way of speaking about and affirming the sovereignty of God, that is, the primacy of his being and value to all contingent being and value. The second is the principle of "transformism" or "conversionism." The somewhat barbarous term "transformism" has reference to that continuous process of *metanoia*— which is itself a consequence of receiving radically monotheistic faith— in which all human thought, valuation, and action, both in its individual and social expression, are redirected toward God. These two themes may also be understood as Niebuhr's answer to two questions that must be asked and answered by any theological ethic that warrants serious consideration. First, "How is God known and what may be known of Him?" Second, "What are the consequences of this knowledge for understanding and ordering moral experience and action?"

The transformation of human life both individually and socially centrally involves the "incarnation" of this radical faith intensively and extensively in "all the realms and offices in which self acts."[14] By means of these two principles Niebuhr sought to show that the question of faith, that is, the question of our ultimate trust and loyalty, is the central issue in ethics. It is impossible for a self to have moral integrity, that is, to be a truly *responsible* self, unless and until all its responses to finite beings are qualified or conditioned by its response to the one faithful and trustworthy God present in all events.[15] The self that lives in ignorance of the fact that the one power upon which it is absolutely dependent is good to the self and all that exists cannot act as a responsible *self, one* self in all its responses to the actions of the many upon it. Niebuhr does not deny that a partial unity can be attained in our social roles. Man has been highly successful in interpreting the many actions upon his systems that display certain constancies in their actions toward the self; but they remain a multiplicity of systems. But the unity of the self as a moral being is possible only in relation to a unity that is beyond all finite beings and finite systems of value. To attain unity as one self responding to the one God present in all events is to have attained salvation.[16]

It is necessary to tread carefully here because Niebuhr is not saying that God is present only to that self who has radical faith. God is present to every self he has created in two ways. First, he is present as that power upon which the self is absolutely dependent as just this contingent self. Second, he is present to each self in all the actions of finite beings upon it. In theological language we must say that each self is at every moment related to God as the Creator and Sustainer of all that exists.

But man is a sinner, a worshiper of false gods. The problem of man's sinfulness must be understood as a fundamental perversion of his own being that is occasioned by his ultimate trust in finite beings.[17] Radical monotheistic faith affirms that whatever is, is *good* because God made it and sustains it, but this does not mean that whatever man does is *right*.[18] Throughout Niebuhr's writings there is a remarkable consistency with respect to his doctrine of sin. Sin, for Niebuhr, is first and foremost distrust in God and disloyalty to him and to the whole realm of being that he has created.[19] On the one hand sin is the absence of right loyalty, the failure to worship the one true God who is "the only trustworthy and wholly lovable reality"; on the other hand it is false loyalty, loyalty to something other than God. Loyalty to such "henotheisms" as humanism, naturalism, and vitalism are false centers of value because "each excludes some realm of being from the sphere of value."[20] In the last analysis sin is idolatry.

This general understanding of sin afforded Niebuhr a basis from which to explore its consequences in the individual and social experience of man. One consequence of sin is the impotence of man to save himself from his disloyalty and rebellion. It is important to notice that for Niebuhr "*moral* evils" are a *consequence* of sin and not strictly speaking a part of the definition of sin itself. He rejects as "moralism" the view that sin "means that men occasionally become disloyal to God or that their disloyalty is real only insofar as they *consciously choose* to be disloyal; it means rather that those to whom God is wholly loyal and who are by nature wholly dependent upon him are in active rebellion against him."[21] The idea that men are blameworthy for this disloyalty only in those cases where they are "consciously and willingly disloyal" is rejected on two counts. It is rejected, first, because Christianity is less concerned with "assessing the blame" and more concerned with "the fact and the cure" and, second, because this idea entails a dubious doctrine of freedom. "The starting-point of the doctrine of sin is not man's freedom but man's dependence; freedom accounts for the fact that man can be and is disloyal, not for the fact that he ought to be loyal."[22] To say that "the start-

ing-point of the doctrine of sin is not man's freedom but man's dependence" means, for Niebuhr, that the "will" is always committed either
to God or to some false god.

Objectively, this means that God or a false god is a "center of value"
and, as such, "the standard of morality, presupposed by morality."[23] All
moral judgments are objectively relativistic, that is, the moral concepts
that are employed in them are neither absolute nor psychologically relative. Moral terms like "good" and "evil," "right" and "wrong" take on
meaning only within a value system where the "chief good" or "center
of value" is not itself a moral value but is "the standard of morality."
Subjectively, this means that man's will is never uncommitted to some
god or value-center. More crucially, Niebuhr asserts that when the will
is committed to a false god it is impossible for man to transfer his trust
and loyalty to God by exercising his will since it is precisely his will that
is committed to the false god.

> Moralism which makes the human free will the source of all good
> and evil cannot understand this impotence. Its savior is the will;
> every problem is solved by an appeal to the will. But there is no
> such thing as a free will in this sense. The will is always committed
> or it is no will at all. It is either committed to God or to one of the
> gods.[24]

This doctrine of sin is, Niebuhr believed, fully consonant with his doctrine of the freedom and grace of God because, if man is ever to know
and love the One beyond all the many finite gods, it will be possible
only because God gives him the freedom to trust and to love him. Niebuhr did not hesitate to follow Luther and Calvin and especially Jonathan
Edwards in embracing the doctrine of "divine determinism."[25]

Yet theocentric ethics is also an ethic of freedom. "Where faith in
God is present the self is free from concern for itself. It has not achieved
freedom from self concern, but has been set free by God through the gift
of faith in him. It is able to accept itself as the forgiven self. . . ."[26] With
the gift of faith in God the possibility of freedom from these kinds of
bondage arises as a promise and is made actual in those moments in
which, with repentance, true faith in God is exercised. This freedom is
not only freedom *from* but freedom *to*. The self is set free to respond
with imaginativeness and creativity in every personal and social situation. Niebuhr indicated that he believed this aspect of Christian ethics
had not been analyzed adequately and it is clear that he saw his own
work as an attempt to supply this lack, building on the foundation laid
in Scripture and tradition.[27]

In *The Meaning of Revelation* Niebuhr has described the way in
which the image of God as faithful self, insofar as it replaces the evil

imaginations of the heart, enables the self to interpret all the events of the past, present, and future as events in which the creative, sustaining, and redeeming activity of God in Christ is always present.[28] Revelation is that event in which the self is given a new image by means of which it is enabled progressively to reinterpret all the events of its individual and social existence as related in a meaningful universe. "Whatever else revelation means it does mean an event in our history which brings rationality and wholeness into the confused joys and sorrows of personal existence and allows us to discern order in the brawl of communal histories."[29] The revelatory event makes all past events meaningful by first helping the self to understand the events of its own remembered past. Not only so, but it is enabled to remember and acknowledge follies and sins that it had repressed and tried to forget as its own, and to accept forgiveness for them. Beyond this, it enables the self to appropriate as its own the past of all human communities.

> To remember all that is in our past and so in our present is to achieve unity as a self. To remember the human past as our own past is to achieve community with mankind. Such conversion of the memory is an important, indispensable part of the soul's conversion.[30]

The "past" Niebuhr refers to here is that enduring "internal history" of selves and their communities that is known only to practical reason and not the serial past of "external history" known to theoretical reason.[31] The "conversion of the memory" is not therefore a single event but, "because the past is infinite and because sin enters anew in repeated efforts to separate ourselves from God and our fellow-men through the separation of our past from them,"[32] it is a continuing process of being converted. In traditional theological language it is sanctification.

The continuing conversion of the individual believer has its social counterpart in the necessary and continuing reformation and reunion of the church.[33] "Our Christian churches are like ourselves, just human entities on which God has taken mercy and which he is converting to himself."[34] Niebuhr had never believed that the reunion of the churches depended upon achieving uniformity of doctrines and liturgies, or of politics or codes or ethics; just as he had never believed that their differences on these matters were the crucial factors dividing them.[35] In his earlier writings he had argued for the independence of the church and protested against the idolatrous attachment of the churches to cultural values and ideologies.[36] In his later work he still believed that idolatry was the besetting sin but that the idols were now within the church itself.[37] "If my Protestantism led me in the past to protest against the spirit of capitalism and of nationalism, of communism and technological civilization, it now leads me to protest against the deification of Scriptures and of the church."[38] Among the many factors that Niebuhr analyzed as responsible for divisiveness and fragmentation within the Christian church, none was more insidious than the self-righteous and defensive attitude displayed by the various traditions within the church in holding defensively and unrepentantly to an image of itself as the true church.[39]

Niebuhr points to the passion of Christ as providing the crucial image for the interpretation of present deeds done and suffered. Through this image we are able to discern "the evidence of a pattern in which, by great travail of men and God, a work of redemption goes on which is like the work of Christ."[40] But the lack of any clear doctrine of atonement in Niebuhr's theology makes it difficult to know, with any precision, what this analogy entails. He specifically rejected all theories "that operate with the symbolism of laws and courts," but he did not develop any clear alternative.[41] This omission is part of the larger set of christological difficulties.

In *Christ and Culture* (1951), in the section entitled "Toward a Definition of Christ," Niebuhr made a very promising start toward a Christology approached through a careful study of the virtues of Jesus as recorded in the Gospels. Unfortunately, he did not develop this view further in subsequent writings but reverted back to that exclusive emphasis on the *work* rather than the person *and* work of Christ that is characteristic of his view in *The Meaning of Revelation* (1941).

It should be pointed out here, too, that while Niebuhr often *refers* to the resurrection of Christ, he did not present any very clear account of how he understood this "event." Given his general rejection of supernaturalism and nature-miracles he doubtless would have viewed any belief in *bodily* resurrection as part of the primitive mythology of supernaturalism. "The resurrection is not," he declared, "manifest to us in physical signs but in his continuing Lordship."[42] Of the resurrection of Jesus Christ "we may know no more than that he lives and is powerful over us and among us."[43] To any inquiry about the ontological status of the object of the pronoun "he," Niebuhr doubtless would have replied that such questions cannot arise in a theology that properly confines itself to what can be known about God or Christ within the limits of value experience.

The revelation of God not only effects a transformation in man's understanding of his personal and social history, but it also transforms his understanding of the moral law. "The first change which the moral law undergoes with the aid of the revelation of God's person is in its imperativeness."[44] We begin to see (1) that our transgressions against the laws our conscience acknowledges, or that our society justly imposes upon us, are also transgressions against God himself; and (2) that "the imperative behind the law is the imperative of the faithful, earnest, never-resting, eternal self."[45] A second change is the recognition that its application is *universalized* and *intensified*. It is intensified in the sense that before God we recognize that we have always employed the law in the service of self and so have corrupted it.[46] When the law we claim to live by thwarts our desires, we correct it and deceive ourselves into believing that no transgression has occurred. The same revelation in which we receive the assurance that we are eternally loved and valued by God also condemns us for corrupting all our moral laws and values. The third and "greatest change" is "the conversion of the imperative into an indicative and of the law whose content is love into a free love of God and man. . . ."[47] This is Niebuhr's way of expressing the primacy of gospel over law.

Among the New Testament writers, Paul understood most clearly that the gospel of the reconciliation of all men to God accomplished by the life, death, and resurrection of Christ meant that God's primary relation to man is one of grace rather than law, and that the imperative moral law (understood as code of conduct) can never by itself make any man "good at the core." The root-virtue from which all actions draw their goodness is faith, which was for Paul, as it was for Niebuhr, wholly a gift of God. Because the Christian life is initiated by the unmerited grace of God, Christian conduct cannot be understood at its profoundest level as obedience to moral imperatives but as freedom to love God and neighbor for their own sakes. When the will of God is given expression in the form of injunctions that men ought or ought not to perform, consequences follow that only serve to further define man's inability to love anything but himself. If such moral injunctions do not goad man's self-will and tempt him to futher transgression of the law, then they intensify his consciousness of guilt and fear of death so that he becomes self-absorbed and burdened with despair. In either case the very imperative form of the law itself "presupposes the presence in man of a desire contrary to the intention of the law."[48] Only when confidence in God as the One who delivers from all evil is received is man released from concern about himself to respond with joyful, grateful, reverent, and loyal love to God and to the neighbor toward whom God has shown the same compassion.

The transformation of ethics effected by the revelation of God in Christ does not mean for Niebuhr, then, that the moral rules and virtues common to a given culture are replaced or supplemented by a new and wholly different morality. The coming of radically monotheistic faith means that our ordinary cultural morality begins to undergo a transformation, for it no longer functions as an elaborate mechanism for maintaining our own existence and value at the expense of the existence and value of other persons and things. Radical faith in God frees man from such anxious self-concern to be a responsible self.

Relativism, Theology, and Ethics

It is sometimes remarked that the Reformed tradition has not developed a moral theology that can come close to rivaling the comprehensiveness, particularity, or profundity of that produced by the Catholic tradition. And that is true whether one thinks about the literature of casuistry that aims at providing help to believers perplexed by the difficulties involved in making morally sound decisions about "hard cases," or whether one looks at the literature on the virtues and vices that seeks to clarify and vivify those dispositions that form or deform a distinctively Christian character. Someone might plausibly reply that even if this is true, it may be explained in part historically in view of the greater length and breadth of the Catholic tradition. More importantly it is to be explained theologically. To emphasize casuistry only encourages a legalism that is an affront to grace; to stress the virtues and vices only strengthens a moralism that is a substitute for faith.

Whatever may be the truth of the matter with respect to the Reformed tradition the foregoing exposition of the principles of radical monotheism and conversionism may suggest that Niebuhr would be sympathetic to this reply. He did not deny the need for casuistry nor did he completely neglect the virtues.[49] In his essay "The Problem of Constructive Protestantism"[50] he argued that while stress on the sovereign grace of God and the sinfulness of man as principles in a Protestant ethic do effectively rebuke all legalism and moralism they do not offer any "standard whereby men could make choices between relative goods and relative evils; it gave them no scale of values whereby their interests could be harmonized and the higher could be made to control the lower."[51] But if he recognized the need for a constructive ethic he did little himself to provide it. Why was this so? The reasons for it are philosophical and complex. The development of constructive proposals for ordering our personal and social life was made difficult in view of his commitment to relativism in two different yet related senses: (1) the *relatedness* of all being and value and (2) the *relativity* of all human knowing and valuing.

He has argued that a positive personal and rational relation between man and God is possible, but that it is qualified from the side of the subject by two limitations in all human knowledge. First, he accepted the Kantian separation between theoretical and practical modes of human cognition[52] and then argued that all knowledge of God is confined to the practical mode.[53] Second, he accepted the historicist assumption that all human experience and knowledge, including experience and knowledge of God, is wholly relative to the historical standpoint of the individual in a specific culture.[54] While it is not possible to do justice here to all or even most of the implications these claims have for his theology, it is my considered conclusion that the whole notion of "relativity" understood ontologically as *relatedness* (to be is to be-in-relation) and epistemologically as *limitation* is at once the most pervasive,[55] the most striking, and the most troublesome concept in Niebuhr's thought.[56]

Some understanding of the first of these, relativity as relatedness, is best gained from a brief look at the way Niebuhr attempted to explain the relation of God to the world by means of a relational theory of value. He argues that value terms do not name qualities of any entity and do not refer to certain modifications of consciousness in persons; rather, they refer exclusively to states of affairs that are actualized when any existent being with capacities or potentialities confronts another being that limits, completes, or complements it.[57] This view clearly involves reciprocity among beings in that each needs others external to itself for the realization of its own inherent potentialities. But when Niebuhr argues that the relation of God to man can be sufficiently explained by means of this relational theory of value, serious difficulties arise. It is not hard to see how God thought of in this way is good for other beings, but it is not so easy to understand how this relation can be exclusively reciprocal. How, for instance, is he to account for the value that created beings have for God? He recognized the problem: "it cannot be said that God has need for any being external to himself."[58] But is this consistent with an exclusively relational theory? He cannot at this point advance arguments in support of values intrinsic to the existence of God without forsaking a purely relational theory.[59]

The modification he suggests does not appear to be warranted. A radically monotheistic faith must, he suggests, "use a sort of psychological relativism" since it is "able only to say that whatever is exists because it pleases God."[60] He does not attempt to resolve the issue of whether ultimately values are relative to some constitutive need in the nature of God or whether they are relative to what pleases him. "Whether the relation is to need or to desire, in any case the starting point is that transcendent absolute for whom . . . whatever is, is good."[61] This either-or cannot stand: his *objective* relativism requires that he support the first of these positions.[62] He did not do so, doubtless for the very good reason that this would impugn the sovereignty of God, the very theological dogma to which he was most committed. This would suggest that his relational theory of value is incompatible with his deepest theological interest. Theologically he was committed to metaphysical dualism and opposed to a monistic view of reality. But the relational theory of value is more compatible with a monistic theory. As George Schrader has shrewdly observed: "It is an important question whether Niebuhr's relational theory of value in itself provides a sufficient safeguard against such a monistic theory. It is not his relational theory as such which provides this safeguard, but rather Niebuhr's specific interpretation and application of the theory."[63]

A similar sort of ambiguity is present in his thinking about relativity in the sense of limitation rather than relatedness. This is particularly evident in his discussion of the role that *historical* relativism plays in his thought. Awareness of the problems posed for theology and ethics by the historically relative character of all knowledge claims was aroused by his early unpublished dissertation on Ernst Troeltsch.[64] He did not share the view of other critics that Troeltsch's emphasis on historical relativism was excessive.[65] Indeed, he took the view that the historically conditioned character of all knowledge had been *"demonstrated* by history and sociology." In every field of inquiry, including theology, "if reason is to operate at all it must be content to work as an historical reason."[66] But it is far from clear that historical relativity in the sense Niebuhr intended has been universally accepted, much less "demonstrated by history and sociology." He simply takes as a fact that certain unnamed social theorists and historians have demonstrated that this is the case.[67] As Paul Ramsey correctly observed, he asks us "to presuppose that a volume entitled 'The Critique of Historical Reason' has already been written, and has clearly established itself in a consensus of 'critical philosophers.' "[68]

It is perhaps too easy to point out the logically self-contradictory character of statements that imply that historical relativism is a universal truth. But to say unqualifiedly that "we are in history as the fish is in water" is to use a misleading analogy. If *all* our knowing is *wholly* determined by our social history as the fish is immersed in water, then how did we come by knowledge of this universal truth? To know that this is true of all our reasoning is only possible for a mind that has transcended its partial perspective and grasped a universal truth. Niebuhr was not, of course, unaware of such an obvious criticism. There is direct evidence throughout his writings that he recognized the problem. He wanted to give full weight to his "conviction of the radically historical character of human existence" without embracing the kind of relativism that would rule out any universal truths and values in theology and ethics.[69] Yet the exact nature of the claims he has made in the name of historical relativism remains ambiguous.

Part of the problem may be due to Niebuhr's failure to observe the distinction between descriptive and normative relativism. Does he in particular contexts claim that judgments in society S_1 differ from those in society S_2 (descriptive relativism) or does he claim that what is really good, right, or true in society S_1 is not good, right, or true for society S_2 (normative relativism)? The truth of descriptive relativism does not logically entail the truth of normative relativism. An awareness of the great variety of beliefs that various people hold to be true and the variability of the values that they cherish at differnt times and places is a strong antidote to the ready acceptance of parochial beliefs and evaluations masquerading as universal principles or values. It was the prevalence of this tendency in all individuals and institutions against which Niebuhr rightly directed much of his most acute, trenchant, and timely moral critique. But the erection of false values or norms does not by itself provide grounds for denying the possibility or actuality of universal principles of moral obligation or moral value.

It was remarked above that Niebuhr did not advance any criticism of the theological or strategic adequacy of the "conversionist" answer to the relation of Christ and culture. It is now important to point out that few interpreters of Niebuhr have provided any sustained evaluation of its theological sufficiency.[70] To my mind the most profound and challenging critique has been provided by John Howard Yoder.[71] As Stanley Hauerwas has ably shown,[72] Yoder's own view cannot with any justice be ignored[73] or dismissed as either a moralistic defense of absolute pacifism or a counsel that Christians should eschew any concern about how they are to live in the world and confine their attention to changing individual hearts.[74] Rather, the importance of Yoder's criticism lies precisely at the point of his questioning the theological and political adequacy of a contemporary Christian social ethic like Niebuhr's that takes the position that the basic Christ-culture issue is whether Christians should withdraw from or take responsibility for the world.

He has argued correctly that the issue is not whether the Christian is to be responsible or not, but rather what form that responsibility is to take in the light of God's action in Jesus Christ. A Christian social ethic that fails to put the issue in this way may only affirm the norm of Christendom under the rubric of "being responsible." In other words, it may simply accept uncritically the idea that the bases for the ethic of society and for that of the church are not essentially different.[75]

The point here is not that critics of Niebuhr have not been alert to ambiguity[76] or other difficulties[77] in his theological and methodological formulations but rather that to a surprising degree they have failed to ask how such difficulties might require a fundamental rethinking of his own version of the conversionist answer provided in works like *Radical Monotheism and Western Culture* (1960) and *The Responsible Self* (1963), essays published after *Christ and Culture* (1951). This is not to imply that Yoder's position may not have difficulties of its own, but it is to endorse the importance of his challenge to the sort of Protestant moral theology H. Richard Niebuhr proposed. That is, he has asked *in what sense* a Christian ethic can be an ethic for the world given the sort of claims Christians make about Christ. Or to put it another way, he has asked in what sense Niebuhr has succeeded in keeping Christian ethics Christian: How do the life, death, and resurrection of Jesus Christ and the establishing of his Kingdom decisively change the world and each Christian's relation to it?

Several sympathetic critics have remarked on Niebuhr's reluctance to affirm the unity of the person *and* work of Jesus Christ, and the significance of the traditional affirmation about incarnation and atonement for informing and guiding self-understanding and action of Christians.[78] For example, while Professor John Godsey affirms that "Jesus Christ is by no means incidental to his theology but is decisive for it," he also observes that his theology "does differ from traditional interpretations of Christianity."

> It is not the story of a supernatural being, the Second Person of the Trinity, who becomes incarnate by assuming human flesh, performs during his lifetime many miracles, atones for the sins of all mankind by suffering death upon a cross, rises bodily from the grave, ascends into heaven where He sits at the right hand of God and from whence He will some day return to judge the living and the dead.[79]

If it is agreed that Jesus Christ is "decisive" for Niebuhr's theology, then he is so only as the man Jesus who perfectly "incarnates" radical faith in God and who by so doing has become a moral son of God. Like many other students of Niebuhr's work I record my gratitude for the incisiveness and power of his analysis of "the cultural problem" but also my sadness that he was unable sufficiently to forsake the presuppositions and preoccupations of liberal Protestant theology to be able to affirm those claims that are distinctively Christian rather than simply theistic—claims that define what it means to confess the incarnation of God in Jesus Christ and the reconciliation of sinners to God through his life, death, and resurrection. Indeed, there is a sad irony here. No contemporary American Protestant theologian has written more often and more strenuously than Niebuhr about the need for the church to maintain its independence and integrity over against the world.[80] But insofar as he neglected to focus attention upon positive christological convictions, just so far he failed to provide the church with the very convictions that define both its integrity as the body of Christ and its independence from the world.

Notes: H. Richard Niebuhr

1. H. Richard Niebuhr, "Reformation: Continuing Imperative," *Christian Century* 77 (1960): 248-49; *The Kingdom of God in America* (New York: Harper Torchbooks, 1959), xii-xvi; *The Meaning of Revelation* (New York: Macmillan Publishing Company, 1941), viii-ix; *Christ and Culture* (New York: Harper and Brothers, 1951, 1956), xii.

2. "I came to understand," he declared, "that unless being itself, the constitution of things, the One beyond all the many, . . . was trustworthy . . . could be counted on by what had proceeded from it . . . I had no God at all" ("Reformation," 248).

3. Ibid., 249. Perhaps the most significant change centered in his development of a more sophisticated and complex understanding of "faith."

4. Niebuhr, *Christ and Culture*, 112-13, 78-79.

5. Ibid., 113, 79-80.

6. Ibid., 232.

7. Ibid., 2 (italics added).

8. Niebuhr, *Revelation*, viii; cf. 116-21, 165-75, 182-91.

9. Ibid., 191.

10. Niebuhr, *Christ and Culture*, 191.

11. Ibid., 194.

12. Ibid., 195.

13. Niebuhr, *The Responsible Self* (New York: Harper & Row, 1963), 126.

14. Niebuhr, *Radical Monotheism and Western Culture* (New York: Harper and Row, 1960), 48.

15. Niebuhr, *Responsible Self*, 121-26, 137-45; *Radical Monotheism*, 47-48; *Revelation*, 78.

16. Niebuhr, *Responsible Self*, 137-38.

17. In his essay "Man the Sinner," *Journal of Religion* 15 (1935): 272-80, Niebuhr has presented a concise and incisive account of his understanding of human sinfulness. The doctrine of sin is an important element in Niebuhr's thought but it is always subordinate to and is only intelligible in terms of the sovereignty of God and man's dependence upon him. "Evangelical ethics is God-centered, not sin-centered. When our fundamental orientation in life is that of persons who live *vis à vis* our own sinful selves rather than *vis à vis* God, the spirit of Evangelical ethics takes flight no less surely than when we live in the contemplation of our own righteousness" (Niebuhr, "Evangelical and Protestant Ethics," in *The Heritage of the Reformation*, ed. E. J. F. Arndt (New York: Richard R. Smith, 1950), 222.

18. Niebuhr, *Radical Monotheism*, 38; *Responsible Self*, 125.

19. Niebuhr, "Man the Sinner," 276-78.

20. Niebuhr, *Radical Monotheism*, 35-37.

21. Niebuhr, "Man the Sinner," 277.

22. Ibid.

23. Ibid., 274.

24. Ibid., 279.

25. Niebuhr, *Kingdom of God*, 175. "Faith, the root-virtue whence all actions draw their goodness, is for Luther completely the gift of God. It is not something under man's control so that he can will to trust as perhaps he can will to believe a proposition about God" (Waldo Beach and H. Richard Niebuhr, eds., *Christian Ethics: Sources of the Living Tradition* [New York: Ronald Press, 1955], 241). For

similar views attributed by Niebuhr to Calvin and Edwards, cf. 270-71 and 387-88, respectively.

26. Niebuhr, "Evangelical and Protestant Ethics," 224.

27. Ibid., 226-27. Niebuhr acknowledged three sources as particularly important in informing his own understanding of faith in God and its consequences for human freedom. They were Paul's Epistle to the Romans, Luther's *Treatise on Christian Liberty*, and Jonathan Edwards's *Nature of True Virtue*.

28. Niebuhr, *Revelation*, 109-32.

29. Ibid., 109; cf. *Radical Monotheism*, 47-48; *Responsible Self*, 125-26.

30. Ibid., 117.

31. Ibid., 59-73.

32. Ibid., 118.

33. Niebuhr, "The Hidden Church and the Churches in Sight," *Religion in Life* 15 (1946): 118-20.

34. Ibid., 117.

35. Niebuhr, *The Social Sources of Denominationalism* (New York: Henry Holt and Company, 1929; New York: Meridian Books, 1957), ch. 1. Niebuhr, "What Holds the Churches Together," *The Christian Century* 43 (1926): 346-48.

36. Niebuhr, "Toward the Independence of the Church," in *The Church Against the World* (Chicago and New York: Willett, Clark and Company, 1935), 123-39; and Niebuhr, "The Christian Evangel and Social Culture," *Religion in Life* 8 (1939): 44-48.

37. Niebuhr, *Radical Monotheism*, 56-60; *The Purpose of the Church and Its Ministry* (New York: Harper and Row, 1956), 29-30, 39-47.

38. Niebuhr, "Reformation: Continuing Imperative," 250.

39. Niebuhr, "The Disorder of Man in the Church of God," in *Man's Disorder and God's Design*, vol. 1, *The Universal Church in God's Design* (New York: Harper and Brothers, 1949), 83.

40. Niebuhr, *Revelation*, 125.

41. Niebuhr, *Responsible Self*, 131.

42. Ibid., 177.

43. Ibid., 143.

44. Niebuhr, *Revelation*, 165 (italics added). Cf. "Evangelical and Protestant Ethics," 226.

45. Ibid.

46. Ibid., 168-70.

47. Ibid., 170.

48. Niebuhr, *Christian Ethics*, 41.

49. Niebuhr, *Christ and Culture*, 11-29; *The Purpose of the Church*, 34-36.

50. Niebuhr, *Kingdom of God*, ch. 1.

51. Ibid., 32.

52. Niebuhr, *Revelation*, viii, 65, 73-74; *Radical Monotheism*, 12-16, 78, 116-17, 127-30; *Responsible Self*, 82-83. Recalling his break with liberal theology over the nature of the relation between God and man, Niebuhr observed that this did not mean that he abandoned "religious empiricism any more than [he] abandoned historicism or neo-Kantian epistemology" ("Reformation: Continuing Imperative," 249).

53. Niebuhr, *Revelation*, 22-38, 156-59.

54. Ibid., vii, 7-22; *Christ and Culture*, 14, 236-37; *Responsible Self*, 46, 98-107.

55. Malcolm Reid, "The Theological Ethics of H. Richard Niebuhr" (Ph.D. diss., Edinburgh, 1974), ch. 4.

in both these senses plays in Niebuhr's thought, see Hans Frei, "The Theology of H. Richard Niebuhr," in *Faith and Ethics*, ed. Paul Ramsey (New York: Harper and Row, 1957), 87-94; Paul Ramsey, "The Transformation of Ethics," ibid., 151-72; George Schrader, "Value and Valuation," ibid., 184-94; Lonnie D. Kliever, *H. Richard Niebuhr* (Waco, TX: Word Books, 1977), 65-72, 170-72.

H. Richard Niebuhr (Waco, TX: Word Books, 1977), 65-72, 170-72.

57. *Radical Monotheism*, 103.

58. Ibid., 112.

59. ". . . Nothing is valuable in itself, but everything has value, positive or negative, in its relations."

60. *Radical Monotheism*, 107.

61. Ibid., 112.

62. Ibid., 113. Cf. "A more adequate value-theory would recognize . . . the relativity of values without prejudice to their objectivity. The interpretation of values as relative to structure and organic needs, rather than to desire and consciousness, provides for such an objective relativism" (Niebuhr, "Value Theory and Theology," in *The Nature of Religious Experience: Essays in Honor of D. C. Macintosh*, ed. J. S. Bixler, et al. (New York: Harper and Brothers, 1937), 113.

63. George Schrader, "Value and Valuation," in *Faith and Ethics*, 182.

64. Niebuhr, *Ernst Troeltsch's Philosophy of Religion* (Ph.D. diss., Yale University, 1924). Troeltsch "helped me to accept and to profit by the acceptance of the relativity not only of historical objects but, more, of the historical subject, the observer and interpreter" (*Christ and Culture*, x).

65. Cf. Baron F. Von Hugel's introduction to Troeltsch's *Christian Thought: Its History and Application* (New York: Meridian Books, 1957); H. R. Macintosh, *Types of Modern Theology* (London: Collins, 1937), 195-98, 204-08.

66. Niebuhr, *Revelation*, 12, 16.

67. Ibid., 7-8. Niebuhr doubtless had Troeltsch primarily in mind as having "demonstrated" the truth of historical relativism.

68. Paul Ramsey, "The Transformation of Ethics," in *Faith and Ethics*, 153.

69. Niebuhr, "Reformation: Continuing Imperative," 249.

70. This is unfortunately true of the author's own Ph.D. diss., "The Theological Ethics of H. Richard Niebuhr" (Edinburgh, 1974).

71. John Howard Yoder, " 'Christ and Culture,' A Critique of H. Richard Niebuhr" (unpublished paper). The perspective from which this critique is given is elaborated in such representative studies as Yoder, *The Christian Witness to the State* (Newton, KS: Faith and Life Press, 1964); "The Otherness of the Church," *Mennonite Quarterly Review* 35 (1961).

72. Stanley Hauerwas, "The Nonresistant Church: The Theological Ethics of John Howard Yoder," in *Vision and Virtue: Essays in Christian Ethical Reflection* (Notre Dame: Fides Publishers, 1974), 197-221.

73. Hauerwas correctly notes that while Yoder has written informed and incisive critiques of the theology of Barth and both Niebuhrs, to date "no one from the more 'orthodox' tradition has attempted a similar assessment of Yoder's positive theological position" (ibid., 199).

74. His theology of culture is not easily recognizable in terms of the description and critique Niebuhr has provided of the "Christ-against-culture movement" (*Christ and Culture*, 40-41, 45-82).

75. Hauerwas, in *Vision and Virtue*, 214.

76. For example, Kliever's careful study, *H. Richard Niebuhr*, 165-75.

77. John D. Godsey, *The Promise of H. Richard Niebuhr* (Philadelphia: J. B. Lippincott Company, 1970), 96-107; Reid, in ibid., 61-71, 208-11, 222-26, 239-42, 262-373.

78. Frei, in *Faith and Ethics*, 104-16; Godsey, *Promise*, 101-02; James W. Fowler, *To See the Kingdom* (Nashville: Abingdon Press, 1974), 245-47.

79. Godsey, *Promise*, 109.

80. See particularly Niebuhr, "Toward the Independence of the Church," in *The Church Against the World;* and *The Purpose of the Church*, 1-47.

THE FUTURE OF REFORMED THEOLOGY

JAMES MONTGOMERY BOICE

In the spring of 1974, when the Philadelphia Conference on Reformed Theology held the first of its many annual meetings, a religion reporter from one of the Philadelphia daily papers called to talk about the conference. "Why should your conference amount to anything?" he asked. "People are disillusioned today; most are apathetic about religion. Many will not even know what the title of your conference, 'The Doctrines of Grace,' or the words 'Reformed Theology' mean. Why should this new effort be successful?"

It was a fair question, one that might be asked of many in the Reformed community.

On this occasion I tried to be as prophetic as one who is not a prophet dares. First, I agreed that many persons are disillusioned today and for that very reason are looking for answers in new places. I pointed to the rebirth of interest in the eastern religions, recent outcroppings of the occult, the Jesus movement, and other contemporary phenomena. I spoke of the striking interest in religious questions among young people, evidenced in part by large numbers of students involved in active churches.

Second, I argued that the doctrines of grace, expressed in the distinctive tenets of the Reformed faith, are true and therefore have a unique ability to capture and enthrall people's minds. They are about God and man, sin and grace, love and judgment. When these are acknowledged to be true, they illuminate the mind and transform the life and conduct of the one perceiving them.

Finally, I noted that there is an undeniable connection between these doctrines and the periods of greatest advance for Christianity in the Western world. Wherever one turns—to the sixteenth-century Reformation in Europe, the seventeenth-century revivals in England and Scotland, the eighteenth-century awakenings in England and America, the nineteenth-century recovery of true religion and godliness in England under Charles Haddon Spurgeon—wherever one turns, it is the doctrines of grace that underlie spiritual awakening. Luther, Calvin, Zwingli, Knox, Baxter, Bunyan, Henry, Edwards, Whitefield, Spurgeon—all were "Calvinists," not to mention the vast host of confessors and martyrs who preceded them in earlier centuries. God used the fearless proclamation of the whole counsel of God, including the distinct doctrines of the Reformed faith, to turn millions to Christ through their ministries.

An Impoverished Movement

Today we do not see a corresponding vitality in the Reformed communions, and while many feel that the Reformed faith is in some sense being rediscovered,[1] we are at best looking for a new Reformation rather than being in the midst or even on the verge of one.

An honest assessment of a possible bright future for Reformed theology must begin with the present weaknesses of those who hold to it. There are a number of them.

1. Fragmentation. To make a significant impact in history, individuals and the institutions they represent do not necessarily have to be part of a carefully constructed organization, but they do have to have a sense of being part of the same essential movement. In the sixteenth century the Protestant Reformers had this awareness in spite of national and eventually denominational differences. They were hurt by these divisions, but they were effective because they sensed that they were part of one movement of the one Spirit of God in spite of them. Since the demise of the Old Princeton movement in the earlier part of this century the Reformed movement in America has lacked that cohesion. Indeed, it has been worse than this. In place of the former general sense of unity came sharp, acrimonious divisions. Presbyterians divided, and then divided and divided again. This is no place to argue whether those old divisions were necessary; no doubt many were. But necessary or not, they destroyed much of the impact Presbyterians had made.

At the same time, more ethnic churches, such as the Reformed Church in America and the Christian Reformed Church, went their own way. Those with distinctives that seemed to demand separation, such as the Reformed Presbyterian Church of North America, looked on detachedly.

Fortunately, the Reformed churches seem to be moving away from the fragmentation of earlier years. One hopeful sign was the National Presbyterian and Reformed Fellowship (now disbanded), which sought to build fuller measures of trust and cooperation between Reformed people in seven key denominations: the Christian Reformed Church; the Orthodox Presbyterian Church; the Presbyterian Church in the United

States; the Reformed Church in America; the Reformed Presbyterian Church, Evangelical Synod; the Reformed Presbyterian Church of North America; and the United Presbyterian Church in the United States of America. Formation of the new Presbyterian Church in America is another hopeful sign, particularly in view of its absorption of the Reformed Presbyterian Church, Evangelical Synod in 1982, and its invitation for a similar joining and receiving of the Orthodox Presbyterian Church in the near future.

More important than mergers is the mingling of Reformed elders from these and other communions in joint projects, plus cooperation among the major Reformed colleges and seminaries. It is not unusual for students and faculty to pass freely from one institution to another.

2. *Intellectualism.* A glory of the Reformed movement has been the number of great minds that have embraced its distinctives, communicating them forcefully to their age. We rightly applaud such intellectual giants as John Owen and Jonathan Edwards. But there is a down side to this great heritage. The very nature of the Reformed system of doctrine, which tends to put reality together and thus make sense of life as other systems of theology do not, tends to produce lovers of theology for its own sake and thus persons detached from life and perhaps even detached from vital fellowship with the God they speak about theologically. It is not without reason that some of our seminaries are more noted for producing theology lecturers than preachers, not to mention evangelists. It is not without justification that many Reformed people are seen as dry, ivory-tower intellectuals (or pseudo-intellectuals) out of touch with contemporary needs.

There is a contemporaneousness that betrays the gospel, of course. But one does not have to fall to this to be relevant. Virtually any outstanding Reformed leader of any previous age coupled his intellectual grasp of doctrines to an equally important and astute grasp of the struggles and issues of his time. Luther, Calvin, Edwards, even Charles Hodge and Benjamin Warfield were engaged in current battles.

3. *Elite Membership.* No one in the Reformed communions has openly tried to make them white, or middle or upper class, but an honest assessment says that this has happened widely nonetheless. Presbyterian and Reformed churches (even liberal ones) have few members of minorities—few blacks, even fewer Hispanics—and even more distressing is the absence of significant numbers of blue-collar individuals. This is not all our fault. The mobility of American society has weakened denominational as well as other ties, and relocating individuals and families tend naturally to group with others of like background. Church growth specialists even commend this as the fastest pathway to numerical growth.

But although what has happened is not entirely any one denomination's fault, it is nevertheless a failure for the Reformed churches and a serious one at that. The greatest failure is a lack of effective evangelism to all classes, particularly the masses. We have a model we could follow. George Whitefield preached, as did the Wesleys, in the fields to the common man. He preached powerful evangelistic sermons that were nonetheless filled with Reformed doctrinal distinctives. He swept the eastern seaboard of the United States with lasting results. We have not done that. We do not even evangelize much. It has been remarked that in earlier ages it was hard to find an outstanding evangelist or missionary who was not a Calvinist but that in our age, by contrast, it is hard to find one who is. No wonder then that we perpetuate an elite, middle-class membership and fail to impact culture as we claim we seek to do.

4. *Lack of Love.* The late Francis Schaeffer, a highly visible Reformed thinker and writer, spoke of a need for observable love, calling it "the mark of the Christian," a mark by which the world has a right to judge whether one is a Christian or not and by which unsaved individuals are to be won to Christ. Schaeffer was no compromiser of doctrinal purity. He left the large Presbyterian Church in the United States of America at the time J. Gresham Machen left it to found Westminster Theological Seminary, and he did not regret that decision. Nevertheless he wrote of a lack of love evident in many of the divisions of those days and other places and deplored it.

> I have observed one thing *among true Christians* in their differences in many countries: what divides and severs true Christian groups and Christians—what leaves a bitterness that can last for 20, 30 or 40 years (or for 50 or 60 years in a son's memory)—is not the issue of doctrine or belief which caused the differences in the first place. Invariably it is lack of love—and the bitter things that are said by true Christians in the midst of differences. These stick in the mind like glue. And after time passes and the differences between the Christians or the groups appear less than they did, there are still those bitter, bitter things we said in the midst of what we thought was a good and sufficient objective discussion. It is these things— these unloving attitudes and words—that cause the stench that the world can smell in the church of Jesus Christ among those who are really true Christians.[2]

I cannot say that I have heard or witnessed the bitter things Schaeffer did in what was admittedly a more volatile time. Perhaps this is good. But I have not witnessed a great deal of love expressed between members of one Reformed communion and another either, or even among members of the same communion. This lack should be a cause of genuine sadness. Until it is rectified it will seriously weaken attempts to revive what is today a potentially great but seriously impoverished movement.

Awakening Giant

The Reformed movement in America may be likened to a sleeping giant, perhaps one even beginning to stir from slumber.

One noticeable sign of this awakening has been the surprising and impressive growth of important Reformed colleges and seminaries. Calvin College and Seminary of the Christian Reformed Church, located in Grand Rapids, Michigan, have long been faithful bastions of genuine Calvinism. They have not weakened over the years. In 1985, with more than 3,800 students in the college and an additional 240 students in the seminary, they have grown even stronger. Covenant College, located at Lookout Mountain, Tennessee, reports more than 500 students. Its sister institution, Covenant Seminary in St. Louis, had a 20 percent increase from 1972 to 1975, and has shown notable growth since. Its current enrollment stands at 150. Even more remarkable is the growth of the Reformed Theological Seminary in Jackson, Mississippi, which has been successful in preparing ministers for both the large United Presbyterian Church in the U.S.A. and the breakaway 125,000-member Presbyterian Church in America. The Jackson seminary has grown from 17 students in 1966 to 243 today. Westminster Seminary in Philadelphia also reports an upswing in attendance after a number of fairly static years. Presently it numbers 470 students, up from 427 in 1983-84. In recent years it has spun off Westminster Theological Seminary (west) in Escondido, California, which now has 70 students, offers three degree programs, and is fully accredited.

Other schools not explicitly Reformed have also grown in the direction of strengthening the Reformed doctrines taught there. A key example is Gordon-Conwell Theological Seminary, South Hamilton, Massachusetts. Another is Trinity Evangelical Divinity School, Deerfield, Illinois.

The last decade has witnessed an upsurge of independent churches in the "Reformed Baptist" tradition. The Bible Fellowship churches have seen a strong movement toward explicit Reformed teaching. One observer estimates that 60 percent of these churches may now be Calvinistic.

All this represents not merely a numerical growth of those committed to an articulate Reformed world-and-life view, but also an increase in the numbers of those trying to articulate it. Ligonier Valley Study Center, formerly in western Pennsylvania, now in Orlando, Florida, has produced much readable Reformed literature for both scholars and laymen. Its recent offering, *Classical Apologetics* by authors R. C. Sproul, John H. Gerstner, and Arthur W. Lindsley,[3] is a significant contribution to the ongoing presuppositionalist versus evidentialist debate in apologetics. Noteworthy also is the success of The Banner of Truth Trust in reprinting classic Reformed literature.

Need of the Hour

As the sleeping giant of Reformed theology awakes, here and there leaders raise their banners and start forward to speak historic Christianity to our day. But they are warning that the mistakes of the past must be renounced and that a whole, balanced Calvinism must be voiced in clear tones and not merely be assumed. It must contain these elements.

1. *A High View of Scripture.* A high view of Scripture as the inerrant Word of God is not in doubt among genuinely Reformed people, but it is not always well articulated either, though it must be. The difficulty is that the unique authority of the Bible is under attack today. Critics say that it is only a human book, that it contains errors, and that it is therefore at best only relatively trustworthy or authoritative. These views sometimes come from people who enjoy "evangelical" reputations and are therefore extremely confusing to more Reformed church members than pastors wish to admit. In such a climate Reformed spokesmen must make it clear that we believe what we believe and do what we do, not because it is the tradition of the Reformed churches, however valuable these traditions may be, but because these are things Scripture teaches and because we want to be ruled by the voice of Jesus Christ through that Book.

This must be applied to ethics, particularly personal ethics. It is a tragedy of our time, from which Reformed people have not escaped, that the breakdown of marriages epidemic in the culture mars our homes as well. This must not be. We cannot be like the world ethically, yet maintain our orthodoxy. We must be people of the Book. We must study the Bible, decide what it says, and then live by it. We must ask: What does God demand of me personally in this age?

We are going to have to do that sooner or later anyway, or else we are going to have to go in the world's way. This is because history does not allow anyone to stand long in an ambiguous position. In Germany during the Nazi era the church went in one of two ways: either it capitulated to the Nazi point of view (which most of the established church did), or else it became increasingly a church of the Book. Those who wanted to live by the Bible eventually established a communion of their own. They signed documents identifying themselves as the "Confessing Church." They did that because, when the drift of the society is against Christian standards, it is impossible to appeal to external norms. One cannot say, "This is backed up in the area of psychology or science or social relations," because most of what is being written in those fields will be contrary to biblical truth. The church must stand on divine revelation. The Reformed churches are not abandoning this base, but they must make it increasingly clear that they are not. "What does Scripture say?" must be their watchword.

2. *The Sovereignty of God.* Another watchword of the Reformed churches is God's sovereignty. Sovereignty means "rule"; so the doctrine of God's sovereignty means that God rules in this world and the universe. From sovereignty we get the doctrines of providence, election, particular redemption, and perseverance. What a wonderful doctrine! Yes, but trials come to us as to others, and in the heat of trials Reformed people often lose sight of God's greatness or at least fail to make their trust in God plain to the surrounding world.

Some years ago the English Bible translator J. B. Phillips wrote a book entitled *Your God Is Too Small.*[4] That title, which is also a statement, might well be spoken to the great majority of professing Christians (including Reformed believers) who, in their ignorance, scale God down to their own fallible perspectives. Or they do something worse. They do not deny that God is sovereign, but they dissociate him from what they go through so that for all practical purposes they live and talk as unbelievers. We need trust in the sovereignty of God on this level. Our model must be the Old Testament patriarch Joseph, by whom hardly a sentence was spoken that did not have the name of God in it.

When Potiphar's wife propositioned him, Joseph replied, "How then could I do such a wicked thing and sin against *God*?" (Gen. 39:9).

When Joseph was thrown into prison and the chief cupbearer and the chief baker of Pharaoh had dreams and told them to Joseph, Joseph instantly replied, "Do not interpretations belong to *God*?" (Gen. 40:8).

When he appeared before Pharaoh and Pharaoh asked for an interpretation of his dream, Joseph responded, "I cannot do it, . . . but *God* will give Pharaoh the answer he desires" (Gen. 41:16). When he interpreted the dream, he began by saying, "*God* has revealed to Pharaoh what he is about to do" (v. 25; cf. vv. 28, 32).

When he saw his brothers again and eventually revealed himself to them, he explained the events of the preceding years by noting, "It was to save lives that *God* sent me ahead of you. . . . *God* sent me ahead of you to preserve for you a remnant on earth and to save your lives by a great deliverance. So then, it was not you who sent me here, but *God*" (Gen. 45:5, 7-8).

Joseph said of his sons Ephraim and Manasseh, "They are the sons *God* has given me" (Gen. 48:9).

At the end of his life he said to his brothers, "Don't be afraid. Am I in the place of *God*? You intended to harm me, but *God* intended it for good to accomplish what is now being done, the saving of many lives" (Gen. 50:19-20).

His last words were, "I am about to die. But *God* will surely come to your aid and take you up out of this land to the land he promised on oath to Abraham, Isaac and Jacob. . . . *God* will surely come to your aid, and then you must carry my bones up from this place" (Gen. 50:24-25).

This is the kind of belief in the sovereignty of God our generation needs—not mere doctrinaire belief, but belief that unfolds in all the wrinkles of life. It is in God that we live and move and have our being.

3. *The Lordship of Christ.* With proclamation of the doctrine of God's sovereignty must go preaching of the lordship of Christ—that Jesus is Lord over all areas of life and that this must be acknowledged and lived by all who call themselves Christians. Calvinists have two fronts in this battle. One front is manned by the world, which seeks to push Christians back onto the reservation. It says that they can practice their religion there, where it will do no harm, but that they are not to think of bringing it into the real world of politics, economics, law, and individual "rights." We must oppose this. We must declare that "the earth is the Lord's and everything in it, the world, and all who live in it" (Ps. 24:1). We must show that "all authority in heaven and on earth" has been given to Jesus (Matt. 28:18) and indicate what this means.

The other front is held by well-intentioned but erring Christians who believe that it is possible to have Jesus as Savior without having him as Lord and even go so far as to say that "Lordship salvation," as they call it, is an errant gospel.[5] There is only one Savior: the *Lord* Jesus Christ. Anyone who believes in a Savior who is not the Lord is not believing in the true Christ and is not regenerate. We must call for commitment to that Christ and must challenge the presumption that claims to be Christian while at the same time disregarding or disobeying Christ's commands.

4. *Human Depravity.* American theology today is lopsidedly Arminian, but it is here rather than at some other point of the Calvinistic system that Reformed people can best make a corrective contribution. Many object to Calvinism for what they perceive to be its arbitrary character, expressed in its doctrine of election. But for most the problem does not lie with election but with the doctrine of depravity that necessitates it. Human nature instinctively holds out for some credit for itself, even in the matter of salvation by "grace." In our theological climate this expresses itself in the conviction that although the offer is of grace—God did not have to try to save anyone—in the final analysis what determines whether an individual is saved or not is his or her faith—whether or not he or she will "receive" Christ or "accept" him.

As Augustine saw long ago, this toehold of depravity weakens what the Bible says of the pervasive and destructive effects of sin and demolishes grace. The Bible does not teach that men and women are harmed by sin only. It says that they are dead in it (Eph. 2:1-3). They are thoroughly corrupted: "The LORD saw how great man's wickedness had become, and that every inclination of the thoughts of his heart was only evil all the time" (Gen. 6:5). So great is this depravity that a person cannot even come to Christ unless God first renews his spirit and thus draws him (John 6:24).

This is not an abstract issue. It is practical. Since most American Christianity is thoroughly Arminian at this point, believing that it is within the individual's own power, unaided by the Holy Spirit, to accept or reject Christ, it follows that most preachers rely on human persuasion, speaking to "felt needs" and using Madison Avenue techniques and other external aids to make conversions. Often such are not true conversions. Techniques like these may fill pews, but the response is matched to the techniques both in quality and duration. Such works quickly fade away. In place of man-centered preaching and human techniques we need a new and utter dependence on God. "Salvation comes from the LORD" (Jonah 2:9). Nothing but this will bring lasting reformation. Moreover, although a proper sense of the biblical doctrine of depravity humbles us even in our preaching, it emboldens us too. For our strength is in the Lord and is seen to be in him. If God is working, we can be bold to act, knowing that God is capable of blessing even the weakest and most unworthy instruments.

5. *Grace.* Loss of the full doctrine of depravity also causes a loss of awareness of grace, regardless of what is said to the contrary. To the extent that human beings receive credit for anything, even for so "small" a matter as their accepting Christ, to that extent the grace and glory of God are diminished. This weakens the church and impoverishes preaching. Adherents to Reformed theology have much to offer at this point. They must preach grace and then grace again. This reminds hearers that salvation is from God and humbles them, but it draws them too. For what most wins people to Christ is not facile promises that Jesus will fix our problems or make us prosperous, a depth that much preaching probes, but the truth that God loves individuals in spite of their sin and that he has acted in utter grace to save them. First, he elects them to salvation, apart from any merit of their own (which, of course, they do not have). Second, he makes atonement for sin through Christ's dying for these individuals. Third, he opens the blind eyes of these people and woos their will through the power of the Holy Spirit, thereby bringing them to trust Christ as their Savior.

These are the most glorious themes that can pass through people's minds. It seems impossible that anyone who has known them could ever grow lax in thinking of them or proclaiming them to others. Yet we do. Reformed believers must recapture their wonder at the grace of God in salvation if they are to be effective in today's religious world.

6. *Godliness*. One of the most striking things said of Reformed leaders of earlier days is that they were godly individuals. This is not just a pious accolade. It is an accurate assessment of the way these men operated as God's servants. Like anyone else, they wanted to succeed in their various responsibilities, whatever they were. But more than this, they wanted to know and please God. That is evident even from the brief analyses of the contributions of some of the men in this volume, people like Charles Hodge, B. B. Warfield, J. Gresham Machen, Cornelius Van Til, R. L. Dabney, and others—and the list omits many other godly preachers and scholars. People were attracted by their personalities (in many cases), stimulated by their wit, and impressed by their intellect. But chiefly they were awed by sensing that these men spent many hours in effectual fervent prayer and consciously lived in God's presence.

This is a crying need in our day. We have many methods and much money. We have churches and schools and committees and organizations. What we most need are godly men and women, people whose lives are thereby blessed and who become great blessings to others.

7. *Work to Do*. A full-orbed, balanced Reformed theology must also stress that when God does the great work of saving individuals, drawing them to Christ, he does not then abandon them to a continuation of the same or even no activity but rather directs them to do meaningful work for him. Many of Christ's sayings about discipleship fall into this area. So does Ephesians 2:10, which uses the idea of election of this call to works: "For we are God's workmanship, created in Christ Jesus to do good works, which God prepared in advance for us to do." It is necessary that believers do these good works, for unless they do, they have no assurance that they really are Christ's followers. Like Jesus himself, Christians are to stand for justice and do everything in their power to comfort the sick, rescue the outcast, defend the oppressed, and save the innocent. We are to oppose those who perpetrate or condone injustice.

In past centuries Calvinists were in the vanguard of social works projects. We point with pride to Calvin's work among the refugees of Geneva, to Whitefield's efforts to raise money for the orphanage in Georgia. Unfortunately, although Reformed people have in many cases continued in that tradition, honesty compels us to acknowledge that we are no longer in the vanguard and may actually lag behind. This is particularly true in the cities, which we, like most white, middle-class Americans, have generally abandoned.

To say that God has ordained specific works for us to do not only says that there is meaningful work to do. It says that whatever work God gives us to do is meaningful. Reformed people need to proclaim this clearly, because the scope of many of today's problems makes individuals feel insignificant. Besides, the people who launch great movements or interact politically are the ones who grab headlines. Little works are unnoticed. Calvinists need to say that this evaluation of what is worthwhile is of the world and that, with God's blessing, the work of even the most overlooked believer is significant. Even more than that, what is done in quiet ways in terms of true commitment to Christ and the standards of the Bible is more important than worldly power or political agitation.

The only lasting and effective basis for national reformation is the transformed lives of citizens. Therefore, Calvinists should lead in "demythologizing the state"[6] and calling on individuals to be different.

8. *Security in Christ.* Jesus was strong in cautioning against presumption. He let no one think that he or she could be a Christian while at the same time disregarding or disobeying his teachings. He said, "My sheep . . . *follow me"* (John 10:27). If we are not listening to Christ and are not following him in faithful obedience, we are not his. However, although he cautioned against presumption, he also spoke the greatest words of assurance for those who did follow him. He said they would never perish. How could they if God himself is responsible for their salvation: "I give them eternal life, and they shall never perish; no one can snatch them out of my hand. My Father, who has given them to me, is greater than all; no one can snatch them out of my Father's hand" (John 10:28-29). Ours is a threatening and insecure world. People need to know that there is a safe haven in Jesus Christ.

9. *Discernible Love.* Earlier I wrote of the Calvinists' past lack in this area. To our shame fighting, hostility, unjustified accusations, bitterness, and an ugly spirit have marred relationships and damaged our work. This must cease if Reformed theology is to have a new birth in American life. Most Americans do not know what love is, bombarded as they are with the media's distortion of love and other basic graces. We must show love by the way we reflect concern and compassion to all people, particularly those who are of the household of faith.

Francis Schaeffer outlines what this means. First, we must ask forgiveness of those we have wronged. Second, we must show forgiveness, refusing to harbor grudges and ill will. Third, we must pay the price of love even when that is costly. Fourth, we must solve problems rather than merely expose them. Fifth, we must maintain oneness in Christ regardless of differences. "Before a watching world an observable love in the midst of differences will show a difference between Christians' differences and other men's differences. The world may not understand what the Christians are disagreeing about, but they will very quickly understand the difference of our differences from the world's differences if they see us having our differences in an open and observable love on a practical level."[7]

A New Day

Will Reformed theology carry the field? Does Calvinism in America have a future? Reformed people have had great days before. They may again, if the flaws that marred earlier efforts are corrected and the love of God infuses their lives and preaching. More than a decade ago I wrote,

> Too often the Calvinists have become theologically brittle and highly critical of other theological positions and of one another. They have refused to work with those who have not expressed themselves in precisely their terms. They have allowed no theological flexibility, even in such uncertain areas as eschatology. But today's upsurge shows signs of being different. Among the younger Calvinists at least there has appeared a new openness in discussion, and there is an awareness of the need for 'observable love' toward all Christians.[8]

With the elements I have listed—faith in the divine inspiration and inerrancy of the Scriptures, belief in the sovereignty of God and a willingness to act in that belief, commitment to the lordship of Christ, awareness of human depravity, a love of grace and its accompanying doctrines, personal godliness, hard work, confidence that God will persevere with his saints, and discernible love—today's Calvinists may yet usher in a new day.

Notes: The Future of Reformed Theology

1. James Montgomery Boice, "Is the Reformed Faith Being Rediscovered?" *Christianity Today,* 28 March 1975, 12-14.
2. Francis A. Schaeffer, *The Church at the End of the Twentieth Century* (Downers Grove, IL: InterVarsity Press, 1970), 144.
3. R. C. Sproul, John H. Gerstner, and Arthur W. Lindsley, *Classical Apologetics: A Rational Defense of the Christian Faith and a Critique of Presuppositional Apologetics* (Grand Rapids: Zondervan Publishing House, 1984).
4. J. B. Phillips, *Your God Is Too Small* (New York: Macmillan Company, 1967).
5. See Charles Caldwell Ryrie, "Must Christ Be Lord to Be Savior?" in *Balancing the Christian Life* (Chicago: Moody Press, 1973). Ryrie is reacting to statements by J. I. Packer in Packer's *Evangelism and the Sovereignty of God* (Downers Grove, IL: InterVarsity Press, 1967), to John R. W. Stott in "Must Christ

Be Lord to Be Savior?" *Eternity*, September 1959, and to an out-of-print work by Arthur W. Pink, *Present Day Evangelism*.

6. Jacques Ellul develops this idea in *The Political Illusion*, trans. Konrad Kellen (New York: Vintage Books, 1972). Ellul regards contemporary appeals to the state to solve our problems as the height of folly and calls upon individuals to resist its ever-expanding encroachment on their lives.

7. Schaeffer, *The Church*, 143-53, esp. 149.

8. Boice, "Is the Reformed Faith Being Rediscovered," 14.

INDEX

313

9234